Discussion of the legal status, responsibilities and rights of men who are fathers – whether they are married or unmarried, cohabiting or separated, biological or 'social' in nature – has a long history. In recent years, however, western societies have witnessed a heightening of concern about whether families need fathers and, if so, what kinds of fathers these should be. A debate about the future of fatherhood has become central to a range of conversations about the changing family, parenting and society. Law has served an important role in these discussions, serving as a focal point for broader political frustrations, playing a central role in mediating disputes, and operating as a significant symbolic 'authorised discourse' which provides an official, state-sanctioned account of the scope of paternal rights and responsibilities. *Fragmenting Fatherhood* provides the first sustained engagement with the way that fatherhood has been understood, constructed and regulated within English law. Drawing on a range of disparate legal provisions, and material from diverse disciplines, it sketches the major contours of the figure of the father as drawn in law and social policy, tracing shifts in legal and broader understandings of what it means to be a 'father' and what rights and obligations should accrue to that status. In thematically linked chapters cutting across substantive areas of law, the book locates fatherhood as a key site of contestation within broader political debates regarding the family and gender equality. *Fragmenting Fatherhood* provides an important and unique resource and speaks to debates about fatherhood across a range of fields including law and legal theory, sociology, gender studies, social policy, marriage and family, women's studies and gender studies.

Fragmenting Fatherhood

A Socio-Legal Study

RICHARD COLLIER

and

SALLY SHELDON

·HART·
PUBLISHING

OXFORD AND PORTLAND, OREGON
2008

Published in North America (US and Canada) by
Hart Publishing
c/o International Specialized Book Services
920 NE 58th Avenue, Suite 300
Portland, OR 97213–3786
USA
Tel: +1 503 287 3093 or toll-free: (1) 800 944 6190
Fax: +1 503 280 8832
E-mail: orders@isbs.com
Website: http://www.isbs.com

Hart Publishing, 16C Worcester Place, Oxford, OX1 2JW
Telephone: +44 (0)1865 517530 Fax: +44 (0)1865 510710
E-mail: mail@hartpub.co.uk
Website: http://www.hartpub.co.uk

British Library Cataloguing in Publication Data

Data Available

ISBN: 978-1-84113-417-8

Typeset by Columns Design Limited, Reading RG4 7DH
Printed and bound in Great Britain by
TJ International Ltd, Padstow, Cornwall

Acknowledgments

We have incurred many debts in the writing of this book. We would like to thank all those at Hart who worked on the book and, in particular, Richard Hart for his patience and understanding as each deadline passed. We are also grateful to Lesley Irvine for her work on the manuscript. Our thoughts on fatherhood have been greatly influenced by the discussions we have had with colleagues over the years, many of whom have given generously of their time in order to offer comments on draft papers, conference presentations or staff seminars drawing on this research. While they are too numerous to list here, we thank all of them. We would especially like to acknowledge the financial support provided by the following: Kent Law School, the ESRC (RES/000–27–0111) (Sally); British Academy (TOB06–07/SRF2005.88 & SG42903) and AHRB (RL/AN8065/APN16739) (Richard).

Earlier versions of some parts of the book have drawn on material which has appeared elsewhere and we are grateful to the publishers for the permission to reproduce it here: see S. Sheldon (1999) 'ReConceiving Masculinity: Imagining Men's Reproductive Bodies in Law' 26(2) *Journal of Law and Society* 129–49; S.Sheldon (2005) 'Fragmenting Fatherhood: the Regulation of Reproductive Technologies' 68(4) *Modern Law Review* 523–53; R.Collier (2005) 'Fathers 4 Justice, Law and the New Politics of Fatherhood' 17(4) *Child and Family Law Quarterly* (2005) 1–29; R.Collier (2001) 'A Hard Time to be a Father? Law, Policy and Family Practices' 28 (4) *Journal of Law and Society* 520–545.

We dedicate this book to our mothers and fathers, with love.

Contents

vii

1

Introducing Fatherhood and Law

Introduction

THE LEGAL STATUS, responsibilities and rights of men who are fathers – whether married or unmarried, cohabiting or separated, biological or 'social' in nature – is a topic with a long and well-documented history. However, in recent years it has been possible to detect a heightening of concern about whether families need fathers and, if so, what kinds of fathers these should be. Discussion of the future of fatherhood has become a ubiquitous feature of a range of legal and social policy debates, the question of what is happening to contemporary fatherhood proving central to conversations about the shifting parameters of the (heterosexual) family. Law, we argue in this book, has had an important role in these discussions, serving as a focal point for broader political frustrations, playing a central role in mediating disputes and operating as a significant symbolic, state-sanctioned discourse of the scope of paternal rights and responsibilities. At stake in contestations around the legal status of fatherhood is, for some, no less than the future of 'the family' itself.[1]

A well-established literature in the fields of sociology and social policy, history, psychology and gender and family studies deals with diverse aspects of the role of fathers and the idea of fatherhood. This book provides, in contrast, the first sustained, socio-legal[2] engagement with the way fathers have been understood,

---

[1] See eg: I Duncan Smith, 'Now They Want to Abolish Fatherhood', *Mail on Sunday* (18 November 2007) News 29; N Dennis and G Erdos, *Families Without Fatherhood* (Institute of Economic Affairs, London, 1993); P Morgan, *Farewell to the Family? Public Policy and Family Breakdown in Britain and the USA* (Health and Welfare Unit, Institute of Economic Affairs, London, 1995); ME David (ed), *The Fragmenting Family: Does it Matter?* (Health and Welfare Unit, Institute for Economic Affairs, London, 1998). For the US context, see: D Blakenhorn, *Fatherless America: Confronting Our Most Urgent Social Problem* (Basic Books, New York, 1995); cf CR Daniels (ed), *Lost Fathers: The Politics of Fatherlessness in America* (St Martin's Press, New York, 1998).

[2] While recognising that 'socio-legal studies' is a notoriously ill defined and contested term, we mean to locate our work within a broad tradition of contextual, critical and interdisciplinary legal scholarship, drawing on studies of law, policy and practice, questions of theory and detailed discussion of legal cases. See further: P Thomas (ed), *Socio-legal Studies* (Dartmouth, Aldershot, 1997); R Cotterrell, 'Subverting Orthodoxy, Making Law Central: A View of Socio-Legal Studies' (2002) 29(4) *Journal of Law & Society* 632.

1

constructed and regulated within English law.[3] In focusing on legal regulation, our aim is to complement the existing literature on fatherhood whilst providing new insights and perspectives on the changing place of fathers in society. Drawing on a range of disparate legal provisions, the chapters to follow sketch some of the major contours of the 'father figure' as drawn in law and social policy.[4] These contours are shaped by common law, legislation, custom and history. They are reproduced within the practices of judges, barristers, solicitors and other legal agents, in the 'everyday' work of the legal profession, the courts and the legal system. They also form part of the broader cultural context in which ideas about fatherhood circulate, are reproduced, challenged and come to shape understandings of family life. The interconnections between fatherhood and law also raise broader questions about the legal regulation of social relationships. In this book, we unpack significant historical shifts within social and legal understandings of what it means to be a 'father' and, importantly, what rights and obligations should accrue to that status. We consider how fatherhood has emerged as a particular *kind* of problem to be addressed by law at different historical moments. Within thematically linked chapters, cutting across substantive areas of law, we locate fatherhood throughout as a key site of contestation within broader debates around the relationship between law, the family and social change.

Fragmenting Fatherhood is, first, an explicitly interdisciplinary work. Knowledge of the substance and operation of legal regulation is crucial to developing an understanding of fatherhood from a political or sociological perspective. Likewise, an appreciation of the content and consequences of law can only be gained via an engagement with the social contexts in which law comes about and operates. Our analysis thus seeks to incorporate perspectives from disciplines as diverse as sociology, politics, psychology, history and social policy. What follows is, second, a theoretical work. In the chapters to follow, we draw on diverse perspectives gleaned from both social and legal theory. We ground our study within an analytic and political frame concerned with both cultural changes around the institution of fatherhood, understood as a set of ideas about men who are parents, and shifts in fathering as a distinctive social (and not simply familial) practice, raising questions of what women and men do in their 'everyday' lives. Whilst it is not our intention to set out a prescriptive range of reform proposals relating to fatherhood, we will, in each of the areas under discussion, consider current policy debates and explore what they can tell us about the legal regulation of fatherhood in a more general sense. In laws regulating reproduction (chapters two and three), marriage, employment and parental responsibility (chapter four),

---

[3] Cf in the US: N Dowd, *Redefining Fatherhood* (New York University Press, New York, 2000).

[4] This is the title of one important earlier study: L McKee and M O'Brien (eds), *The Father Figure* (Tavistock, London, 1982). See also: C Lewis and M O'Brien, *Reassessing Fatherhood: New Observations on Fathers and the Modern Family* (Sage, London, 1987); G Russell, *The Changing Role of the Father* (University of Queensland Press, London, 1983); C Lewis, *Becoming a Father* (Open University Press, Milton Keynes, 1986); R LaRossa, 'Fatherhood and Social Change' (1988) 37 *Family Relations* 451.

divorce and separation (chapter five) and unmarried fathers (chapter six), we locate our consideration of these legal provisions in the context of broader reconfigurations of the relationship between law and fatherhood at different historical moments.

Our choice of subject matter and scope is necessarily selective. Given that the principal focus of analysis is legal regulation, it is not possible to address each and every area of law pertaining to fatherhood.[5] We focus primarily on the law of England and Wales and make no attempt to set out a comprehensive 'map' of all laws relating to fatherhood.[6] The legal regulation of parenthood is a topic already well served by a range of textbooks, monographs and journal articles, and over the years these sources have become more aware of specific issues relating to fathers. In relation to subjects such as family law, employment law, health care law, European law and the growing literature in the field of human rights, a rich body of work provides detailed accounts of substantive legal provisions and the historical development of case and statute law pertaining to many aspects of legal regulation relevant to fathers. In drawing on such work, this book seeks to address some of the most politically significant interconnections of fatherhood, law and social change that have emerged in recent years. The approach undertaken assumes no prior knowledge of either substantive law or the nature of legal methods and legal reasoning. Indeed, far from taking for granted what it means to encounter 'law' in this area, we wish to rethink concepts and categories that have, to date, framed much analysis of fatherhood within legal studies.

I 'Fragmenting Fatherhood'

Our title, *Fragmenting Fatherhood*, is intended to capture a number of aspects of our work. First, the idea of a 'fragmentation' has been deployed by modern theorists of the family, writing from diverse political perspectives, to describe how broad demographic shifts have led to a position in which genetic families

---

[5] Whilst we address a broad range of topics, we do not, for example, explore in detail the legal position of lone fathers, step-fathers in a more general sense, questions of fathers and adoption, laws pertaining to gay fathers, and the status of the father in relation to local authority care proceedings and relocation law. On the first of these, see: RW Barker, *Lone Fathers and Masculinities* (Ashgate, London, 2004); on the last, note M Hayes, 'Relocation cases: is the Court of Appeal applying the correct principles?' (2006) 18(3) *Child and Family Law Quarterly* 351; G Temple-Bone, 'Fathers, Parental Responsibility and Care Proceedings' (2000) *Family Law* 55. Equally, in highlighting the diversity of fatherhood throughout, it is important to note the specificity of experience of some groups of fathers in encountering law. See eg: W Marsiglio, RD Day and M Lamb, 'Exploring Fatherhood Diversity: Implications for Conceptualizing Father Involvement' (2000) 29(4) *Marriage & Family Review* 269.

[6] There is an extensive range of family law textbooks in which detailed discussion can be found of the range of laws relating to parenting and families. See eg: J Herring, *Family Law*, 3rd edn (Pearson Longman, Harlow, 2007); A Diduck and F Kaganas, *Family Law, Gender and the State: Text, Cases and Materials*, 2nd edn (Hart, Oxford, 2006); R Probert, *Cretney's Family Law* (London, Sweet and Maxwell, 2006).

have become increasingly 'split' across households.[7] We would suggest that this 'fragmentation' of families relies, to a significant degree, on a fragmentation of fatherhood that has a number of specific features. As we will explore in more detail in chapter five, the area of divorce and separation has had a particular resonance and importance in contemporary debates about fathering as once 'the social, emotional and economic foundations of the nuclear family begin to shake, fathers typically find themselves parenting at a distance, or not at all'.[8] The idea of fragmentation captures aspects of the disintegration of a model of fatherhood that, in the past, had been held together by a framework of laws around marriage, parenthood and the (hetero)sexual family. As we argue in chapter four, while a distinctive model of the father as 'family man' remains culturally resonant, it has been profoundly challenged as a result of these social changes.[9] It remains the case that, following the breakdown of a relationship, children are overwhelmingly more likely to live with their genetic mother. Men who retain parental roles and responsibilities will thus typically do so whilst living in a different household, perhaps sharing the role of social father with the children's mother's new partner,[10] and, if they themselves have re-partnered, possibly living with and parenting the children of their new partner.[11]

This widespread sub-division of fatherhood involves a very practical kind of fragmentation, therefore, where the work of fathering is shared between two or more men, raising questions about how fatherhood can itself be understood as a

---

[7] C Smart and B Neale, *Family Fragments?* (Polity, Cambridge, 1999); B Almond, *The Fragmenting Family* (Clarendon Press, Oxford 2006); David, above (n 1). In particular, marriage and parenthood have been increasingly separated, with particular attention paid to a significant rise in cohabitation, divorce, lone and step-parenting: J Lewis and K Kiernan, 'The Boundaries between Marriage, Non Marriage, and Parenthood: Changes in Behavior and Policy in Postwar Britain' (1996) 21 *Journal of Family History* 372. See also: Office for National Statistics, 'Living in Britain: General Household Survey 2002, Chapter 3: Households, families and people' (2004), <http://www.statistics.gov.uk/cci/nugget.asp?id=819>, accessed 3 January 2008.

[8] B Simpson, JA Jessop and P McCarthy, 'Fathers After Divorce' in A Bainham, B Lindley, and M Richards (eds), *Children and their Families: Contact, Rights and Welfare* (Hart, Oxford, 2003) at 201–2; see further: Smart and Neale, above (n 7).

[9] Drawing on his own rich empirical material, gleaned from focus groups with fathers, Jonathan Ives expresses this in terms of layers of meaning: 'fathering ideology has been building up in layers, with the "father as carer" model the most recent addition. If we dig below the surface we find the father as gender role model, a little deeper and we find the breadwinner, and deeper still we find the dominant, patriarchal disciplinarian and moral compass': J Ives, 'Becoming a Father/Refusing Fatherhood: How Paternal Responsibilities and Rights are Generated' (DPhil thesis, University of Birmingham, 2007) at 187.

[10] W Marsiglio and R Hinojosa, 'Managing the Multifather Family: Stepfathers as Father Allies' (2007) 69 *Journal of Marriage & Family* 862.

[11] Smart and Neale, above (n 7). See also: M MacLean and M Richards, 'Parents and Divorce: Changing Patterns of Public Intervention' in A Bainham, B Lindley and M Richards (eds), *Children and their Families: Contact, Rights and Welfare* (Hart, Oxford, 2003); B Simpson, *Changing Families: An Ethnographic Approach to Divorce and Separation* (Berg, Oxford. 1998). According to the 2001 census, 87% of step-families involve households made up of a couple with children from the woman's previous relationship, 11% have children from the man's previous relationship, with 3% including children from both partners' previous relationships: Office for National Statistics, above (n 7) at table 3.10.

4

situated social practice in terms of men's movement across particular physical and social spaces. In the above sense, 'fragmentation' draws together themes central to the emerging sociology of personal life around, for example, the changing status of marriage, childhood and parenting, ideas of individualisation, relationality, kinship and the rise of 'fluid' family practices.[12]

Second, the idea of fragmentation may also reflect aspects of the lived experience of parents themselves. This is perhaps most obviously true in the case of those fathers now parenting at a distance, who may find their time with their children parcelled into (possibly court-sanctioned) blocks of time. Beyond this, however, the idea of fragmentation may also resonate with the social experience of parents in a more general sense. Recent empirical research into men's beliefs regarding fatherhood suggests that it can be viewed as a fragmented – even confused – concept, used to denote a number of conceptually distinct kinds of relationships.[13] For example, Ives' empirical research found that the idea of fatherhood was used by men not so much as a fixed term with a unitary meaning but as something to be deployed in quite divergent ways, most notably via reference to a central distinction between the 'father as progenitor' and the 'father as carer'.[14]

Third, *Fragmenting Fatherhood* focuses on the specific legal responses to this changing social context, tracking the evolution of a legal recognition of diversity and heterogeneity in men's 'family practices'. Legal attempts to attach children to more than one 'father' figure mark a potentially significant break with the past, a fracturing of hitherto dominant ideas about fathering and the (sexual) family. While it remains the case, for example, that a child can have no more than one legal father named on his or her birth certificate,[15] law has responded to the demographic changes noted above by developing a range of other ways to recognise and to protect men's connections with their children. A crucial part of this process has been to accept that more than one man can have a legal connection with a child and, thus, to share – or fragment – the rights and responsibilities of fatherhood.[16] At the same time, however, we shall see that traditional ideas about the nature of the biological link between father and child and a father's role and responsibilities have had a tenacious hold on legal understandings of fatherhood in other respects.

---

[12] For discussion of these ideas see further C Smart, *Personal Life* (Polity, Cambridge, 2007) at ch 1, 'A Sociology of Personal Life'. On the idea of situated fathering, W Marsiglio, K Roy and G Litton Fox (eds), *Situated Fathering: A Focus on Physical and Social Spaces* (Rowman & Littlefield, Lanham, MD, 2005).

[13] Ives, above (n 9) at 176.

[14] *Ibid* at 177. Ives suggests the need for a division between 'causal', 'material' and 'moral' fatherhoods, so that the morally meaningful 'fatherhood as carer' can be distinguished from the less morally significant, 'father as progenitor': *ibid* at 187.

[15] Since the introduction of the Adoption and Children Act 2002, a gay male couple are able to adopt a child. However, they will find that they are legally registered as 'parents' rather than 'fathers': for discussion, see Herring, above (n 6) at 635–62.

[16] Eg through parental responsibility and contact orders. For detailed discussion see chs 5 and 6 below.

5

Fourth, as well as tracing broad social trends and emerging themes around the legal treatment of fatherhood, one of the aims of this book is to reveal the points of inconsistency and tension in this development. It will become clear that the rights and responsibilities of fatherhood can be awarded on different bases in different legal contexts. A financial obligation to support a child, for example, is generally grounded in a genetic link with that child, whereas various other relationships, rights and responsibilities associated with fatherhood may require different kinds of connection. While the 'ideal' type of the marital father we describe in chapter four (one parenting his own genetic children within a subsisting married unit) may unite several of these rights and responsibilities, we will discuss in chapters five and six how the legal regulation of fatherhood in other contexts provides for a rather more fragmented approach, as above. This legal treatment of fatherhood suggests a bundle of rights and responsibilities that can be awarded to different men, on different bases and in different contexts, a model that may itself fit closely with men's own attitudes towards fathering in some respects but not in others.[17]

Finally, the idea of 'fragmentation' captures aspects of our own attempt to unpack fatherhood, to scrutinise how it has emerged as a distinctive object of legal regulation and to track the various and shifting understandings relied upon in that process. Notably, we assess how and why fatherhood is treated variously as a genetic relationship, as a relationship with a child's mother, and as a social relationship with a child, and the various factors which affect this choice in specific legal contexts. This theme is particularly clear in chapter three, where we discuss how fatherhood is determined following the use of assisted reproductive technologies. In this context, the fragmentation of fatherhood into different kinds of connections with a child can be seen at perhaps its most radical and explicit. We consider further some of the advantages, and limits, of this theme of fragmentation in chapter seven.[18]

One remaining point of clarification should be made. We do not intend to imply that in some 'golden age' of history, fatherhood, whether understood as social experience or social institution, was ever somehow 'whole' or 'complete' or enjoyed a fixed, unitary character. As we shall see, the meaning of fatherhood in law has long been contested. Nonetheless, it seems to us that the idea of fragmentation does capture something new in recent social shifts which have reshaped the political terrain in which debates about law and personal life now take place. We suggest that the fragmentation of fatherhood is a key and under-explored element of broader and social changes around families and households. Fatherhood itself is a fragmented, fluid and ambiguous concept, an

---

[17] Ives, for example, found that fathers tended not to see fatherhood as a package in which rights and responsibilities necessarily came together. Rather, for his focus group participants, fatherhood tended to be constructed first and foremost as a set of responsibilities, which must be fulfilled before rights are earned: Ives, above (n 9).

[18] See pp 207–208, 234–238.

6

idea that means different things in different contexts, one that has been used historically – and is still used currently – to denote a wide range of relationships between a man and a child.

Having set out what we mean by 'fragmentation', we should also say something about the meaning of 'fatherhood'. Is fatherhood a reflection or statement of simple (or, perhaps, not so simple) biological 'fact', one which relates in some way to the status of a man as progenitor of a child or children? Or should fatherhood be understood as a discourse, an ideology, or perhaps in terms of a power structure? How do legal ideas about fatherhood connect to individual and collective identities, to the social behaviour of women and men, and the value systems of specific communities? How might we integrate recognition of the diversity of fatherhood, the impact of fathers' different identities and the way fatherhood is itself cross-cut by questions of race, class, age, faith, disability and sexual orientation?

As we shall see, an interrogation of the relationship between fatherhood and law involves recognising the importance of each of the above. At the outset fatherhood itself can be distinguished from *paternity*, a term generally taken to refer to the status of a man who has biologically fathered a certain child, and as forming the basis on which the status of fatherhood is then often accorded. Fatherhood, on the other hand, can be understood as a contingent social construction through which the law has sought to attach men to children.[19] While paternity is legally important, therefore, the question of whether a man obtains legal fatherhood has depended historically on other factors that are social in nature, such as, for example and notably, whether he is married to the child's mother. Alongside paternity and fatherhood, we can further distinguish the idea of 'social fatherhood', in which fathering practices occur independently of the presence of a biological or legal relationship between man and child. The diversity of fatherhood therefore encompasses questions not only about biological 'fact' but also the nature of different family practices within households, a recognition of and sensitivity to the specific experiences of groups such as lone fathers, step-fathers, birth fathers, black and ethnic minority fathers, gay fathers and young fathers. There is, we shall see, no 'one' fatherhood which can be identified as the object of law's regulation.

II The Structure of the Argument

The structure of the book is as follows. In this introductory chapter, we locate our analysis in the context of a series of demographic changes that have transformed the social, political and economic frameworks in which debates about fatherhood

---

[19] See: S Sevenhuijsen, 'The Gendered Juridification of Parenthood' (1992) 1 *SLS* 71; S Sevenhuijsen, 'Fatherhood and the Political Theory of Rights: Theoretical Perspectives of Feminism' (1986) 14 *IJSL* 329.

and law reform play out. We interrogate the interconnections that have been made between law and fatherhood in legal studies, and outline the conceptual approach to be adopted in the book. In chapter two, we proceed to trace men's involvement and changes in understandings of a father's rights and responsibilities in what we will refer to as 'natural' reproduction. There exists a common assumption in law and society that reproduction is a time of specifically female responsibility, one in which a woman's role as mother is natural, instinctive and inevitable, an 'umbilical attachment'. Men's experiences of reproduction, in contrast, have tended to be seen in law as somewhat distant and vicarious, mediated by and through the agency of the woman, who stands as a 'gate-keeper' to their involvement. At the present moment, however, in the light of the social changes detailed in this introductory chapter, understandings of men's responsibilities in this area appear to be changing in ways that have consequences for law and policy. Indeed, the issue of men's involvement in reproduction raises, we suggest, some fundamental questions not just about how, but also when, one 'becomes' a father.

In chapter three, building on this discussion, we consider fatherhood in the context of assisted reproduction, an area that raises particularly difficult dilemmas for the legal determination of parenthood. The development of assisted reproductive technologies offers radical possibilities for the fragmentation of fatherhood discussed above, providing the potential to break down parenthood into different constituent parts, thus rendering explicit decisions about which kinds of links (genetic, gestational, social and so on) are most significant in making someone a parent. As noted, in this context the questions surrounding what it is that makes a man 'a father', and the legal consequences of such a determination, have been starkly posed.

The focus of our analysis shifts, in chapter four, to the nature of fathers' rights and responsibilities in the context of the subsisting marital relationships, often assumed as the ideal forum in which to raise children. Historically, the legal institution of marriage has been central in attaching men to children, and we chart the social and legal contours of the married father understood as a distinctive kind of 'family man' in law.[20] Turning then to more recent developments, we track the emergence of a *new* and rather different model of the father as 'family man', a figure marked by rather different assumptions about men's family commitments, employment practices, sexual and intimate relations and, in particular, parenting responsibilities. Whilst a new narrative around fathers and families is emerging within certain legal contexts, however, we will suggest that understandings of fatherhood remain in other respects marked by a considerable degree of continuity. In particular, while a traditional model of the father as 'breadwinner' is being reshaped, contested and politicised within the legal

[20] On the idea of the 'family man' see S Coltrane, *Family Man: Fatherhood, Housework and Gender Equality* (Oxford University Press, Oxford, 1996); R Collier, *Masculinity, Law and the Family* (Routledge, London, 1995) at chs 5, 6.

arena, in certain ways it remains deeply resonant and ideologically powerful, framing still reverberant cultural and legal ideas about what being a 'good father' entails.

Chapters five and six focus on fathering outside the bounds of the legal ideal of this subsisting marital relationship.[21] In chapter five, we consider post-separation fatherhood. It is in this area that the emergence over the past two decades of what we term a 'new politics of fatherhood and law' has been particularly visible. The principal focus of contestation has concerned fathers' legal rights and responsibilities, notably, although not exclusively, in relation to post-separation contact, residence and financial arrangements. We suggest that both divorce and understandings of fathers' responsibilities have been reframed within legal policy debates as particular kinds of social problems, with the family practices of separated fathers, in particular, emerging as a distinct object of policy intervention on the part of law. We explore the contours of the reframing of fatherhood that has occurred in this field, tracing changes around what it means to be a 'good' post-separation father in law. In noting the cultural and political significance of the recent campaigns by some fathers' rights groups and equal parenting organisations, we interrogate how the relationship between fatherhood and law, equality and justice, rights and an ethic of care has been redrawn, a shift that has had significant implications for the development of law and policy.

In chapter six, we move on to consider a second significant 'deviation' from the ideal of the subsisting marital relationship, focusing here on the position of unmarried fathers. These form a diverse group including both single fathers and long-term cohabitants actively engaged in parenting, as well as one-off sexual partners, some of whom may not even know that they have fathered a child. We argue that recent developments relating to unmarried fathers raise further important questions about shifts around understandings of the father as a (heterosexual) 'family man', as well as about the changing place and significance of marriage in attaching men to children. Unmarried fathers, whether gay or straight, cohabiting or living alone, resident or non-resident, are a group which has been collectively viewed as posing some quite specific problems for law and policy makers. Yet as unmarried fatherhood has become an increasingly common and culturally legitimate phenomenon, legal conceptualisations of non-marital births have themselves been challenged in far-reaching ways.

In chapter seven, drawing together some of the themes which have arisen in the course of the book, we re-examine the theoretical and political implications of this study of fatherhood and law. We ask what, at a conceptual level, these

---

[21] By this we mean that law and policy has historically held the ideal of marriage to be the 'best possible' context in which to raise children, as noted above. This does not mean that normative beliefs present in law reflect the 'real lives' of individuals. Equally, and in an analytical division of material that reflects how fatherhood has itself been problematised in law, we recognise that in reality men will move between a range of categories (unmarried, marital, separated and so forth) and may sometimes occupy more than one category simultaneously.

9

developments might mean for future legal scholarship around gender and families and, in particular, what questions this interrogation of a 'new politics' of fatherhood and law might raise for understandings of law, policy, legal theory and law's governance.

In the remainder of this introductory chapter, we will set out in more detail the social, political and theoretical context for our discussion of fatherhood and law. We proceed first to track the evolving social, demographic and political context that forms the backdrop for the discussion to follow, before going on to explore how a growing interdisciplinary research base on fatherhood has raised new questions for policy makers, politicians and legal researchers in thinking about how law relates to fatherhood. We will suggest that one recurrent shortcoming of this research has been around how law itself is conceptualised. We then move on to consider in more detail how such research has fed into social policy and law reform discussions, the emergence of a distinctive 'fatherhood problematic', and how fatherhood has itself been addressed within legal studies more generally. Finally, we outline the conceptual approach to be adopted in this book, setting out a framework of analysis that, we suggest, has made possible new ways of approaching the relationship between law and fatherhood.

III   Contexts of Change: New Families, New Fatherhood?

Over the past three decades, a concern about the legal rights and responsibilities of parents has become a central feature of public and political debate and the focus of a growing academic literature.[22] The changing experiences of mothers and fathers, and contestations regarding what being a 'good parent' entails for both men and women, are issues that pervade academic books and journals, films, advertising, newspapers, the internet and television talk shows alike.[23] At present in the UK conversations about issues as diverse as marriage and divorce, crime, criminality and social disorder, adult and child health, sexuality and reproduction, the changing nature and structure of employment, childcare and 'work–life balance' have each, in different ways, posed questions about the rights, responsibilities and duties of parents towards their children, towards one another and towards the wider society in which they live.

---

[22]   While contestations around fatherhood in the legal arena have a long history, it is particularly in the period from the 1970s onwards that it is possible to trace the origins of contemporary debates: J Eekelaar, *Family Law and Personal Life* (OUP, Oxford, 2006) at 140–41. See further: ch 4, p 114–118. This period has also seen growing research and a policy focus on fathers and fatherhood.

[23]   Fatherhood, understandings of which are shaped by cultural memories and past stories, is also a recurring theme within contemporary novels, plays, poetry and television drama; see for example: S French (ed), *Fatherhood* (Virago, London, 1993). For discussion of fatherhood as a cultural signifier of masculinity, see: C Haywood and M Mac an Ghaill, *Men and Masculinities: Theory, Research and Social Practice* (Open University Press, Buckingham, 2003); for an historical perspective on fatherhood imagery: A Burgess, *Fatherhood Reclaimed: The Making of the Modern Father* (Vermillion, London, 1997).

What lies behind these developments? A now rich interdisciplinary literature has sought to explore social shifts that have reshaped how women and men negotiate the meaning and experience of being a parent. Located within the context of broader structural changes associated with late modernity,[24] a recurring concern in this work has been the entry of ever-larger numbers of women into the workforce and their continuing participation within paid employment after having children. Other key themes include the economic and cultural impacts of globalisation, related processes around individualisation and risk management in social life,[25] changes in relation to children and childhood,[26] development of new reproductive technologies and, not least, the social and political consequences of the second-wave feminist movement.[27] Interlinked with each of these developments, falling marriage and rising divorce rates, an ageing of the population, decrease in the size of families,[28] growth of cohabitation and an acceptance (if partial) of fluidity and diversity in family forms have further contributed to a reassessment of fatherhood and changes in understandings of the legal rights and responsibilities of parents.

The result is a social terrain marked by considerable diversity in household structure and family formation, offering a variety of kinds of 'family connections'.[29] 'Family life' in the UK is now widely seen as in transition, and it is largely, if not unequivocally, accepted at a political level that shifts in legal regulation are required to respond to these 'gender transformations'.[30] The extent of this change should not of course be overstated,[31] and law continues, as we shall see, to reproduce normative ideas of parenting, families and sexualities within certain contexts. Nonetheless, these shifts in employment and childcare practices, for

[24] See eg: A Giddens, *The Transformations of Intimacy* (Polity, Cambridge, 1992); U Beck and E Beck-Gernsheim, *The Normal Chaos of Love* (Polity, Cambridge, 1995). Cf: C Smart, *Personal Life* (Polity, Cambridge, 2007); Eekelaar, above (n 22).

[25] U Beck, *Risk Society: Towards a New Modernity* (Sage, London 1992); U Beck and E Beck-Gernsheim, *Individualization* (Sage, London, 2002).

[26] The literature on which is now considerable. See eg: J Qvortrup *et al* (eds), *Childhood Matters: Social Theory, Practices and Politics* (Avebury Press, Aldershot, 1994); A James, C Jenks and A Prout, *Theorizing Childhood* (Polity, London 1998); A James and A Prout (eds), *Constructing and Reconstructing Childhood* (Falmer Press, London, 1990); U Beck, 'Democratization of the Family' (1997) 4(2) *Childhood* 151.

[27] See eg: S Faludi, *Backlash: The Undeclared War Against Women* (Chatto & Windus, London, 1991); also S.Faludi, *Stiffed: The Betrayal of the Modern Man* (Chatto & Windus, London, 1999).

[28] Office for National Statistics, 'Divorce' (2007), <http://www.statistics.gov.uk/cci/nugget.asp?id=170>, accessed 3 January 2008. For discussion, see: S Cretney, *Family Law in the Twentieth Century: A History* (Oxford University Press, Oxford, 2004).

[29] D Morgan, *Family Connections: An Introduction to Family Studies* (Polity, Cambridge, 1999); E Silva and C Smart (eds), *The New Family* (Sage, London, 1999); Smart and Neale, above (n 7).

[30] S Walby, *Gender Transformations* (Routledge, London, 1997).

[31] It is important to remember, for example, that notwithstanding images of the 'absent' father and historically high levels of divorce, around 7 out of 10 families consist of dependent children living with both their parents, and that 70% of British fathers have contact with their children: C Lewis, *A Man's Place in the Home: Fathers and Families in the UK* (Joseph Rowntree Foundation, York, 2000).

example, alongside corresponding changes in the parental aspirations of both women and men, have a two-fold significance for the legal regulation of fatherhood.

First, there has been an explicit recognition at a policy level that fathering now takes place in these diverse settings. There is no 'one' kind of fatherhood. Alongside married cohabiting fathers, we find rising numbers of unmarried cohabiting fathers, non-cohabiting fathers, men who socially father genetically unrelated children and a growing social and legal recognition of fathering within gay/lesbian partnerships, as well as of the specific issues that can face, for example, black and ethnic minority fathers, young fathers, disabled fathers and fathers of disabled children.[32] It is in this context of continuity, change and diversity that we locate our discussion, as above, of the fragmentation of fatherhood.

Second, debates around fatherhood in the legal arena would appear to have become increasingly politicised. Law assumes a symbolic importance within these conversations about gender and social change, appearing as a key 'battleground' for determining the meaning of such change for women and men, and for collective and individual negotiations of the shifting dynamics of power between the sexes.[33] Is it the case, as some suggest, that law now 'favours' one sex over the other? How, for example, does a political contestation around fatherhood in the context of post-separation contact relate to a wider rethinking of issues of care, dependency, vulnerability and autonomy in society? A heightening of concern regarding fatherhood in recent years reflects not only the social and economic changes outlined above but also the emergence of a distinctive cultural and political landscape around families. In this terrain the increasing visibility of fathers' rights agendas, a 'fathers' rights movement' and 'pro-family', 'pro-father' perspective, associated strongly, although by no means exclusively, with the

---

[32] See for example D.Quinton, S.Pollock and J.Golding, *The Transition to Fatherhood for Young Men: Influences on Commitment* (ESRC Trust for the Study of Adolescence, University of Bristol, Bristol, 2002) available at <http://www.fatherhoodinstitute.org/index.php?id=13&cID=477>, accessed 31 March 2008; J.Harrison, M.Henderson and R.Leonard, *Different Dads: Fathers' Stories of Parenting Disabled Children* (Jessica Kingsley, London, 2007): W Hatten, L Vinter and R Williams, *Dads on Dads: Needs and Expectations at Home and Work* (Equal Opportunities Commission, Manchester, 2002); J Warin *et al*, *Fathers, Work and Family Life* (Family Policy Studies Centre, London, 1999). See also J Weeks, B Heaphy and C Donovan, *Same-sex Intimacies: Families of Choice and Other Life Experiments* (Routledge, London, 2002). Equally, cross-cultural and anthropological studies have shown that '. . . despite idealisation of the heterosexual family, there is no consistent model of what a family is': K O'Donovan, *Family Law Matters* (Pluto, London, 1993) at 34; L Nicholson, 'The Myth of the Traditional Family' in HL Nelson (ed), *Feminism and Families* (Routledge, London, 1997).

[33] See eg: A Hochschild, 'Understanding the Future of Fatherhood' in M van Dongen, G Frinking and M Jacobs (eds), *Changing Fatherhood* (Thesis Publishers, Amsterdam, 1995); S Coltrane, 'The Future of Fatherhood: Social, Demographic, and Economic Influences on Men's Family Involvements' in W Marsiglio (ed), *Fatherhood: Contemporary Theory, Research, and Policy* (Sage, Thousand Oaks, CA, 1995); J Mitchell and J Goody, 'Feminism, Fatherhood and the Family in Britain' in A Oakley and J Mitchell (eds), *Who's Afraid of Feminism? Seeing Through the Backlash* (Hamish Hamilton, London, 1997).

political Right,[34] has undoubtedly been one impetus to this politicisation of fatherhood. Within such a vision, a decline in paternal authority is often linked to the collapse of marriage as a social institution, to higher divorce rates, 'family breakdown' and a toxic mixture of other social problems. In accounts of 'fatherhood in crisis', for example, special significance is attached to the interconnections between the 'fatherless family', rising levels of crime, social disorder and the underachievement of boys.

These kinds of arguments play out in different ways at different moments across areas of law, mediated not just by the specificities of legal systems and cultures and the dominant political climate of the time, but also by a complex interplay of social movements in articulating, and challenging, such views.[35] What is significant about the contemporary politics of fatherhood and law in the UK is the extent to which these debates about fatherhood have shifted to reflect the emergence of a legal paradigm marked by a formal commitment to egalitarianism, gender neutrality and social diversity.

Gender Convergence, Gender Neutrality and Formal Equality

A recurring theme within academic, political and popular cultural accounts of change relating to fatherhood is that of a gender convergence between men and women around a range of social experiences, including those pertaining to family life, childcare, paid employment, intimacy, sexuality, reproduction and consumption. Such accounts suggest that the social practices of parents are being reshaped as a result of the breaking down of hitherto gendered divisions in law and society. Thus, women's increased entry into a once male-dominated public domain of paid labour is linked to the argument that fathers today are (or at least should be) undertaking a greater role in childcare and domestic labour in the home. Allied to this are demands that the gendered cultures of organisations and institutions adapt to these new realities facing fathers by promoting, for example, better work–life balance and the development of father-inclusive practices in service provision.[36] Meanwhile, fatherhood, and the identity of 'being a father', appears increasingly bound up with issues of lifestyle and consumption in ways traditionally associated with women, not least in relation to the interlinking of fatherhood with the commodification of heterosexual masculinities and the male body and male sexuality within many areas of popular culture.[37]

---

[34] See ch 5; also: P Abbott and C Wallace, *The Family and the New Right* (Pluto, London, 1992).

[35] See eg: R Collier and S Sheldon (eds), *Fathers' Rights Activism and Legal Reform in Comparative Perspective* (Hart, Oxford, 2006).

[36] See ch 4.

[37] The development of new forms of commercialised masculinity is an important and, we suggest, under-theorised dimension of contemporary fathering. See eg: S Coltrane and K Allan, '"New" Fathers and Old Stereotypes: Representations of Masculinity in 1980s Television Advertising' (1994) 2(4) *Masculinities* 43. See generally: F Mort, *Cultures of Consumption: Masculinities and Social Space in Late Twentieth Century Britain* (Routledge, London, 1996).

Importantly in terms of law, these debates about gender convergence take place within the context of a legal framework that is marked by a formal commitment to gender neutrality and equality.[38] Whether in relation to the legal claims of separated and unmarried fathers (chapters five and six), attempts to promote paternal responsibility on the part of fathers (chapter four), broader social agendas concerning reproduction (chapter two) or issues of men's health,[39] sexuality[40] and men's violence(s),[41] social policy is now largely expressed in this language of gender neutrality and formal equality. Whilst statutory provision in family law tends likewise to be expressed in formally gender-neutral language, this 'sameness of treatment' approach has itself been criticised, particularly by feminist writers, as having reinforced gendered norms by effacing still extant questions of gender difference.[42] Importantly, such critiques suggest, formal gender equality fails to redress the material basis of dominance, side-stepping issues of social power and the fact that differential treatment may, at times, be necessary to compensate for social disadvantage created by structural conditions.[43] From a rather different perspective, meanwhile, framing policy in gender-neutral terms is also seen as effacing the specificity of men's experiences and exacerbating further the marginalisation of fathers in a range of areas of service provision.[44] Naming them 'parents', for example, results in a silencing of the specific experiences of men. Politically, it is argued, such gender neutrality can cut both ways.

Closely implicated in these debates are broader shifts in the relationship between children's and adults' rights and responsibilities in law,[45] the incorporation of the European Convention on Human Rights through the Human Rights

---

[38] This has a long history. Each of the major developments in family law from the mid-nineteenth century onwards has been seen as directed towards the promotion of equality within the law for women and men. It is not, however, until the Guardianship Act 1973 (s 1) that formal equality is finally achieved between women and men in relation to child custody. Although focused particularly on Canada, for an excellent account of this move see: S Boyd, *Child Custody, Law, and Women's Work* (Oxford University Press, Toronto, 2003). See generally: Eekelaar, above (n 22), chs 5 and 6.

[39] S Robertson, *Understanding Men's Health: Masculinity, Identity and Well-being* (Open University Press, Buckingham, 2007); B Featherstone, M Rivett and J Scourfield, *Working With Men in Health and Social Care* (Sage, London, 2007).

[40] M Kimmell, *The Gender of Desire: Essays on Male Sexuality* (SUNY Press, New York, 2005).

[41] J Hearn, *The Violences of Men* (Sage, London, 1998); S Burton, L Regan and L Kelly, *Supporting Women and Challenging Men: Lessons from the Domestic Violence Intervention Project* (The Policy Press, Bristol, 1998). See ch 7, pp 218–222.

[42] M Fineman, *The Illusion of Equality: The Rhetoric and Reality of Divorce Reform* (University of Chicago Press, London, 1991); Boyd, above (n 38); M Fineman, 'Cracking the Foundational Myths: Independence, Autonomy, and Self-Sufficiency' (2000) 13 JGSPL 13; S Boyd, 'From Gender Specificity to Gender Neutrality? Ideologies in Canadian Child Custody Law' in J Brophy and C Smart (eds), *Child Custody and the Politics of Gender* (Routledge, London, 1989).

[43] Formal equality, it has been argued, resolves only the 'problem' of treating people or situations differently; it does not redress questions of dominance and disadvantage. See: Diduck and Kaganas, above (n 6) at ch 7. In relation to rights, see: Eekelaar, above (n 22).

[44] Ch 4, p 118.

[45] See: A Bainham, *Children: The Modern Law*, 3rd edn (Jordan Publishing, Bristol, 2005).

Act 1998 further entrenching ideas of equality into English law.[46] Across diverse legal fields, and in the context also of broader EU agendas to promote the 'mainstreaming' of gender equality within member states, law has been used to encourage or reinforce certain forms of (gendered) behaviour on the part of parents in ways seen to be compatible with the promotion of equality.[47] In this book, we chart how a coming together of these social and legal changes, and the political debates around formal equality and gender neutrality to which they have given rise, have played out in relation to fatherhood within the legal arena. In the next section, we explore in more detail how research around fatherhood has evolved, and the kinds of questions that this work has raised for law.

IV. Researching Fatherhood, New Questions For Law

The terms 'motherhood' and 'fatherhood' are, simultaneously, both powerful descriptors of the lived experience of individuals and abstract socio-cultural concepts. Parenthood is experienced in ways framed by culturally and historically contingent normative ideas about, for example, gendered divisions of labour, ethics of care and caring, sexuality and economic responsibility.[48] Both motherhood and fatherhood, as we shall see, have been interpreted, constructed and given meaning in ways that are defined and delimited by law. However, motherhood has attracted far more attention than fatherhood, spawning a now vast social policy, social scientific, psychological and medical literature.[49] Likewise, an extensive body of feminist (and other) legal scholarship has explored how mothers have been subjected to identification, explanation and disposition in law as (or, indeed, as not) familial individuals in particularly oppressive ways, ways that, importantly, men as fathers have not.[50] The fact that much less has been written on the relationship between law and fatherhood reflects, in part, this

[46] The Human Rights Act 1998 has, for example, in injecting a public element of rights and justice into intimate relations, led to extensions of marriage to transsexual persons (Gender Recognition Act 2004) and to the recognition of registered same-sex relationships (Civil Partnership Act 2004).

[47] On the reconceptualising of 'responsibility' involved in this process, see: H Reece, *Divorcing Responsibly* (Hart, Oxford, 2003); R van Krieken, 'The "Best Interests of the Child" and Parental Separation: On the "Civilising of Parents"' (2005) 68(1) MLR 25; Eekelaar, above (n 22) at 127–131. See ch 7 below, pp 214–216.

[48] See ch 7 below, p 234.

[49] See eg: A Phoenix, A Woollett and E Lloyd, *Motherhood: Meanings, Practices, Ideologies* (Sage, London, 1991); J Ribbens, *Mothers and their Children: A Feminist Sociology of Childrearing* (Sage, London, 1994).

[50] See eg: M Fineman, *The Neutered Mother, The Sexual Family, and Other Twentieth Century Tragedies* (Routledge, New York, 1995); S Boyd, 'Is there an Ideology of Motherhood in (Post)modern Child Custody Law?' (1996) 5 SLS 495; A Diduck, 'In Search of the Feminist Good Mother' (1998) 7(1) SLS 129; A Diduck, 'Legislating Ideologies of Motherhood' (1993) 2 SLS 461; M Fineman and I Karpin (eds), *Mothers in Law: Feminist Theory and the Legal Regulation of Motherhood* (Columbia University Press, New York, 1995); E Silva (ed), *Good Enough Mothering? Feminist Perspectives on Lone Motherhood* (Routledge, London, 1996).

wider societal scrutiny of motherhood and surveillance of mothers (and of some groups of mothers in particular). Over the last two decades, however, there has been a concerted attempt across the arts, social sciences and humanities to move beyond the mother-focused paradigm that had marked so many earlier studies of parenthood, and to develop a study of fatherhood in its own right.[51]

As a result of this fast-growing body of work, research that is international in scope and diverse in focus, much more is now known about fathers, the complexity and diversity of fathering practices and the all-too-often 'hidden histories' of fathers' lives.[52] Academic research has occupied a particularly power-ful position in the reshaping of our understandings of fatherhood, constituting a form of knowledge often seen as authoritative in both political and policy forums. However, it is also important to recognise here the extent to which popular texts and media such as television, film, child-rearing and parenting manuals, self-help books, newspaper and magazine articles and so on have also shaped understandings of many aspects of the changing experience of fathers, including how fathers relate to law.[53] As Lupton and Barclay suggest, such popular representations can also serve to highlight aspects of fathering that may be absent in the 'expert' literature, not least in seeking to engage with the emotional dimensions of fatherhood, 'with all its hopes, joys and pleasures as well

---

[51] This literature, encompassing disciplines as diverse as developmental and social psychology, sociology, family health and welfare, applied sociological research and writings on masculinity will be referred to as this book progresses. It is not our intention in this chapter to present a literature review of empirical and theoretical research on fatherhood. Rather, we focus on how this academic research has itself constructed certain 'ways of thinking' about law and fatherhood. See ch 2 below for how this shift can also be seen in the biomedical sciences, which are increasingly paying attention to male reproductive biology.

[52] See eg: C Lewis and M Lamb, *Understanding Fatherhood: A Review of Recent Research* (Joseph Rowntree Foundation, Lancaster University, 2007); G Barker *et al*, *Supporting Fathers: Contributions from the International Fatherhood Summit 2003* (Early Childhood Development: Practice and Reflec-tions Series, Bernard van Leer Foundation, The Hague, 2004); C Lewis and ME Lamb, 'Fathers: The Research Perspective' in G Barker *et al*, *ibid*; W Marsiglio, *Fatherhood: Contemporary Theory, Research and Social Policy* (Sage, New York, 1995); A Dienhart, *Reshaping Fatherhood: The Social Construction of Shared Parenting* (Sage, London, 1998); N Rosh White, 'About Fathers: Masculinity and the Social Construction of Fatherhood' (1994) 30(2) *Journal of Sociology* 119; A Doucet, *Do Men Mother? Fatherhood, Care and Domestic Responsibility* (University of Toronto Press, Toronto, 2006); D Lupton and L Barclay, *Constructing Fatherhood: Discourses and Experiences* (Sage, London, 1997); A Doucet, 'Fathers and Responsibility for Children: A Puzzle and a Tension' (2004) 28(2) *Atlantis* 103; L Curran, and S Abrams, 'Making Men into Dads: Fatherhood, the State, and Welfare Reform' (2000) 14(5) *Gender & Society* 662; Dowd, above (n 3); Larossa, above (n 4); R Parke, *Fatherhood* (Harvard University Press, Cambridge, MA, 1996); EH Peters *et al*, *Fatherhood: Research, Interventions and Policies* (Haworth, New York, 2000); F Bozett and S Hanson (eds), *Fatherhood and Families in Cultural Context* (Springer, New York, 1991); Marsiglio, Roy and Litton Fox (eds), above (n 12).

[53] See eg: S Bruzzi, *Bringing Up Daddy: Fatherhood and Masculinity in Post-war Hollywood* (British Film Institute, London, 2005); E Tincknell, *Mediating the Family: Gender, Culture and Representation* (Hodder Arnold, London, 2005) especially ch 3. See generally: D Chambers, *Represent-ing the Family* (Sage, London, 2001). Many self-help books, child-care manuals and newspaper or magazine articles on fatherhood, of course, traverse the boundaries between academic and popular text (written, for example, by academics and university researchers for a wider readership): Lupton and Barclay, above (n 52).

as its anxieties'.[54] This is a theme particularly evident in the emergence of a plethora of autobiographical accounts of fatherhood, whether it be of fathering daughters, fathering sons or of being father*ed*, something which now constitutes a distinctive genre of writing.[55]

Whilst much academic work on fatherhood has been of a historical, theoretical, empirical and policy-focused nature, one of the most significant drivers of the new research agenda has been work developed by psychologists and social policy analysts. It is, Haywood and Mac an Ghaill suggest, the conceptual frameworks, methodologies and substantive concerns of these disciplines that have tended to frame much of the 'new wave' of fatherhood research.[56] Issues of law and legal regulation have nonetheless been a significant feature within this work, although not necessarily in ways that have engaged with what is, from the perspective of legal studies, the problematic nature of law itself. This point requires clarification.

In the UK, a wide range of books, journal articles,[57] and policy reports,[58] have each sought to address many aspects of the experience of fathers. This work has embraced a wide range of concerns encompassing, for example, fathers as step-parents,[59] unmarried and cohabiting fathers,[60] young black and ethnic

[54] Lupton and Barclay, above (n 52).

[55] See eg: B Morrison, *And When Did You Last See Your Father?*, 2nd edn (Granta, London, 2006); G Greer, *Daddy, We Hardly Knew You* (Penguin, Harmondsworth, 1990); D Henry and JA McPherson, *Fathering Daughters: Reflections by Men* (Beacon, Boston, MA, 1999). Reflecting the shifts outlined above, accounts are emerging of the experiences of the children of gay parents. See eg: N Howey and E Samuels, *Out of the Ordinary: Essays on Growing Up With Gay, Lesbian and Transgender Parents* (St Martins Press, New York, 2000); J Drucker, *Families of Value: Gay and Lesbian Parents and their Children Speak Out* (De Capo Press, New York, 1998).

[56] Haywood and Mac an Ghaill, above (n 23).

[57] See eg: B Hobson (ed), *Making Men into Fathers: Men, Masculinities and the Social Politics of Fatherhood* (Cambridge University Press, Cambridge, 2002); B Featherstone, 'Taking Fathers Seriously' (2003) 33(2) *British Journal of Social Work* 239; B Featherstone, 'Fathers Matter: A Research Review' (2004) 18 *Children & Society* 312; K Stanley, *Daddy Dearest? Active Fatherhood and Public Policy* (Institute for Public Policy Research, London, 2005); A Burgess, *Fatherhood Reclaimed: The Making of the Modern Father* (Vermillion, London, 1997); A Burgess and S Ruxton, *Men and Their Children: Proposals for Public Policy* (Institute for Public Policy Research, London, 1996); A Burgess and G Russell, 'Fatherhood and Public Policy' in G Barker *et al*, *Supporting Fathers: Contributions from the International Fatherhood Summit 2003* (Early Childhood Development: Practice and Reflections Series, Bernard van Leer Foundation, The Hague, 2004).

[58] In the UK, research councils, charities and other organisations have funded a range of projects on diverse aspects of fatherhood. See eg: S Dex and K Ward, *Parental Care and Employment in Early Childhood: Working Paper 57* (Equal Opportunities Commission, Manchester, 2007); C Lewis, *A Man's Place in the Home: Fathers and Families in the UK* (Joseph Rowntree Foundation, York, 2000); J Warin *et al*, *Fathers, Work and Family Life* (Family Policy Studies Centre, London, 1999); Equal Opportunities Commission, *Fathers and the Modern Family* (Equal Opportunities Commission, Manchester, 2007); L Burghes, L Clarke and N Cronin, *Fathers and Fatherhood in Britain* (Family Policy Studies Centre, London, 1997); P Moss (ed), *Father Figures: Fathers in the Families of the 1990s* (HMSO, Edinburgh, 1995); G Dench, *The Place of Men in Changing Family Cultures* (Institute of Community Studies, London, 1996).

[59] E Ferri and K Smith, *Step-parenting in the 1990s* (Family Policy Studies Centre, London, 1998). See generally: W Marsiglio, *Stepdads: Stories of Love, Hope and Repair* (Rowman & Littlefield, Lanham, MD, 2004).

17

minority fathers,[61] the role of fathers in preventive services,[62] and the place of fathers in divorce and separation.[63] Notably, much of this scholarship has sought to explore aspects of fathering at the interface of men's employment and family commitments.[64] This research has, at times, quite explicitly taken aspects of law and legal regulation as the object of analysis (for example, in analysing provisions relating to parental leave, or measures aimed at promoting work–life balance). Understandably, however, given the nature of their primary concern and specific disciplinary contexts, such studies have tended not to take *law* as the specific object of analysis – and certainly not in a way informed by developments within social and legal theory.[65] This work has shown a tendency, rather, to conceptualise law in a way informed by the assumptions of legal positivism, a 'black-letter' approach to law which not only provides little grasp of the complex interconnections of law and other disciplines, and the discourses which speak of fathers, but which also constitutes fatherhood as a distinctive kind of social problem.

In this book, we draw on and explore this growing research base around fatherhood whilst, at the same time, integrating insights from legal analysis and jurisprudence around the study of law and families. We consider, in particular, how law relates to these other disciplines and to this contemporary research on fathers. Some sociological scholarship, for example, has sought to address various aspects of the legal regulation of fatherhood in the UK. Yet this work has tended to focus on discrete areas of law: the participation and role of fathers in childcare and domestic labour,[66] law reform proposals relating to unmarried fathers,[67] post-separation non-residential fathers and so forth.[68] What empirically based,

---

[60]   R Pickford, *Fathers, Marriage and the Law* (Family Policy Studies Centre, London, 1999).

[61]   S Speak, S Cameron and R Gilroy, *Young Single Fathers: Participation in Fatherhood – Bridges and Barriers* (Family Policy Studies Centre, London, 1997).

[62]   D Ghate, C Shaw and N Hazel, *Fathers and Family Centres: Engaging Fathers in Preventive Services* (York Publishing Services, York, 2000); B Featherstone, M Rivett and J Scourfield, 'Working with Men in Health and Social Care' (Sage, London, 2007); J.Scourfield, 'The Challenge of Engaging Fathers in the Child Protection Process' (2006) 26(2) *Critical Social Policy* 440. See further ch 4.

[63]   See eg: GB Wilson, 'The Non-resident Parental Role for Separated Fathers: A Review' (2006) *IJLPF* 1; J Hunt and C Roberts, *Child Contact with Non-Resident Parents*, Family Policy Briefing 3, (Department of Social Policy and Social Work, University of Oxford, Oxford, 2004); B Rodgers and J Pryor, *Divorce and Separation: The Outcomes for Children*, (Joseph Rowntree Foundation, York, 1998); J Pryor and B Rodgers, *Children in Changing Families: Life After Parental Separation* (Blackwell, Oxford, 2001). See also M Lamb, *The Role of the Father in Child Development* (John Wiley, New York, 1997). See further ch 5.

[64]   Ch 4, pp 118–120. See also: M O'Brien, *Shared Caring: Bringing Fathers into the Frame* (Equal Opportunties Commission, Manchester, 2005); M O'Brien, *Fathers and Family Support* (National Family and Parenting Institute, London, 2004); M O'Brien and I Shemilt, *Working Fathers: Earning and Caring* (Equal Opportunities Commission, Manchester, 2003); L Haas, P Hwang and G Russell (eds), *Organisational Change and Gender Equity: International Perspectives on Fathers and Mothers in the Workplace* (Sage, London, 2000).

[65]   Cf N Lowe, 'The Legal Status of Fathers: Past and Present' in L McKee and M O'Brien (eds), *The Father Figure* (Tavistock, London, 1982).

[66]   See ch 4 below, pp 128–129.

[67]   See ch 6 below.

[68]   For discussion, see ch 5 below, pp 153–55.

18

disciplinary focused and applied research tends not to do, however, is to address the 'bigger picture' of changes in the nature of legal regulation and governance more generally, to interrogate the interconnections that exist between what is happening *across* diverse areas of law. That is what this book seeks to do.

This can be illustrated via a theme that will resurface in each of the chapters to follow. A number of books and articles, diverse in content, form and political intent, have sought to document various aspects of what have been termed the twin 'crises' of fatherhood and masculinity.[69] Law, once again, has been a central theme in this work, notably through its implication in well-publicised debates around fatherhood, crime and social order.[70] Yet what this literature has tended not to do is to question the representations of law within these accounts, nor to seek to explain how a mutually constituted 'crisis' around fatherhood and masculinities has itself drawn on certain assumptions about the nature of law and legal regulation, ideas that play out in different ways across legal contexts. The reframing of the relationship between law and gender that has occurred as a result of the rise of formal equality agendas and gender neutrality, as discussed above, has, as we shall see, itself been a key feature of the reconstruction of fatherhood as a distinctive social problem and object of legal intervention. We will argue in this book that this shift must be located not in relation to any idea of 'masculine crisis', but rather within the context of broader and longer-term strategies of governance and shifts in relation to ideas of the responsibilities of parenthood contained in law.

What has remained unexplored in accounts of fatherhood and law, therefore, is not simply the problematic nature of how law relates to and draws upon (and is itself drawn upon by) other disciplines such as sociology, psychology and criminology.[71] It is also the changing nature of law and legal regulation itself in relation to understandings of the 'private' (sexual) family and familial autonomy, childhood, elder care and dependency, employment, family life and intimacy and so forth. As such, it is in this context of an expanding literature on fatherhood that we locate this book as part of a broader attempt to develop a new sociology of personal life.[72]

In the light of the social changes discussed above, and in noting this growing research base on fathering, we now go on to assess how fatherhood has emerged as a prominent object of social policy concern and legal intervention within the UK, in particular, we shall suggest, in the years since 1997.

---

[69] The 'crisis of masculinity' has been the subject of a vast literature. See eg: A Clare, *On Men: Masculinity in Crisis* (Chatto & Windus, London, 2000); R Collier, *Masculinities, Crime and Criminology: Men, Heterosexuality and the Criminal(ised) Other* (Sage, London, 1998).

[70] Collier, above (n 69) at ch 5. Fatherhood has, in particular, had a central role in debates about youth crime, social disorder and parental responsibility.

[71] See eg: M King and C Piper, *How the Law Thinks About Children*, 2nd edn (Arena, Aldershot, 1995); M King and J Trowell, *Children's Welfare and the Law: The Limits of Legal Intervention* (Sage, London, 1992).

[72] Smart, above (n 12). See also Fineman (2000), above (n 42); Fineman, above (n 50).

V. Family Law, Family Policy and Fatherhood

The political and research contexts described above reflect a broad consensus that law has a significant role to play in the promotion of social responsibility on the part of men and of a particular kind of 'good', desirable fathering. Precisely what the latter entails has inevitably, however, been contested.[73] Two elements of this process are of particular significance for the discussion of fatherhood to follow in this book. First, the achievement of consensus has relied upon a shift in, and a challenge to, normative ideas of family life, ideas premised on certain assumptions about the nature of heterosexuality and gendered divisions of labour. Second, the emergence of a policy agenda based around 'father-inclusive practice' in the UK has itself focused attention on certain problems relating to men, masculinities and fatherhood that play out in different ways across different areas of social policy. We will here briefly consider each of these issues in turn.

In the period since the election of the New Labour government in 1997, a range of legal reforms have reshaped the parameters of the hetero(sexual) family in a number of respects.[74] Legislation such as the Civil Partnership Act 2004[75] and the Gender Recognition Act 2004,[76] alongside related developments in case law, policy and legal practice (for example, in the field of adoption),[77] have served to challenge ideas of parenting and family life as somehow a priori heterosexual. In other contexts, reforms relating to the legal status of unmarried and cohabitating parents have served to reposition, if not undermine, the place of marriage within family policy, in ways that have reshaped understandings of the responsibilities of fathers.[78] We do not wish to overstate the scope and impact of these shifts here, nor the extent to which such developments are themselves partial, contested and problematic. Marriage, as we shall see, continues to hold a particularly privileged position in law, not least in relation to determinations of the status of fatherhood. If we consider the kinds of partnerships that now attract legal recognition as 'family', there is also perhaps 'less scope for diversity than first

---

[73] See eg: Guardian Editor, 'The Conservatives and Family Policy: Fatherhood and Apple Pie', *Guardian* (21 June 2006) Comment 32; P Wintour, 'Fathers told: Do more for your children' *Guardian* (27 February 2007) News 1.

[74] See ch 4, pp 114–118.

[75] P Mallender and J Rayson, *The Civil Partnership Act 2004: A Practical Guide* (Cambridge University Press, Cambridge, 2005). Cf: S Gavigan, 'Legal Forms and Family Norms: What is a Spouse?' (1999) 14 *Canadian Journal of Law & Society* 127: J Goldberg-Hiller, 'The Status of Status: Domestic Partnership and the Politics of Same-sex Marriage' (1999) 19 *Studies in Law, Politics & Society* 3.

[76] Above n 46. This legislation gives legal recognition to transsexual people and allows them to acquire, subject to certain criteria, a new birth certificate and to marry, as well as affording them full recognition in law for other purposes. See also ch 4, p 116–117.

[77] The Adoption and Children Act 2002 now allows same-sex couples to adopt.

[78] Ch 6. See also: M Stewart, 'Judicial Redefinition of Marriage' (2004) 21 *Canadian Journal of Family Law* 11.

20

appears'.[79] Further, the apparent extension of the idea of 'family' in these developments may be seen as part of a normalising process and extension of law's governance, a 'rolling out' of the responsibilities of parents in ways that well serve the economic and social interests of the neo-liberal state.[80] At the very least, however, these developments represent a significant challenge to hetero-normative definitions of family life and with it, we suggest, traditional under-standings of the role and responsibilities of fathers.

Underscoring these shifts has been a longer-term transformation in family law, one dating back over 30 years (at least), in which the welfare, rights and autonomy of the child has become increasingly central to discussions of law and social policy. This development has been described as a key part of 'the second revolution in family law'[81] that resulted in the reframing of the position of parents and children. The enactment of the Children Act 1989 has been widely seen as encapsulating the historical shift in English and Welsh law from a focus on parental (and, more specifically, paternal) *rights*, towards an increasing focus on gender-neutral, and equal, parental *responsibilities*.[82] Importantly for our present concerns, this shift occurred alongside a rethinking of the place of the father in child welfare and development, a move bound up in complex ways with the explosion of research on fatherhood discussed above. Emerging from a range of disciplines and standpoints, one central theme within this work has been that fathers have a contribution to make to families that transcends the role of breadwinner/provider with which they have historically been associated. Rather, fatherhood is now widely viewed in legal and social policy as a highly significant resource for children, with considerable consensus emerging regarding the posi-tive impact of suitably 'engaged fathers' on child welfare.[83]

---

[79] A Diduck and K O'Donovan, 'Feminism and Families: Plus Ça Change?' in A Diduck and K O'Donovan (eds), *Feminist Perspectives on Family Law* (Routledge-Cavendish, Abingdon, 2006) at p 6.

[80] Boyd, above (n 38); S Boyd, 'Legal Regulation of Families in Changing Societies' in A Sarat (ed), *The Blackwell Companion to Law and Society* (Blackwell, London, 2004); M.Fineman, *The Autonomy Myth* (The New Press, New York, 2004); A Diduck, 'Shifting Familiarity', in J Holder and C O'Cinneide (eds), *Current Legal Problems 2005*, vol 58 (Oxford University Press, Oxford, 2006) 235; van Krieken, above (n 47); R van Krieken, 'Legal Informalism, Power and Liberal Governance' (2001) 19(1) *SLS* 5; B Cossman, 'Family feuds: Neo-conservative and Neo-liberal Visions of the Reprivatiza-tion Project' in J Fudge and B Cossman (eds), *Privatization, Law and the Challenge to Feminism* (University of Toronto Press, Toronto, 2002). Note, for example, Stychin's reading of the 2004 Civil Partnership Act: C Stychin, 'Family Friendly? Rights, Responsibilities and Relationship Recognition' in A Diduck and K O'Donovan (eds), *Feminist Perspectives on Family Law* (Routledge-Cavendish, Abingdon, 2006). Cf Eekelaar, above (n 22) at 120–21.

[81] J Carbone, *From Partners to Parents: The Second Revolution in Family Law* (Columbia University Press, Columbia, 2000). Cf MA Glendon, *The Transformation of Family Law: State, Law and Family in the United States and Western Europe* (University of Chicago Press, Chicago, IL, 1989).

[82] See ch 4, p 103; Eekelaar, above (n 22) at ch 5. Cf (in the US context) MA Mason, *From Father's Property to Children's Rights: The History of Child Custody in the United States* (Columbia University Press, New York, 1994). See further ch 7, pp 223–225.

[83] See eg: E Flouri, *Fathering and Child Outcomes* (John Wiley & Sons, Chichester, 2005); AJ Hawkins and DC Dollahite, *Generative Fathering: Beyond Deficit Perspectives* (Sage, Thousand Oaks, CA, 1997); Lamb, above (n 63); Barker *et al*, above (n 52). This literature is discussed further in ch 5 below at pp 154–155.

Thus, whether in terms of a child's psychological health, future socio-economic status, educational achievement or adolescent development, or in relation to the prevention of youth crime, social and legal policy in the UK has, across diverse fields, been informed by the view that that the mere physical presence of fathers in the lives of their children is not enough. A heightened concern with the effects of divorce and separation on children has provided much impetus for the evolution of this view.[84] However, this repositioning of the father cuts across areas of social policy. The overarching framework of child welfare and development has been a crucial backdrop in the move to promote the above ideas of the 'involved father' and 'father-inclusive' practice,[85] and law, importantly, has had a central role in this process.

Over the past decade in Britain, there has been an explicit attempt to use law to promote a range of father-inclusive practice in service provision across diverse areas of policy and service delivery. In the last three years alone, measures such as the Childcare Act 2006,[86] the Equality Act 2006,[87] policy documents such as *Every Parent Matters*,[88] the National Service Frameworks, Guidance and other developments[89] have sought to increase expectation and encourage local authorities, health care providers and other organisations to include fathers, regardless of social background, in the delivery of services. These initiatives have been

---

[84]   See ch 5 below, pp 153–155.

[85]   J Scourfield and M Drakeford, 'New Labour and the "Problem of Men"' (2002) 22 *Critical Social Policy* 619. See also: Burgess and Russell, above (n 57).

[86]   By which local authorities in England and Wales must identify parents and prospective parents who are considered unlikely to use early childhood services (for example, fathers, who are specifically mentioned) and facilitate access to those services. See eg: Department for Children, Schools and Families, 'Childcare Act 2006: First ever Early Years and Childcare Act', Information Resource Surestart website, <http://www.surestart.gov.uk/resources/general/childcareact>, accessed 4 January 2008. See further ch 4 below, pp 122–124.

[87]   This places upon public bodies (including health, education and children's services) the requirement to publish an 'action plan' for promoting gender equality, to undertake a 'gender impact assessment' and to gather information and consult on how services impact on men and women: Equality Act 2006, s 84.

[88]   Department of Education and Skills, *Every Parent Matters* (Department of Education and Skills, London, 2007). This explicitly states, for example, that fathers, 'irrespective of the degree of involvement they have in the care of their children ... should be offered routinely the support and opportunities they need to play their parental role effectively'. It is now required that information is gathered about fathers and that fathers, across all social groups, are routinely consulted with when planning services: *ibid* at para [3.11]: note also B Daniel *et al*, 'Why Gender Matters for "Every Child Matters"' (2005) 35 *British Journal of Social Work* 1343.

[89]   For example, the *Children's Centre Practice Guidance 2006* and *Planning and Performance Management Guidance 2006*, which place specific requirements on including fathers, and the *Teenage Parents Next Steps: Guidance for Local Authorities and Primary Care Trusts*, which prioritises the need to work with young fathers in the development of service provision around pregnancy and birth: Department of Education and Skills, 'Children's Centre Practice Guidance' Surestart website, 2006, <http://www.surestart.gov.uk/publications/?Document=1500>, accessed 4 January 2008; Department of Education and Skills, 'Planning and Performance Management Guidance', Surestart website, revised November 2006, <http://www.surestart.gov.uk/publications/?Document=1852>, accessed 4 January 2008; Department for Children, Schools and Families, 'Teenage Parents Next Steps: Guidance for Local Authorities and Primary Care Trusts' (Department for Children, Schools and Families, London, 2007). See further ch 2 below.

informed by a significant rethinking of, first, how fathers' involvement impacts on children, as above; second, the behaviour of mothers; and third, the role of fathers in child protection. The promotion of 'good enough' fathering, in particular, is now widely seen as a 'buffer', a protection, against child disadvantage. Thus, fathers have been repositioned as the perceived solution to a range of complex social problems, albeit, as we shall see, in some contradictory ways. This shift has rested on assumptions, however, not just about fatherhood, but also about the reach and power of law in changing the behaviour of parents, an issue that raises important questions about how the relationship between law, families and fatherhood is conceptualised.

VI. Law, Families, Fatherhood: Conceptual Questions

If the centrality of law to attempts to entrench, promote and shape the role of fatherhood is now clear, what then of the place of fatherhood within legal studies? The past two decades have seen a far-reaching reassessment of the regulation of families in legal scholarship.[90] Exploring issues of theory, methodology and the scope and limits of law itself, a diverse literature in law and society and socio-legal studies has opened up new questions about the relationship between law and families.[91] Yet the place of fatherhood within this field of work has often been marginal, with fathers addressed as just one component of a broader analysis pitched at either the investigation of a range of laws pertaining to 'parenthood' and 'the family', or else in relation to some other specific topic (adoption, contact and residence, step-parents, assisted reproduction and so on). Thus, whilst fatherhood has been discussed in the context of numerous studies of, say, law and motherhood, law and masculinities, or the legal regulation of reproduction, it has tended to emerge as an object of analysis merely incidental to the primary focus on some other central theme or issue.

The theoretical and practical critique of the positivist, doctrinal framework that historically dominated much Anglo-American legal study has shifted the scope of the study of law and parenthood. The contribution of critical and socio-legal scholars, critical race and queer theorists, feminist legal writers and scholars of masculinities and law has reframed the kinds of questions now being asked about the relationship between law and fatherhood.[92] As a result, and alongside the growing literature concerned with broader questions about rights

---

[90] For general discussion, and an excellent overview relating to families and family law: Boyd, above (n 80).

[91] For an earlier attempt to address law within a contextual, policy frame: J Eekelaar, *Family Law and Social Policy*, 2nd edn (Weidenfeld & Nicholson, London, 1984); J Eekelaar and M Maclean, *Maintenance After Divorce* (Clarendon Press, Oxford 1986); MDA Freeman (ed), *State, Law, and the Family: Critical Perspectives* (Tavistock, London, 1984).

[92] Boyd, above (n 38); Smart and Neale, above (n 7). For an excellent overview of gender, state and family law: Diduck and Kaganas, above (n 6) at ch 1.

and responsibility pertaining to parenthood in law,[93] new concepts and categories of analysis have emerged through which to approach the legal regulation of fatherhood. This work provides analytic tools through which it is possible to explore how, and why, fatherhood should have become so pivotal to political struggles over the changing nature of contemporary family life. In this section, we first explore how fatherhood appeared within earlier accounts of law and families in legal studies. We then proceed to consider this more recent work, research that, we suggest, raises some rather different questions about law and fatherhood.

Constructing the 'Family Man': Fatherhood, Functionalism and the Public/Private Divide

Earlier socio-legal accounts of the relationship between law and families had tended, first, to rely on a functionalist lens of analysis and, second, to emphasise the division between public and private spheres. Each of these approaches, on closer examination, depicts the relation between law and fatherhood in certain ways. Within functionalist sociology, for example, 'the family' plays a central role in the processes of socialisation and consumption.[94] Mothers and fathers each have distinctive roles in relation to the care of children and paid employment (with the father, broadly, primarily important as familial breadwinner). Within this paradigm, the family provides an orderly means of reproduction, and, through marriage, control of the potentially destructive forces of human sexuality.[95] Law, as a mechanism of enforcing social norms, is seen as deeply implicated within this analysis, and functionalism has had a marked influence on diverse accounts of law and families, informing studies of both family policy and legal practice.[96] Functionalist presuppositions can be seen in both academic work and judicial pronouncements, the latter frequently drawing on the language of sex role theory in accounts of what being a 'good father' entails, a tendency particularly evident in disputes over what used to be called child custody.[97]

The political and conceptual limitations to this approach have been well documented, within both legal studies and sociology more generally.[98] Not only does functionalism misread the nature and effect of legal regulation in relation to families, effacing questions of social power that were to be central to later

---

[93] See further: Eekelaar, above (n 22).

[94] T Parsons, 'The American Father: Its Relation to Personality and to Social Structure' in T Parsons and RF Bales (eds), *Family, Socialization and Interaction Process* (The Free Press, New York, 1955). See further: D Cheal, *Family and State Theory* (Harvester Wheatsheaf, Hemel Hempstead, 1991); Haywood and Mac an Ghaill, above (n 23).

[95] Curiously, this remains a theme of accounts of fatherhood within variations of underclass theory. See eg: C Murray, *The Emerging British Underclass* (Institute of Economic Affairs, Health and Welfare Unit, London, 1990); C Murray, *Losing Ground* (Basic Books, New York, 1984).

[96] Eekelaar, above (n 22).

[97] See further the discussion in Boyd, above (n 38).

[98] See eg: O'Donovan, above (n 32); Collier, above (n 20); J Dewar, *Law and the Family*, 2nd edn (Butterworths, London, 1992). For a useful recent discussion see Smart, above (n 12) at ch 1.

24

feminist work, it also involves a problematic notion of the 'sexed' or 'gendered' subject in the first place.[99] Arguments about the functional male gender role of the father, meanwhile, involve assumptions about the normative nature of paternal/familial masculinity, male sexuality and indeed about what constitutes 'good' fatherhood. As a framework for approaching the relationship between fatherhood and law, functionalism thus rests on a reductionist model of gendered parenting, a model increasingly out of step with the social and demographic changes and equity and diversity agendas outlined above. These shifts pose significant challenges to the hetero-normative definitions of family life so central to functionalist accounts of fatherhood.

A second and rather different framework of analysis has been provided by work focusing on the public/private distinction, a subject that has enjoyed a special significance in accounts of fatherhood within legal, historical and socio-logical studies of parenting. Notably, a fusing of beliefs about fatherhood and heterosexual masculinity has been seen as central to the institution historically of a range of 'sexual divisions' in law.[100] The bodies, identities and emotional lives of fathers have each been understood via reference to men's primary location in the public, rather than the domestic or private, sphere.[101] On closer examination, however, a number of different interconnections exist between the public/private divide and the legal regulation of families, each in ways that involve some historically specific ideas of fatherhood. The relationship between home and the workplace, for example, has been seen in sociological scholarship as mediating the experience of men as both husbands and fathers, with some accounts suggesting a form of masculinity 'subordinated' at work can be productive of a patriarchal, authoritarian model of fatherhood within the home. Elsewhere, the private arena of the home has been explained as a space in which fathers are provided with a secure 'haven' from the demands of their paid labour. Mean-while, in discussions of the rise of the 'companionate marriage' during the post-war period, it is in the home that the father is provided with an opportunity to develop expressive qualities, to nurture, care and 'be a man' in ways that, it is assumed, he is unable to do in the workplace.[102]

Given the centrality of the public/private division to liberalism and liberal legal thought more generally, it is unsurprising to find a range of issues bearing on fatherhood and law in this way framed in terms of the boundary between public powers and private freedoms. Questions such as how, and to what extent, the

---

[99] On the limits of sex role theory see eg: RW Connell, *Gender and Power* (Polity, Cambridge, 1987) at 47–54; T Carrigan, B Connell and J Lee, 'Toward a New Sociology of Masculinity' (1985) 14 *Theory & Society* 551.

[100] For an account of this process see K O'Donovan, *Sexual Divisions in Law* (Weidenfeld & Nicholson, London, 1985).

[101] See further: TL Broughton and H Rogers (eds), *Gender and Fatherhood in the Nineteenth Century* (Palgrave Macmillan, London, 2007); ch 4 below, p 109–110.

[102] Haywood and Mac as Ghaill, above (n 23). Cf C Lasch, *Haven in a Heartless World: The Family Besieged* (Basic Books, New York, 1977).

25

state should intervene in family life; whether personal morality is, and should be, the concern of the law; and the extent to which welfare professionals do or should 'intervene' in the family have each been couched in terms of the dichotomy between the public and the private spheres. Yet over the past two decades, a body of sociological, theoretical and historical work concerned with the relationship between law and families and the gendered nature of the pubic/private division has presented a profound challenge to the idea that the family is – or, as Boyd observes, could ever be – an unregulated private sphere.[103] This critique of the public/private divide has taken a number of forms, each raising various questions about law and fatherhood. Historical research suggests, for example, that the evolution of fatherhood is itself far more complex than a primary reference to the gendered division between public and private would indicate. Great variation can exist in men's practices and experiences, and these do not necessarily correlate with the dominant cultural codes regarding what it means to be a 'father' within specific contexts. Such ideas are themselves mediated by questions about social class, race, locale, sexuality, disability, health and so forth.[104] There are, in short, profound dangers in reading assumptions about fathering practices from the dominant cultural codes around fatherhood at any given moment in time.

At a conceptual level, meanwhile, work has addressed the contingent, social and politically problematic nature of the public/private distinction itself,[105] noting in particular the erasure of the role of law in the constitution of that division, and the silencing of power relations within families that results from approaching legal regulation in terms of 'state intervention'. Feminist work has argued that this dualism has been central to the way in which law has historically served to reinforce unequal social relations along the lines of gender, race, class, sexual orientation and disability.[106] Within such a critique, importantly, certain aspects of fatherhood have themselves been rendered problematic and 'made visible' – the scale and nature of men's violence within families, and the response of the state to such violence, has in particular been reframed as a pressing social problem. This engagement with the gendered dimensions of the public/private distinction can be seen as part of the wider politicisation of fatherhood that has

---

[103] Boyd, above (n 80); F Olsen, 'The Family and the Market: A Study of Ideology and Legal Reform' (1983) 96 *Harvard Law Review* 1497; N Rose, 'Beyond the Public/Private Division: Law, Power and the Family' (1987) 14 *Journal of Law & Society* 61; F Olsen, 'The Myth of State Intervention in the Family' (1985) 18(4) *University of Michigan Journal of Law Reform* 835; Fineman, above (nn 50 and 42, 'Cracking the Foundational . . .').

[104] This is a central theme in the research studies listed above (see nn 52, 57 and 58). See eg: J Brown and G Barker, 'Global Diversity and Trends in Patterns of Fatherhood' in G Barker *et al*, *Supporting Fathers: Contributions from the International Fatherhood Summit 2003* (Early Childhood Development: Practice and Reflections Series, Bernard van Leer Foundation, The Hague, 2004).

[105] S Boyd (ed), *Challenging the Public Private Divide: Feminism, Law, and Public Policy* (University of Toronto Press, Toronto, 1997); M Thornton, 'The Public Private Dichotomy: Gendered and Discriminatory' (1991) 18(4) *Journal of Law & Society* 448; SM Okin, *Justice, Gender and the Family* (Harper Collins, London, 1989); C Pateman, *The Sexual Contract* (Cambridge University Press, Cambridge, 1988); JB Elshtain, *The Family in Political Thought* (Harvester Press, Sussex, 1982).

[106] See eg Boyd, above (n 105); Fineman (2000), above (n 42); O'Donovan, above (n 100).

occurred in the wake of feminism, raising questions about the behaviour of men in relation to what 'goes on' both within and beyond the 'home'.[107] As O'Donovan notes, the public private division historically legitimated 'the law of the father' whilst effacing how 'law is not only central to the concepts of private and public, and to the division between the two, but also plays an important part in the construction of that division'.[108] Such feminist critiques of the public/private have brought to the surface how the division has been infused with gendered notions about the worlds of work, the market, autonomy and individualism, politics, competition and the state. In opening the 'box' of the family and subjecting power relations within the private domestic sphere to critical assessment, however, what also occurred was a 'cracking open' of the concept and terrain of family law itself.[109] This move in legal study, we argue in the next section, has had important implications for how we approach fatherhood and law.

Fatherhood, Feminism and Law's Governance: Towards a 'Critical Family Law'?[110]

Earlier work concerned with the politics of families – notably feminist, socialist-feminist and Marxist critiques of the family and economy produced during the 1970s and 1980s[111] – tended to locate law as just one significant element within a broader structural analysis of power relations within advanced capitalist societies. The figure of the father was positioned in much of this work as the patriarchal embodiment of male authority, his power broadly functional to the interests of the capitalist state.[112] Law continued, however, to be understood largely within the terms of the positivist framework dominating legal studies at the time: a juridical conception of power expressed through the legal form and reflected in social policies. In such accounts the state is positioned as sole point of reference for a range of juridical, administrative and political functions, an implicit unity given to the concept of 'state intervention' itself.[113] In terms of

---

[107] On the concept of which in law: L Fox, *Conceptualising Home: Theories, Power, Policies* (Hart, Oxford, 2006).

[108] O'Donovan, above (n 100) at 3.

[109] Boyd, above (n 80).

[110] M Freeman, 'Towards a Critical Theory of Family Law' (1985) 38 *Current Legal Problems* 153.

[111] See eg: M Barrett and M McIntosh, *The Anti-Social Family* (Verso, London, 1982); E Zaretsky, *Capitalism, The Family, and Personal Life* (Harper & Row, New York, 1976).

[112] This was also very much a theme of men's anti-sexist literature of the time. Note generally the representation of the father in work such as: J Hearn, *Birth and Afterbirth: A Materialist Account* (Achilles Heel, London, 1983). For discussion: Collier, above (n 20)

[113] See C Smart, *Feminism and the Power of Law* (Routledge, London, 1989). Rethinking the public/private dichotomy entails questioning the concept of the state as the '. . . locus of all political power and of the interests which the law as expression of state policy – is deemed to serve': Rose, above (n 103) at 66. See also: N Rose and P Miller, 'Political Power Beyond the State: Problems of Government' (1994) 43(2) *British Journal of Sociology* 173.

developing understanding of the relationship between fatherhood and law, and far from seeing governance as something distributed among diverse elements of the polity, the form and content of legal regulation was largely seen as the barometer of the freedoms of individuals and families.

This form of theorising involved a specific (juridical) conception of power, one that has continued to inform perceptions of the state/law as a reflection of the relative power of men and women.[114] During the 1980s, however, not least as a result of the growing impact of feminist scholarship and post-structuralism within legal studies, legal research increasingly sought to question the kinds of assumptions about the 'power of law' underscoring these accounts of family relations.[115] For some, this meant looking beyond marriage and divorce, and towards the plethora of laws that, in different ways, affected and constituted ideas about families within legal discourse. The parameters of 'family law', as a distinctive field of study, became increasingly problematic as topics hitherto considered outside the subject were now included within socio-legal analyses of family relations.[116] At the same time, in developing the feminist critique of the public/private distinction, other work sought to highlight the historically contingent and conceptually imprecise nature of the relationship between law and the state, the market and family.[117] Noting the 'uneven development'[118] of much law reform in practice, it questioned the limits of thinking about law in terms of legal intervention either increasing or decreasing family 'privacy'. Further, it rejected the assumption that the power of law could itself usefully be understood in terms of a 'zero-sum' equation whereby, it was assumed, an increase in the power of the state (or men) would mean a decrease in the power of the family (or women), and vice versa.[119] In aligning the critique of the public/private outlined above with developments taking place within feminist and post-structuralist thought around the concepts of power, discourse and the (gendered) subject,[120] this work was to inform the study of fatherhood, law and masculinities that developed during the 1990s.

---

[114] For critical discussion: Smart, above (n 113)

[115] *Ibid.*

[116] Increasingly, the scope of 'family law' was seen to include, for example, questions of criminal law and criminology, EU law, employment law, public and constitutional law, social security law, taxation law, immigration law and property law, as well as, more generally, the psycho-social dimensions of human relationships around feeling, expectation and emotion. Each of these areas, as we shall see in this book, has relevance for understanding fatherhood.

[117] Rose, above (n 103).

[118] C Smart, 'Feminism and Law: Some Problems of Analysis and Strategy' (1986) 14 *IJSL* 109.

[119] Smart, above (n 113) at ch 1.

[120] C Smart, 'The Woman of Legal Discourse' (1992) 1 SLS 29; C Smart, *Law, Crime and Sexuality: Essays in Feminism, Essays on Feminism* (Sage, London, 1995).

Fatherhood, Law and the Subject(s) of Men

We noted above how the idea of the 'unregulated private'[121] has the potential to mask questions of power, and that the ostensibly private world of the family is in fact formed by, and through, structures external to it. In building on these insights, an engagement with fathers and fatherhood has become a significant theme both within feminist legal scholarship and in studies of masculinities and law.[122] It is possible, for heuristic purposes, to identify a number of distinctive 'phases' or approaches within this work, each of which has tended to conceptualise men and fatherhood in different ways.[123] For example, from the so-called 'first phase' liberal-progressivist feminist scholarship,[124] through to the work of those feminist writers who later sought to engage with the inherent 'maleness' of patriarchal legal systems, ideas about fatherhood have been linked to different arguments about how law and the power of men interrelate. Within earlier feminist work, the presence of a distinctive masculine culture (or culture*s*) of law was singled out as particularly problematic for women. Hetero-normative definitions of family life, ideas about the 'natural' familial roles of mothers and fathers, were presented as historically enmeshed with a range of sexualised and sexist beliefs. The resulting 'masculinism'[125] of social and legal institutions was seen as evident in the content of judicial pronouncements, in the disavowal of the specificities of women's distinctive experiences, and in the routine sexualisation (and rendering 'Other') of women's bodies within much legal practice. All this, importantly, was seen to have implications for women as mothers in ways that it did not for men as fathers. Rather, the deployment of an idea of the 'masculinity of law' was linked to an erasure of men's 'private lives' in such a way that fatherhood appeared as something distant, disengaged, set apart from women, children and families, away from questions of emotion, vulnerability and dependency.[126]

---

[121] O'Donovan, above (n 32) at 11.

[122] Whilst 'family relations and family law have always been important to men and children also and to their political status, economic activity and claims to citizenship and rights, . . . it is a feminist perspective that has made this link explicit': A Diduck and K O'Donovan (eds), *Feminist Perspectives on Family Law* (Routledge-Cavendish, Abingdon, 2006) at 1. See further: R Collier, 'Feminist Legal Studies and the Subject(s) of Men: Questions of Text, Terrain and Context in the Politics of Family Law and Gender' in A Diduck and K O'Donovan (eds), *Feminist Perspectives on Family Law* (Routledge-Cavendish, Abingdon, 2006).

[123] N Naffine, *Law and the Sexes* (Allen & Unwin, Sydney 1990) at ch 1. It is, we recognise, problematic to categorise together a vast body of feminist work and assume a linear narrative underscoring what is, in fact, a far more complex history. Equally, it is important not to assume a conceptual 'clean break' with earlier (pre-feminist) sociogenic sex role accounts of men, masculinities and fatherhood; see further: R Collier, 'Reflections on the Relationship Between Law and Masculinities: Rethinking The "Man Question"' *Current Legal Problems*, (2003) vol 56 (Oxford University Press, Oxford, 2004) at 345; Carrigan, Connell and Lee, above (n 99); J Conaghan, 'Reassessing the Feminist Theoretical Project in Law' (2000) 27 *Journal of Law & Society* 351.

[124] Naffine, above (n 123) at 3–6.

[125] A Brittan, *Masculinity and Power* (Blackwell, Oxford, 1989) at 4.

[126] See eg: R Collier, 'A Hard Time to be a Father? Law, Policy and Family Practices' (2001) 28 *Journal of Law & Society* 520; R Collier, 'Male Bodies, Family Practices' in A Bainham, S Day Sclater

29

Whilst these earlier feminist studies focused primarily on mothers and motherhood, in so doing they did, in a sense, seek to make fathers visible. Texts such as Atkins and Hoggett's *Women and the Law*, for example, with their discussions of equality and opportunity, motherhood, fatherhood, marriage, violence and 'breadwinners and homemakers', illustrate the attempt that was being made to question the dominant masculine cultures of law, to hold men in families, as well as the legal system itself, to account.[127] Engaging with the gendered assumptions of case law, statute and legal practice, such work provided fruitful insights into how law had historically understood fatherhood. What it did not do, however, was engage with the gendered nature of legal concepts, categories and reasoning,[128] or address the social and legal construction of the 'Woman' of legal discourse.[129] By the mid/late 1980s, in a 'third phase' of feminist scholarship,[130] anti-essentialist work had began to question the way in which feminism had itself ascribed to the category 'woman' a certain ontological status, thereby negating the diverse positionality both within and between women's lives. What was also increasingly recognised in legal studies, however, albeit implicitly, was that there were dangers in conceiving of men as a homogenous group; and, indeed, conceiving of law as an unproblematic embodiment of men's social power.[131] The embrace of essentialist notions of the 'masculinity of law' (as well as, we would suggest, its heterosexuality),[132] served to erase the complexity and heterogeneity in the lives, not only of women, but also of men.[133]

and M Richards (eds), *Body Lore and Laws* (Hart, Oxford, 2002); R Collier, 'In Search of the "Good Father": Law, Family Practices and the Normative Reconstruction of Parenthood' (2001) 22 *Studies in Law, Politics and Society* 133.

[127] S Atkins and B Hoggett, *Women and the Law* (Blackwell, Oxford, 1984); A Sachs and JH Wilson, *Sexism and the Law: A Study of Male Beliefs and Judicial Bias* (Martin Robertson, Oxford, 1978).

[128] See eg: C Mackinnon, *Feminism Unmodified: Discourses on Life and Law* (Harvard University Press, Cambridge, MA, 1987); C Mackinnon, 'Feminism, Marxism, Method and the State: An Agenda for Theory' (1983) 8 *Signs* 635.

[129] Smart (1992), above (n 120); N Lacey, *Unspeakable Subjects: Feminist Essays in Legal and Social Theory* (Hart, Oxford, 1998).

[130] Naffine, above (n 123).

[131] 'Although it may be that it is men as biological entities who exercise most legally constituted forms of power, and indeed men as individuals who benefit most from the oppression of women, the law is not simply a conglomeration of individual, biological men. Neither is it a collection of individuals in this way, even though individuals have a responsibility for how they interpret or enforce the law': C Smart, *The Ties That Bind* (Routledge & Kegan Paul, London, 1984) at 18. This problem, Smart then suggested, may itself be indicative of just '... how difficult it is to talk of structures of power and mechanisms of regulation *without* attributing these to biological agents who then become personifications of power and control': Smart, *ibid* at 17. See also: J Brophy and C Smart (eds), *Women in Law: Explorations in Law, Family, Sexuality* (Routledge & Kegan Paul, London, 1985) at 97, 115.

[132] L Segal, *Straight Sex: The Politics of Pleasure* (Virago, London, 1994) 46; W Hollway, 'Recognition and Heterosexual Desire' in D Richardson (ed), *Theorising Heterosexuality: Telling it Straight* (Open University Press, Buckingham, 1996); C Smart, 'Collusion, Collaboration and Confession on Moving Beyond the Heterosexuality Debate' in D Richardson (ed), *Theorising Heterosexuality: Telling*

This shift in thinking is of particular significance for the study of fatherhood and law. What opens out to analysis here is the contingency, complexity and diversity of men's social experiences, including their experience as fathers. Fusing a feminist critique of law[134] with emerging sociological challenges to dominant notions of masculinity,[135] attempts in legal studies during the 1990s to engage with men 'as the subjects of a discourse of masculinity' brought into view the plurality and contingency of those discourses which speak of men, masculinities and fatherhood across diverse institutional and cultural contexts. It is not difficult to see, in retrospect, why this transition should have taken place within feminism; nor why feminists and pro-feminist scholars should then have sought to turn 'their attention to men and masculinity in a discursive attempt to stop the depiction of women as "the problem", as well as to resist the on-going objectification of women'.[136] However, if it is then (albeit implicitly) recognised that all men do not have equal access to cultural, symbolic or economic capital, and that there is a need to engage with plural 'familial' masculinities, this raises a number of questions about social power and the diversity of men's experiences of being a father.[137] There is, we shall see in this book, no 'one' fatherhood in law, even if law's nature is to seek to regulate experientially and socially complex relationships within generalist categories. In short, in turning attention to the 'Woman' of legal (and, indeed, of feminist) discourse,[138] what was (inescapably) brought into the critical frame was the 'Man' of law, the contingent nature of the male subject of legal feminism and with it, importantly for our present purposes, the nature of the 'father' in law.

Law, Discourse and the Construction of the 'Social Problem' of Fatherhood

We noted above a series of presuppositions regarding the centrality of law to strategies of intervention concerned with 'dealing with' particular social problems. In marked contrast to the dominant epistemological frameworks which

---

it Straight (Open University Press, Buckingham, 1996); C Smart, 'Desperately Seeking Post-Heterosexual Woman' in J Holland and L Adkins (eds), *Sex, Sensibility and the Gendered Body* (Macmillan, Basingstoke, 1996).

[133] Collier, above (n 123).

[134] Smart, above (n 114) at 86; O'Donovan, above (n 32) at 5.

[135] See, for discussion in law: Collier, above (n 123).

[136] M Thornton, 'Neoliberal Melancholia: The Case of Feminist Legal Scholarship' (2004) 20 *Australian Feminist Law Journal* 7 at 12.

[137] See further: W Marsiglio and JH Pleck, 'Fatherhood and Masculinities' in M Kimmell, J Hearn and RW Connell (eds), *The Handbook of Studies on Men and Masculinities* (Sage, Thousand Oaks, CA, 2004).

[138] As others have observed, it had became apparent in the 1990s that differentiation by, for example, race, economic resources and religion made universal claims about the conditions of 'Woman' difficult to maintain; see A Diduck and K O'Donovan (eds), *Feminist Perspectives on Family Law* (Routledge-Cavendish, Abingdon, 2006), EV Spelman, *Inessential Woman: Problems of Exclusion in Feminist Thought* (The Women's Press, London, 1990).

31

have characterised much doctrinal legal scholarship, Rose and Valverde seek to rephrase the question 'what does [family] law govern?' by beginning, not with 'law' itself (whether in the form of statutes, cases or legal practices), but from a series of questions or what they term 'problems or problematizations'.[139] Their focus is the

way in which experience is offered to thought in the form of a problem requiring attention. The analysis of problematization is the analysis of the practices within which these problematizing experiences are formed . . . in order to analyse the ways in which problems form at the intersection of legal and extra-legal discourses, practices and institutions, it is necessary to de-centre law from the outset.[140]

In taking up this notion of the construction of fatherhood as a distinctive 'social problem', we do not wish to suggest that law is unimportant in seeking to understand the relationship between fatherhood and family life. To focus the analytic gaze on how ideas of fatherhood become problematised at particular historical moments is, however, to move away from pre-given notions, whether of fatherhood or law, and to draw attention to how fatherhood is itself formed as a particular kind of social experience, and target for government, at certain moments. Such analysis seeks to explore 'the role of legal mechanisms, legal arenas, legal functionaries, legal forms of reasoning and so on in strategies of regulation'.[141] This frame allows us to analyse how a plurality of different forms of expertise have come together historically in the construction of family policy in England and Wales, the *dramatis personae* of policy formulation and implementation including (at the very least) psychologists, family welfare professionals, lawyers, sociologists, demographers, geographers and economists, as well as politicians and civil servants. The authorities that have defined different aspects of fatherhood as objects of legal intervention have thus worked within a broader regulatory apparatus concerned with the scrutinising of familial well-being and welfare.[142] Such a disciplining of social life has involved not just the individual internalisation of controls within the liberal state,[143] but also issues of sanction,

---

[139] N Rose and M Valverde, 'Governed by Law?' (1998) 7(4) *SLS* 541. See also: JI Kitsuse and M Spector, 'The Definition of Social Problems' (1973) 20(4) *Social Problems* 407.

[140] Rose and Valverde, above (n 139) 545. Cf Smart, above (n 114). On the 'governmentality' approach with which this argument is aligned, see further: N Rose, 'Expertise and the Government of Conduct' (1994) 14 *Studies in Law, Politics and Society* 359; M Valverde, *Law's Dream of a Common Knowledge* (Princeton University Press, Princeton, NJ, 2003); P O'Malley, *Risk, Uncertainty and Government* (The Glasshouse Press, London, 2004).

[141] Rose and Valverde, above (n 139) at 546; See also: M Foucault, 'Governmentality' in G Burchell, C Gordon and P Miller (eds), *The Foucault Effect: Studies in Governmentality* (Harvester Wheatsheaf, London, 1991); N Rose, *Governing the Soul* (Routledge, London, 1995).

[142] J Lewis, 'The Problem of Fathers: Policy and Behaviour in Britain' in B Hobson (ed), *Making Men into Fathers: Men, Masculinities and the Social Politics of Fatherhood* (Cambridge University Press, Cambridge, 2002).

[143] Rose, above (n 141). See also: M Dean, *Governmentality: Power and Rule in Modern Society* (Sage, London, 1999); G Burchell, C Gordon and P Miller (eds), *The Foucault Effect: Studies in Governmentality* (Harvester Wheatsheaf, London, 1991); A Barry, T Osborne and N Rose (eds), *Foucault and Political Reason: Liberalism, Neo-liberalism and Rationality of Government* (UCL Press,

censure and the deployment of power around the construction of ideas about what constitutes a good mother, a good father, a good parent and so forth.[144] Law has played a central role in this promulgation of these ideas about 'good fatherhood', and fathers, as well as mothers, have been subject to surveillance, regulation and discipline through law.

Fatherhood and Family Practices

In developing this idea of the construction of fatherhood as a social problem, the approach we adopt in this book can be aligned with that of recent sociological work which views 'the family' not as a pre-given site in or to which men and women come as fixed and finished gender subjects. Rather, family practices are themselves active forces in the social construction of these ideas about men and women. We would draw a distinction between fathering practices (what fathers do), and cultures of fatherhood (diverse, and by no means consistent, sets of beliefs about fathers that circulate in the social realm, in law, in popular culture, in academic scholarship and so forth). In seeking to engage with this issue of what men do as fathers, David Morgan has suggested that family life might be usefully

> considered through a variety of different lenses and from different perspectives. Thus, family practices may also be gender practices, class practices, age practices and so on . . . *family life* is never simply family life and . . . *is always continuous with other areas of existence.* The points of overlap and connection are often more important than the separate entities, understood as work, family, politics and so on.[145]

In approaching family as 'a constructed quality of human interaction . . . an active process rather than a thing-like object of detached social investigation' an engagement with fathering as social practice seeks to transcend those binaries that have constrained understandings of social practice within liberal legal thought – notably the divisions between public/private, mind/body, hetero/homo(sexual), sex/gender and nature/nurture. This approach serves to question pre-given, taken-for-granted notions of what fathers' family practices might be in the first place. In contrast to those accounts which conceptualise the family as 'a relatively bounded unit exchanging with other, equally relatively bounded units',[146] such a focus on the 'doing' of family life embraces an appreciation of difference and diversity in family forms, including the multifarious ways in which men can 'do' fathering. It resists a slippage into normative models of (heterosexual) family life, something that is, in any case, increasingly untenable in the

London, 1996); J Donzelot, *The Policing of Families* (Hutchinson, London, 1980). A different reading of 'normalisation' can be found in Eekelaar, above (n 22) at 120.

[144] van Krieken, above (n 47).

[145] (Emphasis added) D Morgan, 'Risk and Family Practices: Accounting for Change and Fluidity in Family Life' in E Silva and C Smart (eds), *The 'New' Family?* (Sage, London, 1999) at 13. See further: Morgan, above (n 29). For discussion, Smart, above (n 12), at ch 1.

[146] Morgan (1999), above (n 145) at p 13.

face of the demographic changes and the fracturing of heteronormativity inherent in the new democratic family ideal outlined above.[147]

In what follows, therefore, we seek to recognise the significance of shifting cultural representations of fatherhood, such as those contained in law, whilst also recognising the complexity and diversity of these family practices.[148] In each of the areas of law discussed in the following chapters, we identify dominant discourses at play within the legal arena, and consider how these have contributed towards particular understandings of fatherhood in specific instances. These discourses of fatherhood, we suggest, are expressed both in legal texts (whether written, such as cases and statutes, or oral, as in legal argument), as well as in the social and embodied practices of individuals that take place within the legal arena.[149] They play out at particular historical moments in ways that shape how fatherhood is talked about, and, in the context of law, how the parenting practices of men are constituted as a distinctive kind of social problem. Yet these cultural representations of fatherhood have a problematic relation to social practice, to the question of what men and women do in their 'everyday' lives. The tension and 'gap' between the two will be a key and recurring theme of this book. The forms of fatherhood evident in law, and in much contemporary cultural imagery of parenting, do not necessarily reflect or simply describe a changing reality – whether of 'family life', paid employment or interpersonal relationships. Rather, as Lupton and Barclay suggest, these discourses stand 'in an active relation' to such a reality.[150] Shifting ideas about fatherhood are themselves part of how ideas about reality and knowledge of a rapidly changing world are constituted. The discourses of fatherhood to be found in law are just one, albeit significant, element of this.

As we aim to show in the pages which follow, diverse social practices play a role in the constitution of fathers as distinctively gendered (as masculine/male) 'familial' subjects. Such gendering happens in processes of encoding cultural, social and economic capital within particular contexts (whether workplace, household or community), in the construction of family work as a distinctive form of emotional labour, and in the establishment of normative gendered notions of parental responsibility. Our engagement with the way both structural and discursive practices constitute and give meaning to sexual difference allows us to highlight the differential nature of women's and men's gendered experiences

---

[147] See further: R Collier, 'Straight Families, Queer Lives? Heterosexual(izing) Family Law' in D Herman and C Stychin (eds), *Sexuality in the Legal Arena* (Athlone Press, London, 2000); Stychin, above (n 80).

[148] Lupton and Barclay, above (n 52) at ch 1.

[149] We here follow Lupton and Barclay in considering discourses of fatherhood as ways of representing – whether through talking, writing or visually portraying – ideas about fathers and the practices or material conditions associated with these representations.

[150] These 'discourses [of fatherhood] may be regarded as assemblages of knowledges that serve to produce notions of the human subject': Lupton and Barclay, at 42.

in relation to these family practices,[151] as well as the problems implicit in attempts to promote social justice via the conceptualisation of an ungendered citizen.[152] Such an approach thus serves to question aspects of the idea of gender convergence underpinning the 'new fatherhood' ideal discussed above, as well as the related belief that the consequences of these social changes are, in all contexts, inevitably and necessarily socially progressive.

Conclusion

In the rest of the book, we draw on and develop the themes and issues discussed in this introductory chapter in a detailed exploration of the relationship between fatherhood and law. We pay attention to both the socio-cultural contexts in which discourses of fatherhood are generated and reproduced, and the structural and political contexts in which legal regulation occurs, laws are enacted and enforced, legal agents operate and so forth. In debates around law reform, for example, we consider the way in which certain social groups, institutions and structures shape these debates about law and fatherhood as social problems. Why, and how, have some discourses of fatherhood been favoured in legal arenas over others? In what ways are 'official' perceptions of the relative power of social groups justified and sustained, or, perhaps, challenged by the choices that individuals and organisations make within particular legal contexts? Further, and of particular importance in understanding the complexity of law reform in recent years, what practices of resistance can take place and what alternative knowledge(s) and truth claims are generated as a response to these dominant discourses around fatherhood?

Fatherhood, we have suggested in this introductory chapter, is a rather amorphous phenomenon.[153] There is little doubt that fatherhood has become a site of 'intensely political debate ... a focus for a number of tensions around notions of gender and intimate relationships and the role of the state in "private" life that have emerged in the wake of second-wave feminism and changing economic conditions'.[154] Within recent social scientific research, as well as in numerous popular accounts, there has been a clear and repeated attempt to

---

[151] For example, questions about what (notwithstanding the technological developments discussed in ch 3) bodies are and are not generally capable of. See: E Grosz, 'A Note on Essentialism and Difference' in S Gunew (ed), *Feminist Knowledge: Critique and Construct* (Routledge, London, 1990); E Grosz, *Volatile Bodies: Towards a Corporeal Feminism* (Allen & Unwin, St Leonards, New South Wales, 1994); E Grosz and E Probyn (eds), *Sexy Bodies: Strange Carnalities of Feminism* (Routledge, London, 1995). In the context of families, note the discussion of 'inevitable dependency' in Fineman, above (n 50); M Fineman, 'Feminist Legal Scholarship and Women's Gendered Lives' in M Cain and C Harrington (eds), *Lawyers in a Postmodern World* (Open University Press, Buckingham, 1994).

[152] See further: W Cealey Harrison and J Hood Williams, *Beyond Sex and Gender* (Sage, London, 2002); Collier, above (n 69) at ch 7.

[153] Lupton and Barclay, above (n 52).

[154] *Ibid* at 3.

'establish boundaries around the contemporary concept of fatherhood',[155] to assess how fatherhood should be defined, and to agree the rights and responsibilities which ought properly to follow that status. In the chapters to follow, we chart how these concerns and questions have played out in the field of legal regulation. We do not approach this work with any expectation of finding a single model of fatherhood, or consistent understanding of the role of fathers in law. Rather, understandings of fatherhood have evolved unevenly over time across diverse areas of law, remaining enmeshed in complex ways with the economic, cultural and political contexts in which discourses of parenthood are produced.

[155] *Ibid.*

2

Fatherhood and 'Natural' Reproduction

[H]ighly questionable assumptions still persist in our understandings of men's relationship to human reproduction. It is still assumed that men play a secondary role in biological reproduction. It is still assumed that the male body is relatively invulnerable to the harms of the outside world. Men are the protectors of women, children, and nation and not, therefore, in need of protection from the state or others. It is still assumed that the male body is inherently virile. The ability to biologically father one's children remains a hallmark of one's manhood, and infertility remains a source of masculine shame ... It is still assumed that men are more distant from the health and well-being of children. The challenge lies in sorting out the distinctions between myth and reality in the politics of reproductive masculinity.[1]

Introduction

IN THIS CHAPTER, with our focus on biological fathers, we trace men's involvement, rights and responsibilities following conception resulting from sexual intercourse. For lack of a better term, we will refer to this as 'natural' reproduction.[2] Against the background of cultural assumptions that reproduction is a time of specifically female responsibility, in which the woman's role as mother has been seen as natural, instinctive and inevitable, the role of the father has tended to be viewed as less central and more problematic. Men's experience of reproduction has appeared distant and vicarious, mediated by and through the agency of women. As such, in so far as fathers have historically had responsibilities in reproduction, they have generally been seen as indirect, involving supporting mothers in financial, emotional or other ways.[3] These social understandings,

---

[1] CR Daniels, *Exposing Men: The Science and Politics of Male Reproduction* (Oxford University Press, Oxford, 2006) at160–61.

[2] 'Natural' conception has traditionally been opposed to 'artificial' conception, but use of the word 'artificial' has gradually fallen out of use, partly due to a recognition that our sense of what is natural and what is not is subject to change: for example, as in vitro fertilisation has become more familiar, it has come to be seen as natural because the sperm fertilises the egg without assistance, see: C Thompson, *Making Parents: The Ontological Choreography of Reproductive Technologies* (MIT Press, Cambridge, MA, 2005) at 140.

[3] This is explored further in chs 4 and 5 below.

37

underpinned by medical understandings of male and female reproductive biology, have been entrenched in a range of legal provisions.

Perhaps this is not surprising. After all, reproduction appears a visibly female activity. It is the woman's body that carries and nourishes a foetus and swells to accommodate its growth. This bodily connection grounds the common belief that women must control avoidance of unwanted pregnancy. It has further underpinned concerns that women may injure the foetus through their antenatal (and even pre-conceptual) behaviour. Female reproductive biology has typically been seen as more complex and liable to malfunction than that of men, with both lay and expert opinion accepting, at least until more recent years, that the roots of infertility were more likely to lie with the woman. By comparison, men's involvement before birth seems to pale into insignificance, amounting to nothing more than the ejaculation of a small amount of seminal fluid. Men's bodies are not even directly connected to the moment of conception, which occurs well after the sexual act is complete.[4] As one commentator suggests:

> When his seed is alienated, man is separated from the continuity of the human species, from a sense of unity with the natural process. He does not actually experience a link between generations.[5]

Further, ejaculation has often been codified as primarily a sexual act, rather than a reproductive one: the idea that women are interested in sex for procreation while men desire sexual gratification has retained a stubborn, if loosening, grip on the popular imagination.[6]

In this chapter, we introduce and develop themes that will run throughout this book. One such idea has already been mentioned: the extent to which fatherhood is perceived as a problematic status, standing in marked contrast to the assumed obvious and natural role of the mother. Secondly, claims that men are disenfranchised and disadvantaged relative to women may be particularly significant in a reproductive context, given the constraints which seem to be imposed by biology and the consequent impossibility of formal equality of treatment. Thirdly, this chapter introduces the pervasive influence of the breadwinner/carer divide, discussed further in chapter four, in showing how beliefs regarding gendered parenting roles after birth have also affected law and policy relating to antenatal responsibilities. Fourthly, the chapter casts light on discussions of the nature of fatherhood by raising the question of not so much *who* should count as a father

---

[4] W Marsiglio, *Procreative Man* (New York University Press, New York, 1998) at 50.

[5] G Corea, *The Mother Machine: Reproductive Technologies from Artificial Insemination to Artificial Wombs* (The Women's Press, London, 1988) at 287.

[6] S Sheldon, 'Reproductive Choice: Men's Freedom and Women's Responsibility?' in A Pedain and J Spencer (eds), *Freedom and Responsibility in Reproductive Choice* (Hart, Oxford, 2006). Graycar provides an interesting example of the legal entrenchment of this view in her analysis of the action for loss of consortium, suggesting that courts are more likely to recognise lack of sexual function as an actionable injury in men, and lack of reproductive capacity as an actionable injury in women: R Graycar, 'Sex, Golf and Stereotypes: Measuring, Valuing and Imagining the Body in Court' (2002) 10 *Torts Law Journal* 205.

as *when* fatherhood begins. Finally, and perhaps most significantly, we suggest that men's closer involvement in reproduction, an enhanced sense of men's reproductive agency and shifting understandings of male reproductive biology are together challenging earlier understandings of men's and women's roles in reproduction as radically distinct. As a rhetoric of more involved fathering and less distinct maternal and paternal roles gains dominance in discussions of parenting practices, we suggest that a similar discursive shift may also be taking place in understandings of reproductive responsibilities in law. As in the other contexts discussed in this book, the nature of fatherhood emerges as a focus of dispute and contestation, with the rights and responsibilities of fathers currently in a state of flux.

In what follows we assess the continued currency of the notion that reproduction is 'women's business', tracking the footprints of this idea across relevant law and social policy and noting challenges to it in recent years. We start by discussing the putative father's rights and responsibilities in the context of preventing reproduction through contraception and abortion. We move on to consider issues of men's reproductive health, asking what level of responsibility is implied for foetal welfare. While it is often suggested that the responsibilities of motherhood do not begin at birth, is the same (increasingly) believed of fatherhood? Finally, we will consider the legal framework concerning men's involvement in both pregnancy and birth.

I. Preventing Fatherhood: Contraception and Abortion

Contraception

In the 2002 General Household Survey, the contraceptive pill remained the single most popular method of birth control for women (26%), followed by the male condom (19%), vasectomy (12%) and female sterilisation (9%).[7] The importance of the contraceptive pill in part reflects what has been historically a primary targeting of family planning services towards women.[8] GPs' hostility towards the idea of providing condoms to men, as part of the newly negotiated free family planning service in the 1970s, led the British Medical Association to decide that

---

[7] Office for National Statistics, 'Living in Britain: General Household Survey 2002, Chapter 10: Contraception' (2004), <http://www.statistics.gov.uk/lib2002/downloads/contraception.pdf>, accessed 25 October 2007.

[8] Generally, on the significance of a variety of social, legal and cultural factors in determining contraceptive choice, see C Djerassi, *This Man's Pill: Reflections on the 50th Birthday of the Pill* (Oxford University Press,, Oxford, 2001); J Weeks, *Sex, Politics and Society: The Regulation of Sexuality Since 1800* (Longman, Harlow, 1989).

GPs should not prescribe them, an anomaly that persists today.[9] Early reports expressed concern that having men in family planning settings would 'intimidate women and staff would leave'.[10] This hints at the gulf between attitudes at the time towards female use of contraception, which was seen as a part of responsible and respectable reproductive planning, and male use, which was seen as facilitating promiscuity.

Attitudes have shifted. By the mid-1980s, the Family Planning Association had launched its 'Men Too' campaign, noting that '[i]mproving male involvement does not mean men having a monopoly on decision making, but rather highlights the need to re-examine the balance between the needs of women and men'.[11] However, men remain a small minority of users of sexual health services: in 2004/05, 99,000 users of family planning clinics (FPCs) were men, compared with 1.2 million women.[12] It has been suggested that sexual health policies and services have largely failed to take men's specific experiences and needs into account and that too little effort has been made to attract more male users. This compounds limitations in sex education, which has been criticised for allowing men to grow up with little information and still adhering to the 'traditional' model of sex: 'men should always be ready for it, that sex is about performance rather than fun and pleasure, that contraception is a women's issue and that only straight sex is normal sex'.[13]

There has been one notable exception to the above: vasectomy is a popular method of contraception in the UK. Around 18% of UK men of reproductive age have undergone a vasectomy, a figure that establishes the UK as the joint world leader in this respect.[14] Sterilisation is a slightly more common procedure for men than for women, no doubt due to the fact that it is the cheaper, faster, safer and more reliable procedure of the two, with lower natural reversal rates. In the UK, it was at one time common for consent forms to require the consent of a spouse to a sterilisation operation, although it is likely that this was aimed at

---

[9] T Belfield, 'It Takes Two: Men and Contraception' (2005) 31(1) *Journal of Family Planning and Reproductive Health Care* 3.

[10] *Ibid.*

[11] Cited in Belfield, above (n 9) at 3. Similarly, Marsiglio notes that it was in the 1980s that a concerted large-scale effort was first made in the US to accentuate men's potential role and responsibilities in the areas of family planning and fatherhood: Marsiglio, above (n 4) at 2.

[12] Office for National Statistics, *NHS Contraceptive Services, England: 2004–05* (Office for National Statistics, London, 2005). Although a tiny percentage of the whole, it should be noted that this represents a significant increase on the 60,000 men who attended FPCs in 1994/95: *ibid* at para 2.5.1.

[13] Men's Health Forum, 'Private Parts, Public Policy: Improving Men's Sexual Health', Report by the Men's Health Forum (2003), <http://www.menshealthforum.org.uk/uploaded_files/mhfprivateparts.pdf>, accessed 25 October 2007. It is interesting here that the language of 'sexual' health is deployed, rather than 'reproductive' health, which was the terminology traditionally deployed in the context of female health. See further the discussion of the 'family man' as heterosexual in ch 4 below.

[14] See further T Kerridge et al, *Into View: Views on Vasectomy: the Male Experience* (Marie Stopes International, London, 2003) at 5.

ensuring good domestic relations rather than being legally mandated.Lord Denning was almost certainly mistaken when he ruled in the 1950s that:

when [a sterilisation operation] is done without just cause or excuse [such as to prevent the transmission of hereditary disease], it is unlawful, even though the man consents to it. Take a case where a sterilisation operation is done so as to enable a man to have the pleasure of sexual intercourse, without shouldering the responsibilities attaching to it. The operation then is plainly injurious to the public interest. It is degrading to the man himself. It is injurious to his wife and to any woman whom he may marry, to say nothing of the way it opens to licentiousness.[15]

It has been more credibly suggested that a husband undergoing a vasectomy against his wife's wishes, or without her knowledge, may give her good cause for divorce.[16] Yet Lord Denning's judgment is nonetheless interesting for the strong assertion of a model of familial masculinity which it contains: sex for pleasure alone is immoral and irresponsible, and procreation is understood as a duty owed to one's partner, specifically by a man to his wife. A greatly muted version of these views may still be in evidence in some quarters today.[17]

While more recent advances in contraceptive technologies have tended to focus on female-mediated methods, a view of contraception as a woman's responsibility has been challenged on two further fronts. First, although the advent of the hormonal contraceptive pill was initially heralded as a liberating advance for women, once its health risks became clear in the 1970s, feminists began to advocate the development of birth control technologies for men, arguing that the health risks involved in the use of contraceptives should be shared more equally between the sexes.[18] Second, a rather different concern has been that female contraceptives leave men unable to control their own reproductivity. As Ruddick has put it:

[15] *Bravery v Bravery* [1954] 1 WLR 1169 (CA). See however the judgment of Hodson LJ, Evershed MR concurring. Neither was a husband able to insist that his wife either use or refrain from using contraception, nor a wife to insist that her husband did so: see *Baxter v Baxter* [1948] AC 274 (HL). Cf the discussion of the sexual father, particularly in the context of nullity and consummation cases, in ch 4 below at p 112.

[16] 'It would not be difficult ... to construct in imagination a case of grave cruelty on a wife founded on the progressive hurt to her health caused by an operation for sterilisation undergone by her husband in disregard of, or contrary to, the wife's wishes or natural instincts': [1954] 1 WLR 1169 at 1173 (CA) (per Evershed MR).

[17] Some doctors still request that both partners sign a consent form prior to treatment: Family Planning Association, 'Male and Female Sterilisation', <http://www.fpa.org.uk/information/leaflets/documents_and_pdfs/detail.cfm?contentID=157>, accessed 13 June 2008. Note also statements of guilt made by infertile men regarding their inability to provide their wife with a child: RE Webb and JC Daniluk, 'The End of the Line: Infertile Men's Experience of Being Unable to Produce a Child' (1999) 2(1) *Men and Masculinities* 6 at 15.

[18] J van Kammen and N Oudshoorn, 'Gender and Risk Assessment in Contraceptive Technologies' (2002) 24(4) *Sociology of Health & Illness* 436 at 446. McLaren notes: 'Women, it was realized, had gained more effective methods of birth control only at the price of assuming full responsibility for the inconveniences and risks involved. No one wanted to have to rely again on coitus interruptus, but the

A man's increasingly traceable sperm is used to bind him to economic relations he would not have chosen and often cannot sustain. Now, like a woman, a man can be made materially accountable for, yet socially alienated from, his sexual activities; he may therefore feel that, like a woman (though surely less painfully) he is a victim of his procreative body.[19]

The concern is well illustrated by a series of cases where American men have sued (former) sexual partners, generally claiming that the man's reliance on the woman's misrepresentations regarding sterility or use of birth control has resulted in a pregnancy that the biological father had taken every reasonable step to avoid.[20] Such actions have typically seen men seek recovery from the mother of child support payments for which they now find themselves liable.The US courts have responded by rejecting all such claims, an approach that would almost certainly be followed in the UK.[21] In the one reported UK authority, a Scottish sheriff held that a genetic father should be liable only to make nominal child support payments where his partner had failed to use the contraceptive pills that were in her possession. This verdict was overturned by a strongly critical Court of Second Division.[22] In one unreported English case, a man whose partner had allegedly inseminated herself using a discarded condom was told by the courts that the method of conception did not affect his liability to support the resulting child.[23]

While these cases are rare, they attract a considerable degree of media attention, frequently provoking assertions that the law is favouring women's reproductive rights at the expense of those of men. The analysis of one such case offered by two journalists is typical:

> [The male plaintiff's] complaint touches upon ancient fears and frustrations. For centuries, it was believed that witches stole sperm from men as they slept and made them impotent or even sterile. [His case,] it would seem, has given that mystic tale an updated twist. And some men's groups think he has a point. When it comes to procreation, they complain, women hold all the power.[24]

---

argument could be made that, as unsatisfactory as it might have been, it at least required a high level of male involvement': A McLaren, *A History of Contraception: From Antiquity to the Present Day* (Basil Blackwell, Cambridge, MA, 1990).

[19] S Ruddick, 'Thinking About Fatherhood' in M Hirsch and E Fox Keller (eds) *Conflicts in Feminism* (Routledge, New York, 1990) at 232.

[20] See S Sheldon, 'Sperm Bandits, Birth Control Fraud and the Battle of the Sexes' (2001) 21(3) *Legal Studies* 460 for a discussion of the legal bases of such actions.

[21] *Ibid.*

[22] *Bell v McCurdle* (1981) SC 64.

[23] 'Sperm Stealing', BBC Radio 4 *Woman's Hour* (2003) <http://www.bbc.co.uk/radio4/womanshour/2003_07_thu_01.shtml>, accessed 25 October 2007. See also the Australian case, *Magill v Magill* [2005] VSCA 51 (17 March 2005) on whether a man can use the tort of deceit to sue the mother of a child who has misled him as to paternity.

[24] B Vobejda, 'Sexual Commodities', *Minneapolis Star Tribune* (24 November 1998).

Whereas comeback for undiscussed pregnancy used to be that hapless men were tricked into parenthood, now the objection centres around loss of control. First women stole men's jobs, then their earning power, now their body fluid.[25]

For both commentators, such cases form part of a broader picture of male powerlessness and general 'crisis in masculinity', traced elsewhere in this book. Their discussion is compellingly located within broader concerns about men's procreative powerlessness, an anxiety that arises, albeit in different form, in the context of reproductive technologies. In a particularly striking reversal of early feminist calls for a female contraceptive, one response to this case was to call for a *male*-controlled contraceptive that will allow men to take control of their procreative capacity. The suggestion was that this would be a better way to guard against unwanted parenthood.[26] Locating these cases as part of a more general 'battle of the sexes', such a response suggests that it may be better to arm the perceived weaker party.[27]

This call may soon be answered. Medical commentators report that a male hormonal contraceptive will be available in the next decade.[28] The impact of such a development is unknown. Marsiglio suggests that currently contraceptive decisions are relatively harmonious because female-mediated means are most effective. If, however, a male pill, hormonal injection, or reliable form of reversible vasectomy were commercially marketed, contraceptive decision-making would become more complex and therefore potentially more confrontational.[29] And Djerassi, inventor of the female contraceptive pill, suggests that women would not be happy to rely on a male pill.[30]

Notwithstanding the doubts of these commentators, research suggests that male contraception would be likely to be acceptable to a large number of potential users, and that the majority of women would happily trust their partners to take responsibility for contraception.[31] One study discussing the development of a male contraceptive, and men's willingness to participate in trials relating to it, suggests that men's desire for a male contraceptive is rooted in a wish to be a responsible caring man and to enhance gender equality.[32] Another

---

[25] R Prasad, 'The Sperm that Turned', *Guardian* (11 February 1999).

[26] S McCarthy, 'A Couple's Deal to Use Birth Control is a Deal', *Dallas Morning News* (20 November 1998).

[27] See Sheldon, above (n 20) for discussion of these cases as part of a battle of the sexes.

[28] Belfield, above (n 9); RA Anderson, 'Hormonal Contraception in the Male' (2000) 56(3) *British Medical Bulletin* 717. See Marsiglio, above (n 4) at 77 for an overview of some of the earlier scientific literature and a rather less optimistic conclusion on the availability of a male hormonal contraceptive in the near future.

[29] Marsiglio, above (n 4) at 65.

[30] Djerassi, above (n 8) at 78.

[31] K Heinemann *et al*, 'Attitudes toward Male Fertility Control: Results of a Multinational Survey on Four Continents' (2005) 20(2) *Human Reproduction* 549; AF Glasier *et al*, 'Contraception. Would Women Trust their Partners to Use A Male Pill?' (2000) 15(3) *Human Reproduction* 646.

[32] N Oudshoorn, '"Astronauts in the Sperm World": The Renegotiation of Masculine Identities in Discourses on Male Contraception' (2004) 6(4) *Men & Masculinities* 349.

sees all but a minority of men rejecting the idea that contraception is a woman's responsibility, with a far greater proportion agreeing that it was important for a man to take responsibility for contraception within a relationship.[33] Narratives of male control and masculine powerlessness seem not to speak to the given views of at least these study participants, whose stated vision is one of mutuality and equal responsibility.

Abortion

Provision of Abortion Services

Abortion decision-making has also historically been an area of female responsibility, albeit one exercised under the close scrutiny of a traditionally male-dominated medical profession.[34] While the putative father enjoys no legal rights, however, there has been a growing awareness of the important role that men play in abortion decisions.[35] In line with a broad trend across social and health service providers,[36] there has also been an emerging sense that more should be done to meet men's specific needs and experiences. A recent survey of the small number of empirical studies concerning the impact of abortion on men found, for example, that men can experience ambivalent reactions towards an elective abortion, including relief, grief, powerlessness and a desire to support their partners.[37]

A survey at one of the British Pregnancy Advisory Service's largest London clinics, found that a man, usually a partner, accompanied two-thirds of women seeking abortion.[38] There is further evidence to suggest that the perceived (un)suitability of partners as fathers is extremely relevant to women's termination decisions. In describing their motivation for seeking abortion, women talk extensively not just about their own current inability to be a good mother, but

---

[33] Kerridge *et al,* above (n 14).

[34] S Sheldon, *Beyond Control: Medical Power and Abortion Law* (Pluto, London, 1997).

[35] It should be noted that this evidence has been overwhelmingly gathered from interviews with women seeking abortion and service providers, rather than men themselves, but see A Kero *et al,* 'Ethics and Society: The Male Partner Involved in Legal Abortion' (1999) 14(10) *Human Reproduction* 2669. This study of 75 men involved in legal abortion found that more than half wanted the woman to have an abortion, 20 submitted themselves to their partner's decision and only one wanted the woman to complete the pregnancy.

[36] Eg K Stanley (ed), *Daddy Dearest? Active Fatherhood and Public Policy* (Institute for Public Policy Research, London, 2005).

[37] CT Coyle, 'Men and Abortion: A Review of Empirical Reports Concerning the Impact of Abortion on Men' (2007) 3(2) *The Internet Journal of Mental Health* <http://www.ispub.com/ostia/index.php?xmlFilePath=journals/ijmh/vol3n2/abortion.xml>, accessed 25 October 2007. Coyle found 28 relevant studies conducted since 1973.

[38] British Pregnancy Advisory Service, 'Background Information on Men and Abortion', Press Release (14 May 2001).

also the inadequacy of their partners to be good fathers, and the state of their relationships.[39] One researcher who studied abortion decision-making in a number of UK clinics notes:

The men were so important ... they were there in the waiting rooms, in the counselling rooms, at the clinics. And even if they weren't there in person, they were still there, in that these women's relationships were just so, so important in their decision to end the pregnancy, so they always talked about the man in their life during the counselling session and the state of their relationship.[40]

In one of the few studies directly to question men about their motivation in seeking terminations, the respondents cited a desire to have children in a context where they were able to provide qualitatively good parenting and, specifically, to father within functioning family units.[41]

Abortion, then, has been formally carved out as an issue of special importance for women and, for many years, low priority was given to the interests of putative fathers. Currently, while the law fails to give men any legal rights, in practice often more effort is made to include the man in termination decisions. In 2001, the largest UK provider of abortion services produced a leaflet with information for men both about the abortion procedure and how they may best support their partners through it.[42] Such changes to men's involvement in terminations reflect a broa .er trend to include men across a range of health and childcare service provisions, which we discuss in chapter four. Burgess's review of how well public service provision is meeting the needs of fathers suggests a widespread sense that service provision needs to be reoriented to promote men's involvement.[43] Similar trends to those described above can also be seen in moves to encourage men's involvement in antenatal classes and services supporting early years childcare.[44] Yet currently, Burgess suggests, while engaging with fathers is praised, failing to do so is tolerated.

---

[39] M Lattimer, 'Abortion Discourses: An Exploration of the Social, Cultural and Organisational Context of Abortion Decision-Making in Contemporary Britain' (DPhil thesis, University of Sussex, 2000). See also: E Lee *et al*, *A Matter of Choice? Explaining National Variations in Teenage Abortion and Motherhood* (Joseph Rowntree Foundation, York, 2004).

[40] Statement by M Lattimer (personal communication).

[41] Kero *et al*, above (n 35). See also AB Shostak *et al*, *Men and Abortion: Lessons, Losses and Love* (Praeger, New York, 1984) for a large, if dated, US study concluding that any image of men as largely uninvolved and uninterested bystanders in the abortion process misunderstands the experience of many.

[42] British Pregnancy Advisory Service, *Men Too!* (abortion information leaflet) (British Pregnancy Advisory Service, London, 2006), <http://www.bpas.org/images/pdfs/Men_Too_Mar06_FINAL.pdf>, accessed 25 October 2007.

[43] A Burgess, 'Fathers and Public Service', in K Stanley (ed), *Daddy Dearest? Active Fatherhood and Public Policy* (Institute of Public Policy Research, London, 2005).

[44] See below and ch 4, respectively.

Putative Fathers' Rights in Disputed Termination Decisions

While many termination decisions are made in a consensual way, with men involved in the decision-making process, putative fathers have never been granted any legal rights in termination decisions.[45] Under the Abortion Act 1967, a woman can access abortion services where two doctors agree that a termination is justified with reference to one of a number of contra-indications (most commonly, risk to her health).[46] The Act characterises abortion as a medical matter, to be considered in consultation with one's doctor.[47] Understanding abortion as a matter of women's health created a space for the provision of abortion as a matter of clinical discretion and left little space for consideration of the needs of the putative father. Clinicians' broad interpretation of the terms of the statute and the provision of abortion through the charitable sector has since led to a situation where termination is readily available for most women, at least during the first trimester of pregnancy.[48]

Notwithstanding the above, however, abortion remains controversial and the question of fathers' rights has been one significant point of contestation. Putative fathers have brought a number of well-publicised, but ultimately unsuccessful, challenges in UK courts, in each case attempting to secure an injunction to restrain their (ex-)partners from terminating a pregnancy. The first challenge involved a married couple: Mr Paton argued that he had a right to have a say in the destiny of his child and that his wife 'had no proper legal grounds for seeking a termination of her pregnancy and that, not to mince words, she was being spiteful, vindictive and utterly unreasonable in seeking to do so'.[49] His claim was located within the context of his (deteriorating) marital relationship. The court refused an injunction on the basis that a husband had no legal right to stop his wife having, or a registered medical practitioner performing, a legal abortion. The foetus was incapable of having any rights of its own until it was born and had a separate existence from its mother.[50] To succeed, the action must therefore have rested on the rights of Mr Paton but the courts will not grant injunctions to enforce or restrain matrimonial obligations.[51]

---

[45] For the possibility of according some rights to a woman's husband during the passage of the abortion legislation through Parliament, see DC Bradley, 'A Woman's Right to Choose' (1978) 41(4) MLR 368.

[46] Abortion Act 1967, s 1(1)(a).

[47] See generally Sheldon, above (n 34).

[48] There is significant regional variation in state funding, however, and the women who may find it most difficult to overcome the various legal hurdles created by the 1967 Act are likely to be those who are most vulnerable: see S Sheldon, 'The Abortion Act 1967: a Critical Perspective' in E Lee (ed), *Abortion Law and Politics Today* (Macmillan, Basingstoke, 1998) at 46–7.

[49] *Paton v BPAS* [1978] 2 All ER 987.

[50] *Ibid* at 989.

[51] Mr Paton's subsequent challenge in the European Court of Human Rights equally failed: *Paton v UK* [1980] ECHR 408. While it was recognised that a potential father was sufficiently closely affected by the termination of his wife's pregnancy to be able to claim status as a victim, the right to respect for

The second case involved a similar application by Robert Carver, President of the Oxford University Pro-Life group.[52] Following *Paton*, Carver was forced to concede that he had no legal standing to bring an action based on a claim of biological paternity. However, he argued that he had a sufficient personal interest to do so as his ex-partner's proposed termination would be a crime concerning the life of the foetus, which was already at a later gestational age (between 18 and 21 weeks) than that in *Paton* and was 'capable of being born alive'.[53] Carver failed to convince the judges who heard his case but triumphed outside the courts as the attendant publicity left his ex-partner feeling unable to go through with the termination. He went on to raise their child and gained some media attention during the campaigns around subsequent parliamentary attempts to restrict access to abortion in the late 1980s,[54] with one pro-life MP commending him for showing 'that abortion is not only an issue for women and that men are prepared to shoulder the responsibility'.[55] Rather than grounding his action in his relationship with the pregnant woman (as Mr Paton had done), Carver aligned his interests with those of the foetus, relying on medical understandings of foetal development and asserting his desire to parent. This parallels a broader shift in the campaigning of fathers' rights activists, further explored in chapter five below: the alignment of men's interests with those of children, and the opposition of these interests against those of women, who may be portrayed as self-interested or otherwise unconcerned with child welfare.

Given such clear precedents, the few further cases in the UK have been brought with little hope of success. This might suggest that the men's endeavours were fuelled less by a desire to win and more by the chance to air their frustrations and, possibly, the hope that their partners might have second thoughts faced with the inevitable publicity.[56] While rare, these cases illustrate some putative fathers' anger, pain and frustration with a law that accords them no rights in this area. Some commentators have understood their challenges as an attempt to reassert patriarchal control over women. Thus, Fegan, for example, commenting on the Canadian context, suggests that these cases:

> look suspiciously like a 'backlash' against women's independence in reproductive decision-making … Apart from representing some 'paternal instinct' to protect the

family life could not be interpreted so widely as to confer on the father a right to be consulted or to make applications about an abortion his wife intends to have performed.

52   *C v S* [1987] 2 WLR 1108, [1987] 1 All ER 1230.

53   If so, then the act of aborting it would have constituted the offence of child destruction under s 1(b) of the Infant Life (Preservation) Act 1929. This case could no longer occur in the same form, as s 37 of the Human Fertilisation and Embryology Act 1990 specifically uncoupled the application of the Abortion Act from that of the 1929 Act.

54   See eg C Langley, 'Anti-abortion man raises baby alone', *Sunday Times* (17 January 1988).

55   David Alton, cited in M McNeil, 'Putting the Alton Bill in Context' in S Franklin *et al* (eds), *Off-centre: Feminism and Cultural Studies* (HarperCollins Academic, London, 1991) at 149, 154.

56   Although one of the cases did test whether Scots law accorded fathers any greater rights: *Kelly v Kelly* [1997] 2 FLR 828.

foetus, such claims might be argued to be more indicative of a patriarchal desire to restore women to the 'proper' model of 'femininity'.[57]

As Fegan recognises, however, these cases might also stem from the men's 'paternal instinct', a desire to be involved fathers (and, no doubt, a reflection of the increased social expectations that they will claim such a role, discussed further in chapter four). While Mr Paton asserts his rights as a husband, subsequent plaintiffs have asserted their desire to father, and Robert Carver, at least, has evidenced a commitment to this role. Some other commentators, meanwhile, have noted a problematic disparity between calling for men to be more greatly involved and responsible in other areas of reproduction, yet denying them any role in termination decisions. As McDonnell points out:

> Though feminism has never actually worked out a position on the role of men in abortion, in practice we have designated only one appropriate role for them, that of the 'supportive man' … So to a large extent, what we have encouraged in men is a passive, auxiliary role in abortion, allowing them to participate in a way that is helpful, but perhaps not, in some important sense, truly meaningful.[58]

It looks probable that the Abortion Act 1967 will be subject to reform, via amendments tabled during the course of the Human Fertilisation and Embryology Bill 2007 through Parliament. Any such reform is likely to be influenced by the authoritative review relating to the workings of the 1967 Act conducted by the House of Commons Science and Technology Committee, which has already played significant role in dissuading parliamentarians from bringing down the upper time limit within which abortion is legally available.[59] The issue of fathers' rights was not considered in this report (which focused exclusively on scientific developments) and did not emerge as a significant issue in the reform agenda presented either within or outside of Parliament.

---

[57] E Fegan, 'Fathers, Fetuses and Abortion Decision Making' (1996) 5 SLS 75 at 79 (references omitted). Note our own suspicion of the backlash thesis: R Collier and S Sheldon, 'Fathers' Rights, Fatherhood and Law Reform – International Perspectives' in R Collier and S Sheldon (eds) *Fathers' Rights Activism and Law Reform in Comparative Perspective* (Hart, Oxford, 2006).

[58] K McDonnell, *Not an Easy Choice: A Feminist Re-examines Abortion* (Women's Press, Ontario, 1984).

[59] House of Commons Science and Technology Committee, *Scientific Developments Relating to the Abortion Act 1967, Twelfth Report of Session 2006–07 (Volume I)*, HC 1045-I. The findings detailed in this report appear to have played a central role in dissuading MPs from reducing the upper time limit within which abortion is available (see the Bill's Committee Stage in the House of Commons, HC Debs Vol 476, Cols 222–290 (20 May 2008). It is likely that modernizing amendments will be introduced when the Bill reaches its Report stage. Those aspects of the 2007 Bill which relate to fatherhood are discussed in ch 3 below.

II. Reproductive Agency, Antenatal Responsibility and Foetal Welfare

Evolving Understandings of Men's Role in Reproduction

In chapter one, we noted the growth of a range of cultural anxieties around childhood and parenting. While these anxieties extend to the pre-natal period, it is perhaps not surprising, given the more corporeal nature of mothers' engagement with reproduction, that they have traditionally been focused mainly on women. It is the woman who has been expected to moderate her actions in the interests of the well being of her future child, as the 'excessive consumption of drugs or alcohol and the excessive smoking of cigarettes' by pregnant women pose dangers to foetal health, as do 'unsuitable or inadequate maternal diet and workplace hazards such as exposure to radiation or harmful chemicals of various kinds'.[60] Considerable social pressure may be brought to bear on women who fail to guard against such risks as the opprobrium directed towards a heavily pregnant woman smoking in public demonstrates.

Where are fathers in this discussion? An explanation for their absence can be found in Daniels' reading of scientific research and reports in the popular media, which suggests that traditional ideals of masculinity have skewed the science of male reproductive health and understandings of men's relationship to human reproduction.[61] In particular, Daniels tracks the impact of four interrelated assumptions that combine to form the basis of a dominant understanding of male reproductivity: first, the view that men are secondary in biological reproduction; second, that they are less vulnerable to reproductive harm than are women; third, that they are virile, ideally capable of fathering their own biological children, with an inability to do so a source of personal shame and shrouded in comparative secrecy; and finally, that they are relatively distant from the health problems of the children they father.[62] Each of these elements is revealed in the areas of legal regulation discussed in this chapter and each, as Daniels suggests, has increasingly become subject to social contestation in ways which have posed new challenges for the law.

For a long time it had been assumed that only female transmission of mutagens (toxins which affect the foetus or the sperm/ova which create it) was possible. This, Daniels suggests, could be seen as part of a broader ignorance of male reproductive biology, one which persisted well into the final quarter of the

---

[60] J Fortin, 'Legal Protection for the Unborn Child' (1988) 51 MLR 54 at 75.

[61] See Daniels, above (n 1) and 'Between Fathers and Fetuses: The Social Construction of Male Reproduction and the Politics of Fetal Harm' (1997) 22(3) *Signs: Journal of Women in Culture and Society* 579 at 582.

[62] Daniels, above (n 1).

twentieth century. While gynaecology grew in importance throughout the nineteenth century, the first journal to focus on male reproductive health, *Andrologie*, was not established until 1969 and it was only in the late 1970s that andrology was fully established as a medical specialty, albeit one which remains small and marginal today compared to gynaecology. This lack of research into male reproductive capacity has had clear consequences. Well into the 1970s, men were believed either to be invulnerable to harm from the toxicity of drugs, alcohol and environmental or occupational hazards, or rendered completely infertile by any sufficiently serious exposure.[63] Sperm that crossed the line from virile to vulnerable by being damaged by reproductive toxins were assumed to be incapable of fertilisation. The converse was also true: men not rendered infertile by their toxic exposures were assumed to be immune from any other reproductive risk.[64] Today, however, it is accepted that there is a range of factors, including pesticides, radiation, metals, and heat exposure, that can affect sperm and male fertility, and male genetic damage has now established itself as an increasingly significant topic for obtaining research funding.[65]

The heightened interest in male reproductive fragility is not confined to scientists. It has also entered the public consciousness through well-publicised reports of declining sperm counts, increased rates of diseases of the male reproductive system, and the extensive media attention paid to men who have alleged that toxic exposure suffered during military service has resulted in a range of injuries, including reduced fertility and risk to the health of future children.[66] Declining sperm counts are attributed most commonly to environmental causes, but also to a bewildering range of other factors including:

> the use of plastic diapers on boys, increased rates of sexual activity, the shift from boxer to jockey shorts, the rise of male obesity and dietary changes in men, increased use of drugs and alcohol, the shift from factory to sedentary work, maternal use of drugs during pregnancy, the use of hard bicycle seats, even the advent of feminism and the decline of war![67]

Such reports have greatly increased public awareness of male-mediated infertility, historically viewed as a female problem. Yet while only 12% of the men in a

---

[63] *Ibid* at 33.

[64] Daniels (1997), above (n 61) at 582.

[65] K Messing, *One-eyed Science: Occupational Health and Women Workers* (Temple University Press, Philadelphia, 1998) at 146–7.

[66] While there has been substantial discussion as to the existence of 'Gulf War Syndrome', a large-scale survey found that if Gulf War veterans' partners did become pregnant, conception had taken longer to achieve, and the pregnancy was less likely to run full term, see: N Maconochie *et al*, 'Infertility among Male UK Veterans of the 1990–1 Gulf War: Reproductive Cohort Study' (2004) 329 BMJ 196–201. For an extensive consideration of the evidence relating to US veterans' exposure in the Gulf and Vietnam Wars, see Daniels, above (n 1) at ch 5.

[67] Daniels, above (n 1) at 48. For two well-publicised contributions to the popular debate, see T Colborn *et al*, *Our Stolen Future: How We are Threatening Our Fertility, Our Intelligence and Our Survival* (Plume Books, New York, 1997); and H Fisch, *The Male Biological Clock: The Startling News About Aging, Sexuality, and Fertility in Men* (Free Press, New York, 2005).

recent UK survey had viewed their own fertility as a concern when thinking about starting a family,[68] the most comprehensive epidemiological study of infertility to date suggests that men are the sole cause or a contributing factor to infertility in more than half of all couples around the globe.[69] And it has been estimated that 2.5 million men in the UK (almost one in ten of the male population) could have fertility problems.[70] Further anxiety has been provoked by a reported increase in rates of male reproductive disease, including cancers of the male reproductive system.[71]

Intriguingly, in describing such events, many commentators have implicitly reached for the imagery of male defeat in gender wars, deploying a language of 'feminization' or 'chemical castration' of men.[72] Daniels rightly notes that discussion of the scientific data has involved:

> a debate not just about the evidence but about manhood. Assumptions of masculinity were implicated in the belief or rejection of the evidence that male reproductive health was at risk. Gendered norms of manhood intensified the response in both directions, with sharply critical attacks at one extreme and predictions of global doom at the other. Indeed, in the end, the question was not whether male reproductive health was at risk at all, but how the perception of risk was obscured by these norms of masculinity. Evidence of reproductive risk was deeply entangled with … the idea that men are less vulnerable than women to the harms of the outside world. The male body has been codified as relatively invulnerable to risk. The evidence suggested that this was no longer assured.[73]

This shift in understanding of male reproductive biology has also had a clear impact on the advice given to prospective parents. Significantly, men as well as women are now called upon to moderate their behaviour in order to improve their chances of a successful conception, paying attention to diet, exercise, weight, smoking and alcohol intake.[74] There is a sense here in which male and female reproductive biology seems to be on a convergence course, both increasingly seen as subject to similar dangers. Such advice suggests a growing sense that men, like women, are reproductive (as well as sexual) agents who must be responsible risk-managers, attentive to the fragility of their reproductive bodies and careful

---

[68] C Nordqvist, 'Infertility affects 2.5 million males in the UK' *Medical News Today* (13 September 2005), <http://www.medicalnewstoday.com/articles/30585.php>, accessed 25 October 2007, discussing a report commissioned by Norwich Union Healthcare. See also Webb and Daniluk, (n 17) at 13.

[69] See MR Dudgeon and MC Inhorn, 'Men's Influences on Women's Reproductive Health: Medical Anthropological Perspectives' (2004) 59 *Social Science & Medicine* 1379 at 1388, discussing a WHO-sponsored study of 5,800 couples in 33 centres in 22 countries.

[70] Nordqvist, above (n 68).

[71] Daniels, above (n 1) at ch 3.

[72] *Ibid*, particularly at 31–2.

[73] *Ibid* at 68.

[74] Eg Baby Centre, 'Diet for a healthy dad-to-be' (article reviewed 2007), <http://www.babycentre.co.uk/preconception/dadstobe/dietforadadtobe/>, accessed 25 October 2007.

to maximise their chances of a successful conception and a healthy child. The importance of seeing men as reproductive agents can be briefly demonstrated through two examples.

The first is a study which found that, while HIV+ women are routinely given reproductive advice, heterosexual HIV+ men were given very little information despite the known risks of paternal transmission.[75] This was not because the men were not interested: over half of those interviewed stated that they would value consultations regarding fertility and fathering. That sexual intercourse would continue to play a role in HIV+ men's lives and that they should wish to be responsible sexual agents is assumed: information is regularly provided regarding safer sexual practices. Reproduction, however, is presented as a less central matter of concern for men and, while women are expected to be responsible reproductive decision-makers, far less is expected of men and far less assistance (and surveillance) is provided of their reproductive decision-making. These men are seen as active *sexual* but not *reproductive* agents.[76]

Second, however, a far greater recognition of men's reproductive agency can clearly be seen in developments in genetic medicine. Increasing knowledge in the area of genetics calls on individuals to make appropriate reproductive choices with a view to the health of future offspring, thus generating new forms of 'genetic responsibility'.[77] One relevant study focused on a web chatroom for Huntington's Disease (HD) sufferers, where the most frequently posed ethical question concerned the decision to have children in the light of knowledge of being genetically at risk or pre-symptomatic.[78] Men at risk of HD have the potential to transmit more severe and earlier onset forms of HD to their offspring. Novas and Rose suggest that 'once the field of reproductive decision-making becomes structured by knowledge of molecular risk, each individual becomes obliged to inform themselves of the potential genetic risks that may be transmitted in the course of reproducing their genetic selves'.[79] Men, like women, are thus called upon to manage their own genetic health and to act responsibly with regard to the health of their future offspring. Such ideas of individual responsibility for managing risk, as we shall see in other contexts discussed in this book, increasingly frame understandings of fatherhood.

---

[75] L Sherr and N Barry, 'Fatherhood and HIV-positive Men' (2004) 5 *HIV Medicine* 258.

[76] And as Daniels has noted, according men a less central place in reproduction than women has both privileged and burdened men: 'It has privileged men by casting them as less responsible for concerns of reproduction, less vulnerable to the harms of the outside world, and more distant from the children they produce. But at the same time it has led to a distorted view of men in human reproduction, a neglect of the male reproductive system, and a devaluation of the male role in producing healthy children': Daniels, above (n 1) at 30.

[77] C Novas and N Rose, 'Genetic Risk and the Birth of the Somatic Individual' (2000) 29(4) *Economy and Society* 485.

[78] *Ibid.*

[79] *Ibid* at 504.

This impetus to act as a responsible reproductive agent may be implicitly enforced via social and medical mechanisms and mediated through other people's expectations of the *right* thing to do. For example, a gay man with no desire for children may feel obliged to accept a reproductive advice session with a genetic counsellor in order to be seen to act responsibly with regard to his hereditary disorder.[80] Men, envisaged as reproductive agents and future fathers, may expect to be judged on how well they exercise the responsibility that accompanies that agency, facing medical, familial and broader social disapproval if they make 'irresponsible' choices.[81] As Novas and Rose note, the subject that is constructed in the contemporary genetic consultation is not merely a subject at genetic risk, but also a responsible subject who exercises choices wisely, both for himself and for others.[82] For putative fathers and mothers alike, the norms of reproductive health suggested by genetics are thus shaped through concern for one's future children.[83]

The shifts discussed above have important potential legal ramifications. If the health and welfare of future children can be affected not just by the actions of their mothers before birth, but also by those of their fathers, then the existence of a duty to prevent such harm becomes at issue, as does the question of whether legal liability should be attached to failure to fulfil it. Two examples serve to illustrate the radically divergent understandings of male and female antenatal responsibilities which have historically characterised English law regarding such duties: foetal protection legislation and policies, and parental liability for congenital disability (where a child is born with an impairment resulting from events which take place before her birth).

Foetal Protection Legislation and Policies

A concern with the health of future children has resulted in a range of statutes and regulations seeking to prevent women who are or who might become pregnant from working in contact with certain toxic substances.[84] Further, the same concern has led some employers to implement their own 'foetal protection' policies.[85] However, today the known risks of male transmission of toxins have made it increasingly difficult to justify the exclusion of women alone from these

---

[80] See S Sheldon, 'ReConceiving Masculinity: Imagining Men's Reproductive Bodies in Law' (1999) 26(2) *Journal of Law & Society* 129 at 148 for such an incident.

[81] Compare the dynamic at play in the context of divorce and separation, where separating partners are expected to act 'responsibly': ch 5 below.

[82] Novas and Rose, above (n 77) at 495 (references omitted).

[83] *Ibid* at 504.

[84] See Sheldon above (n 80) and M Thomson, 'Employing the Body: the Reproductive Body and Employment Exclusion' (1996) 5 SLS 243 for more details of UK and EU law.

[85] Such substances may affect the foetus by producing defects in the conceptus (teratogens), or may cause mutation in the genetic structure of either sperm cells or the ova leading to hereditable genetic defects, which may result in spontaneous abortion or birth defects (mutagens).

workplaces. Scientific research has shown, for example, that male exposure can affect sperm quality directly or that toxins can be carried home to pregnant women on the clothes or in the hair of male workers. Male reproductive exposures are now proven to cause, or strongly suspected of causing, not just fertility problems but also miscarriage, low birth weight, congenital abnormalities, cancer, neurological problems and other childhood health problems.[86]

There has been only one reported, unsuccessful, attempt to challenge a foetal protection policy in the UK. In *Page* (1981), the Employment Appeals Tribunal upheld the legality of an employer's decision to dismiss a 23-year-old female tanker driver who would be brought into contact with a particular chemical, believed dangerous to pregnant women. Ms Page's claim that she did not wish to become pregnant and was willing to provide her employer with an indemnity to that effect did not help her given that she was 'clearly of a child-bearing age'.[87]

While *Page* illustrates the problems that foetal protection policies can pose for women, a second case from another jurisdiction demonstrates their potential consequences for men. The Johnson Controls Company was sued in the US following its introduction of a 'foetal protection policy' excluding 'women who are pregnant or capable of bearing children' from jobs involving exposure to lead, on the basis that such exposure could harm their reproductive capacity and result in children being born with congenital defects.[88] Some women chose to become sterilised in order to avoid losing their jobs, others accepted transfers to positions with lower pay. Some employees, however, responded by legally challenging the policy and, eventually, the US Supreme Court held that the policy constituted unlawful sex discrimination. Not surprisingly, the company's actions provoked much critical comment, tending to focus on the dilemma facing women forced to choose between their jobs and their reproductive capacity.[89] Less widely noted was the fact that one of the plaintiffs was a man. Donald Penney had complained that he was denied a request for leave of absence for the purpose of lowering his lead level because he intended to become a father. Whilst the dangers to male reproductivity resulting from lead exposure were already well known at this time, Penney argued that he too was subject to discrimination, being refused the possibility of taking advantage of the very health measures which were being imposed on his female colleagues.

Foetal protection policies on both sides of the Atlantic have been criticised for making the assumption that all women are potential child-bearers unless they are medically incapable of conceiving. This, it has been argued, denies female agency

---

[86] See generally RH Blank, *Fetal Protection in the Workplace* (Columbia University Press, New York, 1993); Thomson, above (n 84); M. Thomson *Reproducing Narrative: Gender, Reproduction and the Law* (Ashgate, London, 1998); CR Daniels, *At Women's Expense: State Power and the Politics of Fetal Rights* (Harvard University Press, Cambridge, MA, 1993); Daniels, above (n 1).

[87] *Page* v *Freight Hire (Tank Haulage Co.) Ltd* [1981] IRLR 13.

[88] *International Union, United Automobile Workers* v *Johnson Controls Inc*, 499 US 187 (1991).

[89] Eg Daniels (1993), above (n 86).

and posits maternity as women's natural, inevitable and primary function.[90] What is also implicit in the Johnson Controls case, however, is blindness to men's reproductive needs. Donald Penney's agency is also ignored. He is refused the possibility of prioritising his body's reproductive capacity over and above its ability to labour, as surely as this prioritisation is forced on his female colleagues. This raises the possibility that potential fathers may find themselves unable to make responsible reproductive decisions regarding the health of their future children. While the primacy of parenthood is here dictated to women, it is denied to men; or, if considered, fatherhood is recognised in terms of the breadwinner imperative to remain in work to provide for one's family.[91]

Liability for Injuries Sustained Before Birth

A second case study reflecting many of the same assumptions can be found in the regulation of liability for injuring the foetus *in utero* or through events prior to conception. While the UK has not followed the US in prosecuting women who drink alcohol or take drugs during pregnancy, the issue of whether mothers and fathers should be liable to pay damages to their future offspring for harm suffered as a result of their actions before birth has been considered.[92] The Congenital Disabilities (Civil Liability) Act 1976 provides that a child will, in certain circumstances, be able to sue for damages where an occurrence before its birth results in some physical or mental disability. The 'occurrence' envisaged by the legislation includes anything which 'affected either parent in his or her ability to have a normal, healthy child' or which 'affected the mother during her pregnancy, or affected her or the child in the course of its birth'.[93]

The Act contains an almost complete exclusion of a right to sue one's mother (but not one's father) providing that, except in the case of negligent driving where insurance payouts would be available, a woman will not be liable to her eventual child for antenatal injury.[94] Four reasons in support of the exclusion of maternal liability were stated in a report preceding the legislation. These were clearly not believed equally applicable to fathers. First, it was noted that the relationship between mother and disabled child is one of the most stressful that can exist and to add legal liability to pay compensation would be bound to

---

[90] It is noteworthy that foetal protection policies have typically been used to exclude women from particular traditionally male industries – normally chemical and heavy manufacturing – whilst retaining men in them. See Thomson, above (nn 84 and 86).

[91] The idea of the father as breadwinner is most fully explored in ch 4. It is important to note here the class dimension of many of these debates, employment frequently taking place in an industrial context itself transformed in a number of respects as a result of global economic change.

[92] Such charges brought in the US have included manslaughter and supplying drugs to a minor: see Daniels, above (n 61); R Roth *Making Women Pay: The Hidden Costs of Fetal Rights* (Cornell University Press, Ithaca, NY, 2000).

[93] Congenital Disabilities (Civil Liability) Act 1976, s 1(2)(a) and (b), respectively.

[94] *Ibid*, s 2.

increase tension. Second, some possible allegations, such as maternal smoking and gin drinking, would be 'unseemly' and difficult to prove. Third, there would often be no fund from which the mother's liability could be paid without hardship to the rest of the family. Creation of a right of action that could seldom be satisfied would 'exacerbate the bitterness which a disabled child so often feels when it grows conscious of its condition'. Finally, the existence of such an action might become a weapon between parents in a matrimonial conflict, to the further detriment of a disabled child.[95]

Although the Law Commission in 1974 clearly saw the greatest threat of injury as occurring through the body of the pregnant woman, it did recognise that harm to either genitor could be the cause of abnormalities in a child subsequently conceived. However, it perceived no need to extend the same special exemption from liability to fathers. Here there was neither the same 'physical identification' between father and foetus, nor the same enormous variety of ways in which paternal conduct could cause a congenital disability. Neither did the Law Commission accept that the threat of legal action was as great here, as available allegations would be far more limited (and, presumably, less 'unseemly'). It was also assumed that the damage that would result from litigation within a close familial relationship would not automatically rule out the possibility of suing the father.[96]

The above reasoning reveals important assumptions at the time regarding parenting arrangements following birth, most notably that the mother will be the primary carer and the father the breadwinner for the family.[97] The Law Commission focused exclusively on preventing disruption to the woman's *familial* role, being persuaded that maternal liability should be limited because of the dangers to the family were it to be allowed. This implication that the mother is at the centre of the family is further seen in the assumption that the mother will be a child's primary carer (this is clear in the positing of the mother/disabled child relationship as the *most* stressful one) and this relationship should be characterised by love rather than litigation.[98] Although the Law Commission is aware of literature setting out appropriate behaviour for the pregnant woman, it feels that the legal enforcement of such behaviour would be 'unseemly'.

Recriminations towards the father regarding his occupational exposure or dangerous lifestyle choices are assumed, by implication and in contrast, to be less troubling. The refusal to allow an action that may bring bitterness, or contribute to tension in the child's relationship with the mother (primary carer), can be contrasted with a willingness to accept the legitimacy of an action where the

---

[95] Law Commission, *Report on Injuries to Unborn Children*, Cmnd 60 (1974) 22–3.
[96] *Ibid* at 35.
[97] Ch 4 below, pp 109–111.
[98] Also, as a carer rather than breadwinner, the mother is unlikely to have independent income to meet such a claim. Whether the labour market shifts outlined in ch 1 have changed this position is a moot point.

child's father (economic provider) has acted irresponsibly. Tort law's role is one of imposing financial responsibility for negligent acts and this fits easily with the man's responsibilities to the child which are seen, primarily, as economic.[99] As was seen above, a woman can be excluded from employment via foetal protection policies because of her duty, as a mother, to provide a safe environment for her foetus. However, her child cannot sue regarding her antenatal behaviour, as that would juridify what should be an exclusively affective relationship. The man will not be excluded from employment given that his duty, as a father, is to provide financially for his family. However, in principle, the man who, through his negligence, has injured his unborn child, may be called upon to make financial reparation.

The presumptions that underpin the provisions discussed above seem also to rely on radically different understandings of male and female bodies and their reproductive functioning. The female body is here understood as frail and susceptible to injury and thus an appropriate object of protection. It is constructed as permeable and penetrable – open to the invasion of foreign substances – and thus volatile, dangerous to itself and to others (particularly the foetus within) and, as such, in need of (medical) surveillance, supervision and legal protection. This understanding of the woman's body has been implicitly contrasted against an idealised male norm. The 'normal' idealised male body is seen as stable, safe, bounded and impermeable. It is not liable to dysfunction, and hence is not in need of constant medical control. It is strong and invulnerable, not liable to succumb to penetration by foreign bodies such as toxins. It is self-contained, bounded, isolated and inviolate, not connected to other bodies. Its relationship to reproduction is one of bodily distance, being, as it is, physically disengaged from pregnancy. These understandings of men's and women's bodies resonate in obvious ways with contemporary gender wisdom about male and female social roles: men are seen as stronger, harder, not connected to reproduction; their bodies are more stable, less likely to dysfunction; women are understood as weaker, softer, intimately connected to reproduction; their bodies are less stable, more likely to dysfunction.[100]

Challenges for Law

Law inevitably fossilises the values of the era in which it was created. While still in force today, the Congenital Disabilities (Civil Liability) Act 1976 was drafted more than 30 years ago and reflects the assumptions of that time. It is far from clear that a contemporary Parliament would wish to draw a distinction between mothers' and fathers' respective liabilities along these same lines and, if it did so

---

[99] This fits closely with a more general legal enforcement of a man's financial responsibility for his biological children by way of child support legislation (see ch 5).

[100] Compare ch 4, p 112.

57

choose, no doubt it would justify its decision in terms which accord more closely with contemporary understandings of male and female reproductive responsibilities and the current force of the rhetoric of gender equality.[101] The scale of such transformations in understandings of fathers' roles and responsibilities will be tracked throughout this book. Likewise, *Page* was heard over 25 years ago. Whether a judge hearing the case today would feel equally comfortable making a claim that a woman's statement that she did not wish to become pregnant did not help her given that she was 'clearly of a child-bearing age' is similarly moot.

Over the course of the decades since *Page* was decided and the 1976 Act debated and passed, there has been a striking evolution in men's relationship to reproduction. Beliefs about men's fertility and reproductive health increasingly mirror, we have suggested, our beliefs about women. Men, we are now told, can also suffer from ticking biological clocks and a 'male menopause'.[102] Increased attention has also been paid to fathers' experience of postnatal depression, an illness hitherto more typically associated with women.[103] And concerns regarding the health consequences of delaying having children have been increasingly extended to include men, recent research suggesting that older fathers are associated with a range of child health risks including reduced life expectancy and autism.[104]

Some insight here might be offered by the large literature discussing men's experience of sympathetic pregnancy symptoms in Couvade syndrome. Writing some years ago, the anthropologist Mary Douglas suggested understanding Couvade syndrome in correlation with a weak definition of marriage and a strong interest on the partner's part in asserting his claim to woman and child. The 'Couvading husband', suggests Douglas, is saying: 'Look at me, having cramps and contractions even more than she! Doesn't this prove I am the father of her child?'.[105] Douglas's analysis suggests a broader possibility for contextualising the above reconceptualisation of reproduction as a shared and more equal experience within the general social trends regarding marriage and living patterns detailed in chapter one. In a context where marriage cannot be relied on as

[101] Current concerns might lead, for example, to discussions less focused on the problems of gin drinking, furniture polish and 'those extraordinary things which women do to themselves', and more on the dangerous possibilities of cocaine, ecstasy and alcohol abuse. Debates focused in such a way might produce rather different conclusions, as is clear from the way in which these issues have played out in the US. See Daniels, above (1993) (n 86), and D Roberts, *Killing the Black Body: Race, Reproduction and the Meaning of Liberty* (Vintage Books, New York, 1997).

[102] Fisch, above (n 67).

[103] ME Areias *et al*, 'Correlates of Postnatal Depression in Mothers and Fathers' (1996) 169 *British Journal of Psychiatry* 36; JF Paulson *et al*, 'Individual and Combined Effects of Postpartum Depression in Mothers and Fathers on Parenting Behavior' (2006) 118(2) *Paediatrics* 659.

[104] K Horsey, 'Older Fathers May Increase Chance of Dying Before Adulthood', citing study published in the European Journal of Epidemiology, http://www.bionews.org.uk/new.lasso?storyid=3862 (accessed 13 June 2008). A Reichenberg *et al*, 'Advancing Paternal Age and Autism' (2006) 63(9) *Archives of General Psychiatry* 1026 at 1032.

[105] M Douglas, *Implicit Meanings: Selected Essays in Anthropology*, 2nd edn (Routledge, London, 1999) 173.

a lifelong commitment, grounding claims to one's child within a range of direct biological experiences may become more important.

What we may be witnessing here is a convergence of cultural understandings of men's and women's relationship to reproduction. Implicit, and sometimes explicit, in the literature are calls for men to be treated 'equally' with women and angry rejections of the same, revealing the development of scientific understandings in this area to be neither uncontroversial nor uninfluenced by broader social developments.[106] As Daniels argues, discussion of the science swiftly falls into discussion of the role of men. The ideal man, she suggests, is expected to be virile, and relatively invulnerable to harm. Public exposure of men's private reproductive troubles thus threatens to throw into question not just the health of the male body but deeper ideals of masculinity as well.[107] This interlinking of ideas about fathers, masculinity and heterosexuality is, as we shall see elsewhere in this book, a recurring theme in the legal regulation of fatherhood.

III. Fathers, Pregnancy and Childbirth

The above discussion tracks what might be described as a 'traditional' view of reproduction coming increasingly under attack. Similar understandings pervade the literature on men's involvement in pregnancy and birth, and similar challenges to this marginalisation of fathers are equally in evidence. While fathers' experience of antenatal care can vary widely, some common themes emerge from the existing research. These are captured by one writer's suggestion that the essence of men's experience is that of 'labouring for a relevance'. Men, she argues, grapple with the reality of pregnancy and child, and struggle for recognition as a parent from the mother, co-workers, friends, family and society.[108] This may be contrasted with cultural assumptions concerning the reality, centrality and immediacy of maternal identity. While women have the experience of pregnancy to draw upon, the man's knowledge appears vicarious, disconnected and abstract, being mediated through the woman's body.[109]

> [T]he expectant father has traditionally been a vicarious knower in the sense that his knowledge of the fetus has been limited to external visual and tactile sources of information. He may sense the fetus, but only via his pregnant partner's body and only then with her permission. His knowledge of the fetus is disembodied and, therefore, more disconnected and abstract than hers. Whereas maternity has traditionally been an experience providing women with reproductive continuity from conception through

---

[106] As we shall see in other contexts elsewhere in this book: eg, ch 4, ch 5.

[107] Daniels, above (n 1).

[108] PL Jordan, 'Laboring for Relevance: Expectant and New Fatherhood' (1990) 39(1) *Nursing Research* 11.

[109] Cf the discussion of how mothers can mediate aspects of a father's interaction with children: see ch 5.

59

gestation to birthing and nursing a child, paternity is only an 'abstract idea'. Biological fatherhood is a discontinuous experience, the genetic/inseminator role separated in time and space from the nurturer role.[110]

Men frequently speak of a desire to be involved in the pregnancy but a difficulty in engaging with its reality, citing a sense of remoteness and redundancy and a lack of 'evidence' about the growing foetus.[111] This distance from reproduction contributes to an assumption of greater and instinctive female expertise in reproduction and parenting, with men frequently portrayed as having no natural parenting abilities.[112] Some men also suggest that, unlike women, their lack of continuous physical experience leaves them able to opt in and out of involvement with pregnancy, with an element of choice that their partners lack. Women's pregnant embodiment can therefore be understood as an anchor, firmly grounding the reality of the baby within their day-to-day existence.[113] A man's lack of such an anchor can contribute to an experience of their involvement in reproduction as 'volunteers', while the women are 'draftees'.[114]

A substantial literature suggests that the organisation of what is, after all, typically referred to as 'maternity' care may serve to foster and support such a vision of participation in reproduction as optional for fathers, an issue which we consider further in chapter four in the context of policies aimed at the promotion of 'active fathering' across a range of health care contexts.[115] Torr's overview of services supporting men's parenting found, for example, that antenatal services for fathers tend to be thinly spread and reactive, with an emphasis on the father's role as supporter, his own needs overlooked.[116] This is clearly in evidence in men's involvement in antenatal medical appointments and classes and at birth. It is also relevant in the historical lack of attention to men's emotional needs in the event that the pregnancy is miscarried. Research suggests that the attendance of many fathers at antenatal appointments can be infrequent and sporadic, men often expressing uncertainty as to whether they are either wanted or required.[117]

---

[110] M Sandelowski, 'Separate but Less Unequal: Fetal ultrasonography and the Transformation of expectant mother/fatherhood' (1994) 8(2) *Gender & Society* 230 at 234.

[111] J Draper, '"It's the first scientific evidence": Men's Experience of Pregnancy Confirmation' (2002) 39(6) *Journal of Advanced Nursing* 563; J Draper, 'Blurring, Moving and Broken Boundaries: Men's Encounters with the Pregnant Body' (2003) 25(7) *Sociology and Health & Illness* 743.

[112] J Smith, 'The First Intruder: Fatherhood, a historical perspective' in P Moss (ed), *Father Figures: Fathers in the Families of the 1990s* (HMSO, Edinburgh, 1995) at 20. See also J Sunderland, 'Baby entertainer, bumbling assistant and line manager: discourses of fatherhood in parentcraft texts' (2000) 11(2) *Discourse & Society* 249.

[113] Draper (2003), above (n 111) at 753.

[114] K Czapanskiy, 'Volunteers and Draftees: The Struggle for Parental Equality' (1991) 38 *UCLA Law Review* 415. Compare ch 4 below.

[115] Ch 4, p 122–125; this policy agenda includes the involvement of health visitors, GPs, community paediatric teams and family support and resource units in the 'promotion' of this vision of men's participation.

[116] J Torr, *Is There a Father in the House? A Handbook for Health and Social Care Professionals* (Oxford, Radcliffe Medical Press, Oxford, 2003). See also Jordan, above (n 108).

[117] D Singh and M Newburn, *Becoming a Father* (National Childbirth Trust, London, 2000).

There is one notable exception: the foetal ultrasound scan has now established itself as an integral part of the cultural script of expectant fatherhood, serving to 'expand men's physical and emotional involvement in childbearing beyond their biological role in conception and their supportive role during childbirth',[118] providing men with their first 'real evidence' of the pregnancy.[119] Some women talk about taking vicarious pleasure in a partner's enjoyment at the ultrasound appointment. Others describe feeling left out, reporting that they were not easily able to see the screen themselves and suggesting that the doctors were catering to their partners.[120] Such descriptions hint at the potentially double-edged nature of greater paternal involvement for women, with the possibility that it might be perceived as a potential challenge to the centrality of the mother's role, a tension we explore in more detail in later chapters.[121]

Men's participation in antenatal classes is likewise influenced by a number of structural factors. Such classes are generally given by women, aimed at women and often held during the day with, at most, one 'fathers' evening'.[122] A number of articles in midwifery journals castigate childbirth educators for overlooking the needs of fathers and, perhaps surprisingly for a profession historically so closely associated with the needs of women,[123] increasingly adopt a tone of equality of mothers' and fathers' needs.[124] Central to this invocation of equality is a movement away from viewing birth primarily as a medical event. If health care professionals aim to provide the best possible experience of a milestone in one's life, then the needs of the father become far more important than if their exclusive goal is a medically safe delivery. Torr suggests that fathers are less marginalised if the birth takes place at home, and it is the midwife not the father who leaves after the delivery.[125]

Prospective parents may obtain much of their information from reading. Yet it has been noted that fathers are often given relatively little information either before or after birth as part of antenatal care, and virtually none of it is given to them directly. And while giving information via the mother may be convenient, it may also foster a sense that she is the gatekeeper to the child.[126] A number of

[118] Sandelowski, above (n 110) at 235; J Draper, ' "It was a real good show": The Ultrasound Scan, Fathers and the Power of Visual Knowledge' (2002) 24(6) *Sociology of Health & Illness* 771 at 789. See also M Sandelowski, 'Channels of Desire: Fetal Ultrasonography in Two Use Contexts' (1994) 4(3) *Qualitative Health Research* 262.

[119] This description was used by some of the men interviewed by Draper, above (n 118) at 780.

[120] Sandelowski, above (n 118).

[121] See ch 4 below, for discussion of a similar tension with regard to early years childcare.

[122] M Nolan, 'Caring for Fathers in Antenatal Classes' (1994) 4(2) *Modern Midwife* 25. See also VA Bedford and N Johnson, 'The Role of the Father' (1998) 4 *Midwifery* 190; R Early, 'Men as Consumers of Maternity Services: a Contradiction in Terms' (2001) 25 *International Journal of Consumer Studies* 160.

[123] The word 'midwife' itself derives from the profession's central vocation to be 'with woman'.

[124] Nolan, above (n 122); Bedford and Johnson, above (n 122).

[125] Torr, above (n 116) at 57.

[126] The mother's role as 'gatekeeper' is further explored below, particularly in the context of unmarried fathers: see ch 6.

authors have noted the lack of relevant literature specifically written for fathers.[127] Burgess's analysis of pregnancy books aimed at the general public is particularly critical, finding that images of women in them outnumbered those of men by 200 to 1, with fathers addressed rarely and even then with patronising enthusiasm.[128] Further, the information available often fails to engage with men's specific concerns around pregnancy,[129] no doubt contributing to the fact that only a very small proportion of those reading pregnancy and parenting literature are men.[130] The registered charity, the Fatherhood Institute (formerly Fathers Direct), has attempted to respond to this by publishing its own *Dad's Pack*, a series of glossy flashcards aiming to provide basic information for new fathers, and launching a twelve point action plan to prevent fathers from being 'shut out' of maternity services.[131]

It has also been suggested that where something goes wrong with the pregnancy, men's experience of loss has been neglected, with such support as is available post-miscarriage being centred on the woman and the man's own feelings denied, his proper role being to 'stay strong' for his partner.[132] Yet one recent study found that men and women grieved differently and that men should not simply be an 'add-on' to any strategy designed to support women.[133] A number of agencies have now started providing materials which deal with miscarriage and the loss of a young child specifically for men.[134]

However, while the above picture may reveal men's involvement in antenatal care to be limited and patchy, it has nonetheless been subject to a sea change over the last 50 years. Nowhere is this more dramatically illustrated than by statistics regarding fathers' attendance at birth, which has risen from 5% in the 1950s to as much as 97% in the early 1990s. In the space of just one decade (1970s–1980s), fathers' birth attendance rose almost threefold from 35% to 90%.[135] While fathers' admittance to labour and delivery may now seem entirely normal, it was

---

[127] Eg, Burgess, above (n 44).

[128] *Ibid* at 115. See also: C Lewis, *Becoming a Father* (Open University Press, Milton Keynes, 1986).

[129] B Chalmers and D Meyer, 'What men say about pregnancy, birth and parenthood' (1996) 17 *Journal of Psychosomatic Obstetrics and Gynecology* 47.

[130] Singh and Newburn, above (n 117) 42.

[131] See Fatherhood Institute, *The Dad Deficit: the Missing Piece in the Maternity Jigsaw* (London, Fatherhood Institute, 2008), A Burgess, *Maternal and Infant Health in the Perinatal Period: the Father's Role* (London, Fatherhood Institute, 2008) and the various resources on the importance of fathers' involvement in the antenatal period collected at http://www.fatherhoodinstitute.org/index.php?id=2&cID=733 (accessed, 13 June 2008). For more on the Fatherhood Institute see ch 4 below, p 125.

[132] See: The Miscarriage Association, *Men & Miscarriage* (The Miscarriage Association, Wakefield 2006).

[133] See: M Johnson and S Baker, 'Co-occurrence of Positive and Negative Affect Following Miscarriage', ESCRC Report; RES-000–22–0192. A summary is available at <http:www.esrcsocietyto-day.ac.uk>, accessed 28 October 2007.

[134] Eg The Miscarriage Association, above (n 132).

[135] Smith, above (n 112) at 21. Analysis of data from the Millennium Cohort Study suggests slightly lower attendance: K Kiernan and K Smith, 'Unmarried Parenthood: New Insights from the Millennium Cohort Study' (2003) 114 *Population Trends* 26 at 26–33.

anything but uncontroversial. Before the 1970s, some hospitals formally excluded fathers, citing a number of objections to their presence, including the risk of infection and their propensity to faint.[136] The motives of those men who wished to attend the birth were also questioned until comparatively recently.[137] In clear contrast, reports of the 2005 UK election campaign saw little adverse comment on the delay of the launch of the Liberal Democrats' election manifesto in order to allow the Party leader to attend the birth of his child.[138] Even the one reported exception to this, an elderly peer who noted that 'you wouldn't have had a wimp taking days off to go and have babies in my day', explicitly locates his disapproval in the values of an earlier era.[139] The trend towards fathers attending birth is now so pronounced that current concerns focus more on the possibility that men may be pressurised to attend.[140] The NHS has been moved to give specific advice to fathers-to-be that their presence at the birth is not compulsory.[141] However, while now admitted to the birth, men may still find themselves uncertain of their role in the delivery suite. The dominant experience for many appears to remain that, rather than attending to witness an important event in own lives, men are there as 'little more than another assistant in the childbirth scenario'.[142]

The legal context for antenatal medicine presents a similar vision of limited paternal involvement. Given that the foetus is growing inside the woman's body, it is impossible to give a father any formal legal rights to participate in medical decisions regarding the pregnancy without also giving him significant control over the pregnant woman. And pregnant women are treated as no exception to the principle of English law that the only person who can give consent to medical treatment on behalf of a mentally competent adult patient, is that patient herself.[143] This principle is not affected by the consequences of refusal of treatment for a foetus, even late in pregnancy. Even where the woman is

---

[136] Lewis reports a letter published in the *British Medical Journal* in 1961 promoting 'a more enlightened attitude to normal obstetrics ... where the father is welcomed and encouraged to be present at the delivery'. This provoked a response characterised by a rather different idea of the father's proper place: 'Let us not pander to morbid curiosity and sensationalism, nor to those featherbrains who wish to be in the van of a new fashion, by encouraging a highly unnatural trend with the mumbo-jumbo of pseudo-psychology. The proper place for the father, if not at work, is the "local" whither instinct will usually guide him. Family men may be baby-sitting, unless ejected by mother-in-law': Lewis, above (n 128) at 57.

[137] Burgess, above (n 44) at 121.

[138] S. Laville et all 'Kennedy Rushes to Pregnant Wife' Guardian (12 April 2005).

[139] Lord Beaumont of Whitley, cited in S Graudt, 'The Reckoning', *Observer* (24 April 2005).

[140] J Hall, 'Attendance not compulsory' (1993) 89(46) *Nursing Times* 69.

[141] The second edition of the NHS Magazine *You're Pregnant* featured a new supplement of advice and information for new dads, entitled '37 Things Every Man Should Know Before He Becomes a Dad'. Number 4 in the list is 'You don't have to be at the birth' and advises: 'Some loving partners feel very anxious about being there for the birth. If it's worrying you talk to your partner about it. Don't wait until you're in the delivery room.'

[142] R Mander, *Men and Maternity* (Routledge, London and New York, 2004) at 81. See also: Torr, above (n 116) at 53; J Draper, 'Whose Welfare in the Labour Room? A Discussion of the Increasing Trend of Fathers' Birth Attendance' (1997) 13 *Midwifery* 132.

[143] *Re T (Adult: Refusal of Treatment)* [1992] 4 All ER 649; *Re MB* [1997] 2 FLR 426.

63

completely incapacitated, there is no legal right for the putative father to make decisions regarding antenatal care, although he may be consulted regarding what the woman might have wanted had she been competent. English law is different in this respect from that of the US, which accords the next of kin greater rights to make treatment decisions. This is graphically illustrated by a series of US cases where pregnant women have been ventilated at the request of male progenitors wishing to save the life of the foetuses the women are carrying. In one such case, the putative father of a foetus was granted the formal status of protector of the foetus by appointing him its guardian ad litem.[144] Whatever respect might be accorded to a man's wishes in practice, in the UK there would be no formal legal basis for according him any decision-making rights in such a case.[145]

Conclusion

Above, we have traced a dominant understanding of reproduction as a matter of female expertise, responsibility and control, a view entrenched in a range of legal provisions. We have noted putative fathers' corresponding frequent sense of marginalisation and lack of control in this sphere, a theme that will reoccur frequently in different parenting contexts discussed later in this book. Such a sense may be implicated in men's choice to opt out of any involvement in pregnancy and birth, or to engage only as occasional supporters of their partners or as 'volunteers'.[146] However, efforts to bring men in from the margins involve challenging the centrality of the female role. The problem of how to include men and recognise their needs while not undermining women and denying theirs is thrown into clear relief in this context and poses significant challenges both for service providers and law-makers. How is it possible to recognise the significance for men of abortion and important treatment decisions in pregnancy, while protecting women's autonomy and bodily integrity in this area? In the light of shifting and contested understandings of male and female reproductivity, how should we guard the bodies of all potential parents? How do these questions relate to the broader social shifts around the allocation of risk and responsibility discussed in chapter one? Does the current movement away from radically different towards convergent understandings of male and female reproduction provide the basis for some kind of formal equality of treatment? Yet how might recourse to ideas of equality help us, given the significant biological differences at play here?

---

[144] *Poole v Santa Clara County Kaiser Hospital* (1986) Petition No 604575, Super Ct of Santa Clara County.

[145] English law would not recognise the possibility of appointing a guardian ad litem for a foetus. An early attempt to make a foetus a ward of court in order to protect it from the actions of the pregnant woman similarly failed: *Re F (In Utero)* [1988] Fam 122.

[146] Czapanskiy, above (n 114).

Conclusion

Significantly, in this chapter, we have also tracked a number of challenges to the marginalisation of fathers, a greater desire to involve men more closely both in birth control and antenatal care, and a growing sense of men as reproductive agents with responsibilities to their future offspring. Health care professionals are increasingly encouraged not just to facilitate men's involvement as supporters of women, but also to recognise men's own needs as reproductive agents and putative fathers. Ideas of equality between mothers and fathers form a frequent reference here. Against this developing backdrop, certain aspects of the web of legal rights and responsibilities outlined above might appear dated, relying on assumptions that no longer reflect either popular opinion or the current state of scientific knowledge. Men's reproductive capacity is increasingly seen as vulnerable, at times equally so as that of women. Beliefs regarding infertility as a largely female problem are giving way to understandings that implicate men as just as likely to contribute to a failure to conceive. Finally, the understanding of male reproductive biology as less likely to cause harm to the foetus, which underpinned foetal protection policies and liability for congenital disability legislation, has come under attack. As has long been the case for women, there is now a clear sense that men too have responsibilities to their future offspring and that these responsibilities are not only financial (a theme to which we return in chapters four and five). Rather, potential fathers should moderate their behaviour in certain ways prior to conception, taking seriously their duties as responsible reproductive agents. It has been suggested that fathers' sense of responsibility towards children may be closely linked to their sense of responsibility towards their partners, rather than directly to those children per se.[147] While such a sense resonates with aspects of what we called a 'traditional' view of reproduction, it is clear from the above discussion that this view of paternal responsibilities is under challenge.[148]

There is a striking fit between the evolving understandings outlined above and the current rethinking of men and women's responsibilities with regard to parenting explored elsewhere in this book. Specifically, a movement towards conceptualising reproduction as a matter of more central concern for men, with male bodies more closely implicated in foetal health, presents a striking parallel to the evolution in contemporary understandings of the 'good father' as not just a breadwinner and remote disciplinarian, but also a hands-on carer and active

---

[147] Marsiglio, above (n 4) at 95.

[148] Most notably from evolving knowledge of genetics. A more direct relationship to the foetus is also asserted in those abortion cases where men have sought to align their interests with those of the foetus, in opposition to those of the pregnant woman, who is constructed as selfish and either hostile or indifferent to its welfare. Such a portrayal of the pregnant woman has been described, particularly by feminist authors, as part of a deeply problematic, adversarial construction of pregnancy, which pits the woman against the foetus, assuming a conflict between female and foetal rights. See, for example, S McLean, *Old Law, New Medicine: Medical Ethics and Human Rights* (Pandora, London, 1999) at 52. More significantly for our purposes, the alignment of male and foetal interests strongly parallels the alignment of men's interests with those of children in the contact and residence disputes discussed in ch 5 below.

65

presence in his children's lives.[149] It may not be coincidental that claims that birth brings families together are increasingly being made at a time when the traditional nuclear family appears to be under threat.[150] A sense of men's closer involvement in reproduction and direct relationship to the foetus/child may be a response to fears that this relationship can no longer be so easily or firmly anchored in men's relationships with those children's mothers.[151] It may also serve to ground challenges to mothers' perceived role of 'gatekeepers' to their children.

Before we move on, it is worth noting one last issue raised by the above discussion. In subsequent chapters, we will address more explicitly the complex issue of what it is which makes one a father. The additional question raised in this chapter is not just *what* makes a father, but also *when* is a father made? Whilst gestation may render fixing upon the beginning of motherhood contentious, is the start of fatherhood now any clearer?[152] Does a man become a father at the birth of his child, or sometime before or after that event? For lawyers the answer is clear: a legal person exists only from birth, so the legal statuses of mother and father can only make sense from that point onwards. But, ethically speaking, many feel that individuals do have rights and responsibilities before that point which could accurately be characterised as parental. And, in psychological terms, men may begin to feel like fathers at different moments: at birth; before birth (in planning for a child's future, feeling a foetus move within a partner's body or witnessing those movements through ultrasonography); or some time after birth (through developing a relationship with a child).[153] What is clear from the discussion in this chapter is that increasing awareness of their own reproductive biology may make men more aware of themselves as potential fathers long before birth. Men may decide to follow a particular diet, stop smoking or moderate alcohol intake to improve chances of conception, or take up a less risky or more stable career in anticipation of the responsibilities of fatherhood. Likewise, when a HD sufferer considers whether to become a father, he foregrounds his paternal responsibility to a future possible child. Diagnostic technologies and genetic knowledges have carved out a new context for fatherhood, one that more strongly

---

[149] See chs 4 and 5 below, and R Collier, *Masculinity, Law and the Family* (Routledge, London, 1995) on the construction of the 'good father', ch 5.

[150] Lewis, above (n 128) at 60–61.

[151] See eg ch 6 below at p 202 for discussion of a more general trend for law to focus less on men's responsibilities to their partners, and more on their responsibilities to their children.

[152] JL Shapiro writes that birth is the biggest experience of men's lives, as '[i]t is how we become fathers'. JL Shapiro, 'When Men are Pregnant' in JL Shapiro, MJ Diamond, M Greenberg (eds), *Becoming a Father: Contemporary, Social, Developmental and Clinical Perspectives* (Springer, New York, 1995) at 119.

[153] Marsiglio notes: 'seeing my son, and then holding him in my arms, brought to life my new identity as a father': Marsiglio, above (n 4) at vii. Thomas Laqueur, however, suggests that fatherhood is to do with 'emotional investment' in a child – a labour of the heart, not the hand – and that this may begin before birth: TW Laqueur, 'The Facts of Fatherhood' in M Hirsch and E Fox (eds), *Conflicts in Feminism* (Routledge, New York, 1990) at 219.

implicates men's responsibilities before birth. These developments may be rendering the beginning of fatherhood almost as indeterminate as the beginning of motherhood.

3

Fatherhood and Assisted Reproduction

Introduction

IN THIS CHAPTER, we move on to consider fatherhood in the context of assisted reproduction.[1] Assisted Reproductive Technologies (ARTs) offer the potential to break down parenthood into different constituent parts, thus rendering explicit decisions about which kinds of links (genetic, gestational, social and so on) are most significant in making someone a parent. As such, the question of what it is that makes a man a father is here posed in a particularly stark way. ARTs also graphically illustrate what we have described as the 'fragmentation of fatherhood', where different aspects of the traditional father role may be shared among a number of men. A child may have (legally recognised) relationships with a genetic father, with the mother's husband, and with one or more other men who are involved in social parenting roles. In the context of ARTs, where these roles are less likely to be concentrated in one man, there is also the possibility of an additional father figure: the man (neither husband nor genitor) who embarked on a course of treatment services with the mother. The fragmentation of fatherhood may thus be particularly radical in this context and, given a desire to limit the potential resulting confusion, law's efforts to contain that fragmentation even more marked. The mass of regulation in this area provides a significant body of documentation in which to trace the choices that law-makers have made in this regard and, given that these issues are back before Parliament at the time this book goes to press, much of this documentation is extremely topical.

It is no surprise that ARTs' ability to complicate – and limit – paternal ties and, more specifically, to facilitate procreation outwith heterosexual relationships have

---

[1] See ch 2, n 2 for the problematic nature of this terminology, and below p 71 for exactly what we include within 'assisted' reproduction. Our discussion in this chapter does not extend to self-insemination using sperm of a known donor outside of a licensed clinic, some cases of which are discussed in ch 6 below at pp 192–193.

served as a significant flashpoint in the articulation of cultural anxieties regarding fatherhood and the so-called 'crisis in masculinity' described in chapter one. This perhaps received its clearest expression in concerns regarding the idea of so-called 'virgin births' but extends considerably beyond that.[2] Women who make use of ARTs are sometimes characterised as neglectful of the interests of children where they attempt procreation without a suitable father figure, or as selfish in deferring motherhood in order to concentrate on a career. One clinic manager is quoted as suggesting:

> People want everything now. If they can't have a baby now, they want IVF. They think it's no different from putting your name down for a handbag. Some people are horrified by the idea that they have to have sex two to three times a week. About 10 per cent of people I see don't have time to have sex.[3]

The provision of ARTs in the UK is a fast-growing, highly regulated industry. In addition to raising the concerns sketched above, it has provoked a large (often feminist) literature suggesting that ARTs involve unnecessary interventions on the bodies of otherwise healthy women, increasing pressure to conceive and further stigmatising childlessness. Critics cite the high costs and low success rates of many treatments and complain that invasive procedures on women are often carried out as treatment for a male-mediated infertility. One such very popular procedure is Intra-Cytoplasmic Sperm Injection (ICSI), a treatment for low sperm motility. The dramatic increase in use rates of ICSI demonstrates the importance that potential parents attach to a genetic link between the social father and his future child.[4] Further, the use of ICSI has lessened (although by no means removed) the asymmetry between men and women in a context where women were previously the near-exclusive focus of medical attention: ICSI brings men in from the margins.[5] This mirrors some of the developments discussed in the last chapter regarding a greater focus on male reproductive health. Yet ICSI involves *ex utero* creation of embryos – with women required to undergo egg harvesting and embryo implantation procedures – in a context where there may be no female reproductive health problem.

To date, little research has been done on men's experience of ARTs. One US study found that men's infertility was perceived as compromising their sense of

---

[2] See below for discussion (n 26) and accompanying text.

[3] C Edwardes and A Alderson, 'Women Bypass Sex in Favour of "Instant Pregnancies"' *Daily Telegraph* (25 September 2005) <http://www.telegraph.co.uk/global/main.jhtml?xml=/global/2005/09/25/nivf25.xml> accessed 21 November 2007.

[4] ICSI involves injecting sperm directly into an egg, dramatically increasing the chance of a successful fertilisation in the presence of low sperm counts or poor motility. Use of donor semen has fallen from 25,000 insemination treatments in 1992–93 to just 6,000 in 2002–03, a decline which seems clearly attributable to the increase in ICSI over the same period (from virtually zero to over 15,000 treatments): Human Fertilisation and Embryology Authority, 'Factsheet on Sperm, Egg and Embryo Donation' (Human Fertilisation and Embryology Authority, London, 2004).

[5] C Thompson, *Making Parents: the Ontological Choreography of Reproductive Technologies* (MIT Press, Cambridge, MA, 2005) at 124–5.

masculinity in the clinical setting because it betokened a lack of virility and stopped them from becoming fathers. The researcher uncovered a prevalent belief that 'if you can't father a child, then you are not really a man', with the emphasis on impregnation and its implications of sexual prowess.[6] Considerations of fertility are here deeply linked to cultural ideas of virility.[7] This may go to the heart of why the preservation of genetic links is so important for many, and is a significant underpinning to the 'geneticisation' of paternity that forms a central theme of this chapter and of chapter six.

The legal backdrop to the discussion that follows is provided by the Human Fertilisation and Embryology Act 1990 (the 1990 Act). At the time of writing, the 1990 Act looks likely to be amended by the Human Fertilisation and Embryology Bill 2007 (the 2007 Bill).[8] If passed in its current form, the 2007 Bill will make significant changes to the detail of the 1990 Act, while leaving relatively intact the broad principles which underpin it. This chapter describes the law as it currently stands as well as noting, where relevant, the changes likely to be made by the 2007 Bill.

The 1990 Act drew heavily on a report prepared by a Committee of Inquiry chaired by the philosopher Mary Warnock (the Warnock Report) in the 1980s.[9] It establishes a regulatory regime, overseen by the Human Fertilisation and Embryology Authority (HFEA), for embryo research and for those infertility treatment services that involve creation of embryos outside of a woman's body and/or use of any donated gametes.[10] Where treatment includes neither the external creation of embryos nor sperm obtained from a donor via a licensed clinic, then the treatment will not be covered by the 1990 Act. In such circumstances, legal fatherhood is governed by common law principles providing that where the woman is married, her husband is presumed to be the legal father and where she is unmarried, or where the presumption of her husband's paternity is rebutted by genetic proof, then the genetic father is deemed the legal father.[11] This has particular significance for lesbian couples who achieve parenthood through self-insemination using the sperm of a friend, as we will see in chapter six below.[12]

---

[6] *Ibid* at 136. See also the discussion of the 'sexual father' in ch 4 below at p 112.

[7] Women, in contrast, suggested that it was the fact of having no children, rather than the physical inability to procreate which was more stigmatising: *ibid* at 128. See, further: E Reynaud, *Holy Virility: The Social Construction of Masculinity* (Pluto, London, 1983).

[8] Human Fertilisation and Embryology Bill HL (2007–08) [6], originally entitled the Human Tissue and Embryos Bill. At the time this book goes to press, the Bill has completed its passage through the House of Lords and had its second reading in the House of Commons.

[9] Committee on Human Fertilisation and Embryology, 'Report of the Committee of Inquiry into Human Fertilisation and Embryology' ('the Warnock Report'), Cmnd 9314 (1984).

[10] 1990 Act, ss 2–3.

[11] For more detail, see ch 6 below at pp 180–181. The 2007 Bill would not change this state of affairs.

[12] The impossibility of having a legally fatherless child outside of a licensed clinic has been explained as due to the unique ability of physicians to 'de-bless' sperm, robbing it of its mystical power of attributing paternity: T Laqueur, 'The Facts of Fatherhood' in M Hirsch and E Fox-Keller (eds), *Conflicts in Feminism* (Routledge, London, 1990) at 217.

In what follows, we discuss those aspects of the 1990 Act that relate to (putative) fathers' legal status, rights and responsibilities in this context. First, the Act requires clinics to consider a child's welfare when deciding whom to accept for treatment, explicitly directing that account be taken of that child's need for a father. Second, the Act contains 'status provisions', determining who should be treated as the parents of children conceived via infertility treatment services. Third, one aspect of these provisions has received particular attention: whether a child desired by a couple together, but conceived after the death of the husband/partner, should be deemed legally fatherless. Fourth, the Act addresses the issue of surrogacy. Fifth, the question of whether children born of donor insemination (DI) should have access to information identifying their genetic parent/s has been the focus of substantial debate, litigation and statutory reform. Finally, the Act has been the basis for litigation regarding the disposal of stored embryos. Each of these matters is addressed below.

I. Child Welfare and the Need for a Father

The provision of the 1990 Act to have generated the most critical commentary is section 13(5), which provides that:

> A woman shall not be provided with treatment services unless account has been taken of the welfare of any child who may be born as a result of the treatment (including the need of that child for a father), and of any other child who may be affected by the birth.[13]

If enacted in its current form, the 2007 Bill will serve to change the phrase '(including the need of that child for a father)'.[14] The original rationale for including this phrase and the growing consensus in favour of its revision is discussed below.

Exactly what was meant by consideration of the 'need of that child for a father' in the 1990 Act is far less clear than one might imagine, although this provision is evidently not prescribing the need for a genetic father through proscribing parthenogenesis.[15] In an early commentary, Douglas takes the section as '*presumably* meaning a man who will fulfil the social role of father'.[16] Yet even if this

---

[13] This is supplemented by guidance offered in the HFEA Code of Practice: 'where the child will have no legal father, the centre should assess ... the prospective mother's ability to meet the child's/children's needs and the ability of other persons within the family or social circle willing to share responsibility for those needs': HFEA, 'Code of Practice: Edition 7.0' (2007), <http://cop.hfea.gov.uk/cop>, accessed 21 November 2007 [G.3.3.3]. This suggests a reading of s 13(5) as aiming to ensure the provision of a social father.

[14] 2007 Bill, cl 14(2)(b).

[15] RG Lee and D Morgan, *Human Fertilisation and Embryology: Regulating the Reproductive Revolution*, 2nd edn (Blackstones, London, 2001) at 222. Their own interpretation of the section is that 'the woman seeking treatment should have a male partner'.

[16] Emphasis added. G Douglas, *Law, Fertility and Reproduction* (Sweet & Maxwell, London 1991) 1273.

presumption is correct, the meaning of 'the social role of father', and why such a figure is important, remain relatively unexplored in this context. Are social fathers necessary to ensure the presence of a second 'hands-on' carer? If so, is the need just for any two carers to be present? Are fathers necessary because they provide a distinctively gendered style of parenting? Is the aim to ensure financial provision for children? Or are fathers deemed important for their symbolic function in completing the nuclear family?

In Parliament during the late 1980s and early 1990s, the desirability of protecting the heterosexual nuclear family was generally assumed,[17] and the debates preceding the 1990 Act were no exception. MPs at the time were divided only on how far it is legitimate to intervene in enforcing this preferred model over other possible living arrangements. Nonetheless, three analytically distinct grounds for asserting the importance of fathers can be discerned. First and most prominent, is the role of father as financial provider.[18] The 1990 Act was passed at a time of significant concern about increasing social security expenditure on single-parent families, with the Child Support Act 1991 under contemporaneous discussion.[19] As such, it is not surprising that financial issues occupied members of both Houses of Parliament. The following comment from the Earl of Lauderdale is typical:

> To allow and encourage by state provision – it is at the taxpayers' expense ultimately – begetting of children into what are designed to be one-parent families does not make sense as regards serious sociological responsibility.[20]

Second, the importance of fathers as 'hands-on' carers is also considered, with Lady Saltoun commending the 'inestimable benefit of a father's loving care',[21] presenting a distinctly male model of parenting, where fathers are important for the healthy psychological development of children into the well-adjusted spouses and parents of tomorrow:

> Children learn primarily from example, by copying what they see. It is by example that a boy learns how to be a responsible husband and father and how to treat his own children in turn. It is by example that a girl learns how to be a wife, from seeing how her mother cares for her father. The father is enormously important, if only as a role model.[22]

---

[17] As evidence of this same climate, see also the Child Support Act 1991, and the infamous s 28 of the Local Government Act 1988.

[18] Ch 4 below, pp 109–110.

[19] See ch 5 below, pp 150–153, and, for an excellent overview of the run-up to reform: G Davis *et al*, *Child Support in Action* (Hart Publications, Oxford, 1998) at ch 1.

[20] *Hansard*, HL, vol 516, col 1103 (6 March 1990).

[21] *Hansard*, HL, vol 515, col 801 (6 February 1990). Precisely what is meant by 'hands-on' care is open to debate: see ch 4 below. See also the early custody/residence and access/contact cases, for similar arguments regarding the need for a father figure.

[22] *Hansard*, HL, vol 515, col 788 (6 February 1990).

Third, however, by far the clearest and most frequent message to emerge from these debates is a strong moral assertion of the marital unit as the only acceptable forum in which to raise children. This unit is seen as the only sure start in life for children and, indeed, its decline is credited with causing much that is wrong in society.[23] The importance of providing a 'stable' base for children is frequently asserted, with 'stability' standing as shorthand for heterosexual marital monogamy. Douglas notes that the House of Lords' proposed amendments to the draft legislation were overwhelmingly concerned with preventing women with dubious sexual attitudes from having children, yet seemingly indifferent to others who might be deemed unsuitable as parents.[24] And even those speakers who are reluctant to confine child-bearing to the marital unit are often convinced that it must remain the preserve of the stable, cohabiting heterosexual couple:

> People have an absolute right to be themselves, to reject contact with men or to shun any physical contact with them. That is their choice. But that is not the same as accepting that there is some automatic or inalienable right to child bearing. Child bearing is not a right. It is part of the unfathomable life force. That is why man and woman together must take responsibility for the well-being and love of the child.[25]

The underlying anxiety that 'people' (which, given the context, clearly means women) are attempting to 'reject contact with men' also provides an interesting insight into one subtext to these debates. The worry was one that was shortly to grip the country regarding so-called 'virgin births': were women who had never had sex with a man really to be helped to conceive children?[26] A close reading, then, might suggest that parliamentarians were less concerned with the need to ensure a financial provider or hands-on (male) carer than they were with the symbolic value of ensuring children were only born into (quasi-)marital units. Of course, the importance accorded to committed heterosexual relationships in the debates might also reflect these parliamentarians' belief that such relationships would ensure a father's presence for the reasons given above: financial provision and a second carer who could bring specifically male attributes to bear. There are two compelling reasons for doubting this, however.

[23] See eg: *Hansard*, HL, vol 515, col 767 (6 February 1990) (per Lord Ashbourne); HC vol 174, cols 1024–5 (20 June 1990) (Wilshire).

[24] G Douglas, 'Assisted Reproduction and the Welfare of the Child' (1993) 5 *Current Legal Problems* 53 at 58.

[25] *Hansard*, HC, vol 174, col 1023 (20 June 1990) (per David Blunkett MP). Poignantly, Blunkett has since been involved a high-profile struggle regarding two young children born following his sexual relationship with publisher, Kimberley Quinn. See eg: G Hinsliff, 'Blunkett blasted for "intrusion" in Kimberly Quinn paternity battle', *Observer* (6 March 2005), <http://observer.guardian.co.uk/politics/story/0,,1431623,00.html>, accessed 21 November 2007.

[26] The *Daily Mail*'s article 'Storm Over Virgin Births' drew attention to a letter in *The Lancet* regarding a single woman with no history of sexual activity seeking donor insemination: 'Storm Over Virgin Births'. *Daily Mail* (London. 11 March 1991). See: D Cooper and D Herman, 'Getting "The Family Right": Legislating Heterosexuality in Britain, 1986–1991' (1991) 10 *Canadian Journal of Family Law* 41 at 43.

First, if the need really was for either financial provision or two carers, then there is no reason to discriminate between homosexual and heterosexual couples. If what is required is at least one carer and one breadwinner, the gender of the parties should make no difference. In the course of the debates, no parliamentarian makes this point, although references to the distinctive attributes of male parents are surprisingly infrequent. The subsequent furore regarding 'virgin births' was, likewise, specifically concerned with women being able to have children when they were not in a relationship with a man. At that time, no distinction was made between single women and those in lesbian relationships.[27]

Second, that the perceived importance of fatherhood lies primarily in its symbolic function of completing the nuclear family is emphasised by the privileged place accorded to widows within the debates. If the need for the father was rooted in the desire for a male breadwinner or hands-on carer, then presumably widows should provoke the same concerns as other single parents. In numerous interventions, however, parliamentarians make favourable mention of widows. They seek either to explain why their disapproval of single parents is not intended to include criticism of widows' ability as mothers, or alternatively use the example of widows to demonstrate the possibility of good single-parent mothering in order to argue that treatment services should not be restricted to married couples.[28] In the parliamentary discussions of the 2007 Bill, reference to widows seems to have almost entirely disappeared from the debates. In contrast, in 1990, widows emerge as a special, deserving category of woman, providing clear indication that it was not single-parent families per se, but the intentional creation of children outside of a heterosexual (ideally marital) union which was the key source of concern.[29]

We return to this point shortly, but first we should enter a caveat. It should be noted that the 1990 Act does allow for the possibility of children who will be legally fatherless: clinics need only 'consider' a child's need for a father, not ensure that one is available. This wording was a compromise measure following the narrow failure of an amendment proposing to make treatment of anyone other than married couples a criminal offence. Further, any reproductive freedom offered by this provision is left firmly within the hands of clinicians, who will act as gatekeepers to the provision of infertility treatment services: some clinics have

---

[27] Cooper and Herman, above (n 24). In the debates regarding the 2007 Bill, such a distinction is often (at least implicitly) present in frequent references to the high quality of parenting which can occur in lesbian relationships.

[28] See eg: *Hansard*, HC, vol 174, cols 1026–7 (20 June 1990) (per Peter Thurnham MP).

[29] This fits with the tentative guidance given by the Warnock Report: 'many believe that the interests of the child dictate that it should be born into a home where there is a loving, stable, heterosexual relationship and that, therefore, the deliberate creation of a child for a woman who is not a partner in such a relationship is morally wrong': Warnock Report, above (n 9) at [2.11].

refused treatment to those not in stable heterosexual relationships.[30] In their guide to the 1990 Act, Morgan and Lee are clear that the policy underlying the legislation was actively to discourage treatment for infertile people who live outside the umbrella of the nuclear family:[31] assisted conception was, for the most part, to be for the 'married, mortgaged, middle classes'.[32]

Twenty years on, the 2007 Bill foresees the deletion of the phrase mandating consideration of the child's need for a father. This can be seen as a reflection of shifting attitudes towards the family and, specifically, the criticism that the provision discriminates against single women and lesbian couples.[33] Notably, the government has suggested that the current law is 'framed in terms of heterosexual couples' and may need to be changed so as better to 'recognise the wider range of people who seek and receive assisted reproduction services in the 21st century'.[34] A House of Commons Select Committee specifically recommended reform of section 13(5) on the basis that:

> The requirement to consider whether a child born as a result of assisted reproduction needs a father is too open to interpretation and unjustifiably offensive to many. It is wrong for legislation to imply that unjustified discrimination against 'unconventional families' is acceptable.[35]

More recently, the Joint Parliamentary Committee charged with scrutinising the draft legislation recommended retention of this provision, albeit in a form which makes it clear that it should be understood as requiring consideration of the need for a second parent, who may be either a father or a second 'female parent'. Intriguingly, the Committee states:

---

[30] See eg: Douglas, above (n 24); D Steinberg, *Bodies in Glass: Genetics, Eugenics Embryo Ethics* (Manchester University Press, Manchester, 1997); A Plomer, I Smith, and N Martin-Clement, 'Rationing Policies on Access to In Vitro Fertilisation in the NHS, UK' (1999) 7 *Reproductive Health Matters* 60.

[31] D Morgan and R Lee, *Blackstone's Guide to the Human Fertilisation and Embryology Act 1990*, 1st edn (Blackstone, London, 1991) at 155–6.

[32] *Ibid* at 159–67.

[33] This is reflected in the official guidance issued to clinics by the HFEA which, in its most recent formulation, directs that there should be a presumption in favour of offering treatment unless there is evidence that the child to be born or any existing child of the family is likely to suffer serious, physical or psychological harm: HFEA, 'Revised Guidance: Welfare of the child and the assessment of those seeking treatment', <http://www.hfea.gov.uk/en/505.html>, accessed 21 November 2007. The extent to which lesbian couples are subject to discrimination in practice emerges as a point of disagreement in the consideration of the 2007 Bill at Committee Stage in the House of Commons: see eg HC Debs Vol 476 (20 May 2008), particularly the interventions by Emily Thornberry MP at Col 171, John Hemming MP at Col 174, and Evan Harris MP at Col 200.

[34] G Hinsliff, 'Gay Couples to Get New Rights to Fertility Treatment', *Observer* (15 August 2004), quoting a spokeswoman for the Department of Health who cites the Civil Partnership Act 2004 as providing the impetus for a reassessment of this provision. Section 13(5) of the 1990 Act also seems inconsistent with the Adoption and Children Act 2002, allowing same-sex couples to adopt.

[35] Science and Technology Select Committee, 'Human Reproductive Technologies and the Law', HC (2004–05) 7-I at [101] (Recommendation 21).

In making this recommendation, we do not seek to discriminate against single women seeking treatment and we recommend that in such circumstances ... the requirement to consider the need of a child for a second parent should, as now, not be a barrier to treatment.[36]

How it is possible to prefer a two-parent model while not so discriminating receives no further attention. The government declined to redraft the legislation in line with this recommendation, suggesting that this would not add significantly to the requirement that the welfare of the child be taken into account before treatment is provided.[37] Various further possibilities for how this section might be amended were discussed during the Bill's progress in the House of Lords. The House ultimately decided against any formulation which made explicit reference to either a 'father' or a 'second parent', preferring instead to require that account must be taken of the child's need for 'supportive parenting'.[38] Having survived various attempts further to amend this section during the Bill's Committee Stage in the House of Commons, it now seems highly likely that this is the wording which will pass into law.

Section 13(5) has been criticised for opening up women's lives to surveillance. Women have been refused treatment on the basis of age and a past history of prostitution.[39] However, men's lives are also scrutinised, albeit in different ways. Thompson notes pressure on men in US IVF clinics to behave as 'good patients' as well as compliant, supportive and committed husbands. These qualities, she suggests, are taken as indications of men's worthiness to become 'good' fathers.[40] In the UK context, where consideration of the need for a father has been legally mandated, it would be surprising if similar processes were not at work, not least given the cultural and legal shifts relating to father-inclusive policies detailed elsewhere in this book. Further, while not concerned with section 13(5), legal scrutiny of men's ability to act as good fathers can be seen in some of the cases discussed below,[41] as well as in litigation on the matter of whether prisoners and their partners should be allowed access to facilities for assisted insemination.[42] A case on this last issue made it as far as the European Court of Human Rights, where one judge opined:

---

[36] See: Joint Committee on the Human Tissue and Embryos (Draft) Bill, 'First Report', HC (2006–07) 630-I at [243].

[37] Government Response to the Report from the Joint Committee on the Human Tissue and Embryos (Draft) Bill, Cm 7209 (HMSO, London, 2007)at [57].

[38] Amendment No 108, moved by Lord Darzi of Denham:*Hansard*, HL Deb, vol 698, col 55 (21 January 2008).

[39] See *R v Sheffield AHA ex parte Seale* (1994) 25 BMLR 1 and, in a case which predated the legislation, *R v Ethical Committee of St Mary's Hospital, ex parte Harriot* [1988] 1 FLR 512.

[40] Thompson, above (n 5) at 133.

[41] See the cases brought under the status provisions, discussed below at pp 80–89.

[42] *R (Mellor) v Secretary of State for the Home Department* [2001] EWCA Civ 472, [2002] 1 QB 13; *Dickson v UK* (App no 44362/04), ECHR, 18 April 2006. For a discussion on how the welfare principle plays out in the decisions made by the Prison Service in these cases, see: H Codd, 'Slippery Slope to Sperm Smuggling' (2007) 15 *Medical Law Review* 220.

77

I am far from persuaded that kick-starting into life a child in the meanest circumstances, could be viewed as an exercise in promoting its finest interests. The debut of life in a one-parent family, deprived of the presence of the father and a father-figure, offspring of a life prisoner convicted for the most serious crime of violence, would not quite appear to be the best way of giving a child-to-be a headstart in life.[43]

II. Diane Blood, Deceased Fathers and the Privileging of Widows

The Right to Use Her Husband's Sperm

The tremendous sympathy extended to widows in discussions of single motherhood, noted above, was also evident in responses to what probably remains the most high-profile challenge to the powers of the HFEA.[44] Diane Blood had married in 1991. Towards the end of 1994, she and her husband, Stephen, decided to try to start a family. Before this could happen, however, Stephen contracted meningitis and lapsed into a coma. Shortly before he died, Diane Blood asked for samples of his sperm to be collected by electro-ejaculation for later use. The clinic complied but, unfortunately for Blood, the 1990 Act laid down stringent consent requirements for the posthumous use and storage of gametes, requirements which were not met in her case.[45] As such, the HFEA refused leave for the sperm either to be used by Blood in the UK or to be exported for use in a Belgian clinic. Blood successfully challenged the latter aspect of the HFEA's decision, convincing the Court of Appeal that the HFEA had not properly considered her right to obtain medical services elsewhere in the European Union. She celebrated her victory, delivered on the day after Stephen's birthday, by draping a 'Happy Birthday' banner over his gravestone, telling reporters: 'this is the nicest present he could have … This was always my husband's wish as well as my own. And I am here to carry out his wishes.'[46]

Given the social and legal antipathy often displayed towards single mothers (ostensibly on the basis of their children's need for a father), and the fact that the fertile Mrs Blood was attempting to use techniques portrayed as a last resort for those unable to conceive, one might have expected some criticism of her

---

[43] *Dickson v UK, ibid* at [16]. The majority judgment appears to have been more strongly influenced by considerations of the UK's margin of appreciation than Dickson's unsuitability as a father.

[44] *R v Human Fertilisation and Embryology Authority, ex p Blood* [1999] Fam 151 (HC); [1991] Fam 151 (CA).

[45] Consent must be written, counselling offered and certain information provided before such consent is obtained: 1990 Act, Sch 3.

[46] Cited in K de Gama, 'Posthumous Pregnancies: Some Thoughts on "Life" and Death' in S Sheldon and M Thomson (eds), *Feminist Perspectives on Health Care Law* (Cavendish, London, 1998) at 271.

actions.[47] However, clear sympathy for her was pervasive in the courts, media and, later, Parliament. This hinged on Blood's explicit self-portrayal as a respectable married woman, epitomising all the attributes of a good mother: committed to her husband, pious, serene and gentle.[48] Central to her story were ideas of what her husband would have wanted and of their joint desire for a child: her actions were 'patently in the name of the father'.[49] Blood's deceased husband clearly could not offer shared childcare or financial support, but was nonetheless a symbolic presence throughout the case, acting as vital legitimation for his wife's desire for a child.[50]

The Right for Deceased Fathers to be Named on Birth Certificates

Following her success in the Court of Appeal, treatment in Belgium, and eventual delivery of two sons, Ms Blood returned to the courts to challenge a further provision of the 1990 Act: that where sperm (or an embryo created using such sperm) was used after the sperm provider's death, that man was not to be treated as the father of the child.[51] Her contention that this breached her children's human rights was accepted, and the Human Fertilisation and Embryology (Deceased Fathers) Act 2003 was passed to remedy the problem. The 2003 Act draws on, but goes beyond, the recommendation in a report commissioned after the first *Blood* case, which had suggested that children should have an 'essentially symbolic' acknowledgement of their deceased father on their birth certificates where he had made a written statement of intention regarding the posthumous disposal of gametes.[52] It provides for such acknowledgement for those children conceived after a man's death using his sperm or an embryo created with his sperm, and equally where an embryo was created from donor sperm before a man's death where a couple had embarked on infertility treatment services together. Unusually, the legislation has retroactive operation and, contrary to the report's recommendation, allows for birth registration even in the absence of

---

[47] See: H Biggs, 'Madonna Minus Child Or: Wanted: Dead or Alive! The Right to Have a Dead Partner's Child' (1997) 5(2) *Feminist Legal Studies* 225 at 231. The then Chair of the HFEA described *Blood* as the 'most famous case of infertility treatment for convenience': R Deech, 'Assisted Reproductive Techniques and the Law' (2001) 69 *Medico-Legal Journal* 13 at 18.

[48] Biggs, *ibid*. See generally: D Morgan and RG Lee, 'In the Name of the Father? *Ex parte Blood*: Dealing with Novelty and Anomaly' (1997) 60 MLR 840, for the sympathetic language in the judgment of the Court of Appeal.

[49] Morgan and Lee, *ibid* at 842, footnote(s) omitted.

[50] S Millns, 'Making Social Judgments which Go Beyond the Medical' in J Bridgeman and S Millns (eds), *Law and Body Politics: Regulating the Female Body* (Aldershot, Dartmouth, 1995) at 97–8.

[51] Unreported (HC, 1 March 2003), challenging s 28(6)(b).

[52] S McLean, *Review of the Common Law Provisions Relating to the Removal of Gametes and of the Consent Provisions in the Human Fertilisation and Embryology Act 1990* (Department of Health, London, 1998) at [3.2].

written consent for those men who died before the 2003 Act came into force.[53] Importantly, recognition of paternity is to have no legal force in terms of succession. The 2007 Bill extends these provisions further to apply to lesbian couples.[54]

This reform illustrates the important symbolism of registering a father (and now, for lesbian couples, a 'female parent') even where no consequences will flow from such recognition. Yet it also suggests an interesting change in attitudes from the time of the 1990 Act, illustrated by the *volte-face* of the architect of that reform. Mary Warnock came out as a strong supporter of Blood, despite earlier strong pronouncements against posthumous conceptions, made while chairing the Committee of Inquiry that preceded 1990 Act. Warnock explains her change of heart partly in terms of the removal of the legal implications of recognising fatherhood but, intriguingly, also comments on the possibility of disruption to other family relationships:

> The committee of inquiry was fairly strongly opposed to the use of assisted conception to bring about the birth of a posthumous child largely on the grounds of the possible psychological damage that might be caused if, for example, a widow who had remarried and had other children decided to use her first husband's sperm and to have a child by that husband after all.[55]

Warnock now dismisses this possibility as 'rather fanciful'. Nonetheless, the need to record the father's name as a simple matter of recording 'the historical truth'[56] now outweighs the kind of concern that had prevailed less than 15 years previously. For the architect of the 1990 Act, recognition of paternity is no longer seen as a threat to future family arrangements. Rather, it is accepted that a child can have a legally recognised link to more than one 'father', with this construed as a benefit rather than a potentially harmful, disruptive and confusing state of affairs. The fierce protection of the heterosexual nuclear family form entrenched in the 1990 legislation gives way to a more fluid and complex sense of familial relationships. The recognition of lesbian co-parents is part of this same process and will be further considered in the context of our discussion of the status provisions, to which we now turn.

III. The Status Provisions

The initial refusal of the status of legal father to men who had died before their sperm or embryos were used was part of a broader raft of provisions setting out who should be treated as mother and father of a child born following infertility

---

[53] The 2003 Act only applies to those pregnancies conceived after the coming into force of the 1990 Act: Human Fertilisation and Embryology (Deceased Fathers) Act 2003. s 3.

[54] 2007 Bill, cls 45–6, 52.

[55] *Hansard*, HL, vol 650, col 1151 (4 July 2003); see also: Warnock Report, above (n 27) at [45].

[56] *Ibid.*

treatment services, collectively referred to as 'the status provisions'. Attribution of the status of mother in the 1990 Act proves relatively straightforward, taking just over 100 words to provide that, excluding in the case of adoption, the birth mother and no other is to be treated as the legal mother of the child. As will be seen below, this is true whether or not the egg used to conceive the pregnancy was the woman's own and regardless of the provisions of any surrogacy arrangement that she may have made.[57] The 2007 Bill maintains this grounding of legal motherhood in gestation, even in the face of the problem of how legally to recognise a lesbian co-parent. Under the proposed reforms, the latter will not be able to claim the status of legal 'mother' but she can be legally recognised as a 'female parent' provided that certain conditions are met.[58] The 2007 Bill also provides that references to the 'father' of a child elsewhere in law should be read as applying to the 'female parent' created by its operation.[59] Thus, intriguingly, although lesbian co-parents cannot count as legal mothers, if the Bill is passed, they will in many circumstances count as legal fathers.

The legal designation of the 'father' in the 1990 Act is substantially more lengthy and complicated than that of 'mother' and will become even more so if the 2007 Bill passes into law. In brief, under the 1990 Act, where a child results from those ARTs regulated by the 1990 Act, the woman's husband will be the father unless it can be shown that he did not consent to the treatment.[60] Marriage retains a similarly privileged place as the preferred way of attributing paternity in the 2007 Bill, which retains this provision.[61] If no father exists by virtue of marriage then, under the 1990 Act, an unmarried man will be deemed the legal father where treatment services were provided for him and the woman together.[62] As will be seen below, 'treatment together' has been understood by the courts to involve a 'joint enterprise' to create a child, signalling the relevance of intention in grounding fatherhood. While significantly rewriting these provisions, the 2007 Bill remains true to their spirit. The proposed reform abandons reference to 'treatment together' in favour of setting out a list of 'agreed fatherhood conditions' which will apply in cases where no father is designated by virtue of marriage. The conditions turn on the ongoing and written consent of both parties to the man being treated as father of a child resulting from treatment, and the woman not having since consented to anyone else being treated as either the child's father or female parent.[63]

---

[57] 1990 Act, s 27.

[58] 2007 Bill, cls 48–53. These provisions exactly map the conditions by which a man can be recognised as a father.

[59] 2007 Bill, cl 59(2); cl 59(5) provides a list of exceptions to this rule.

[60] 1990 Act, s 28(2). In the absence of consent, there is nonetheless a rebuttable presumption that the husband is the father; s 28(5), saving the common law presumption of paternity.

[61] 2007 Bill, cl 41. This centrality of marriage is explored in significantly more detail in ch 4.

[62] 1990 Act, s 28(3).

[63] 2007 Bill, cl 43. This serves to ensure that a child should not be able to have more than two legal parents. The clause also provides that the man and woman must not be within the prohibited degrees of relationship foreseen in incest legislation with one another.

Unmarried male partners can thus gain the same parental rights as married men, although without the presumption of consent that occurs in marriage. Where someone is treated as a father by virtue of one of these provisions, no other man is to be treated as the father of the child. Where sperm is obtained through a licensed clinic, meanwhile, a sperm donor is not to be treated as the legal father. As such, where treatment services are provided for a single woman or a woman in a same-sex relationship, the resulting child will be legally fatherless.[64] If the 2007 Bill does pass into law, however, a child may acquire a 'female parent' in addition to its mother where a lesbian woman is in a civil partnership[65] or where 'agreed female parenthood conditions' (which closely track the 'agreed fatherhood conditions' discussed above) are met.[66]

Intriguingly, the law retains an exception for succession to any dignity or title of honour, which are not affected by the provisions set out above.[67] Brazier describes this as revealing a 'characteristically British obsession with heredity', suggesting that the imperative for the nobility is that the 'bloodline must not be polluted'.[68] Whilst this provision is phrased in gender-neutral terms, Brazier observes, it must be read in the context of a patrilineal inheritance system where titles pass down via male line.[69] In the context of nobility, it would seem, genetic links are crucial to fatherhood.

We noted in chapter two that fatherhood has often been seen as problematic and uncertain, whereas the woman's bodily connection to the growing foetus in pregnancy renders motherhood a more grounded, straightforward status. In line with this analysis, fatherhood in the context of ARTs also appears as a more fragile and contested role, its establishment dependent on a complex web of provisions. The elaborate definitions of legal 'fatherhood' contained in the 1990 Act and 2007 Bill might, in themselves, be taken as suggesting an attempt to contain the perceived disruptive potential of ARTs in relation to paternity, legitimacy and contact rights.[70] In the status provisions, Parliament attempted to foresee every possible reproductive scenario and to provide in the 1990 Act for the resulting family arrangements to conform as closely as possible to a nuclear

---

[64] That legally fatherless children can only be created where sperm is obtained through a licensed clinic and a doctor oversees the process might suggest that the doctor, in some way, operates as a kind of surrogate or 'coital' father: M Johnson, 'A Biomedical Perspective on Fatherhood', in A Bainham *et al* (eds) *What is a Parent? A Socio-legal Analysis* (Hart, Oxford, 1999) at 54. See ch 6, pp 192–193, for discussion of a case where a lesbian couple make use of the sperm of a known donor outside of a clinic.

[65] Where legal parenthood of the civil partner will be presumed unless it can be shown that she did not consent to the treatment.

[66] 2007 Bill, cls 48–51. Clause 52 provides for a deceased woman to be recognised as a female parent in conditions analogous to those by which deceased men are recognised as fathers, as discussed in Section II above.

[67] See: 1990 Act, s 29(4).

[68] M Brazier, 'Reproductive Rights: Feminism or Patriarchy?' in J Harris and S Holm (eds), *The Future of Human Reproduction* (Oxford University Press, Oxford, 2000) at 67.

[69] *Ibid* at 69. The Warnock Committee was influenced by similar concerns: see above (n 9).

[70] Steinberg, above (n 30) at 181.

family model.[71] The 2007 Bill might be seen as representing a similar attempt in a changed world, where the increased acceptance of same-sex relationships produces still further complications. Inevitably, however, such foresight has its limits and the status provisions have raised some difficult cases for the UK courts, just two of which are considered here.[72] These cases illustrate that, whilst bound to operate within the limits of the status provisions and their entrenchment of the nuclear family norm, a certain degree of judicial creativity has allowed for recognition of some more complex family forms relying, notably, on a fragmentation of fatherhood.

Re R[73]

Ms D and Mr B together sought treatment services involving the use of donor semen. When they separated, D continued the treatment with her new partner, Mr S, not telling the clinic about the change in relationship and relying on the formal consent previously supplied by B. When D gave birth, B sought parental responsibility and contact orders with respect to the child, R.[74] In the first instance hearing, all parties conceded that B was R's legal father. Not called on to find on that issue, Hedley J ordered indirect contact and for B to be given photographs of R, reasoning that he would be an important stabilising member of her family and better placed to explain the circumstances of her conception than the mother. The judge assumes that at least one man must be present in a fathering role and is not persuaded that Mr S will be so 'indefinitely'. As such, B's claim for a greater presence in R's life would be strengthened by the absence of S but, significantly, the presence of S does not preclude B's involvement.

B's application for parental responsibility was adjourned, to be granted if he maintained his commitment to indirect contact for the next couple of years, but B was to be treated as in the same position as a natural father despite the lack of any biological link with R. This decision gave rise to two separate appeals. In the first, the Court of Appeal stated it was not prepared to overturn Hedley J's ruling on contact, commending the judge on having taken the view that the fact of biological parentage could be relevant to the welfare of a child. The Court was

---

[71] 'The definition of paternity ... reflects, more than anything, the type of parents whom the state is prepared to reproduce through the provision of fertility services: namely, the two parent, heterosexual, preferably married, parents': J Dewar, 'The Normal Chaos of Family Law' (1998) 61 MLR 467 at 482.

[72] Many of these cases turn on the meaning of 'treatment together' under s 28(3), see generally: S Sheldon, 'Fragmenting Fatherhood: the Regulation of Reproductive Technologies' (2005) 68(4) MLR 523.

[73] The name was changed in the Court of Appeal. See: *Re R (Contact: Human Fertilisation and Embryology Act)* [2001] 1 FLR 247; *Re D (Contact: Human Fertilisation and Embryology Act 1990)* [2001] 1 FLR 972 (B's appeal on the issue of contact); *Re R (A Child) (IVF: Paternity of Child)* [2003] EWCA Civ 182, [2003] Fam 129 (D's appeal on the issue of paternity). For simplicity here, we call the case *Re R* throughout.

[74] *Re R (Contact)* (HC), above (n 73).

happy to accept his view that B would be better able to deal with the 'delicate issue of the circumstances of [R's] conception and birth'.[75] In the second appeal, brought by D on the issue of paternity, however, the Court found that B could not be considered the legal father under section 28 and, as such, R would be legally fatherless.[76] Mr B's appeal on this point was dismissed in a unanimous judgment of the House of Lords. However, if the 2007 Bill passes into law, a future B would be recognised as the legal father as the terms of the 'agreed fatherhood conditions' discussed above would include him.[77]

Re R demonstrates a trend described elsewhere in this book: an increased weight attached to genetic factors in grounding fatherhood and the growing currency of a child's 'right to genetic truth'. Here, however, this does not play out in any straightforward way: although B does not share a genetic link with R, he can claim some limited paternal rights because of the role he can play in explaining her genetic origins. Significantly, neither court appears overly concerned by the possibility that introducing B into R's life is liable to cause confusion or to disrupt the family unit which her mother claims to be building with S. The benefits gained by knowing something about one's genetic origins outweigh any potential negative impact.[78]

Re R also illustrates a second significant shift that will resonate in discussion of the contact and residence disputes discussed in chapter five: a perception that men increasingly embrace responsibilities with regard to their children. Here we have a man fighting to establish his paternal rights to (and to be involved in caring for) a child with whom he has neither a genetic nor a social relationship.[79] Yet the account that B gives of his motivation suggests a man desperate to act as a father to a child whom he deeply believes to be his own. He explains:

> [R] is my daughter totally and completely. As a man, when you choose to have a child by anonymous donor, they check your height, build, blood group, eye colour and appearance to match the donor with the person. So when the child is born it will have the characteristics of both the father and the mother . . . A child is not a product of one person, but of two ... I have simply loved [R] from the moment I heard she was born.[80]

What it is that B believes grounds his paternal status in this case escapes an exact articulation but might, perhaps, be best captured by Laqueur's suggestion that

---

[75] *Re D (Contact)* (CA), above (n 73) at [38] (per Hale LJ).

[76] *Re R (A Child) (IVF: Paternity of Child)* (CA), above (n 73). The question of whether treatment was provided for the woman and man together should be answered at the time that the embryo was placed in the mother.

[77] See above (n 63) and accompanying text.

[78] The courts' ruling here is clearly in line with an existing line of jurisprudence regarding contact and parental responsibility orders. See ch 5 below pp 155–8 and ch 6, pp 194–200.

[79] Note here the interplay of the twin discourses of justice and care, outlined in ch 5.

[80] A Chrisafis, 'Parenthood Postponed', *Guardian* (20 February 2001), <http://www.guardian.co.uk/law/story/0,,440294,00.html>, accessed 21 November 2007.

fatherhood is grounded in a man's 'emotional investment' in a child.[81] We will return to this issue of the emotional dynamics of parenting in chapter five.

The Leeds Teaching Hospitals NHS Trust v Mr A, Mrs A and Others[82]

A second dispute regarding legal fatherhood arose on a rather different but equally unusual set of facts. Mr and Mrs A had consented to the creation of embryos using only their own gametes and to the embryos' use only for their own treatment or for research. Unfortunately, Mrs A's eggs were erroneously fertilised with the sperm of Mr B, who was undergoing the same treatment at the same clinic with his wife. Mrs A subsequently gave birth to twins. Although the As were both white, it was clear that the twins were of mixed race, and DNA tests proved that Mr B was their genetic father. All parties accepted that the As would raise the children, but Mr A and Mr B both sought declarations of legal paternity.

The Court found that Mr A could not be considered the legal father, as he had not consented to the placing in his wife of the embryos in question, which were fundamentally different from those he had intended should be created. Neither could what had occurred be considered 'treatment together', as this implies a joint enterprise, yet that would be undermined by Mr A's lack of consent to the use of another man's sperm.[83] Whilst the Court's finding that such a fundamental mistake undermined Mr A's consent is a plausible one, it was not the only one available.[84] Exactly what was included in Mr A's consent and what kind of mistake would undermine it, were clearly questions that allowed scope for some discretion. Indeed, due regard to parliamentary intention might have suggested a finding in Mr A's favour, given the clear desire to protect the sanctity of the nuclear family described above. This makes the broad principles and values upon which the Court draws to support its decision all the more interesting.

As was seen above, the 1990 Act is characterised by a concerted effort to ensure each child has only one mother and one father. In *Leeds*, however, the UK's then most senior family law judge was clearly of the view that attributing legal fatherhood to Mr B was not liable to disrupt the twins' nuclear family:

> The effect of the decision of the court ... does not create any greater difficulty for the twins than the unfortunate circumstances surrounding their conception and birth. Although they lose the immediate certainty of the irrebuttable presumption that Mr A is their legal father, they will remain within a loving, stable and secure home. They also retain the great advantage of preserving *the reality of their paternal identity*... To refuse

---

[81] Laqueur, above (n 12).

[82] *The Leeds Teaching Hospitals NHS Trust v Mr A, Mrs A and others* [2003] EWHC 259 (QB), [2003] 1 FLR 1091.

[83] 1990 Act, s 28(2)–(3). Further, the Court held that s 28(3) applies only to unmarried couples.

[84] The Court itself recognises that it would also have been possible to read the legislation in such a way as to find Mr A was the legal father: [2003] EWHC 259 (QB) at [58].

to recognise Mr B as their biological father is to distort the truth about which some day the twins will have to learn through knowledge of their paternal identity. The requirement to preserve the truth will not adversely affect their immediate welfare nor their welfare throughout their childhood. It does not impede the cementing of the permanent relationship of each of them with Mr A.[85]

Thus, while the 'reality' of paternal identity is seen as premised on genetic links, it is recognised that a family structure can be 'stable and secure' and in the best interests of the twins, even where it includes more than two 'parents'.[86] Dame Butler-Sloss, P. continues:

Through no fault of theirs, [the twins] have been born children of mixed race by a mistake which cannot be rectified. Their biological mother and their biological father are not married and cannot marry. They may not be able during their childhood to form any relationship with their biological father. They have inherited two cultures but, in reality, can only gain real benefit from one during their childhood. Of all the parties who have undoubtedly suffered from this mistake, the twins, who at present know nothing of it, have had their human rights most obviously and seriously infringed.[87]

This passage is noteworthy for a number of reasons, not least the assumption that the twins have 'suffered' from the fact that their biological parents are not married and the fact that forming a relationship with their genetic father may be impossible (even though this is a broadly accepted reality for the many children born of DI). There is also a troubling implication that to be born of mixed race is a misfortune, which the twins have suffered 'through no fault of theirs'. Had the twins not been of mixed race, would the Court have decided this case in the same way? Speculatively, it might appear that the idea that the twins had 'inherited two cultures' might have seemed less compelling had all four 'parents' shared a common ethnic background.[88] Considerations of race appear thinly veiled in the suggestion that 'culture' is genetically inherited and that where one derives from two distinct cultures, understanding of both is desirable.[89]

Many commentators have criticised the Court's decision in *Leeds* for failing to value social parenting over the 'mere' genetic link, and thereby identifying the wrong man as the 'real' father:

---

[85] (Emphasis added). [2003] EWHC 259 (QB) at [56]–[57] (per Butler-Sloss, P).

[86] This resonates with Hedley J's assertion in *Re D* that R could benefit from contact with two 'fathers': [2001] 1 FLR 972.

[87] [2003] EWHC 259 (QB) at [55].

[88] Dorothy Roberts argued that the obsession with preserving genetic ties in the US is intimately connected with the 'high value placed on whiteness and the worthlessness accorded blackness', see: D Roberts, 'The Genetic Tie' (1995) 62 *University of Chicago Law Review* 209 at 210. While grounded in the US experience, Roberts' suggestion that considerations of race increase the significance of genetic links seems relevant here.

[89] The Court might also have been influenced by the fact that visible difference in skin colour would make secrecy impossible in any case. See: M Johnson, 'Genes, Genealogies and Paternity: Making Babies in the Twenty-first Century' in A Pedain and J Spencer (eds), *Freedom and Responsibility in Reproductive Choice* (Hart, Oxford, 2006) at 63–5.

[I]n this case, where legal paternity is placed next to biological paternity, the genetic connection seems to be regarded as more important than the social one … But what is the reality of their paternal identity? The twins' biological father is Mr B – this much is indisputable. But declaring him to be the legal father too begins to make him look like the 'real father'. But Mr A intended to be their father. He was there at conception (even though he wasn't responsible for it), during the pregnancy, at the birth and, more importantly, he has been their father every day since their birth and intends to be their father until the day he dies. Shouldn't that be regarded as the 'reality' of their paternal identity?[90]

Such a reading accepts the historically entrenched parameters of decision-making in this area, assuming that the search must be for the candidate (and one candidate alone) who will best fit the role of 'real father' and criticising the Court for making the wrong choice in prioritising genetic over social links. However, we would suggest that the decision in *Leeds* is more complicated and substantially more interesting than this. The Court is explicitly prepared to countenance more than one father (and two parents) in the twins' lives, and to assert this as a positive, serving to foster awareness of their cultural background and enrich their familial situation. Rather than seeing *Leeds* solely within terms of a shift away from social towards genetic fatherhood, it is better contextualised within a movement towards recognising a fragmentation of fatherhood, with a number of different parental figures potentially important for different reasons. The recognition of the genetic father is possible precisely because it does not threaten the social family. As such, *Leeds* reflects the same shift evidenced in *Re R* and some of the other developments discussed above: a movement away from the 1990 Act's imposition of the nuclear family model towards a sharing of the legal trappings of fatherhood. One father figure is better than none but, in some circumstances, two may be better than one.

Finally, *Leeds* clearly illustrates that the fragmentation of parenthood into social and genetic roles is a profoundly gendered phenomenon.[91] If *Leeds* had involved the implantation into Mrs A of embryos created from the gametes of Mrs B and Mr A, or even from the gametes of both Mr and Mrs B, Mrs A would still have enjoyed an unequivocal legal claim to be considered the mother of any resulting children.[92] While motherhood is legally firmly rooted in gestation, fatherhood is an altogether more complex and fragmented status, and genetic links are far more central to its establishment.

Should the 2007 Bill be passed in its current form, it is uncertain whether a future Mr A would be more fortunate in gaining recognition as the legal father. A court may well feel bound to follow the clear precedent of *Leeds* in holding that a

---

[90] J Tizzard, 'Who's the Daddy?', *Bionews* (3 March 2003), <http://www.ivf.net/ivf/index.php?page=out&id=132>, accessed 22 November 2007. See also: TH Murray and GE Knaebnick, 'Genetic Ties and Genetic Mixups' (2003) 29 *Journal of Medical Ethics* 68 at 68–9.

[91] S Day Sclater, A Bainham and M Richards, 'Introduction', in A Bainham *et al* (eds) *What is a Parent? A Socio-legal Analysis* (Hart, Oxford, 1999).

[92] See above (n 57) and accompanying text.

married man's consent to treatment had been undermined by the mistaken use of another man's sperm, and he could not thus be recognised as a father on the basis of his marriage to the woman receiving treatment. What is less clear is whether he would be able to establish himself as father through reference to the 'agreed treatment conditions' which focus on his subsisting consent to 'being treated as the father of any child resulting from treatment provided ... under the licence'.[93]

Transgender Fathers

Finally, must one have been born a man to be recognised as a father? In the case of *X, Y and Z v UK* (1997), X (a female-to-male transsexual) and his partner, Y, had together obtained infertility treatment services using donor semen.[94] X had been present throughout the treatment, had acknowledged himself to be the father of any children conceived and was now playing an active parenting role. Despite all this, he was told that he could not be registered on the birth certificate of the resulting child, Z. X took his case to the European Court of Human Rights, where the majority of the Court held that, while his privacy rights under Article 8 were engaged, they had not been violated. Any potential disadvantages suffered by the applicants were limited since X was not prevented from acting as a social father and could apply for a joint residence order, which would give him parental responsibility. One of the judges commented that 'it is self-evident that a person who is manifestly not the father of a child has no right to be recognised as her father'.[95]

At the time that this case was brought, English law defined a person's sex by reference to biological criteria at birth and did not recognise that it can be changed by reassignment surgery.[96] This position has been radically altered by the Gender Recognition Act 2004 which, under certain conditions, allows for legal recognition of an individual's new gender. Previous parental roles are not affected by this, raising the intriguing possibility than someone might simultaneously be a mother to children born prior to gender reassignment and a father to

---

[93] This broad wording would seem clearly to encompass treatment even when a mistake has taken place. However, the Court in *Leeds* held that the old s 28(3) applied only to unmarried men. If a similar restriction is read into the relationship between cls 41 and 42–3 of the 2007 Bill, then a future Mr A would not benefit from the broader working of cl 43.

[94] *X, Y and Z v UK* (App no 21830/93) (1997) 24 EHRR 143, [1997] 2 FLR 892.

[95] *Ibid* at 175 (per De Mayer). See: A Bainham, 'Sex, Gender and Fatherhood: Does Biology Really Matter?' [1997] CLJ 512 at 515. More recently, in *Goodwin v UK* (App no 28957/95) (2002) 35 EHRR 18, [2002] 2 FLR 487, and *I v UK* (App no 25680/94) (2003) 36 EHRR 53, [2002] 2 FLR 518, the Court has found that a failure to recognise a change in status for post-operative transsexuals no longer fell within a state's margin of appreciation, as an emerging consensus in favour of granting legal recognition could be discerned.

[96] *Corbett v Corbett* [1971] P 83, [1970] 2 WLR 1306; *R v Tan* [1983] QB 1053, [1983] 3 WLR 361; *B v B* [2001] 1 FLR 389.

those conceived after it via infertility treatment services.[97] The correct terminology for someone who now finds himself or herself to be a male 'mother' or female 'father' remains elusive, with Parliamentarians tending to resort to the gender-neutral 'parent',[98] a semantic strategy also invoked in the context of same-sex couple adoption. This side-steps the issue of whether being a 'father' means nothing more than being a male parent, or whether 'fathering' is a distinctive style of parenting, which can be performed by individuals of either gender but which will more typically be associated with men.[99] We return to this issue in chapter seven.

IV. Surrogacy

In surrogacy, one woman carries a child with the intention of giving it up to 'commissioning parents' on birth. The child may be conceived from her own egg and the commissioning father's semen ('partial' surrogacy) or result from an embryo created *ex utero* using both the ova and the sperm of a commissioning couple. Not all partial surrogacy arrangements are regulated by the 1990 Act, which applies only where donor gametes are used or an embryo is created outside a woman's body. In other cases, legal parenthood will be determined by the common law rules set out above.[100] Where the 1990 Act does apply, the surrogate will be the legal mother and the legal father will be her husband or, where she is unmarried and treatment was provided for her together with another man, then that man will be the legal father.[101] Where all goes according to plan, the 1990 Act allows the commissioning couple to adopt the child via a special fast-track procedure.[102]

---

[97] Equally, a male-to-female transsexual would remain the father of any children born when he was a man and might, simultaneously, be recognised as (an adoptive) mother to children in her new sexual identity. See Gender Recognition Act 2004, s 12: 'The fact that a person's gender has become the acquired gender under this Act does not affect the status of the person as the father or mother of a child.'

[98] The rather evasive answer to the following parliamentary question illustrates this point: 'Miss Ann Widdecombe (Maidstone and The Weald) (Con): ... If a woman who has lived her life as a woman, has been registered at birth as a woman and has borne children decides that she wishes to change gender to become fully a man, and the birth certificate is rewritten to reflect that, who is the legal mother of those children? Mr Lammy: She is the parent of those children and she has acquired a new gender.' *Hansard*, HC, vol 418, col 52 (23 February 2004) (Miss Ann Widdecombe MP; Mr. David Lammy, Parliamentary Under-Secretary of State for Constitutional Affairs).

[99] See further: A Doucet, *Do Men Mother? Fatherhood, Care and Domestic Responsibility* (University of Toronto Press, Toronto, 2006).

[100] See above, p 71.

[101] Under the 1990 Act, s 27, s 28(2) and (3) respectively.

[102] The child must be in the care of the couple; the surrogate mother and legal father must give full, voluntary, informed and unconditional consent; the child must be genetically related to at least one of the commissioning couple; the application must be made within six months of the birth, and no money other than reasonable expenses must have been paid: 1990 Act, s 30. The 2007 Bill rewrites these provisions and extends them to same-sex couples: 2007 Bill, cl 60.

Surrogacy is also subject to an additional piece of legislation. The Surrogacy Arrangements Act 1985 prohibits commercial surrogacy and provides that surrogacy arrangements are unenforceable.[103] Most of the cases that have reached the courts have turned on this latter issue. In one case that predated the legislation, *A v C* (1985), a couple paid a prostitute £3,000 to act as a surrogate mother. She was inseminated with the man's sperm but ultimately refused to hand over the child. The Court of Appeal refused to enforce such an 'irresponsible, bizarre and unnatural'[104] arrangement and denied the father access to the child, reasoning that there was:

> absolutely no advantage to this child in continuing to be in contact with the father, except possibly a financial advantage to which I attach no significance whatever, in this case. If the father is to continue to turn up in the mother's house or to keep meeting her somewhere to take over the child, or to meet some member of her family to take over the child and return the child, the whole of this sordid story will be revived weekly or monthly as the case may be. The mother's position will be handicapped, and the handicapping of her position handicaps the child.[105]

While generally subsequent cases have also refused to remove a child from its mother, they have tended to adopt a far less condemnatory tone.[106] In a second case with similar facts, the Court held that, although the commissioning couple were in many ways more suitable as parents (offering a two-parent household, more stimulating intellectual environment, and better financial situation), it was in the children's best interests to be with their mother.[107]

How a contemporary court would find regarding the award of contact rights and parental responsibility is, however, another matter. A man in the position of the commissioning father in *A v C* would seem to have at least as great a claim to paternal rights as the genetic father in *Leeds* and, given his genetic link with the child, a somewhat stronger claim than that of the complainant in *Re R*. Further, as will be seen below, debates surrounding the removal of donor anonymity have advanced a strong notion of a child's right to the 'genetic truth'.[108] *A v C* is a product of the era that produced the 1990 Act, reflecting the same desires to protect the nuclear family and the same fears of reproductive methods that might serve to threaten it. It appears dated in the light of the legal and broader social developments since that time. We would suggest that if and when another disputed surrogacy case come before the courts, due regard to the shifting legal

---

[103] See: Surrogacy Arrangements Act 1985, s 2 and s 1A, respectively.

[104] [1985] FLR 445 (QB).

[105] *Ibid* at 458 (per Ormrod LJ), see also: *ibid* at 460–61 (per Cumming-Bruce LJ).

[106] Mason et al suggest: 'The British cases indicate that the public, as represented by the judiciary, are sympathetic to surrogate motherhood – an attitude which probably derives more from the *fait accompli* nature of the proceedings than from any basic empathy with the practice. It can be taken that no further decisions will be driven by antagonism': JK Mason *et al, Law and Medical Ethics* (Butterworths, London, 2002) at 105.

[107] *Re P (Minors) (Wardship: Surrogacy)* [1987] 2 FLR 421.

[108] See pp 92–95.

landscape described in this chapter and elsewhere in this book could well lead to a commissioning father being granted both contact rights and, possibly subject to a demonstration of ongoing commitment to the child, parental responsibility. Such a conclusion is given further force by a recent, albeit highly unusual, residence dispute that demonstrates the limits of the strong presumption in favour of a maternal preference. Here, an 18-month old child had been born as a result of partial surrogacy. Notwithstanding the fact that the child had lived with his mother since birth, the Court of Appeal upheld the transfer of residence to the father.[109] The decision turned on the fact that the mother had deliberately embarked upon a course of deception for the purpose of having another child, never having had any intention of giving up the baby. This deception led the trial judge to the view that the commissioning couple would make better parents.[110]

Before we move on, it is worth noting that the possibilities offered by surrogacy may be particularly significant for gay fathers. A gay male couple who had twin children, conceived using an egg donated by one woman and their own sperm, and carried by a US surrogate, attracted significant media attention. The couple were granted the right to have both their names on the US birth certificate, being reported as 'the first children of Britons to be registered with two fathers and no mother'.[111] While the US birth certificate does not mean that both men will be recognised as legal fathers under English law, the twins have now been given permission to stay in Britain, without being granted British citizenship.[112] Celebrating this victory, one of the two fathers commented that:

> The nuclear family as we know it is evolving. The emphasis should not be on it being a father and a mother, but on loving, nurturing parents, whether that be a single mother or a gay couple living in a committed relationship.[113]

Despite this 'evolution' in attitudes, the family later reported having encountered so much public hostility and media scrutiny that they had decided to move to Spain.[114]

---

[109] *Re P (A Child)* [2007] EWCA Civ 1053.

[110] See the summary of his reasoning and the Court of Appeal's approval of it, at *ibid*, para 4.

[111] W Woodward, 'Gay Couple Celebrate Birth of Twins Aspen and Saffron', *Guardian* (London, 13 December 1999), <http://www.guardian.co.uk/uk_news/story/0,,245638,00.html>, accessed 22 November 2007.

[112] BBC News (World Service), 'Gay Dads' Twins Stay in Britain' (25 January 2000), <http://news.bbc.co.uk/1/hi/world/europe/618862.stm>, accessed 22 November 2007.

[113] NewsPlanet Staff, 'UK Dads First With US Birth Cert.', <http://www.planetout.com/news/article-print.html?1999/10/28/5>, accessed 22 November 2007.

[114] G Tremlett, '"Hate mail drove us out of Britain. Now we've found a place in the sun"' *Observer* (8 February 2004). <http://observer.guardian.co.uk/uk_news/story/0,,1143435,00.html>, accessed 22 November 2007.

V. Donor Insemination and Anonymity

The growing importance attributed to genetics, clear in some of the developments above, is perhaps most explicitly in evidence in the context of donor insemination (DI). As seen above, the 1990 Act provided that the mother's husband or partner would be a child's legal father, with the donor remaining anonymous and playing no role in his genetic child's life. Donor anonymity was here adopted as a strategy by those who:

> wish[ed] both to accept gamete donation and to resolve some of the problems it presents to notions of the 'ordinary family'. It preserved as many as possible of the conventional features of the family by helping to set a barrier around that unit.[115]

The family to be protected was not just that of the infertile couple, but also the future family of the sperm donor.[116] In recommending donor anonymity, the Warnock Committee was influenced by the argument that banking detailed donor profiles would 'introduce the donor as a person in his own right'.[117] Ensuring donor anonymity, on the other hand, 'would give legal protection to the donor but it would also have the effect of minimising the invasion of the third party into the family'.[118] Intriguingly, only 20 years later, again Warnock's own position has shifted dramatically,[119] a change of heart firmly in line with shifting public opinion, a growing recognition of a child's 'right to genetic truth' and a clear trend in the jurisprudence of the European Court of Human Rights.[120]

Following much popular debate, media interest and public consultation, the law has now been changed so that, on reaching the age of 18, children born from sperm, eggs or embryos donated after April 2005 have the right to know the donor's identity.[121] Parents currently have no corresponding duty to tell their

---

[115] E Haimes, 'Recreating the Family? Policy Considerations Relating to the "New" Reproductive Technologies' in M McNeil, I Varcoe and S Yearley (eds), *The New Reproductive Technologies* (Macmillan, Basingstoke, 1990) at 169.

[116] As Ruth Deech explained: 'the donors ... are unlikely to donate if they think that in 20 or 30 years time their identity will be revealed and the child will visit, maybe at a time when those donors, typically medical students, are married and have families and have forgotten all about this or have suppressed it': Deech above (n 47) at 18.

[117] Warnock Report above (n 9) at para [3.2].

[118] *Ibid* at [4.22].

[119] Now being that 'all such deception is an evil': M Warnock, *Making Babies: Is there a Right to Have Children?* (Oxford University Press, Oxford, 2002) at 66. See also: J Eekelaar, *Family Law and Personal Life* (Oxford University Press, Oxford, 2006).

[120] *Mikulić v Croatia* (App no 53176/99) ECHR, 7 February 2002, *Odièvre v France* (App no 42326/98) (2003) 38 EHRR 43.

[121] Human Fertilisation and Embryology Authority (Disclosure of Donor Information) Regulations 2004, SI 2004/1511. See: Department of Health, 'Donor Information: providing information about sperm, egg and embryo donors', Consultation paper (20 December 2001), <http://www.dh.gov.uk/en/Publicationsandstatistics/Publications/PublicationsPolicyAndGuidance/DH_4005810>, accessed 22 November 2007. The Regulations, approved without a vote, do not have retrospective application.

children how they were conceived.[122] Thomson suggests that this reform must be located in the context of changing popular perceptions of sperm donors, who are now less likely to be medical students and more likely to be older men who already have families of their own. The older sperm donor, he suggests, is seen as a 'safer' figure, whose involvement is understood as altruistic and non-threatening.[123] This analysis is supported by a subsequent report tracing the shifting profile of gamete donors, and an accompanying HFEA press release entitled 'Stereotype of hard-up medical students a thing of the past':

> we can now move away from the misconception of donors as young students to the new realm of 30-something family men. This experience of family life must help donors to understand the incredible value that the donation has in helping others who have experienced difficulty in having children of their own.[124]

The positive tone of the above is interesting in the light of medical knowledge that advancing age is connected to a decrease in a man's sperm quality and increased risks to the health of his offspring.[125]

Such debates regarding donor anonymity have frequently reflected the terms used by Tizzard above, accepting a binary divide between social and genetic fathers with disagreement focused on the question of which should count as 'real' fathers. Such an understanding has underpinned some commentators' condemnation of this reform as part of a misguided shift towards a geneticisation of fatherhood.[126] Without denying the increased importance attributed to genetic ties, Thomson's analysis suggests a reading of the removal of donor anonymity which may be located within more relaxed attitudes towards donor insemination and a growing belief that knowledge of one's genetic paternity is not necessarily disruptive of one's social family and relationship with one's social parents.[127]

Rose and Another v Secretary of State for Health and Another[128]

An increased openness to the importance of the sperm donor as genetic father is further illustrated by *Rose*, a case that preceded the announcement of reform

---

[122] The Joint Parliamentary Committee charged with scrutinising the 2007 Bill recommended that the government consider the possibility of recording the circumstances of conception on a child's birth certificate, in order to give this right more substance, but there is no indication that this will be acted upon. See Joint Committee, above (n 36) at [276].

[123] M Thomson, *Endowed: Regulating the Male Sexed Body* (Routledge, New York, 2007) at ch 5.

[124] Human Fertilisation and Embryology Authority, 'Who are the UK's Sperm Donors? Fertility Regulator Presents National Picture of the People Who Donate', Press release, October 2005, <http://www.hfea.gov.uk/en/1109.html>, accessed 22 November 2007.

[125] See ch 2 p 58; Thomson, above (n 123).

[126] Tizzard, above (n 90). See further, J Bristow, 'Seeds of Suspicion' *Spiked*, http://www.spiked-online.com (21 January 2004), who suggests it signifies 'the importance the government attaches to knowing about one's biological "roots", despite the upheaval this is likely to cause one's "social" (real) family'.

[127] Thomson, above (n 123). See further: C Smart, *Personal Life* (Polity, Cambridge, 2007).

[128] [2002] EWHC Admin 1593, [2002] 2 FLR 962 (QB).

regarding the provision of information to children born of donor gametes.[129] The disclosure of information sought in *Rose* is presented as necessary not to provide a genetic father who can replace the social father, but rather to give a further source of information about an individual's own genetic identity. The first complainant tells the Court:

> these genetic connections are very important to me, socially, emotionally, medically, and even spiritually ... [N]on-identifying information will assist me in forming a fuller sense of self or identity and answer questions that I have been asking for a long time ... With the revelation of my donor conception I am now unable to complete medical history forms ... I do not know about half of my ethnicity or racial identity.[130]

Again, the symbolic importance of fatherhood is asserted, with the need for knowledge of one's genetic parentage expressed not just in terms of the practicalities of medical information, but as a 'spiritual' need. The judge accepts this claim, noting: '[h]ere what the claimants are trying to obtain is information about their biological fathers, something that goes to the very heart of their identity, and to their make up as people.'[131]

The second complainant, EM, is still a young child and it is her mother who is asserting her right to this information, explaining:

> I believe that secrecy can be very destructive to individuals and to families and I would like to be able to protect our daughter as much as I can from this ... If in the future our daughter wanted to make contact with the donor then we would completely support her and help her in this.[132]

The provision of information regarding her genetic father emerges as important in cementing EM's relationship with her social parents. Honesty is an important value within that relationship and ignorance of her genetic father's identity will thus undermine the social family. Contacting the donor would be a matter for the family unit as a whole, in no way undermining the affective bonds upon which it is predicated. While, as a matter of empirical fact, it seems that most heterosexual couples have chosen not to reveal much detail regarding the circumstance of conception to their DI child,[133] this case suggests some parents intend to be more open and do not view this as a threat to their own familial stability. It also

---

[129] The claimants relied on Arts 8 and 14 of the ECHR, asserting discrimination relative to adoptees, and also between donor offspring born before the 1990 Act came into force, and those born thereafter.

[130] [2002] EWHC Admin 1593 at [87]–[88].

[131] *Ibid* at [33].

[132] *Ibid* at [12].

[133] One recent European study found that only 8% of children born of donor insemination had been told about their genetic origins: S Golombok *et al*, 'The European Study of Assisted Reproduction Families: the Transition to Adolescence' (2002) 17(3) *Human Reproduction* 830.

indicates that the courts are receptive to this understanding of disclosure, which is supported by a growing body of research outlining the harm of keeping secret a child's genetic origins.[134]

These developments are, we suggest, more complex than merely involving the articulation of a more geneticised vision of fatherhood. Rather, we again see the fracturing of fatherhood into constituent parts, a correlative proliferation of men with some claim to be considered 'a father', and a recognition that knowledge of one's genetic father may not necessarily disrupt one's relationship with one's social father. In *Rose*, the courts simply recognise a fact long known to them in some of the other family law contexts explored in the chapters to follow: that various ways of grounding paternal rights, obligations or status may be advanced on behalf of different men. Access to one's genetic father, particularly when he is imagined within the terms of safe, familial masculinity,[135] is not perceived to be in competition with protection of the social family. Rather, the former complements, and can even strengthen, the latter.

VI. Rights in Stored Embryos

Finally, we come to the rather different issues raised in the case of *Evans v Amicus Health Care*.[136] Faced with the removal of both of her ovaries due to cancer, Natallie Evans had requested that some eggs be harvested from her and fertilised using the sperm of her then partner, Howard Johnston, to create embryos for their future use. Following the breakdown of the relationship, Johnston asked the clinic to destroy their embryos. Evans responded by bringing an action requesting that she should be allowed to use her stored embryos in order to become pregnant. Her desire to have her own genetic child was thus pitted against his clear wish not to be forced into unwanted paternity. The resulting court case raised a number of complex legal issues regarding interpretation of the 1990 Act and its compatibility with the Human Rights Act 1998.[137] Ultimately, Evans was defeated by the 1990 Act's clear provision that embryos that have been created in vitro can only be used within the terms of 'an effective consent' from each of the parties whose gametes were used to create it. Such consent, moreover, can be varied or revoked at any time up until the moment that the embryos are used.[138]

Evans' appeals in the domestic courts and to the European Court of Human Rights failed to overturn this judgment and there is, it would seem, nothing in

---

[134] E Lycett *et al*, 'Offspring Created as a Result of Donor Insemination: A Study of Family Relationships, Child Adjustment, and Disclosure' (2004) 82(1) *Fertility and Sterility* 172.

[135] See further ch 4.

[136] [2003] EWHC Fam 2161, [2004] EWCA Civ 727; *Evans v UK* (App no 6339/05) ECHR, 7 March 2006, 10 April 2007 (Grand Chamber).

[137] S Sheldon, '*Evans v Amicus Health Care*: Revealing Cracks in the "Twin Pillars"?' [2004] *Child & Family Law Quarterly* 437.

[138] 1990 Act, Sch 3, paras 6(3) and 4, respectively.

the proposed reforms of the 1990 Act that would have helped her. Nonetheless, it seems likely that the drafters of the 2007 Bill did have a case such as this in mind. The Bill maintains the status quo that either party may withdraw consent to the use of embryos, with the result that they would then be destroyed. However, it does make provision for a man in Johnston's situation to be able to withdraw his consent to being treated as the father of a child, while still allowing the woman to make use of the embryos without his involvement.[139]

For many, *Evans* was fundamentally concerned with the relative rights of men and women in reproductive decision-making. It was seen as raising issues like 'whether in a world in which many people have come to accept a woman's right of choice as to whether she should have a child or not the genetic father should have the equivalent right – a right greater than that conferred by nature'.[140] As such, it is perhaps not surprising that many commentators appealed to ideas of gender equality in an attempt to resolve it. Yet *Evans* also illustrates how slippery such arguments can be in reproductive contexts, where men and women can rarely, if ever, be deemed equally situated. This point is well illustrated by the conclusion of the judgment of Wall J:

> it is not difficult to reverse the dilemma. If a man has testicular cancer and his sperm, preserved prior to radical surgery which renders him permanently infertile, is used to create embryos with his partner; and if the couple have separated before the embryos are transferred into the woman, nobody would suggest that she could not withdraw her consent to treatment and refuse to have the embryos transferred into her. The statutory provisions, like Convention Rights, apply to men and women equally.[141]

Wall J's attempt to 'reverse the dilemma' equates the fact that Johnston cannot force Evans to undergo an invasive medical procedure followed by nine months of unwanted pregnancy and the pain and risks of childbirth, with the fact that Evans cannot insist on making use of the embryos herself. In other words, it focuses exclusively on genetic links at the expense of any consideration of gestation. We return to the problematic nature of equality arguments in the context of parenting in chapter seven.

Genetic links are thus central to *Evans*. Evans' medical condition does not make it impossible for her to carry a pregnancy and give birth to a child; what she

---

[139] 2007 Bill, cl 21(3)(6C), requiring that the clinic must inform the woman that the man's consent to being treated as a parent has been withdrawn before going ahead with her treatment. Whether it would have been possible under the 1990 Act for Johnston to withdraw his consent to being treated as a parent while still allowing Evans to make use of the embryos was never explored in *Evans* as Johnston made it clear that he would not wish to make use of such a possibility. See: Sheldon, above (n 137).

[140] [2004] EWCA Civ 727 (per Arden LJ). The same judge later notes: 'if Evans' argument succeeded, it would amount to interference with the genetic father's right to decide not to become a parent. Motherhood could surely not be forced on Evans and likewise fatherhood cannot be forced on Johnston': *ibid* at [111].

[141] See: [2003] EWHC Fam 2161 at [320]; S Sheldon, 'Gender Equality and Reproductive Decision Making' (2004) 12(3) *Feminist Legal Studies* 303 for further discussion on this point.

will lose with the destruction of the stored embryos is the chance to have a child which is genetically her own. Likewise, Johnston has made it clear that he did not want to have a genetic child in the world unless he could be actively involved in parenting. He is guided not just by the legal and financial burdens of fatherhood, telling the Court of Appeal that his 'clear position was one of fundamental rather than purely financial objection'.[142] Johnston thus rejects the idea of fatherhood as being merely a legal status with financial obligations, and describes a sense of paternal responsibility to one's genetic children and a more involved, hands-on understanding of fatherhood in keeping with broader cultural and policy shifts around fatherhood increasingly dominant across many of the areas discussed elsewhere in this book.

Conclusion

While the above analysis of the regulation of ARTs over the last two decades paints a picture of complex, shifting and at times contradictory understandings of fatherhood, some common themes can be discerned. Notably, a belief that fathers are important is prevalent, although exactly what for remains less clearly stated. It was suggested that, for the architects of the Human Fertilisation and Embryology Act 1990, fathers' significance was grounded primarily, though not exclusively, in their symbolic role of completing the nuclear family. The tenacious grip of the nuclear family form has also been clear in more recent developments discussed above: for example, provisions for the naming of deceased fathers on birth certificates and beliefs that we can or should identify 'the real' father of a child. Implicit in this appeal to authenticity is the nuclear family norm of exclusivity: each child can have only one 'real' father. Claims asserted on behalf of any other man are implicitly denigrated to the lesser status of pretence.

Less than 20 years on, the Human Fertilisation and Embryology Bill 2007 paints a still more complex picture. While the nuclear family model is maintained in so far as it is impossible to have more than two parents, the reforms described above reveal a growing acceptance of single-parent and same-sex parent families. As well as reflecting this liberalisation in attitudes, the replacement of the 'need for a father' provision with the much vaguer 'need for supportive parenting', might also represent a weakening of the idea that both mother and father are essential as role models for the adequate gender socialisation of a child. This shift, in itself, mapping to the broader shifts around gender neutrality and child welfare detailed in chapter one, reflects some uncertainty in this context about whether there is anything distinctive about men's parenting.[143] The changes to the status provisions described above reveal an interesting tension between the desire to extend the nuclear family model beyond its historical heterosexual boundaries

---

[142] [2004] EWCA Civ 727 at [32].
[143] Doucet, above (n 99).

combined with a continuing adherence to its one mother/one father form. While the 2007 Bill accepts the extension of the two-parent family to include a lesbian couple, it seems a step too far to accept what might appear as no more than the logical consequence of that move: that a child born to a lesbian couple should have two legal mothers.[144]

Throughout this book we detail the range of different factors that have, in particular social and legal contexts, been considered relevant to the legal determination of fatherhood and award of paternal rights and responsibilities. Scrutinising the interplay of these various factors has been particularly complex in the context of ARTs. Genetic links, marital ties, the intention to create a child and the desire to act as a social father have all figured in legal attempts to plot a way through the complex dilemmas discussed above. Nonetheless, we can here discern a particular reliance on two of these factors, often operating in significant tension. First, a more central role has been accorded to intention in the regulation of ARTs, with both the 1990 Act and the 2007 Bill treating men's consent as central to the establishment of legal fatherhood. At its extreme, a man's intention to create a child can ground his status as a legal father even when he is not married to the child's mother, is not the genetic father and is dead at the time of embryo implantation. The great importance which the 1990 Act attaches to consent can also be seen in *Evans* and the idea that unintended parenthood cannot be forced on an unwilling party.[145] Finally, intention is significant in gamete donation: egg, sperm and embryo donors are not parents because the act of donation signals their clear intention not to become so.

Second, we join those commentators who have recognised an increased priority accorded to genetics in some of the developments analysed above, most obviously in the removal of gamete donor anonymity.[146] We witness the strength of feeling relating to the importance of ensuring a genetic link between father and child in the widespread use of scientific technologies developed to allow men with fertility problems to father their own genetic children. Techniques like ICSI also mark a movement towards bringing men in from the margins, a move we track in this book as occurring across diverse areas of law: recognising the

---

[144] While there is no provision for a gay male couple both to acquire parental status under the reformed status provisions, they can enter into a surrogacy arrangement and make use of the fast-track adoption procedure in the same way as a heterosexual or lesbian couple: 2007 Bill, cl 60. Presumably, the failure to extend the status provisions to include two male parents results from the fact that, while it is relatively easy to see how a lesbian co-parent can acquire parenthood in the same way as a non-genetic father (where the test depends on consent), it is far from clear how a gay male co-father might acquire parenthood in the same way as a mother (ie through gestation). The need for one gestational and one genetic/intentional parent shows again how the heterosexual model frames our thinking here.

[145] With welfare, 'consent' is one of the 'twin pillars' said to provide the ethical support for the regulatory regime established in the 1990 Act: Sheldon, above (n 137). See also the comments of Arden LJ, above (n 140).

[146] Eg: R Deech, 'Family Law and Genetics' (1998) 61 MLR 697, arguing that we may be moving towards a culture of family law based on genetic evidence and not behaviour and responsibility.

existence of male infertility and developing the means of addressing it make the (products of the) male body increasingly subject to the medical gaze. The significance of genetic links was central to the ethical dilemma in *Evans* where the parties were divided by a fervent desire to achieve genetic parenthood (Evans) and to avoid it (Johnston). *Evans* also illustrates the role that focusing on genetics (where contributions of men and women are readily judged the same) plays in foregrounding ideas of equality, a theme that will be further developed in chapters six and seven.

Notwithstanding the above, and as noted in chapter one, we have argued in this context against seeing the evolving law as a 'zero sum game' where recognising genetic links necessarily detracts from valuing other kinds of connections. Rather, we have argued that a greater emphasis on genetics has been accepted, at least in part, because of a growing belief that knowledge of and contact with a genetic father is unlikely to disrupt unduly a child's social family and the fathering carried out within it. At its strongest, it has been claimed that knowledge of one's genetic father can serve to protect and enrich relationships with one's social parents. As such, while the 1990 Act reflected and entrenched the idea that we should have just one legal mother and father, its treatment at the hands of the judiciary suggests a willingness to recognise further father figures standing outside the boundaries of the nuclear family. To put it another way: while the nuclear family may be crucial to the regulatory framework established by the 1990 Act, it is subject to clear emerging cracks, albeit ones which follow rather familiar fault lines, with parental rights most readily granted to those who most closely approximate to some part of the traditional role prescribed for the father within it.

The 1990 Act was the product of a particular moment and specific set of anxieties centring round the radical possibilities offered by ARTs, at a time when traditional family values were seen as under threat. The Act was passed by a Conservative government, which had overseen various other initiatives attempting statutorily to fortify a sexual hierarchy of families which would protect the nuclear family, thus marginalising gay and lesbian parenting.[147] Looking at the 1990 Act in the context of the broader social trends in living arrangements described in chapter one, and some of the developments in family law discussed below in the following chapters, it might seem that the 1990 Act's adherence to the model of the nuclear family was an anachronism even when the law was passed, representing an attempt to stem the tides of change. Subsequent developments in the law regulating ARTs, culminating in the 2007 Bill, may represent nothing more than an attempt to revise and interpret the 1990 Act in the light of the evolving principles and values utilised in the broader family law context, discussed elsewhere in this book. Notably, greater recognition of same-sex and

---

[147] Cooper and Herman, above (n 24); citing Local Government Act 1988, s 28, and guidelines about placing foster children in lesbian and gay households.

single-parent families has had a clear impact here. Further, that the balance has shifted away from a reliance on marriage towards a focus on genetics and intention is unsurprising at a time when marriage is increasingly under threat. Change has been mandated by a sense that fathers' relationships with their children can no longer be securely anchored in men's relationships with those children's mothers.[148] Finally, in many of the cases discussed above, we have seen men's desire to claim an active involvement in the lives of their children and, in cases like *Re R* and *Leeds*, a judicial endorsement of the same. This dynamic is likewise at play in *Evans* in Johnston's refusal to father a child in a context where he could not take on an active parenting role.

In this chapter we have suggested that ARTs form just one, albeit particularly radical, example of the fragmentation of fatherhood. The law's attempt to respond to such fragmentation is part of an ongoing and complex process of the renegotiation of familial rights and responsibilities against a changing scientific, social and demographic landscape. In the next three chapters, we move on to explore the negotiation and regulation of fathering relationships in a number of different family forms: intact marital units, post-separation and in unmarried relationships (whether or not they involve cohabitation).

---

[148] See further ch 6.

4

Marital Fatherhood

Introduction

HAVING CONSIDERED HOW one 'becomes' a father, the focus of our analysis now shifts to the period after birth. In the next three chapters, we deal, respectively, with fathers in the context of subsisting marital relationships, separated fathers and, finally, fathers who are unmarried.[1] Marriage has long played a central role in how law has sought to attach men to their children, with the subsisting marital relationship frequently lauded by politicians across the political spectrum as the best possible framework within which children might be raised. However, the demographic changes described in chapter one, not least an increase in the rates of unmarried childbirth and relationship breakdown, alongside a falling marriage rate, have severely challenged the possibility of relying on marriage as a way of grounding legal fatherhood, as well as those rights and responsibilities with which it has traditionally been accompanied. In chapters five and six, we trace how the law has responded to these changes in relation to separated and unmarried fathers.

In this chapter, however, we begin by scrutinising the law's traditional 'ideal type' of fatherhood within the subsisting marital family, charting some significant shifts in how law has assessed fathering practices within this unit. We noted in chapter one that our focus in this book would be on how law has 'problematised' fatherhood in a number of different ways across different legal contexts. In stark contrast to its non-marital counterpart, the marital family has historically been assumed in law to be essentially unproblematic, with the role played by fathers within it requiring little scrutiny or social support. However, we will suggest in this chapter that this has changed dramatically in recent years, with the nature of fathers' relationships with children in subsisting family units increasingly seen as a key political issue and object of policy intervention. This has involved a significant shift in understandings of what constitutes a good/bad father, and, more specifically, a move away from the idea that a 'good father' need

---

[1] As noted previously, this is an analytical division of material which reflects the way that fatherhood has been variously problematised in law. In reality, men will move between these categories and may sometimes occupy more than one of them simultaneously.

be only a remote disciplinarian and breadwinner towards an increased expectation that men will be 'engaged', 'hands-on' fathers, parents who will 'be there' for their children. This move has been accompanied by a growing concern at policy level to promote what has been termed father-inclusive practice in the delivery of services, and to facilitate a form of 'active fathering' on the part of men.[2]

The development of family law and policy in the period from the late nineteenth century to the present day has reflected this shift in dominant norms of fatherhood, moving from a position in which men held exclusive rights over their children, to one where, by the mid-twentieth century, fathers had been reconstituted in law primarily as familial 'breadwinners'. During this period, as women seemingly displaced men as legal guardians, the question of what constitutes a 'good father' was reframed, largely, if by no means entirely, via reference to the economic link between a man and his family. In more recent years this move from 'rights to responsibilities' in law has taken a further turn, however. Encapsulated in the idea of 'new fatherhood', contemporary fathers are now widely expected to have – and to desire – a closer, more emotionally involved and nurturing relationship with their children.[3] This shift has been described as a move from 'cash to care' in how fatherhood has been repositioned across areas of law and policy.[4] British fathers 'are now expected to be accessible and nurturing as well as economically supportive to their children. They are increasingly self-conscious about juggling conflicts between looking after children and having a job'.[5]

In this chapter, we will focus our discussion on the nature of these shifting ideas about fathers' responsibilities during subsisting marital relationships, while fully recognising the impact of these same ideas on the other 'kinds' of fathers considered in later chapters. We explore here how beliefs about men and masculinities, economy and society, gender and sexuality have each attached, at particular moments, to dominant understandings of fatherhood and paternity in law. We question, in particular, how law has constructed an ideal of the married father as a distinctive kind of 'family man'. Developments around the responsibilities of fathers, we argue, raise important questions about the 'gap' that can exist between cultures of fatherhood and understandings of fatherhood(s) as a social practice, as introduced in chapter one. They also raise the issue of what can, and cannot, be expected from law reform in seeking to 'change' the parenting practices of men and women, a theme we return to in the context of separated

[2] D Bartlett, A Burgess and K Jones, *A Toolkit for Developing Father-inclusive Practice* (Fathers Direct, London, 2007); A Burgess and D Bartlett, *Working With Fathers* (Fathers Direct, London, 2004); The Fatherhood Institute, *The Difference a Dad Makes* (The Fatherhood Institute, London, 2007).

[3] For a useful summary see: M O'Brien, *Shared Caring: Bringing Fathers into the Frame* (Equal Opportunities Commission, Manchester, 2005).

[4] See eg: B Hobson (ed), *Making Men into Fathers: Men, Masculinities and the Social Politics of Fatherhood* (Cambridge University Press, Cambridge, 2002) particularly ch 1.

[5] O'Brien, above (n 3).

fathers in chapter five. Whilst a particular model of the father as 'family man' and 'breadwinner' has been embedded historically in law, a range of policy agendas around the provision of care, notably at the interface of family and employment law, have served to transform and challenge many aspects of these earlier understandings of fatherhood. This has involved a profound rethinking of the responsibilities of fathers. It has also brought about a more far-reaching reconstruction of fatherhood as a particular kind of social problem and object of legal intervention.[6]

We begin by charting the historical shift referred to above, a shift away from a model of fatherhood based in rights and authority, identifying key features of what being a responsible father has involved at various moments. We proceed, in section II, to outline some significant changes to these ideas of paternal responsibility, paying particular attention to understandings of the father as family breadwinner. As a critical case study of these changes, we focus on recent policy debates around the issue of 'work–life' balance. This is an area in which law has been used, quite explicitly, to bring about a shift in fathering practices. In section III, we look in detail at the assumptions underpinning these debates, and consider the extent to which understandings of fathers' responsibilities in law at the present moment are marked by themes of both continuity *and* change. Unpacking the conceptual basis of these debates suggests that diverse, and frequently contradictory, beliefs about family life, gendered divisions of labour, paid employment, sexualities, class and masculinities inform contemporary understandings of fatherhood in law. Dealing with different discourses about the 'problem of men'[7] emerging in these debates around fatherhood, responsibility and family life, has, we suggest, become a key feature of legal policy debates across diverse areas of law.

I. (Re)Constructing the 'Family Man' as Breadwinner: From Rights to Responsibility

The 'Empire of the Father'

What 'being a father' involves in law is, as we have already seen, far from straightforward. It has been through reference to the institution of marriage that fathers have historically been legally 'attached' to a child. While establishing an

---

[6] On the notion of the 'problematisation' of fatherhood see ch 1, p 32.

[7] J Scourfield and M Drakeford, 'New Labour and the "Problem of Men"' (2002) 22 *Critical Social Policy* 619. See further ch 7 p 216.

authoritative determination of biological paternity has posed considerable problems for legal systems,[8] the importance of the bond between a father and his 'legitimate' child has been such that, in the past, neither husband nor wife could give evidence of 'non-access' (lack of sexual intercourse) if the effect would be to 'bastardise' a child born during marriage.[9] Through reference to the legal fiction of the presumption of legitimacy (in effect a presumption of paternity), the law has been able to create a legal relationship between a woman's husband and children, notwithstanding any doubts regarding the existence between them of a genetic link.[10]

At common law, married fathers were invested with sole rights of custody and control over their legitimate children. Writing in the eighteenth century, Blackstone had declared that it was only at the time a child reaches the age of 21, that the 'empire of the father ... gives place to the empire of reason'.[11] The mother, in contrast, was 'entitled to no power, but only to reverence and respect'. By the early nineteenth century, inroads were already being made into this model of paternal rights, and a move away from the common law 'empire of the father' had begun.[12] Nonetheless, it was only in those cases where the conduct of the father was considered 'exceptionally culpable' that fathers' rights were to be curtailed.[13] Whilst the courts did give some consideration to the welfare of the child, this had to be seriously threatened in order to justify judicial interference with paternal rights. Much cited as an example of this father right position, the case of *Re Agar-Ellis*[14] remains instructive.[15] Here, the court upheld the right of the father – as the 'natural guardian' of his legitimate child – to make decisions for that child, and to enforce his right of custody in the common law courts. As a father, he 'knows far better as a rule what is good for his children than a court of justice can'.[16] The rights of fathers were 'natural' and 'sacred' because of the reciprocity of paternal obligation and prerogative.[17] Fathers' rights, given their natural

---

[8] See further ch 6; also: C Smart, '"There is of course the Distinction dictated by Nature": Law and the Problem of Paternity' in M Stanworth (ed), *Reproductive Technologies: Gender, Motherhood and Medicine* (Feminist Perspectives Series, Polity, Cambridge, 1987).

[9] *Ibid.* Note: *Banbury Peerage Case* (1811) 1 Sim & St 153, 57 ER 62.

[10] This situation has been transformed by the emergence of DNA testing; see: T Freeman and M Richards, 'DNA Testing and Kinship' in F Ebtehaj, B Lindley and M Richards (eds), *Kinship Matters* (Hart, Oxford, 2006). See also ch 6, below.

[11] W Blackstone, *Commentaries on the Laws of England: Volume I* (Clarendon Press, Oxford, 1765) 453.

[12] The Court of Chancery had, for example, by this time acquired powers to make children Wards of Court or Wards in Chancery: I Pinchbeck and M Hewitt, *Children in English Society, Volume II: From the Eighteenth Century to the Children Act 1948* (Routledge & Kegan Paul, London, 1973).

[13] S Maidment, *Child Custody and Divorce: The Law in Social Context* (Croom Helm, London, 1984) at112, cited in A Diduck and F Kaganas, *Family Law, Gender and the State: Text, Cases and Materials*, 2nd edn (Hart, Oxford, 2006) at 305. See eg: *Re Flynn* (1848) 2 De G & SM 457, 64 ER 205.

[14] (1883) 24 Ch D 317.

[15] On the facts of this case see: R Collier, *Masculinity, Law and the Family* (Routledge, London 1995) at 186–7.

[16] (1883) 24 Ch D 317 at 338 (per Bowen LJ).

[17] *Ibid* at 327 (per Brett MR).

ordination, meant that a court 'whatever be its authority or jurisdiction, has no right to interfere'.[18] The law was not concerned with the care of children, still less with what the role of fathers might be in practice. Fathers' rights were, rather, symbolic,[19] the embodiment of patriarchal authority, with a man's control within, and over, his family interlinked to a concern with the maintenance of social order and orderly transmission of property.[20]

Re Agar-Ellis illustrates the dominant attitudes of the period towards family, parenting, gender, class and property. This was a social context in which, it is important to remember, the legal 'disabilities' seen to befall married women flowed from the fact that a wife's legal existence at common law had been incorporated into that of her husband.[21] Whilst equitable doctrines developed by the court of Chancery subsequently sought to lessen the harshness of these common law rules, divorce itself remained heavily restricted, and, importantly, permeated by sexual double standards.[22] Cases such as *Agar-Ellis* may now appear anachronistic, but, as we shall see elsewhere in this book, the questions they raise about the interlinking of paternal authority and social order retain a certain resonance in aspects of contemporary debates about the politics of fatherhood and law. What happened, therefore, to change this position?

During the latter part of the nineteenth and first half of the twentieth centuries, significant reforms were introduced which enabled mothers to seek custody and access to their children, albeit in prescribed circumstances.[23] The Guardianship of Infants Act 1886 empowered courts to make such an order as it thought fit, having regard not only to the conduct and wishes of the parent, but also the welfare of the infant.[24] The Guardianship of Infants Act 1925, meanwhile, provided that the court, in deciding questions relating to the custody or upbringing of a child, should henceforth have regard to the welfare of the child as the 'first and paramount consideration'. Whilst the 1925 Act was itself politically

---

[18] *Re Plomley* 47 LT 284 (per Bacon VC).

[19] To interfere with the rights of the father 'would be to ignore the one principle which is the most fundamental of all in this history of mankind, and owing to the full play of which man has become what he is': *Re Agar-Ellis* (1883) 24 Ch D 317 at 337 (per Brett MR).

[20] Within a legal system in which property rights based on ownership and inheritance have historically passed through the male line, the significance of whether a man is sure that a particular child was 'his' has understandably been considerable: K O'Donovan, *Sexual Divisions in Law* (Weidenfeld & Nicolson, London, 1985) at 40.

[21] L Holcombe, *Wives and Property: Reform of the Married Women's Property Acts* (University of Toronto Press, Toronto, 1983).

[22] See further ch 5.

[23] See eg: Custody of Infants Act 1839; Divorce and Matrimonial Causes Act 1857; Custody of Infants Act 1873.

[24] Guardianship of Infants Act 1886, s 5(4).

contested,[25] this 'paramountcy principle' continues, through the Children Act 1989, to inform child law to the present day.[26]

The detailed development of the responsibilities of married fathers in case law throughout the twentieth century, as well as in the period subsequent to the enactment of the Children Act 1989, is beyond the scope of this chapter. Like the indeterminate nature of the welfare principle,[27] as well as more recent elaborations of welfare and responsibility in the light of the Human Rights Act 1998, these issues have been considered in depth elsewhere.[28] For our present purposes, it is necessary to look more closely at how, throughout this period of apparently egalitarian and progressive reform, ideas about fathers and fatherhood were themselves reconstructed in a number of far-reaching ways.

Law and the 'Modernising' of Fatherhood[29]

It is important to note the potential disjuncture between, on the one hand, ideas about fathers' responsibilities contained in legal discourse at particular moments and, on the other, the socially diverse material realities of fathering practices. While the model of fatherhood outlined above may well have registered with those men socialised into the 'civilized self-control ... rigidity of character structure' which marked the middle-class Victorian Man,[30] a case such as *Agar-Ellis* presents a judicial construct of a particular ideal of paternal masculinity. The idea of fatherhood invoked here – that of the Victorian *paterfamilias* – only ever related, however, to the lives of some fathers, and class, geographical (such as rural/urban), religious and ethnic differences, all influenced the legal

---

[25] S Cretney, '"What will women want next?" The Struggle for Power Within the Family 1925–1975' (1996) 12 *Law Quarterly Review* 110. See also: J Eekelaar, *Family Law and Personal Life* (Oxford University Press, Oxford, 2006) at 140–4.

[26] Lord Mackay, 'Perceptions of the Children Bill and Beyond' (1989) 139 NLJ 505. See further: H Reece, 'The Paramountcy Principle: Consensus or Construct?' (1996) 49 *Current Legal Problems* 267. The Children Act 1989 provides that when a court determines any question with respect to a range of circumstances concerning children, 'the child's welfare shall be the court's paramount consideration': Children Act 1989, s 1(1). On the 'welfare checklist' see: Children Act 1989, s 1(3). Note also: *J v C* [1970] AC 668.

[27] Reece, above (n 26).

[28] See eg: H Fenwick, 'Clashing Rights, the Welfare of the Child and the Human Rights Act' (2004) MLR 889; S Choudhry and H Fenwick, 'Taking the Rights of Parents and Children Seriously – Confronting the Welfare Principle under the Human Rights Act' (2005) 25 *Oxford Journal of Legal Studies* 453.

[29] The notion of modernisation has been used in several studies of fatherhood, in particular within US literature. See eg: R Larossa, *The Modernization of Fatherhood: A Social and Political History* (University of Chicago Press, Chicago, 1997). See also: Collier, above (n 15).

[30] P Cominos, 'Late Victorian Sexual Respectabilty and the Social System' (1963) 8 *International Review of Social History* 18, cited in M Richards, 'Fatherhood, Marriage and Sexuality: Some Speculations on the English Middle-class Family' in C Lewis and M O'Brien (eds), *Reassessing Fatherhood: New Observations on Fathers and the Modern Family* (Sage, London, 1987) at 27.

authority of fathers in different ways.[31] It would be misleading to assume, therefore, that a model of authoritarian fatherhood, and the 'separate spheres' ideology underscoring this particular depiction of domestic arrangements, was ever diffused throughout the social order. Culturally resonant and embedded in law as these ideals may have been at the time, they did not necessarily map to the experience of fatherhood on the part of all men, women and children.

This does not mean that to talk of shifting representations of fathers' rights and responsibilities within statute and case law has no value. As noted in chapter one, law is of particular significance as an authorised, 'official' symbolic discourse reflecting changing ideas about fatherhood as a social institution. Law regulates and structures 'everyday' lives, and the shifts that subsequently occurred through-out the twentieth century can tell us much about changing social attitudes to parenthood, childhood and child welfare, equality and responsibility.[32] Yet these legal constructions of the rights, obligations and responsibilities of fathers must be socially, economically and politically located within the context of broader and longer-term changes in family structures, adult–child relations and, we will suggest below, forms of governance.[33]

Historical and sociological work provides further insight here. The changes discussed above took place against a backdrop marked by the transformations of the agricultural and industrial revolutions of the eighteenth and nineteenth centuries. The separation of the private/home and public/work spheres within law and liberal philosophy, in tune with the perceived (gendered) psychological characteristics of the sexes, was of central importance in informing the 'moderni-sation' of fatherhood during this period. Feminist and masculinities scholarship has more recently identified the formation of a distinctive kind of masculine (rational, authoritative)[34] social subject emerging in this process – a 'public man'[35] – as a key element in the entrenchment of men's social power.[36] The home and domestic sphere was to be reconstituted, for certain men at least, as a place of

[31] See further: J Mangan and J Walvin (eds), *Manliness and Morality: Middle Class Masculinity in Britain and America 1800–1940* (Manchester University Press, Manchester, 1987); J Tosh, *A Man's Place: Masculinity and the Middle-class Home in Victorian England* (Yale University Press, London, 1999) at 195; JR Gillis, *A World of Their Own Making: Myth, Ritual and the Quest for Family Values* (Harvard University Press, Cambridge, MA, 1996).

[32] The reforms of the late nineteenth and early twentieth centuries were the result of political struggles for women to secure equal status in relation to their children. See the excellent discussion in: S Boyd, *Child Custody, Law and Women's Work* (Oxford University Press, Oxford, 2003) at chs 2 and 3; MJ Bailey, 'England's First Custody of Infants Act' (1994) 20 *Queen's Law Journal* 391.

[33] See eg: R van Krieken, 'Legal Informalism, Power and Liberal Governance' (2001) 10(1) SLS 5; R van Krieken, '"The Best Interests of the Child" and Parental Separation: On the "Civilising of Parents"' (2005) 68(1) MLR 25.

[34] On the links between masculinity and rationality see eg: V Seidler, *Rediscovering Masculinity* (Routledge, London, 1989).

[35] S Whitehead, *Men and Masculinities* (Polity, Cambridge 2002) at 113–124 on the 'heroic male project'.

[36] J Hearn, *Men in the Public Eye* (Routledge, London, 1992).

Marital Fatherhood

comfort and renewal predicated on the caring provided by women.[37] The subsequent shifts in fatherhood that occurred during the mid- to late nineteenth and early twentieth centuries did not simply result, however, from a reconstitution of the public/private dualism. They were also the product of a complex interweaving of law, medicine, psychology, religion and science, all of which (in different ways) are implicated in the production of normative beliefs about family life, childhood, sexuality and parenting.

The changes which occurred around fathers' rights and responsibilities in law during this period must thus be located within the context of this broader reconfiguration of gender relations interlinked to changing ideas and practices around, for example, children and childhood,[38] health and illness,[39] sexuality[40] and social class.[41] The shifting strategies of governance concerned with instituting gendered divisions around ideas of public and private masculinities[42] – about the (heterosexual) family, the nature of 'good' motherhood, fatherhood and so forth – were also engaged in the constitution of a particular kind of social body and understanding of social order. During this process, a new way of talking about (gendered) parenthood emerged. Importantly, while mothers were subject to levels of surveillance, scrutiny and regulation by law in ways that fathers were not,[43] ideas about the married family man and the 'good' father were also transformed in a number of far-reaching ways. In the move away from the 'empire of the father' towards the model of the family as an egalitarian, complementary household unit, the welfare principle has been central to what has been a complex social and legal reassessment of both mothering and fathering. It is to this that we now turn.

[37] See work cited above at n 31. See also: L Davidoff and C Hall, *Family Fortunes* (Hutchinson, London 1987); L Davidoff *et al*, *The Family Story: Blood, Contract and Intimacy, 1830–1960* (Addison Wesley Longman, Harlow, 1999).

[38] See ch 1 above (n 26); Pinchbeck and Hewitt, above (n 12); I Pinchbeck and M Hewitt, *Children in English Society: Volume 1: From Tudor Times to the Eighteenth Century* (Routledge & Kegan Paul, London, 1969).

[39] M Foucault, *Madness and Civilisation* (Tavistock, London, 1967).

[40] M Foucault, *The History of Sexuality: Volume 1: An Introduction* (Penguin, Harmondsworth, 1981).

[41] See above (n 31).

[42] The period 1870–1920, Hearn argues, 'appeared as the historical means by which men and masculinities came from the heroic "heights" of industrial capitalism in the mid-nineteenth century to become "modern men" of this century': Hearn, above (n 36) at 96.

[43] See: Boyd, above (n 32); M Fineman, *The Neutered Mother, The Sexual Family, and Other Twentieth Century Tragedies* (Routledge, New York, 1995); A Diduck, 'In Search of the Feminist Good Mother' (1998) 7(1) *Social and Legal Studies* 129; A Diduck, 'Legislating Ideologies of Motherhood' (1993) 2 SLS 461; M Fineman and I Karpin (eds), *Mothers in Law: Feminist Theory and the Legal Regulation of Motherhood* (Columbia University Press, New York, 1995); E Silva (ed), *Good Enough Mothering? Feminist Perspectives on Lone Motherhood* (Routledge, London, 1996).

108

Constructing the 'Family Man': Making the Modern Father in Law

The development of the welfare principle within case law and legal practice has involved establishing the 'best interests of the child' as the paramount consideration in any case which involves decisions affecting a child's upbringing. In the determination of what is best for the children, however, not all voices have been equal, and law has drawn on powerful normative discourses regarding the respective roles of mothers and fathers.[44] From the late nineteenth century onwards, informed by the emerging scientific paediatric discourses and changing ideologies of childcare of the time – as well as their own personal prejudices[45] – judges had begun to reflect these shifts in thinking about family and parenting. By the 1920s (with the welfare principle entrenched in the 1925 Act), the role of the wife/mother was increasingly emphasised in a social and legal celebration of the values of the family and marriage,[46] running alongside, and contributing to, the decentring of men as legal guardians noted above. Within this process, the good father ideal was to be reconstituted via reference to rather different assumptions about the role and responsibilities of the father as family breadwinner.

By the mid-twentieth century, the assumption that households would be organised on a sexual division of labour between a (male) primary breadwinner and (female) child rearer had been entrenched across a range of areas of law and policy. At the macro-level, for example, beliefs about the father as breadwinner were embedded in the model of the 'male wage'. The idea of 'providing for the family' bound men, as financial providers, within an economic system that structured household economies via the allocation of the role of primary wage earner to one family member (usually the man).[47] Post-war debates about the level, structure and distribution of wages, taxes and welfare benefits reflected the idea that men and women had different primary commitments towards their families. Sociological research, meanwhile, whilst showing that fathering practices in the UK were heavily contingent on factors such as socio-economic background and region, broadly reflected the extent to which these divisions had become embedded in household economies and prevailing cultural norms.[48] During the 1950s and 1960s, this model of the father as breadwinner was reproduced extensively within the domains of leisure, advertising and the

---

[44] C Smart, *Feminism and the Power of Law* (Routledge, London, 1989) at ch 1.

[45] Boyd, above (n 32).

[46] M Richards, 'Fatherhood, Marriage and Sexuality: Some Speculations on the English Middle-class Family' in C Lewis and M O'Brien (eds), *Reassessing Fatherhood: New Observations on Fathers and the Modern Family* (Sage, London, 1987) at 32; Boyd, above (n 32) at ch 1.

[47] H Land, 'The Family Wage' (1980) 6 *Feminist Review* 55.

[48] See eg: M Young and P Wilmott, *Family and Kinship in East London* (Pelican, Harmondsworth, 1957); cf M Young and P Wilmott, *The Symmetrical Family* (Penguin, Harmondsworth, 1973).

media.[49] Likewise, the texts of law (cases, statutes) of this period are, unsurprisingly, replete with assumptions about the 'natural' familial roles and responsibilities of men and women in relation to childcare, domestic labour, paid employment and the respective positions of mothers and fathers within the workplace and the home.[50]

Judicial views of the different responsibilities of men and women are particularly evident in the field of (pre-1989) child custody law, an area in which law has been widely seen as promulgating ideas of gender difference and which has itself been subject to much critical discussion.[51] Case law reflected dominant cultural beliefs that structures of masculinity and femininity were broadly compatible with (if not functional to)[52] prevailing models of fatherhood and motherhood. In particular, judges utilised a popularised version of sex-role theory and sex-typing through which to legitimate decisions about where, and with whom, a child should live following their parents' divorce.[53] More generally, understandings of men's familial responsibilities, as well as of the paternal masculinity of the father, were seen primarily in terms of an economic resource.[54] This is most clearly reflected in the history of the obligation to maintain, and, subsequent to the enactment of the Child Support Act 1991, it has pervaded debates around the administration of child support.[55] Paid employment has been interpreted as having a central part to play in the maintenance of a secure and stable masculine identity across many other areas of law, with assumptions about a father's primary commitment to his work seen as largely, if not entirely, precluding his extensive participation within both childcare and domestic labour.[56]

The entrenchment of these gendered assumptions about the respective roles of fathers and mothers in law cannot, however, be confined to the area of economic provision. The judiciary has also drawn on elaborate constructions of 'appropriate' masculine and feminine duties and responsibilities in the household, in such a way as to sustain, and legally endorse, a range of broader sexual divisions in

---

[49] L Segal, *Slow Motion: Changing Masculinities, Changing Men* (Virago, London, 1990) at ch 1.

[50] See below, pp 111–114 and ch 2.

[51] Boyd, above (n 32) on 'Maternal Rights to Custody 1900–70' (ch 3), esp at pp 49–54. See also, for discussion, work cited above at n 43; C Smart and S Sevenhujsen (eds), *Child Custody and the Politics of Gender* (Routledge, London, 1989); C Smart, *The Ties That Bind: Law, Marriage and the Reproduction of Patriarchal Relations* (Routledge & Kegan Paul, London, 1984).

[52] Cf: T Parsons and F Bales, *Family Socialization and Interaction Process* (Free Press, Glencoe, 1955).

[53] It is notable, for example, how structural functional accounts of sex-role segregation (ch 1) informed judicial views of the 'natural' roles and responsibilities of mothers and fathers, in ways premised on the opposition of the male breadwinner and female homemaker. For an early critique of the reductionism in this approach, see: A Oakley, *The Sociology of Housework* (Martin Robertson, London, 1974).

[54] RW Connell, *Gender and Power* (Polity Press, Cambridge, 1987) at 106. See further: Whitehead, above (n 35) at 124–38.

[55] See further ch 5 at p 150.

[56] Collier, above (n 15).

law.[57] The indeterminate and open-ended nature of the welfare principle has provided the scope for legal decisions to embody these gendered assumptions about men and women in the determination of what is 'best' for children. Judges have, to degrees, through developing principles of equity, introduced notions of fairness into the legal recognition of domestic labour and childcare as work of equal significance to paid employment. In this way, the law has sought to compensate for the economic disparities that can arise from how parties organise their family lives, not least in the area of post-divorce financial provision.[58] There has, nonetheless, been a 'flip side' to such paternalism, in the way in which law has constructed a strong correspondence between maternity, childcare and a woman's 'natural' familial role, often resulting in the vilification of those women who fall outside these traditional codes of femininity and motherhood.[59] Assumptions about the nature of fatherhood have themselves played a central role in this process. Households lacking suitable paternal masculinity have been cast as dysfunctional, with the father seen as an essential and desirable presence in the lives of children and the family. Significantly, therefore, in the move from rights to responsibility, it has not been through recourse to legal rights that married fathers have been bound to the familial. Rather, a distinctive model of normative heterosexual masculinity has been evoked in the discursive production of the father as a particular kind of responsible 'family man'.[60] It is this to which we now turn.

Unpacking the 'Family Man'

We noted above how, from the late nineteenth to the mid-twentieth century, shifts occurred in gendered ideas about parenting in law. The complex nexus of assumptions that constituted fathers as a desirable presence within families during this period can be grouped together via reference to three key themes. These are beliefs, first, about fatherhood as *heterosexual* (the sexual father);

[57] R Auchmuty, 'Unfair Shares for Women: The Rhetoric of Equality and the Reality of Inequality' in A Bottomley and H Lim (eds), *Feminist Perspectives on Land Law* (Routledge-Cavendish, London, 2007); O'Donovan, above (n 20); S Atkins and B Hoggett, *Women and the Law* (Blackwell, Oxford, 1984).

[58] See eg: *White v White* [2001] 1 AC 596; *Miller v Miller* and *McFarlane v McFarlane* [2006] UKHL 24, [2006] 2 AC 618 – interpreted as an effort on the part of the judiciary to move towards a substantive, as opposed to formal, model of equality in the area of post-divorce financial provision. For discussion see: Eekelaar, above (n 25) at 144–5; A Diduck, 'Fairness and Justice for All? The House of Lords in *White v White*' (2001) 9 *Feminist Legal Studies* 173. On the development of principles since then see: Diduck and Kaganas, above (n 13) at 258–71.

[59] A theme particularly evident in the field of crime and criminal justice: A Lloyd, *Doubly Deviant, Doubly Damned* (Penguin, Harmondsworth, 1995); H Kennedy, *Eve was Framed* (Vintage, London, 1993).

[60] R Collier, 'A Hard Time to be a Father? Law, Policy and Family Practices' (2001) 28(4) *Journal of Law & Society* 520; R Collier, 'In Search of the "Good Father": Law, Family Practices and the Normative Reconstruction of Parenthood' (2001) 22 *Studies in Law, Politics and Society* 133. On the 'family man' see: S Coltrane, *Family Man: Fatherhood, Housework and Gender Equality* (Oxford University Press, Oxford, 1996); Whitehead, above (n 35) 150–55.

second, about the father as family *breadwinner* (the worker father); and, third, around the idea of the father as a figure of *authority* within the household (the father as patriarch). Each of these has, we will proceed to argue, been subject to significant challenge not only as a result of social, economic and cultural shifts, but also as a consequence of changing forms of governance of family practices that reflect, in part, the increased centrality of ideas of formal equality and gender neutrality in law.

First, ideas about fatherhood in law have been historically enmeshed with beliefs about the normative nature of heterosexuality.[61] Legal marriage, the mechanism by which law has historically sought to attach men to children, has been, and, indeed, remains, an institution by statute open only to a man and a woman.[62] Marriage itself is based on a form of sexual consummation (intercourse) which has, in the past, involved law in an elaborate assessment of the bodies, sexualities and identities of both women and men.[63] 'Natural' sexual intercourse in law has been seen as something that does, or at least should, take place within the institutionalised context of marriage. Exemplifying how the father has appeared in this area of law as a distinctive kind of 'embodied' being, case law pertaining to marriage and divorce has entailed the judiciary making assumptions regarding the natural (hetero)sexual 'fit' between the bodies of women and men. This has occurred in ways that have rested upon assumptions about the 'potent', genito-centric, naturalistic and essential nature of male sexuality in marriage, a distinctive model of the father as heterosexual.[64]

Second, as we saw above, fatherhood has been constructed via reference to a range of sexual divisions associated with the dualism between the public and private spheres. In particular, a belief in the primacy of the demands of labour has underpinned the cultural legitimacy of men's disengagement from childcare and domestic labour. This breadwinner ideal, however, has not only involved culturally specific ideas about masculinity, it has also rested on assumptions about the nature of the male subject understood as a certain kind of rational, calculative individual.[65] The good father in this regard corresponds to the characteristics associated with the 'man of law' within a strand of feminist legal scholarship.[66] He is a man who acts in the public domain on behalf of his

---

[61] J Carabine, 'Heterosexuality and social policy' in D Richardson (ed), *Theorising Heterosexuality: Telling it Straight* (Open University Press, Buckingham, 1996).

[62] Matrimonial Causes Act 1973, s 11(c).

[63] L Moran, 'A Study of the History of Male Sexuality in Law: Non-Consummation' (1990) 1 *Law and Critique* 155; R Collier, '"The Art of Living the Married Life": Representations of Male Heterosexuality in Law' (1992) 1 *SLS* 543.

[64] A Hyde, *Bodies of Law* (Princeton University Press, Princeton, NJ, 1997) 172; R Collier, 'Male Bodies, Family Practices' (2002) in A Bainham, S Day Sclater and M Richards (eds), *Body Lore and Laws* (Hart, Oxford, 2002). See further ch 2, above.

[65] Collier, above (n 15) at 213–14.

[66] N Naffine, *Law and the Sexes: Explorations in Feminist Jurisprudence* (Allen and Unwin, Sydney, 1990) at 105. See ch 1, pp 29–30.

family,[67] a man physically and emotionally disengaged from the 'day-to-day' care of children. As a distinctive kind of gendered subject he appears, in marked contrast to mothers, a peculiarly *dis*embodied being, a figure bounded and constituted as male in ways dependent on his separation from other men, and, crucially, on a hierarchical difference from women. In chapter two, in the discussion of antenatal responsibilities, we saw the impact of these assumptions even before a child is born.

Third, and interlinked with the above, this figure of the father as family man has been inscribed in law with assumptions about men's economic power, prerogative, social respectability and authority. Bound up within the narrative of the modernisation of fatherhood, outlined above, has been as a process of rendering fathers 'safe' in law. This has relied on a cultural and legal bifurcation, between, on the one hand, paternal masculinities deemed to be responsible, respectable and familial, and, on the other, a multitude of dangerous, deviant and/or irresponsible masculinities seen to fall outwith the embrace of the 'safe' family man.[68] Central to the construction of the responsible and good father, therefore, has been an assumption that he is somehow different to the undomesticated, irresponsible and (potentially) dangerous male.[69] However, this 'good dad/bad dad'[70] dualism has itself been mediated by assumptions about social class, race, ethnicity and sexuality. These divisions have played out in different ways across areas of law, not least with regard to how cultural understandings of men's violence(s) in the family are bound up with ideas about fathers' authority claims, and in the classification of certain fathers (but not others) as 'errant', 'feckless' and 'deadbeat', as evidenced in debates around child support provision.[71] Meanwhile, the broader interlinking of fatherhood with ideas of male economic responsibility, authority and prerogative has had other consequences. It is, in particular, the interconnection of male authority and men's violence that has, in a sense, been the 'hidden history' of fatherhood in law. As Hearn has observed, 'the social and historical meaning of fatherhood includes the treatment of children as possessions ... even a man who is a "nice" father carries with him the possibility of becoming a "nasty" or violent one'.[72]

---

[67] 'Our man of law might be seen as the archetypal tough-minded businessman – the entrepreneur' embodying an ideal of manliness which 'encourage[s] accomplishment, autonomy and aggression – all in the service of an intense competition for success in the market-place': Naffine, above (n 66). Cf EA Rotundo, 'Patriarchs and Participants: A Historical Perspective on Fatherhood' in M Kaufman (ed), *Beyond Patriarchy: Essays by Men on Pleasure, Power and Change* (Oxford University Press, Toronto, 1987) at 37; Davidoff and Hall, above (n 37) at 110.

[68] Collier, above (n 15).

[69] *Ibid.* See also: R Collier, 'Men, Masculinities and Crime" in C Sumner (ed), *The Blackwell International Companion to Criminology* (Blackwell, Oxford, 2003).

[70] F Furstenberg, 'Good dads-bad dads: Two faces of fatherhood' in AJ Cherlin (ed), *The Changing American Family and Public Policy* (Urban Institute Press, Washington, DC, 1988).

[71] Ch 5, p 151.

[72] J Hearn, 'Child Abuse and Men's Violence' in Violence Against Women Study Group (ed), *Taking Child Abuse Seriously* (Unwin Hyman, London, 1990) at 76.

In identifying the above elements of the father as family man in law, we make no claim that this model, and these assumptions, ever necessarily reflected the social realities of men's family practices. As we observed earlier, there is no clear and inevitable correlation between the representations of parenting found in legal discourse, and how men and women actually live their lives. Thus, with regard to the idea of there being a modernising of fatherhood throughout the twentieth century, 'it is difficult to find any support for either a universal progressive democratization of family life or of the thesis of general cultural diffusion'.[73] Nonetheless, this interlinking of fatherhood, heterosexuality, male authority and breadwinner masculinity has had a strong cultural resonance. A key element of normative familial masculinity has been understood 'as naturally active ... as forming the identity of the male ... the key to a man's constitution, his character'.[74] Importantly, these gendered beliefs are not only reflected in law, they have also been a significant factor in the social conditions under which men and women are employed, bear and raise children, and live their lives.

In the remainder of this chapter, we turn our attention to what may (or may not) have changed in relation to the model of the 'good father' in law outlined above. While the legacy of these ideas about fatherhood persists, we will argue in the next section that this model of the father as family man has fractured, been challenged and called into question by the economic, social, cultural and political changes of the past three decades. It is a model of fatherhood, we suggest, which increasingly fails adequately to describe the complexity of the 'new fatherhood(s)' emerging in law and social policy.

II Making the 'Father Figure'?: Reconstructing Responsible Fatherhood

Fragmenting the 'Breadwinner Father': Contexts of Change

Three interlinked developments have together served to challenge the model of fatherhood outlined above. We will trace each of these in turn, before proceeding to explore, in more detail, how a rather different understanding of the responsibilities of married fathers, and of familial masculinity,[75] has emerged within social policy and law. A significant aspect of this change has been social care

---

[73] L McKee and M O'Brien, *The Father Figure* (Tavistock, London, 1982) at 18. See further: A Burgess, *Fatherhood Reclaimed* (Vermilion, London, 1997) especially at 35–73.

[74] O'Donovan, above (n 20) at 67.

[75] On how these relate to the idea of 'the problem of men', see Scourfield and Drakeford, above (n 7).

agendas that, over the past decade in particular, have assumed an increasing importance at the interface of family and employment law.

Fatherhood, the Changing Family and Child Development

First, the place of the father in child welfare and development has been subject to significant reassessment. We will see in chapter five how this shift has informed new understandings of the role of fathers in the context of post-separation parenting, but the development is no less significant in the way it has destabilised aspects of the above model of the father as family man. As noted in chapter one, research across disciplines has contributed to the increasingly dominant political and policy consensus that fathers have a significant, positive contribution to make to families, one which, importantly, transcends the traditional role of provider.[76] As in debates around the effects of divorce on children (chapter five), fathers are now widely seen to have a vital contribution to make to child development, offering a positive economic, social and developmental resource for children.[77] Whether in terms of a child's psychological health, future socio-economic status, educational achievement or adolescent development, social policy has, across a range of fields in the UK, increasingly been informed by the view that that the mere physical presence of fathers in the home is not enough.

The Children Act 1989, introducing the concept of 'parental responsibility', is a pivotal moment in this development. Section 2(1) of the Act provides that, in cases where a child's father and mother are married to each other at the time of birth, they shall each have parental responsibility for the child. 'Parental responsibility' encompasses 'all the rights, duties, powers, responsibilities and authority which by law a parent of a child has in relation to the child and his property', including 'the rights, powers and duties which a guardian of the child's estate … would have had in relation to the child and his property'.[78] The Act encapsulates the historical legal shift from 'rights to responsibility' outlined above. Yet it also reflects what had already become, by the late 1980s, a broader political and policy acceptance of the view that fathers' relationships with their children should, wherever possible, be encouraged by law.[79] At the same time, it is important to note how economic concerns informed these policy attempts to promote paternal responsibility. In this regard, the continued legacy of an economic model of fatherhood should not be underestimated, particularly in relation to the gendered nature of child support obligations and, subsequent to the Child Support Act 1991, the development of policy and politics around the administration of child support. Nonetheless, the emergent framework of child welfare and development, and the repositioning of the role of the father it entailed, has been a key

---

[76] See for example the work cited in ch 1, above (nn 52 and 57).

[77] See ch 1, above (nn 63 and 64).

[78] Children Act 1989, s 3(1). On the acquisition of parental responsibility by the unmarried father see ch 6 below.

[79] See ch 5, ch 6.

element in the process whereby law has, increasingly, sought to promote the idea of the 'involved father' in family life in ways which transcend the primary economic nexus.[80]

Fatherhood, Economy and Women's Employment

Second, and interlinked with the above, changing patterns of labour market participation have further driven the emergence of wider policy agendas seeking to 'bring fathers in the frame'.[81] A political concern to encourage and facilitate the employment of women, and tackle the social pressures resulting from their increased participation in the workforce, has profoundly disturbed the traditional family man ideal premised on men's disengagement from childcare and domestic labour.[82] As we saw in chapter one, employment statistics reveal a transformation in the labour market behaviour of men and women over the past 30 years.[83] Far from being assumed the norm, full-time, waged employment for men,[84] the nature of men's subjective commitments to paid employment, as well as understandings of its consequences for both families and individuals, has emerged as a policy issue – and, more specifically, as an obstacle to promoting both women's employment and functional, 'balanced' family life within the new globalised economy. Thus, it has been argued that legal reforms are required to provide a more 'modern' infrastructure of economic and social support, one that might, in turn, promote the caring commitments of *both* mothers and fathers both within, and beyond, families.[85]

Fatherhood, Heterosexuality and Marriage

Finally, the association between fatherhood, masculinity, and heterosexuality discussed above has also been disturbed in a number of ways such as to fragment the traditional model of the family man in law. While economic, cultural, demographic and relational[86] shifts around families have challenged ideas around

---

[80] See ch 1, p 20.

[81] O'Brien, above (n 3).

[82] R Crompton, *Restructuring Gender Relations and Employment: The Decline of the Male Breadwinner* (Oxford University Press, Oxford, 1999).

[83] Equal Opportunities Commission, *Facts About Men and Women in Great Britain 2006* (Equal Opportunities Commission, Manchester, 2007); M O'Brien and I Shemilt, *Working Fathers: Earning and Caring* (Equal Opportunities Commission, Manchester, 2003).

[84] C Handy, *The Empty Raincoat: Making Sense of the Future* (Arrow, London, 1994); R Sennett, *The Corrosion of Character: Personal Consequences of Work in the New Capitalism* (WW Norton, New York, 1999).

[85] See eg: Equal Opportunities Commission, *Fathers: Balancing Work and Family* (Equal Opportunities Commission, Manchester, 2003); S Dex and K Ward, *Parental Care and Employment in Early Childhood: Working Paper 57* (Equal Opportunities Commission, Manchester, 2007); W Hatten, L Vinter and R Williams, *Dads on Dads: Needs and Expectations at Home and Work* (Equal Opportunities Commission, Manchester, 2002); J Warin *et al*, *Fathers, Work and Family Life* (Family Policy Studies Centre, London, 1999).

[86] L Jamieson, *Intimacy: Personal Relationships in Modern Society* (Polity, Cambridge 1998); A Giddens, *The Transformation of Intimacy* (Polity, Cambridge, 1992).

the father as breadwinner, changes in relation to the institution of marriage have further undermined a model of familial responsibility and heterosexuality that, in the past, had legally bound fathers to families. It is true that, in law, marriage remains an essentially heterosexual union of one woman and one man, as noted above. However, marriage is no longer the sole vehicle used in family law to safeguard (legal) fatherhood, with a range of other legal concepts and techniques used to attach men to children.[87] Changes to adoption law allowing same-sex couples to adopt,[88] the legal recognition of civil partners[89] and of the social parent within same-sex households, alongside legal responses to growing numbers of non-marital births,[90] have each served to disturb hitherto heteronormative understandings of family life, and thereby challenge the place of marriage as the primary determinant of paternal rights and responsibilities. The elimination of illegitimacy as a legal concept, alongside increased legal recognition of the relationships of unmarried cohabitants, has further diminished the former primacy of the marriage tie between husband and wife in determining legal paternity.[91] Such developments are enmeshed with the broader re-visioning of the place of the father within the child development paradigm discussed above. Taken together, however, they have generated an increased emphasis within law on biological fatherhood and the social bonds between father and child, supplementing and even supplanting the focus on the traditional family based on marriage between a man and a woman (as well as those legal fictions with which it has been historically associated).[92]

Where does this leave us? From a position in which marriage had been the primary mechanism for grounding fathers' rights, fathers are now seen to have a more direct, unmediated relationship to their children. This is the background to the rise of a distinctive kind of 'new fatherhood' in law, one where the father takes an active, nurturing role. We explore this idea in relation to post-separation fatherhood in chapter five and unmarried fathers in chapter six. At this stage, we turn to look more closely at what this has meant for the development of policy around fathers' responsibilities within 'intact' families. In the next section, we will explore how these ideas coalesced in the social policy objectives of the New Labour government in Britain in the years since 1997. We consider, in particular,

---

[87] On the position of unmarried fathers see ch 6 on fatherhood in the context of post-separation family life see ch 5.

[88] Adoption and Children Act 2002.

[89] P Mallender and J Rayson, *The Civil Partnership Act 2004: A Practical Guide* (Cambridge University Press, Cambridge, 2005); *Wilkinson v Kitzinger* [2006] EWHC 2022, [2007] 1 FLR 295.Pre-dating the 2004 Act, note: *Fitzpatrick v Sterling Housing Association* [2001] 1 AC 27, [2000] 2 FLR 271. See also: *Ghaidan v Godin-Mendoza* [2004] UKHL 30, [2004] 2 AC 557.

[90] See further ch 6 below. Note, in particular, A Barlow *et al*, *Cohabitation, Marriage and the Law: Social Change and Legal Reform in the 21st Century* (Hart, Oxford, 2005) at chs 1 and 2.

[91] See ch 6.

[92] C Smart and B Neale, *Family Fragments?* (Polity, Cambridge, 1999).

how an idea of the 'new democratic family' embodies certain assumptions about the new fatherhood and, specifically, the changing nature of paternal responsibilities.

The 'New Father', the 'New Democratic Family' and the Problem of Men

The values of social justice, emancipation, gender neutrality, equality and social cohesion, each implicit in the above shifts around parenting, employment and marriage, have been integral elements of the 'Third Way' political thought which has informed the economic and social policy agendas of the New Labour government.[93] These values have shaped the introduction of various policy objectives relating to family life; the promotion of equality between women and men; the need to find a new balance between individual and collective responsibilities; a concern to protect the vulnerable; and, importantly for debates around fatherhood, the idea that there can be no rights without responsibility, and that to be a responsible citizen, whether male or female, is to be economically productive.[94] A particular model of (gender-neutral) familial responsibility has been central to the promotion of these values, and parental responsibility has itself been a recurrent theme within policy debates, not least around issues of family life, crime and citizenship, from as early as the 1998 consultation document *Supporting Families*.[95] The new democratic family is marked by a commitment not simply to formal equality between men and women, to mutual rights and responsibilities, but also to a negotiated authority over children, a joint commitment to co-parenting and a political acceptance that law has a role to play in promoting 'responsible' parenting and lifelong obligation to children on the part of both women and men.[96]

Each of these themes track back to political and policy concerns which pre-date 1997. We do not wish to overstate what is new about this development. However, as Lewis has observed, within the UK, the kinds of social care agendas around fatherhood with which these values have become associated had, prior to

[93] A Giddens, *The Third Way* (Polity, Cambridge, 1998); Scourfield and Drakeford, above (n 7); C Annesley, 'New Labour and Welfare' in S Ludlam and MJ Smith (eds), *New Labour in Government* (Macmillan, London, 2001). See particularly: B Featherstone and L Trinder, 'New Labour, Families and Fathers' (2001) 21(4) *Critical Social Policy* 534; K Rake, 'Gender and New Labour's Social Policies' (2001) 30(2) *Journal of Social Policy* 209; M Powell (ed), *New Labour, New Welfare State* (The Policy Press, Bristol, 1999). See also: A Etzioni, *The Parenting Deficit* (Demos, London, 1993).

[94] R Plant, 'Citizenship and Social Security' (2003) 24(2) *Fiscal Studies* 153.

[95] Home Office, *Supporting Families: A Consultation Document* (HMSO, London, 1998). A useful account of this document is contained in F Wasoff and I Dey, *Family Policy* (Gildridge, Eastbourne, 2000).

[96] See further ch 5.

118

the election of New Labour in 1997, been 'almost non-existent'.[97] Previously, policies around social care had been based largely upon the assumption that childcare was, predominantly, a private concern of the conjugal family; specifically, in practice, the mother. This can itself be seen as the legacy of the male breadwinner model we outlined above. State-provided child-care in the UK has been historically restricted, not universal in nature, and in some respects limited to those children and families deemed to have 'social problems'. Thus, the typical arrangement, in the majority of cases where mothers of young children were employed outside the home, involved the private organisation of childcare, whether through family members and kin, other informal care arrangements or else private and employer-provided nurseries.[98]

In marked contrast, the 'ratcheting up' of social care agendas over the past decade has drawn, quite explicitly, on each of the three themes outlined in the previous section: on changing ideas of child welfare and development, the shifting labour market participation of women and men, and social changes around marriage and parenting.[99] The new democratic family ideal underpinning much New Labour social policy has entailed a commitment to a rather different notion of family life and, with it, a qualitatively different ideal of the 'good father'. It envisages, in particular, a new sense of familial responsibility on the part of men. It presumes a model of family life in which there is a significant convergence in the lives of women and men in relation to their experiences and expectations of both the workplace and their families.[100] It entails, moreover, a view of 'active' parenting on the part of fathers as part of a re-visioning of familial roles, hitherto based on ideas of natural gendered divisions of domestic tasks and childcare. 'Making the father figure', by promoting good, effective and socially positive fathering, is now widely, if not universally, accepted as a desirable objective of government. The question, therefore, of what men do (and do not do) as fathers is explicitly called into account as an object of policy intervention. This has resulted in the emergence of a distinctive policy agenda, one framed around the social problem of fatherhood and the place of fathers in the provision of social care.[101] The role played by men in intact families has now been firmly written onto the policy agenda.

How then has the UK government sought to achieve this model of democratic family life? And how, in particular, has law been used so as to promote active

---

[97] J Lewis, 'Balancing Work and Family: The Nature of the Policy Challenge and Gender Equality' (Working Paper for GeNet Project 9: *Tackling Inequalities in Work and Care Policy Initiatives and Actors at the EU and UK Levels:*) http://www.genet.ac.uk/projects/project9.htm, at 2.

[98] See further: Daycare Trust, *Informal Childcare: Bridging the Childcare Gap for Families* (Daycare Trust, London, 2003).

[99] Prime Minister's Strategy Unit, *Building on Progress: Families* (Cabinet Office, London, 2007).

[100] M Kilkey, 'New Labour and Reconciling Work and Family Life: Making it Fathers' Business?' 5 *Social Policy & Society* 167; R Collier, '"Feminising the Workplace"? (Re)constructing the "Good Parent" in Employment Law and Family Policy' in A Morris and T O'Donnell (eds), *Feminist Perspectives on Employment Law* (Cavendish, London, 1999).

[101] Scourfield and Drakeford, above (n 7).

fathering? In the next section, we will explore these issues and the more precise framing of the 'problem of fatherhood' they have involved, through reference to the debate surrounding so-called work–life balance. This has become a significant feature of political agendas in the UK around parenting, families and employment, and, at the time of writing, shows no signs of losing its prominence.[102] Approached here as a critical case study of how social care agendas have served to reframe the responsibilities of fathers in law and policy, developments around work–life balance illustrate some of the tensions and contradictions which, we now wish to suggest, underscore the model of the 'new fatherhood' in law.

Promoting the New (Paternal) Responsibility: Care, Fatherhood and 'Work–Life' Balance

Children and 'families' seem to be everywhere in policy reform in recent years. From economic and fiscal policy to employment policy to social security policy, if the goal is to 'help' as many people into work as possible, government now seems to appreciate that a person's caring responsibilities must not be ignored.[103]

In the period since the election of the Labour government in 1997, a range of legislative reforms and policy initiatives have been introduced to support both fathers and the professionals who work with them.[104] Competing imperatives have informed these initiatives. First, the European Union has been a key driver of many of these changes, with discussions of fatherhood and work–life balance taking place in the context of EU attempts to promote a 'mainstreaming' of gender equality.[105] Second, the emergence of work–life balance agendas is enmeshed within broader conversations and concerns about child welfare, the

[102] In the first Queen's Speech since Gordon Brown became Prime Minister, for example, the government announced a proposed extension of the right to request flexible working for those with children up to the age of 17: Philip Webster, 'Flexible Working Hours for Millions' *The Times* (7 November 2007) <http://ste-edition.timesonline.co.uk/tol/news/politics/article2821194.ece>, accessed 24 January 2008.

[103] Diduck and Kaganas, above (n 13) at 94 (citations omitted). See also: A Diduck, 'Shifting Familiarity' 58 *Current Legal Problems* 235.

[104] Featherstone and Trinder, above (n 93); Collier, above (n 100).

[105] F Beveridge, S Nott and K Stephen (eds), *Making Women Count: Integrating Gender into Law and Policy-making* (Ashgate, Aldershot, 2000); C McGlynn, *Families and the European Union* (Cambridge University Press, Cambridge, 2006). Note the UK's adoption of Art 33(2) of the EU Charter of Fundamental Rights: 'To reconcile family and professional life, everyone shall have the right to protection from dismissal for a reason connected with maternity and the right to paid maternity leave and to parental leave following the birth or adoption of a child': Charter of Fundamental Rights of the European Union [2000] OJ C364/1.

120

changing nature of work and the shifting commitments and aspirations of both women and men towards their employment and 'family lives'.[106]

It is against this backdrop that the past decade has seen a heightened focus on questions of work–life balance across numerous newspaper, radio and television reports, as well as academic[107] and 'self-help' books,[108] articles,[109] and research studies.[110] While the core division between 'work' and 'life' is a socially constructed binary, we take the term work–life balance to refer to the connections between an individual's work and personal domains including the structural (time commitment, geographical location, family size) and psychological (job/life satisfaction, stress, general health and well-being) aspects of this relation. In the policy debates that have occurred in this area the potential beneficiaries of reconciling parents' commitments to work and home include; women and men, whether as employees, members of families or wider social/kinship networks; children;[111] businesses;[112], ultimately, the State itself, which will reap the benefits

---

[106] On the significance of the 2003 Green Paper *Every Child Matters* in relation to developing 'joined up' policy around child welfare, see ch 5, p 159; HM Treasury, *Every Child Matters*, Cm 5860 (HMSO, Norwich, 2003); B Daniel *et al*, 'Why Gender Matters for "Every Child Matters"' (2005) 35 *British Journal of Social Work* 1343

[107] The general literature is now voluminous. See for example: AR Hochschild, *The Second Shift: Working Parents and the Revolution at Home* (Piatkus, London, 1989); A Hochschild, *The Time Bind: When Work Becomes Home and Home Becomes Work* (Metropolitan Books, New York, 1997). Also: J Williams, *Unbending Gender: Why Family and Work Conflict and What To Do About It* (Oxford University Press, New York, 2000); S Lewis and J Lewis (eds), *The Work–Family Challenge: Rethinking Employment* (Sage, London, 1996).

[108] It is noticeable that the majority of books in this area have taken the form of popular 'self-help' guides.

[109] Eg: S Lewis, 'Family Friendly Employment Policies' (1997) 4(1) *Gender, Work and Organization* 13.

[110] In addition to work cited above, see eg: B Hayward, B Fong and A Thornton, *The Third Work-Life Balance Employer Survey: Main Findings*, Employment Relations Research Series 86 (Department for Business, Enterprise and Regulatory Reform, London, 2007); S Dex and C Smith, *The Nature and Pattern of Family-Friendly Employment Policies in Britain* (The Policy Press, Bristol, 2002); S Dex, *Families and Work in the Twenty-first Century* (Joseph Rowntree Foundation, York 2003); S Bond *et al*, *Family Friendly Working? Putting Policy Into Practice* (The Policy Press, Bristol, 2002); Women and Equality Unit, *Improving Life at Work: Advancing Women in the Workplace* (Department of Trade and Industry, London, 2003) at ch 7; T Hogarth *et al*, *Work Life Balance 2000: Baseline Study of Work Life Balance Practices in Great Britain* (Department for Education and Employment, London, 2000); M Fine-Davis *et al*, *Fathers and Mothers: Dilemmas of the Work-Life Balance*: Social Indicators Research Series (Kluwer Academic Publishers, Dordrecht, 2004); R Taylor, *The Future of Work Life Balance* (Economic and Social Research Council, Swindon, 2002); D Houston and JA Waumsley, *Attitudes to Flexible Working and Family Life*, Family and Work Series (The Policy Press, Bristol, 2003).

[111] The care of children will be qualitatively improved by spatial and temporal shifts in the working lives of their parents and/or other carers.

[112] Businesses will become more efficient and profitable as a result of retaining and recruiting a committed staff. This profitability encompasses issues of both organisational efficiency and productivity: S Bevan *et al*, *Family Friendly Employment: The Business Case* (Department for Education and Employment, London, 1999).

of more flexible responses to the demands of the 'new economy' within an increasingly competitive global market.[113]

Two themes pertaining to the responsibilities of fathers have particular relevance in the arguments supporting the notion of work–life balance. First, 'father-sensitive'[114] legislation is advocated in order to encourage and promote a different kind of family practice on the part of men. Second, fathers' long and/or inflexible working hours are seen to have a deleterious impact on individuals, families and society. Such work patterns clash, in particular, both with the ideal of the nurturing father contained within the child welfare and development model described above, and with the egalitarian, gender-neutral, new democratic family ideal. We turn now to the impact of these ideas on specific legislative reforms and policies.

'Policies for Working Families': Making the 'Father Figure'

A range of legislative reforms in England and Wales, in the areas of childcare, welfare, employment and taxation, have been presented by the government as constituting a coherent, thought-out and comprehensive package of policies for working families.[115] Encompassing the fields of economic and fiscal management,[116] employment[117] and social security law, a key aim has been to 'enhance family life while making it easier for *both men and women* who work to avoid conflicts between their responsibilities at home and at work'.[118] Published in 1998, the Green Paper *Meeting the Childcare Challenge* set out an early commitment on the part of the new government towards ensuring the availability of good-quality, affordable childcare for all children.[119] Along with the Sure Start

---

[113] Also of relevance in this context is concern about falling fertility rates: HM Treasury *et al*, *Choices for Parents, The Best Start for Children: A Ten Year Strategy for Childcare* (HM Treasury, London, 2004).

[114] O'Brien, above (n 3).

[115] For discussion of the principles that the government sought to follow in reforming employment law in this area, Collier, above (n 100).

[116] Chancellor of the Exchequer, *Investing For Our Future: Fairness and Opportunity for Britain's Hard-working Families: 2005 Budget Report* (HM Treasury, London, 2005).

[117] Department for Trade and Industry, *Work and Families: Choice and Flexibility: A Consultation Document* (Department for Trade and Industry, London, 2005).

[118] M Beckett, *Hansard*, HC, vol 312, col 1105 (21 May 1998, emphasis added). See further: C Henricson, *Government and Parenting: Is there a Case for a Policy Review?* (Joseph Rowntree Foundation, York, 2003); L Harke and S Lewis, 'Work Life Policies: Where Should the Government Go Next?' in N Birkitt (ed), *A Life's Work: Achieving Full and Fulfilling Employment* (Institute for Public Policy Research, London, 2001); S Lewis and J Lewis, 'Work, Family and Well-Being: Can the Law Help?' (1997) 2 *Legal and Criminal Psychology* 155–67.

[119] Secretary of State for Education and Employment, Secretary of State for Social Security and Minister for Women, *Meeting the Childcare Challenge: A Framework and Consultation Document*, Cm 3959 (Department for Education and Employment, London, 1998). The National Childcare Strategy embraces both formal childcare and support for informal arrangements for children aged 0–14. It seeks to both raise the quality of care and make childcare more affordable and accessible. Also of note in this early tranche of reforms are the National Minimum Wage Act 1998, the 'Out of School

programme,[120] the initiatives that followed have sought to support mothers and fathers by increasing the availability of childcare, and improving the health and emotional development of young children, whilst encouraging the workforce participation of both women and men.

The White Paper *Fairness at Work*,[121] also published in May 1998, set out proposals concerning the implementation of the EU Directives on Parental Leave,[122] Working Time and Part-Time Work.[123] The executive summary of the document launching the National Childcare Strategy captures government thinking in this area particularly clearly. In highlighting just why the Childcare Strategy and the working time and parental leave provisions are needed, the then Secretaries of State for Education and Employment, David Blunkett, and for Social Security and the Minister for Women, Harriet Harman, declared their joint belief that:

> it is essential to support childcare ... Society is changing as more women go out to work ... and fewer people live in large families ... Childcare is good for children ...it is good for their parents and others who look after them ... and it is good for the economy.[124]

Childcare' initiative and a series of consultation papers on early education and day care; see: Low Pay Commission, *The National Minimum Wage: Protecting Young Workers: Fifth Report* (HMSO, London, 2004).

[120] 'Sure Start is the Government's programme to deliver the best start in life for every child by bringing together early education, childcare, health and family support': Department for Children, Schools and Families, 'About Sure Start: Sure Start and the Government' (Sure Start website) <http://www.surestart.gov.uk/aboutsurestart/about/thesurestartunit2/>, accessed 25 January 2008. A key aim of Sure Start has been to support service development in disadvantaged areas whilst providing financial help for parents to afford childcare. Note that the policies and programmes of Sure Start apply in England only.

[121] Department for Trade and Industry, *Fairness at Work*, Cm 3968 (1998). This was described on the day of its publication by the then Secretary of State for Trade and Industry as a 'further landmark in our drive to create both a more prosperous and a fairer Britain': M Beckett, *Hansard*, HC, vol 312, col 1103 (21 May 1998).

[122] The Parental Leave Directive, originally adopted by the member states of the EU (with the exception of the UK) in June 1996, provides employees with a right to a minimum of three months' unpaid leave on the birth or adoption of a child to enable them to take care of that child. It also provides for employees to take time off work for urgent family reasons: Council Directive 96/34 of 3 June 1996 on the framework agreement on parental leave concluded by UNICE, CEEP and the ETUC [1996] OJ L145/4. See also EU Directive on Part-Time Work (97/81/EC). On the background to the directive see: Collier, above (n 100). See also: H Wilkinson and I Briscoe, *Parental Leave: The Price of Family Values?* (Demos, London, 1996).

[123] Council Directive (EC) 93/104 of 23 November 1993 concerning certain aspects of the organization of working time [1993] L 307/18, implemented in the UK by the Working Time Regulations 1998, SI 1998/1833. The Directive specifies, amongst measures such as minimum daily and weekly rest periods, rest breaks and annual paid holidays, a limit of 48 hours a week on the average time which employees can be required to work (except by voluntary agreement). On the UK 'opt-out' from the 48-hour average limit on the working week, see: Department for Business Enterprise and Regulatory Reform, 'Working Time Opt-out' (Information resource) <http://www.berr.gov.uk/employment/employment-legislation/working-time-regs/opt-out/page24607.html> accessed 28 January 2008.

[124] D Blunkett and H Harman, 'Foreword' in *Meeting the Childcare Challenge: A Summary* (Department for Education and Employment, London, 1998) at [1]. These themes are taken up in *Supporting Families*, above (n 95), especially ch 4.

This work–life balance agenda has since been extended. Following the enactment of the Employment Act 2002, employers now have a legal duty to consider requests for flexible working-time arrangements from parents of children under the age of six.[125] Significantly, for the first time, the Act grants statutory paternity leave to fathers, and provides that parents may also be entitled to unpaid parental leave in order to care for their child or make arrangements for the child's welfare.[126] All employees have the further right to take a reasonable period of time off work in order to deal with emergencies involving dependants.[127] Meanwhile, there has been a formal recognition that parenting practices can be influenced in positive ways by systems of taxation of income from employment, and by the allocation of income from social benefits.[128] Thus, in addition to the provision of established universal benefit to carers of children,[129] the introduction in the Tax Credits Act 2002 of the Child Tax Credit and the Working Tax Credit[130] has created new tax advantages for those parents who care for children.[131] More recently, in 2004, as part of a 'ten year strategy'[132] around childcare, the government announced a further emphasis on the social importance of providing high quality, flexible childcare by which *all* parents, mothers and fathers, will be better supported in the choices they make about work and family responsibilities. The Work and Families Act 2006 enhances measures already introduced by extending maternity and adoption pay from 26 weeks to 52 weeks and widening the scope of the existing law to enable carers of adults to request to work flexibly. It also, significantly, introduces a scheme that provides employed

[125] O'Brien and Shemilt suggest that take-up of flexible working was generally low before this requirement was introduced: M O'Brien and I Shemilt, above (n 83).

[126] The Paternity and Adoption Leave (Adoption from Overseas) Regulations 2003, SI 2003/921. Fathers who have completed six months of service with their employer at the fifteenth week before the baby is due may take one or two consecutive weeks' paternity leave at any time in the eight weeks following the baby's birth. These fathers are entitled to Statutory Paternity Pay during their paternity leave. Adopting parents are now entitled to similar rights to those vesting in natural parents. In addition, an unmarried same- or opposite-sex partner may be entitled to paternity or adoption leave: *ibid.*

[127] Dependants are here defined as spouses, partners, children, parents or anyone who lives with the employee as part of his or her family.

[128] See Diduck and Kaganas, above (n 13) at 107–10.

[129] Notably in the form of Child Benefit, a universal cash payment paid to the parent with care. This has been assumed to be the mother unless the mother applies for another person to receive it. Subsequent to the Child Trust Funds Act 2004 the government has also issued a voucher automatically to all carers receiving Child Benefit to start an account for all children born on or after 1 September 2002.

[130] These came into effect in April 2003: Child Tax Credit (Amendment) Regulations 2003, SI 2003/738, and Working Tax Credit (Payment by Employers) (Amendment) Regulations 2003, SI 2003/715. See further: A Mumford, 'Working Towards Credit for Parenting: A Consideration of Tax Credits as a Feminist Enterprise' in A Diduck and K O'Donovan, *Feminist Perspectives on Family Law*, Feminist Perspectives Series (Routledge-Cavendish, London, 2006).

[131] The amount which is received depends on level of income and caring responsibilities. This measure is designed to provide benefits to those with lower incomes, including elements that seek to take account of caring responsibilities.

[132] HM Treasury *et al*, above (n 113).

fathers with a new entitlement to take leave to care for a child, and an entitlement to receive pay while they are on leave.[133]

The above initiatives are just part of the broader picture whereby the government has sought to promote an active, engaged model of fatherhood. Funding has also been made available to a range of groups and organisations at both national and local levels seeking to provide fathers with advice, skills and information, and otherwise to promote their involvement in child-rearing and family life. Especially noteworthy is the Fatherhood Institute (formerly Fathers Direct),which aims to improve the interpersonal and parenting skills of fathers, and encourage positive relationships between children and fathers. The work of the Fatherhood Institute embraces not simply advice and information provision, but also support for projects concerned with reflecting the diversity of fatherhood.[134] Elsewhere, albeit with different remits and histories, the Family Welfare Association,[135] the National Family and Parenting Institute,[136] and Parentline Plus,[137] are also involved with a range of issues around fathers and fatherhood. The promotion and support of fathering at the local level, meanwhile, is reflected in the growth of community-based father support groups,[138] as well as in the wide range of professionals and practitioners working with families now involved in developing strategies and practices aimed at involving and supporting fathers.[139] Diverse in terms of aims, funding structure, membership and constituency, what unites these individuals and organisations is a commitment to developing services that might support fathers. It is at this local level, in particular, that there has been an attempt to acknowledge and engage with the heterogeneity of fathering practices and identities, not least in relation to issues around socially vulnerable fathers within a multi-faith and multi-ethnic population.

[133] Work and Families Act 2006, s 3.

[134] The Fatherhood Institute, particularly in its former guise of Fathers Direct, has secured a relatively high profile within political debates around fatherhood and has also sought to promote dialogue between different stakeholders. See eg: Fathers Direct, 'Family Sector Leaders Meet Government and Issue Call for Transformation of Separated Family Policy' (Press Release) (2 May 2006) <http://www.fatherhoodinstitute.org/index.php?id=4&cID=467> accessed 29 January 2008.

[135] Family Welfare Association, 'About Us', <http://www.fwa.org.uk/about.html>, accessed 29 January 29 2008.

[136] Family and Parenting Institute, 'About Us', <http://www.familyandparenting.org/aboutUs>, accessed 29 January 2008.

[137] Parentline Plus, 'Who We Are', <http://www.parentlineplus.org.uk/index.php?id=15>, accessed 29 January 2008.

[138] See eg: T Lloyd, *Fathers Group Evaluation* (Working With Men, London, 1996); A Richardson, *Fathers Plus: An Audit of Work With Fathers Throughout the North East of England 1998* (Children North East, Newcastle, 1998).

[139] This includes, for example, health visitors, GPs, community paediatric teams and family support and resource units.

To summarise: over the past decade a range of legislative reforms[140] have reflected the need to promote a more 'active', 'nurturing' form of fathering. A refocusing on the male parent across health and welfare service provision, at both national and local levels, has led to the growth of measures seeking to promote more effective fathering practices. In the final section of this chapter, we interrogate some of the assumptions about fatherhood that have underscored these developments, and assess both the possibilities, and limitations, of such legal attempts to change the behaviour of fathers. First, it is necessary to consider in more detail how ideas about the relationship between fatherhood and law have been interconnected in these developments, and how, in particular, they have served to challenge, transform and fragment the traditional model of the father as family man and breadwinner discussed above.

III Gender Equality, Gendered Lives: The Limits of the 'New Fatherhood'?

An initiative such as the Ten Year Strategy, concerned with the provision of flexibility and choice, availability, quality and affordability in childcare, illustrates a revealing shift in the way debates in this area have been framed.[141] As an official statement of policy, the link between quality childcare and child development is here explicit. However, it is not simply a question of parental and, in particular, maternal employment driving these changes. Rather, providing choice in quality childcare is not only good for the social and psychological development of children, it also has a key role to play in tackling child poverty.[142] We have moved in the UK, that is, from a position in which questions of labour market participation preoccupied politicians towards what appears to be a heightened policy focus around the interconnections of care, welfare, child poverty and the developmental needs of children. This has resulted in a further refocusing on, and an explicit recognition of, the role of fathers in the provision of 'high quality care',[143] throwing into question several aspects of the model of the father as

---

[140] These must be seen alongside numerous ministerial statements which have also sought to attack negative cultural stereotypes of fathers as somehow inherently abusive or uninterested in children.

[141] Diduck and Kaganas, above (n 13) at 95.

[142] HM Treasury, *Child Poverty Review* (HM Treasury, London, 2004).

[143] A measure such as the introduction of tax credits has been designed, it is true, to encourage more lone parents and second earners in couples to return to work. Initiatives around parental and paternal leave, meanwhile, like the Work and Families Act 2006, share an intention to keep skilled women in the workforce. Here, however, there is an acceptance that the private sector may be limited in the regulation of childcare provision: A Diduck and F Kaganas, *Family Law, Gender and the State: Text, Cases and Materials*, 2nd edn (Hart, Oxford, 2006) citing HM Treasury and others, *Choices for Parents, The Best Start for Children: A Ten Year Strategy for Childcare* (HM Treasury, London, 2004) at [2.44].

breadwinner outlined above.[144] Significantly, as child development is linked to ideas about the employment of parents in ways that are very different from, say, 30 years ago, there is a recognition that the care of children can no longer be seen exclusively as a 'woman's issue', and that 'fathers matter' too.

In our discussion of the family man in law, above, we noted a series of interconnections between paid employment and the idea of a secure, stable and distinctly masculine parental role and identity. This model of gendered work, we suggested, has been fragmented, however, with employment now seen as facilitating increased individual self-esteem, improved social networks, and psychological well-being for both sexes alike.[145] The 1998 White Paper *Fairness at Work* succinctly describes the government intention to recognise

> the *special responsibilities of both parents*. We place great demands on them. Most need to work to give their children a secure life, but children need their parents' time, too, if family life and society are to be cohesive. The White Paper sets out policies that will enhance family life while making it easier for *both men and women* who work to avoid conflicts between their responsibilities at home and at work.[146]

Whereas the earlier 'family-friendly' debates of the 1980s and 1990s tended to imply the development of policies aimed at those with specific needs – primarily, by implication at least, women with childcare responsibilities[147] – in these more recent policies the focus has shifted away from need and towards questions of equality of family responsibilities. The preamble to the Parental Leave Directive similarly states that the Directive is to act 'as an important means of promoting equal opportunities and treatment between men and women' by enabling both 'to reconcile their occupational and family obligations'. This has resulted, we suggest, in a problematisation of those practices and assumptions traditionally associated with fatherhood, men and masculinities.[148]

We wish neither to overstate this theme of equality and gender neutrality,[149] nor to ignore what remains a policy acceptance, in certain contexts, of gendered differences in relation to both employment and family life. Nonetheless, as Hobson and others observe, this policy shift around fatherhood is repositioning fathers' responsibilities away from the breadwinner model towards one of care,

---

[144] HM Treasury, above (n 143) at Annex A, paras 2.15, 2.16., 2.17 and 2.19.

[145] *Ibid* at [2.28].

[146] (Emphasis added). M Beckett, *Hansard*, HC, vol 312, col 1105 (21 May 1998).

[147] One result, it has been argued, is that there has all too often been a tendency to relegate such issues to the margins of policy debate, leaving mainstream, strategic employment operations continuing to be played out around a 'male model' of employment and family life.

[148] Scourfield and Drakeford, above (n7). See further ch 7.

[149] It is well documented, for example, that the period away from full-time work following the birth of children has a detrimental effect on the working lives of mothers, not least in terms of a drop in earnings, in ways it does not for fathers: O'Brien and Shemilt, above (n 83); Women and Equality Unit, *Individual Incomes of Men and Women 1996/97 to 2002/03: A Summary* (Department of Trade and Industry, London 2004); D Grimshaw and J Rubery, *The Gender Pay Gap: A Research Review* (Equal Opportunities Commission, Manchester, 2001); H Metcalf and A Korou, *Towards a Closing of the Gender Pay Gap* (Department of Trade and Industry, London, 2003).

and, in so doing, is bringing the UK into closer policy alignment with its northern and western European neighbours.[150] A rather different question concerns how this framework of gender neutrality itself relates to the desire and ability of fathers to play a greater role in their children's lives, in particular during their early years, as well as what this role might entail in practice. It is to this issue that we now turn.

Change, Continuity and Fathering Practice

We have seen above that one aim of the Children Act 1989, much like the Child Support Act 1991, was to encourage greater responsibility for children on the part of fathers. The 1989 Act is founded on assumptions about gender-neutral parenting, the belief that children might equally easily and competently be cared for by both fathers and mothers. In contrast, at least in formal terms, to the gendered ideologies which had informed past determinations of issues such as where and with whom a child should live, neither the mother nor father is now favoured. This gender-neutral framework notwithstanding, however, a wealth of research evidence suggests that parenting remains in many respects an activity deeply infused with social relations of gender.[151] This, in itself, may not render anomalous those assumptions about gender neutrality contained within the Act. It does raise questions, however, for the new fatherhood ideal contained within these debates around work–life balance. If there has been a policy acceptance that fathers *should* change, and that law has a role to play in facilitating such change, there is less agreement as to what extent fathering practices *have* changed – and, importantly, whether law might succeed in achieving these aims, given that it is itself based on certain assumptions about the nature of the father as a gendered subject.

To clarify: there is substantial evidence that the social experience of fatherhood (and of being fathered) has shifted, and is shifting, in both quantitative and qualitative respects. There is reason to believe, for example, that children and childhood have assumed a different significance and duration within the life experience of many fathers. Further, as children demand a labour (cognitive, affective and manual) that stands in marked contrast to dominant practices associated with fatherhood ideals at earlier historical moments, many men's relationships to children during (and after) marriage are changing.[152] Whilst

---

[150] B Hobson, AZ Duvander and K Halldén, Men's Capabilities and Agency to Create a Work Family Balance: The Gap Between European Norms and Men's Practices', Paper given at 'Fatherhood in Late Modernity: Cultural Images, Social Practices, Structural Frames', Conference (April 2007) (copy of paper with authors). See also: HM Treasury *et al*, above (n 113) at [2.40].

[151] Boyd, above (n 32); Fineman, above (n 43).

[152] W Hatten, L Vinter and R Williams, *Dads on Dads: Needs and Expectations at Work and Home* (Equal Opportunities Commission, Manchester, 2002); Dex and Ward, above (n 85); L Sayer, AH Gauthier and F Furstenberg, 'Educational Differences in Parental Time with Children: Cross-National Variations' (2004) *Journal of Marriage and Family* 1152. See further: G Barker and others, *Supporting*

women still do the majority of caring for children, evidence suggests that growing numbers of fathers feel personally committed to 'doing their share', particularly in contexts marked by high levels of part-time maternal employment and low levels of state-provided childcare. Accordingly, the reforms we have detailed may, one might assume, be welcomed by large numbers of men as well as women.[153]

In certain other respects, however, there is reason to believe that changes to fathering practices have not been so marked. Research evidence suggests, for example, that there have been only marginal changes in many men's participation in domestic work, and, in particular, childcare. Interpretations of time-use/ budget surveys, in the UK as well as internationally, suggest that the amount of time most fathers spend with their children has increased modestly over the past two decades.[154] Further, it is clear that many men experience real difficulties in combining paid work with childcare and their other commitments, even if they desire more 'balance' between the competing demands, and pleasures, of work and family lives.[155] Whilst recognising significant regional and international variations, as well as the complexity of conceptualising men's choice and agency in this area,[156] a compelling case can be made that many men have not changed significantly in relation to their participation in, and in their commitments to, childcare and domestic labour. There is reason to believe, moreover, that paid

Fathers: Contributions from the International Fatherhood Summit 2003, Early Childhood Development: Practice and Reflections Series (Bernard van Leer Foundation, The Hague 2004); C Lewis and ME Lamb, 'Fathers: The Research Perspective' in G Barker and others, *Supporting Fathers: Contributions From the International Fatherhood Summit 2003* (Early Childhood Development: Practice and Reflections Series, Bernard van Leer Foundation, The Hague, 2004).

[153] Note, eg the research above (n 152).

[154] O'Brien and Shemlit, above (n 83); J Hearn and K Pringle, *European Perspectives on Men and Masculinities* (Palgrave Macmillan, Basingstoke, 2006); R Crompton and C Lyonette, *Who Does the Housework? The Division of Labour Within the Home: British Social Attitudes 24th Report* (National Centre for Social Research, Sage, London, 2008), suggesting that, in 1989, around a third of men believed that a man's job is to 'earn money', with women looking after home and family, whilst by 2008 this figure had reduced to nearly 17%. UK Time Use Surveys have tended to suggest that men spend, on average, significantly less time caring for children and engaged in domestic labor per day compared with women. Whilst there is evidence that some fathers decrease the hours they spend at work shortly after the birth of a first child, such an adjustment appears generally short-lived. Fathers in the UK work broadly the same hours as non-fathers and, significantly, typically state that they do not wish to reduce their hours of work: Office for National Statistics, *UK 2000 Time Use Survey: Dataset*, 2nd edn (Office for National Statistics, London, 2002); Office for National Statistics, *Key Statistics for Local Authorities in England and Wales: Census 2001* (Office for National Statistics, London, 2003); E Dermott 'Time and Labour: Fathers' Perceptions of Employment and Childcare' in L Pettinger *et al* (eds), *A New Sociology of Work?*, Sociological Review Monographs (Blackwell, Oxford, 2006) at 91. Whilst both parents' working hours have risen since the 1980s, the mother's childcare role appears to be sustained despite rising maternal employment. However, it appears both mothers and fathers, but especially fathers, have increased the amount of time they spend on childcare since the 1970s. Cf: AH Gauthier, T Smeeding and F Furstenberg, 'Are parents investing less time in children? Trends in selected industrialized countries' (2004) 30(4) *Population and Development Review* 647.

[155] R Crompton and C Lyonette, 'Gender, Attitudes to Work and Work life Balance' in R Crompton and C Lyonette, 'Project Seven: Class, Gender, Employment and Family', <http://www. genet.ac.uk/projects/project7.htm>, accessed 31 January 2008; New Ways to Work, *Balanced Lives: Changing Work Patterns for Men* (New Ways to Work, London, 1995).

[156] See further ch 7; also Hobson, Duvander and Halldén, above (n 150).

employment and the 'breadwinner ethic' still remain of central significance in the formation of a distinctive masculine identity for many men, and that not just fathers, but also other family members, perceive being a 'good father' as something bound up with the role of the breadwinner.[157] As Smart and Neale note:

> for the majority of heterosexual couples who follow traditional child-care arrangements, fatherhood still does not routinely provide an identity for a man nor necessarily an active, involved relationship with children … men's behaviour may well be changing [but] for the majority of fathers, fathering is something that they have to fit into a schedule dominated by paid employment, which tends to mean that their core identity is generated elsewhere.[158]

Alongside the important question of how fathers' relationships with children are often mediated by mothers (both during and after marriage),[159] this raises the issue of the 'gap' between, at the policy level, changing cultures of fatherhood, and the materiality of fathering understood as a distinctive, if heterogeneous, form of family practice. As we saw in chapter one, while the experience of 'being a father' is mediated by social class, race, ethnicity, and geographical location, as well as by a man's health and stage of life, it continues to involve, for many men, a trade-off between the domains of work and family. Many of the practices associated with good fathering remain firmly entrenched within the parameters of other aspects of conventional heterosexual masculine behaviour. Far from constituting any 'rupture' with the past, from this perspective we can see a considerable level of continuity with the model of the traditional father as 'family man' outlined above.[160]

One area in which family practices remain profoundly gendered is that of the financial and moral decisions parents take in arranging childcare and in deciding to have children in the first place. Some research suggests, for example, that the identities of mothers can be bound up with their relationships with children in a way that is not necessarily the case for many fathers.[161] The identities of fathers, in contrast, appear interlinked with still powerful economic and cultural imperatives around the meaning and value of paid work. Thus, while both men and women may have to negotiate issues of work–life balance, these can be experienced in very different ways. This failure to address questions of gender difference has been described as part of the 'rationality mistake' within New Labour's family policy. Mothers, it is argued, tend to make decisions about entering paid work, and the scale of their participation in it, whilst seeing a moral and practical

---

[157] Warin *et al*, above (n 85); O'Brien and Shemilt, above (n 83).

[158] Smart and Neale, above (n 92) at 118.

[159] Smart and Neale, above (n 92).

[160] Lewis and O'Brien, above (n 30) at 9.

[161] See eg: B Neale and C Smart, 'Caring, Earning and Changing: Parenthood and Employment after Divorce' in A Carling, S Duncan and R Edwards (eds), *Analysing Families: Morality and Rationality in Policy and Practice* (Routledge, London, 2002).

responsibility to care for children as their primary duty.[162] The responsibility to be a good mother,[163] that is, is experienced by many women as largely incompatible with the taking on of significant paid work commitments. This is not the case, however, or at least not in the same way, for the majority of fathers, who retain identities bound up with a primary commitment to undertaking the breadwinner role, albeit that this is an identity that has, undoubtedly, been modified. Attitude research from the UK, as elsewhere in Europe, suggests that there is little general desire on the part of either men or women for a move to a full-time, dual earner model.[164]

This raises the issue, therefore, of what individuals, as mothers and fathers, feel to be the morally proper thing to do when situated within particular circumstances in the context of their own personal lives and family connections.[165] It further raises the question of how wider cultural beliefs and the social infrastructure around care interact, so as to support, facilitate or undermine particular caring practices on the part of men.[166] We have seen in this chapter that legislation in the area of social security and employment has sought to shift a dominant structure of parenting away from a male breadwinner to a dual earner model.[167] However, the complicated moral and economic rationalities by which both mothers *and* fathers make decisions about their work–life balance suggest that the gender-neutral parenting ideal on which this policy has rested stands in a complex relation to individual aspirations and actual practices. Thus, evidence suggests many mothers still feel constrained in taking their full leave entitlement due to financial reasons.[168] Many fathers, meanwhile, encounter deeply entrenched institutional, cultural and organisational resistance to taking up what

---

[162] A Barlow, S Duncan and G James, 'New Labour, the Rationality Mistake and Family Policy in Britain' in Carling, Duncan and Edwards, above (n 161); S Duncan *et al*, 'Motherhood, Paid Work and Partnering: Values and Theories' (2002) 17 *Work, Employment & Society* 309; A Barlow and S Duncan, 'New Labour's Communitarianism, Supporting Families and the "Rationality Mistake": Part I' (2000) 22(2) *Journal of Social Welfare and Family Law* 23; A Barlow and S Duncan, 'New Labour's Communitarianism, Supporting Families and the "Rationality Mistake": Part II' (2000) 22(2) *Journal of Social Welfare and Family Law* 129.

[163] See further: V Gillies, *Marginalised Mothers: Exploring Working Class Experiences of Parenting* (Routledge, London, 2006).

[164] Hobson, Duvander and Halldén, above (n 150).

[165] V Gillies, 'Meeting Parents' Needs? Discourses of "Support" and "Inclusion" in Family Policy' (2005) 25(1) *Critical Social Policy* 70; G Marks and DM Houston, 'Attitudes Towards Work and Motherhood Held by Working and Non-Working Mothers' (2002) 16(3) *Work, Employment and Society* 523. According to Barlow and others, lone mothers who chose not to take up paid work did so on the basis of what they believed was 'the morally proper thing to do as a mother': Barlow *et al*, above (n 162).

[166] Burgess, above (n 73) at ch 5.

[167] J Lewis, 'Individualisation, Assumptions about the Existence of an Adult Worker Model and the Shift towards Contractualism' in A Carling, S Duncan and R Edwards (eds), *Analysing Families: Morality and Rationality in Policy and Practice* (Routledge, London, 2002).

[168] See above (n 149).

limited leave provision is available,[169] and can experience powerful subjective commitments to the breadwinner model of fathering. The desired goal for both men and women may be something more akin to a 'one-and-one-half' earner model of the kind most easily accommodated by women's part-time work.[170] Notwithstanding the introduction of paternity leave for fathers, the expectation of many parents continues to be that, in the majority of cases at least, the mother will take primary responsibility for childcare and the early development of the child.[171]

We have identified in this chapter a division between, on the one hand, fatherhood understood as a social institution, and, on the other, the practices of fathers at the interpersonal, micro-political level of an individual man's close and reciprocal relationships with women, children and other men. What we can see in the debates about social care and work–life balance discussed in this section is a conflation of descriptions and prescriptions of men's behaviour. If we think of the new father as a cultural ideal we can understand shifting legal principles as normative claims about how policy makers consider contemporary fathers *should* behave. Yet cultural discourses at the level of law stand in a complex relation to the other social changes informing the 'everyday' interaction between fathers and their children. These changes, we have suggested, are reshaping the relationship between fatherhood and law in some very different and at times contradictory ways.

Concluding Remarks: Policy, Practice and the Contradictions of the New Fatherhood

In this Chapter we have presented a socio-historical reading of fathers' rights and responsibilities. Focusing on the constitution of the 'family man' in law within the context of subsisting marital relationships, we have unpacked how a range of assumptions about gender and sexuality, masculinities, social class, child welfare and childcare, inform the production of the paternal subject within legal discourse at different historical moments. Law, we have seen, has embodied and reproduced assumptions about how parents do and should work and care for young children. These ideas have mapped, although not in any straightforward way, to dominant theories of child development and welfare, as well as to infrastructures of care within and beyond family and kinship networks. We

---

[169] See further: B Hayward, B Fong and A Thornton, above (n 110); O'Brien and Shemilt, above (n 83) at 13. Full-time UK male workers work the most hours of any of their EU counterparts, at a mean of 46 hours per week.

[170] A Manning and B Petrongolo, *The Part-time Pay Penalty* (Women and Equality Unit, London, 2004).

[171] Research into views of fathers, for example, points in different directions. See eg: M Thompson, L Vinter and V Young, *Dads and their Babies: Leave Arrangements in the First Year*, Working Paper Series No 37 (Equal Opportunities Commission, Manchester, 2005).

traced a shift, from the late nineteenth to the late twentieth century, from 'rights to responsibility' in law. In more recent years however, we suggested, a coming together of economic, cultural and political developments has served to reframe the question of what constitutes a 'good father' and responsible 'family man' in law. On one level this narrative can be read as a transition from the model of the father as a distant authority figure and breadwinner, to a paradigm marked, increasingly, by the new fatherhood, in which fathers are now viewed as having a central role to fulfill in meeting the day to day needs of children.[172]

Yet this story is, on closer examination, far more complex. It is certainly tempting to read the above narrative as one of linear progression, in which the position of men in families has been 'modernised', subject to change that occurs in identifiable stages. Such a view would be misleading. Writing in 1987, Richards suggested that, as our historical understanding of fatherhood increases, so does our ability to understand the present.[173] Notably, the shifts in understandings of the responsibilities of fathers traced in this chapter are more complex and multi-layered than the modernisation thesis would suggest. Social class, race, ethnicity and geographical location (for example, under-explored regional variations in meanings of fatherhood) are each important factors influencing family structures and fathering practices within specific locales and communities. At the same time, both the experience of caring and social responsibilities associated with fatherhood are mediated by individual biography and life history. The micro-political realities of fatherhood, the 'everyday' experience of breadwinning, domesticity and child nurturing, that is, all occur at the interface of structure and individual agency. Significantly, therefore, given the distinction identified in this chapter between fatherhood as practice and fatherhood as culture, between descriptions and legal prescriptions of a father's behaviour, any focus on shifting representations of the responsibilities of married fathers in law runs the risk of subordinating those fatherhood practices and experiences which might appear 'off radar'. This may be true, for example, of the sense of responsibility experienced by many non-cohabiting and separated fathers, as well as grandfathers, young fathers, disabled fathers, gay fathers and fathers from black and ethnic minority groups.[174]

The shifts charted in this chapter do reveal how hitherto hetero-normative ideas about parenting and families have been disturbed, challenged and fragmented. At the same time, however, we have noted the continued legacy and hold, not least in terms of collective cultural memory, of these earlier ideas about

---

[172] K Stanley, *Daddy Dearest? Active Fatherhood and Public Policy* (Institute for Public Policy Research, London, 2005).

[173] Richards, above (n 30) at 33–4.

[174] See eg: T Shakespeare, K Gillespie-Sells and D Davies, *The Sexual Politics of Disability: Untold Desires* (Cassell, London, 1996); J Weeks, B Heaphy and C Donovan, *Same-sex Intimacies: Families of Choice and Other Life Experiments* (Routledge, London, 2001).

fatherhood.[175] In recognising the co-existence of change and continuity, we suggest that fathers continue, in certain contexts, to be situated as guarantors of social and familial order, as subjects associated with a primary economic obligation and responsibility. The idea, for example, that a father's primary commitment and identification will – and should – be with paid employment remains powerful. And, as we shall see in chapter five, the obligation on men to provide financially for their children continues to be emphasised particularly strongly in certain areas of law (notably in respect of the Child Support Act 1991). The experience of fatherhood continues to involve, for most men, a temporal and spatial trade-off between the domains of work and family.

This raises the question of how parental choice has been understood within the work–life balance debates discussed above. What has often been unclear is how choice is constrained and bound up with the gendered rationalities considered in this chapter, particularly in terms of how men's capabilities and agency figure in the policy promotion of work–family balance.[176] As Lewis asks, regarding the limits of legal intervention:

> Are men to be cajoled or coerced? Probably not, but if it is increasingly assumed that women and men will be more self-provisioning – for example, in respect of pensions – then the bottom line is that women and men must be in a position to make genuine choices to work and to care.[177]

Notwithstanding the policy package we have outlined in this chapter, what remains unclear is how it might be made possible for fathers to choose to care. Heterosexual relationships and the roles of men and women as parents continue to be ideologically reproduced in such a way that dominant ideas of fatherhood continue, in many respects, to associate fathers with a sense of physical detachment and emotional disengagement from domestic labour and the 'day-to-day' care of children. Research has highlighted significant obstacles towards greater participation on the part of those men who *do* wish to care for children. In relation to policies discussed above, such as the introduction of Sure Start services and the emergence of father support groups within the context of social

---

[175] It is important not to lose sight of how psychologically powerful and resonant questions of cultural memory and the 'stories' that men and women tell about their families can be. See, for discussion: C Smart, *Personal Life* (Polity, Cambridge, 2007).

[176] Hobson, Duvander and Halldén, above (n 150); J Lewis and S Guillari, 'The Adult Worker Model Family, Gender Equality and Care: The Search for New Policy Principles and the Possibilities and Problems of a Capabilities Approach' (2005) 34(1) *Economy & Society* 76; A.Sen, 'Capability and Well-being' in M Nussbaum and A Sen (eds), *The Quality of Life* (Oxford University Press, Oxford, 2003).

[177] Lewis, above (n 97).

and health care provision,[178] research suggests fathers' take-up of support continues to be limited.[179] Many fathers do not see *themselves*, indeed, as in need of support.[180] A growing literature tracks the possible reasons for the low participation rates of fathers in family support services, as well as the practical barriers that can deter them from accessing such services in the first place. The way in which fathering practice is itself often mediated through the agency of mothers further complicates this picture, an issue we consider in chapter five.[181]

As Jane Lewis has argued, it is ultimately far from clear what the policy aim has been in this area.[182] Is it to promote gender equality, or to foster child welfare and development? Or is it to improve the 'quality of life' of individuals? Is it primarily economic, to get mothers 'into work', whether by degrees of force or the subsidising of childcare services? It may well, of course, be each and all of the above, but this does not mean that these policy aims are compatible. Writing a decade before the election of the New Labour government, Lewis and O'Brien noted how the heterogeneity of styles of fathering serves to invalidate the making of any general claims about 'the father'.[183] In the same way, we would suggest, the idea of the new fatherhood is itself misleading, obfuscating as much as it reveals about discussions of the complexities of men's parenting.

This brings us to the material basis of social practice and the economic and political dimensions of struggles around paternal responsibilities in law. The model of the male breadwinner, we have suggested in this chapter, along with the structure of welfare provision on which it has been based, is fracturing as a result of factors such as the increased fluidity in civil status, rising rates of 'family breakdown' and labour market change, issues we explore further elsewhere in this book. Far from interpreting the modernisation narrative as a progressive embrace of gender neutrality and formal equality, however, it is possible to see developments in this area as embedded within broader trends toward fiscal conservatism and economic retrenchment. Political concerns to promote a privatisation of economic responsibilities in families over the past 30 years have informed debates around fathers' responsibilities to a considerable degree. They pervade, notably, the history of the much maligned Child Support Agency (CSA), which sought

---

[178] N Lloyd, M O'Brien and C Lewis, *Fathers in Sure Start: The National Evaluation of Sure Start (NESS)* (Institute for the Study of Children, Families and Social Issues, Birkbeck, University of London, London, 2003); F Williams and H Churchill, *Empowering Parents in Sure Start Local Programmes* (HMSO, London, 2003).

[179] B Daniel and J Taylor, *Engaging with Fathers: Practice Issues for Health and Social Care* (Jessica Kingsley Publishers, London, 2001); D Ghate, C Shaw and N Hazel, Fathers and Family Centres: Engaging Fathers in Preventative Services (Joseph Rowntree Foundation, York, 2000); Lloyd, O'Brien and Lewis, above (n 178).

[180] R Edwards and V Gillies, 'Support in Parenting: Values and Consensus Concerning who to Turn to' 33(4) *Journal of Social Policy* 623.

[181] See also ch 5, pp 165–167.

[182] Lewis, above (n 97). Note also: I Dey and F Wasoff, 'Mixed Messages: Parental Responsibilities, Public Opinion and the Reforms of Family Law' (2006) 20 *International Journal of Law, Policy and the Family* 225.

[183] Lewis and O'Brien, above (n 30) at 6.

since the early 1990s to oblige fathers, via an administrative mechanism, to provide financial support for their biological children.[184] In specific relation, meanwhile, to work–life balance, it is curious how the social care policies charted in this chapter have expanded in the UK at the very moment that other, more established, social policies around care have either stagnated or contracted.[185] Employers in England and Wales are not at present obliged to provide day care facilities for their workers' children.[186] Further, it is clearly economic imperatives and the 'bottom line' of Treasury concerns around public expenditure that, in many respects at least, have framed these debates about the responsibilities of fathers.[187] More generally, the perceived demands of globalisation and market competition structure the labour market and work patterns in the UK in ways that continue to be profoundly 'family-unfriendly' for all parents, women and men.

Instead of presenting, therefore, a narrative of decline in the father as bread-winner discourse, it is preferable to see the heightening of neo-liberal economic and political agendas within western states as having resulted in a reframing of the economic and cultural terrain in which these debates about individual parental 'choice' take place. The 'father as breadwinner' model, and the masculinities with which it has been associated, have not been supplanted in law. Rather, they exist alongside, and in tension with, the new ideology of the 'father as carer'. It is assumed that both men and women should be engaged in paid employment. Yet the conditions in which they do so are marked not only by the 'gendered rationalities' discussed in this chapter, but also by increased insecurity, high levels of casualisation and entrenched polarisation within the workforce.[188] In such a context, much childcare and domestic labour now passes to third parties, whether statutory or market providers; or, increasingly, in certain parts of the country, and amongst some privileged social groups in particular, to migrant workers. Such a passing on of care and domestic labour does not mean that structures of power and inequality have faded away. Rather, they are being displaced within an increasingly global and mobile economy in ways that cut across traditional gendered class and race divisions.

In this chapter, we have looked at law's ideal model of fatherhood – that which occurs in the subsisting marital unit, and traced some important shifts in what it means, within this model, to be a 'good' father. We suggested that fathering in this context has increasingly been problematised, rendering it an appropriate object of policy intervention. In the two following chapters, our focus moves beyond the

---

[184] The CSA has now been replaced by the Child Maintenance and Enforcement Commission. See further ch 5.

[185] Lewis, above (n 97).

[186] For a detailed discussion and visioning of the scale of reform required to institute such changes (and in the US context) see: M Fineman, *The Autonomy Myth* (Free Press, New York, 2004).

[187] Cf: J Carbone, *From Partners to Parents: The Second Revolution in Family Law* (Columbia University Press, New York, 2000).

[188] Sennett, above (n 84).

136

legal treatment of fatherhood within this subsisting marital unit, to areas that fall outwith it. In chapters five and six, we focus on post-separation fatherhood and unmarried fatherhood, respectively. We have already noted that such a division of material clearly leaves scope for overlap: for example, any father, married or unmarried, may face the work–life balance issues addressed in this chapter and benefit from some of the policy initiatives discussed above. Yet consideration of how law has understood fatherhood within these different contexts reveals some important differences in how fathering is problematised therein.

5

Post-separation Fatherhood

Introduction

IN THE PREVIOUS chapter, we traced a number of shifts in the nature of fathers' rights and responsibilities in the context of subsisting marital relationships. Focusing on the social and legal contours of the idea of the father as 'family man', we charted the emergence of a father figure marked by rather different assumptions to those which had prevailed at earlier historical moments. Notwithstanding the heightened cultural visibility of a 'new fatherhood' narrative, however, we suggested that legal understandings of fatherhood remain marked by a considerable degree of continuity, particularly in terms of the still resonant breadwinner model of paternal responsibility. In this chapter and the next we move on to consider law's treatment of fatherhood outside the subsisting marital relationship, focusing first on the idea of the 'good father' in laws regulating post-separation parenting.[1] We will see how the model of new fatherhood traced in the last chapter has played out in some different ways in the field of divorce law. It is in family policy debates regarding the area of post-separation fatherhood (or, more accurately, fatherhoods), in particular, that the emergence of a new politics of fatherhood and law has become, in recent years, increasingly significant.

The principal focus of these contestations around law reform has been the issue of fathers' legal rights and responsibilities, notably, although not exclusively, in relation to post-separation contact, residence and financial arrangements. It is particularly in this context that a range of fathers' rights groups has sought to 'refashion and reposition fatherhood in the legal and cultural imaginary',[2] drawing explicitly on the ideas of equality and the image of the caring father as

---

[1] As noted in the previous chapter, the separation of material between chs 4, 5 and 6 is for analytical convenience. Our discussion of post-separation fatherhood in this chapter includes those men who have previously lived with their children, whether married to the children's mothers or not. It will, however, involve extensive consideration of the evolution of divorce law as one important locus of debate regarding appropriate post-separation fathering.

[2] C Smart, 'The Ethic of Justice Strikes Back', in A Diduck and K O'Donovan (eds), *Feminist Perspectives On Family Law* (Routledge-Cavendish, London, 2006) at 123.

139

sharer of responsibilities introduced in chapter four.[3] What is happening in the field of post-separation fatherhood and law serves as a case study for revisiting the broader interconnections of law, gender and social change discussed in this book. It is most obviously in this area that men have been asserted to be the 'new victims' of family law.[4] Legislation, case law and the practices of judges, solicitors and various court–appointed officials have each been described as biased and discriminatory towards fathers, out of step with the changing realities of family life discussed in chapter one. Here we interrogate these claims and explore how certain ideas about separated fathers' legal rights and responsibilities have themselves been redrawn in the context of the rise of the new fatherhood. Interrogating the legal and political terrain in which debates around post-separation fathering are now taking place sheds different light on the theme of fragmentation around fatherhood in law discussed in earlier chapters. Further, developments in this area raise important questions not just about the politics of law and gender in a more general sense, but also the very possibilities, and limits, of using law reform to regulate and change family practices.

Our argument is structured in five sections. We begin, in section I, by setting out the social context of present debates about fatherhood, divorce and post-separation parenting. We proceed, in section II, to outline the changing place of the father in the history of divorce law. Interrogating how a distinctive 'divorce problem' has reframed understandings of fatherhood in recent years, we consider the idea of the non-resident father as a 'victim' of family law. The emergence of a new orthodoxy around post-separation parenting within family policy has, we will suggest, served to reconstitute the father in a number of contradictory ways. In section III, we detail the framework of legal regulation that has resulted from (and, in turn, informed) this policy shift. We focus, in particular, on provisions introduced to facilitate contact between non-resident parents and children, aiming to foster a new kind of paternal responsibility on the part of men. In section IV, we unpack the assumptions underscoring these debates and explore the ideas they contain about the gendered nature of post-separation parenting. In the concluding section, we draw together the arguments of the chapter in support of the claim that a new political terrain has emerged around post-separation fatherhood, one that raises important questions about the shifting relationship between gender, care, rights and equality in law.

---

[3] See further: R Collier and S Sheldon (eds), *Fathers' Rights Activism and Legal Reform in Comparative Perspective* (Hart, Oxford, 2006) for recent discussion of the activities of the fathers' rights movement (FRM) in a number of countries.

[4] Collier and Sheldon, above (n 3); R Collier, 'From "Women's Emancipation" to "Sex War"?: Beyond the Masculinized Discourse of Divorce', in S Day Sclater and C Piper (eds), *Undercurrents of Divorce* (Aldershot, Dartmouth, 1999).

I   A Context: The Changing Nature of Post-separation Parenting

Debates about fathers' legal rights and responsibilities in the area of post-separation parenting take place in a context marked by a paradox. As seen in our discussion of the 'crisis' of fatherhood in chapter one,[5] there is evidence to suggest relationships between adult partners are becoming increasingly fragile. Much discussion of post-separation fatherhood focuses attention on the consequences of these changes in terms of 'family breakdown', raising questions about issues such as child poverty, youth crime and criminality and the idea of a 'crisis' in childhood.[6] The figure of the 'absent father' has been a key feature of these debates, linking men's (lack of) familial and economic responsibility to wider concerns about marriage breakdown and social disorder.

The above approach highlights the fractured, fragmented nature of contemporary fatherhood and fathering practices, locating them within a shifting network of social relationships between adults and children. An alternative reading, however, is possible. There is also evidence to suggest that relationships between men and children have become more enduring and are, in significant respects, qualitatively different from previous historical moments. Many men, that is, are now seeking a closer, more 'involved', 'hands-on' and nurturing relationship with their children, not only during subsisting marital and cohabiting relationships but also, and in particular, in the context of post-separation parenting. Divorce is increasingly culturally presented as a context that offers not only distinctive challenges for fathers, but also new opportunities and possibilities for men's parenting, calling for a new kind of fathering, a reappraisal of the model of the father as 'family man' discussed in chapter four. It is in the area of post-separation fatherhood that the nature of the division between fatherhood as practice (what men do), and fatherhood as culture (social ideas, beliefs about fatherhood) has played out within the legal arena in a particularly politically contested way. This combination of fragile adult relationships and the discourse of the more engaged, 'hands-on' father has, we shall see, proved a toxic mixture in debates around law reform. Before we proceed to explore these issues, it is necessary to look more closely at what is known about post-separation fatherhood.[8]

---

[5] See above p 13.

[6] See: F Williams, 'Troubled Masculinities in Social Policy Discourses: Fatherhood' in J Popay, J Hearn and J Edwards (eds), *Men, Gender Divisions and Welfare* (Routledge, London, 1998).

[7] There has, notably, been a growth in the publishing of self-help books aimed at separated fathers. See, for example: S Barker and A Einstein, *How to Be a Great Divorced Dad* (Foulsham, Slough, 2007).

[8] Given the increasing functional similarities between marriage and cohabitation, many of the following arguments around post-separation fatherhood apply to both categories.

Fathers, Divorce and Contact

It is estimated that almost one in three children in England and Wales will experience parental divorce before the age of 16.[9] Although statistical evidence of the number affected by the separation of cohabiting parents is difficult to establish, there are also growing concerns about the social impact, and potential legal consequences, of the breakdown of cohabiting relationships.[10] Divorce law is historically marked by shifts in understandings of fatherhood that reflect the social, economic and cultural contexts that frame the ideas about paternal responsibility detailed in chapter four. Drawing on a now extensive research literature, it is possible to paint a picture of the social context in which this debate about post-separation fatherhood and law has taken a rather different turn in recent years.

In around 90 per cent of cases, children living in lone-parent families in England and Wales live with their mothers.[11] A key concern in family policy debate has been around the number of non-resident parents (primarily fathers) who 'lose touch' with their children following divorce.[12] A significant proportion of children, however, do stay in contact with their fathers,[13] and the term 'absent father' should thus be used with a degree of caution.[14] Diverse relationships are encompassed by the term 'absence', and, in the UK as elsewhere, discourses around absent fatherhood have tended to involve moral assessments about the

---

[9] J Hunt with C Roberts, *Family Policy Briefing 3: Child Contact with Non Resident Parents* (Department of Social Policy and Social Work, University of Oxford, Oxford, 2004). It is estimated that around 45% of marriages will now end in divorce: Office for National Statistics, *Population Trends* (Palgrave Macmillan, London, 2008), http://www.statistics.gov.uk/downloads/theme_population/Population_Trends_131_web.pdf, accessed 30 March 2008. Around 150,00 children experienced parental divorce in England and Wales in 2001, 68% aged 10 or under and 24% under five.

[10] See eg: Social Policy Justice Group, 'Fractured Families: The State of The Nation Report', Policy Statement (December 2006), <http://www.centreforsocialjustice.org.uk/default.asp?pageRef=174>, accessed 17 December 2007; Law Commission, 'Cohabitation: The Financial Consequences of Relationship Breakdown', Law Com No 307, Cm 7182 (2007).

[11] See further: A Blackwell and F Dawe, *Non-resident Parental Contact: Based on Data from the National Statistics Omnibus Survey for The Department for Constitutional Affairs: Final Report* (Office for National Statistics, London, 2003); Hunt with Roberts, above (n 9).

[12] See eg: B Simpson, P McCarthy and J Walker, *Being There: Fathers After Divorce* (Newcastle Centre for Family Studies, University of Newcastle Upon Tyne, Newcastle, 1995); B Simpson, J Jessop and P McCarthy, 'Fathers After Divorce' in A Bainham, B Lindley and M Richards (eds), *Children and their Families: Contact, Rights and Welfare* (Hart, Oxford, 2003).

[13] R Creasey *et al*, 'Family networks and parenting support in England and Wales' in C Attwood and others, *2001 Home Office Citizenship Survey: People, Families and Communities* (Home Office Research, Development and Statistics Directorate, London, 2003). It is important not to exaggerate the extent of change and the fact that most children do grow up in stable family settings. At the same time a growing number do not live with resident fathers and there is a marked increase in the number of fathers who move between households: M.O'Brien, 'Social Science and Public Policy Perspectives on Fatherhood' in M E Lamb (ed) *The Role of the Father in Child Development* (John Wiley, New Jersey, 2004).

[14] J Bradshaw *et al*, *Absent Fathers?* (Routledge, London, 1999).

social behaviour of men and women which are mediated by assumptions about social class, ethnicity, race and locale. In the UK, this was particularly evident in the debates of the early 1990s around child support, which were dominated by representations of the 'feckless', 'deadbeat' and 'errant' father.[15] The figure of the absent father has assumed, more generally, an iconic status within 'pro-family' accounts of social change of the kind traditionally associated with the political Right, not least in variations of underclass theory.[16]

If the idea of father absence is both empirically and conceptually problematic, the question about post-separation fatherhood which has vexed policy makers, politicians and parents in recent years can be clearly stated: what can be done to improve the nature and quality of post-separation contact between non-resident parents (the majority of whom are fathers) and children? Research suggests that meaningful post-separation relationships between non-resident fathers and their children can be extremely difficult to establish and maintain, due to a combination of interpersonal, psychological and material/economic factors.[17] In particular, conflicts around separation may be intertwined with subsequent life-changes, such as when one or both parents choose to re-partner. These transitions can result in potential difficulties relating to financial arrangements, as well as negotiations around the presence of step-parents, step-siblings and step-children.[18] A rich research literature around post-separation fatherhood provides crucial insights into the difficulties that can arise and the conditions in which post-separation parenting on the part of fathers might be most successfully established and maintained.[19]

It is, notwithstanding the above, important to note that most post-separation parenting arrangements are, in fact, uncontested. For the vast majority, arrangements are made 'in the shadow of the law' in ways that, on the surface at least, appear consensual.[20] Only in a far smaller number of cases, estimated at around

---

[15] S Westwood, '"Feckless Fathers": Masculinity and the British State' in M Mac an Ghaill (ed), *Understanding Masculinities: Social Relations and Cultural Arenas* (Open University Press, Buckingham, 1996); R Collier, 'The Campaign Against the Child Support Act, "Errant Fathers" and "Family Men"' [1994]) *Family Law* 384; J Wallbank, 'The Campaign for Change of the Child Support Act: Reconstituting the "Absent" Father' (1997) 6 *Legal Studies* 191. These ideas, of course, continue to circulate: BBC News 'Shame bad fathers says Cameron', (22 February 2007), <http://news.bbc.co.uk/1/hi/uk_politics/6385781.stm>, accessed 30 March 2008.

[16] See further R Collier, *Masculinities, Crime and Criminology: Men, Heterosexuality and the Criminal(ised) Other* (Sage, London, 1998) at 129–33.

[17] For an excellent overview of this literature, see: GB Wilson, 'The Non-resident Parental Role For Separated Fathers: A Review' (2006) *International Journal of Law, Policy and the Family* 1.

[18] Parentline Plus, *Stepfamilies: New Relationships, New Challenges*, Report (Parentline Plus, London, 2005); M Smith *et al*, *A Study of Step Parents and Step Parenting* (Thomas Coram Research Unit, Institute of Education, London, 2003). On the legal position of step-parents see: A Diduck and F Kaganas, *Family Law, Gender and the State: Text, Cases and Materials*, 2nd edn (Hart, Oxford, 2006) at 161–3.

[19] Wilson, above (n 17); M Maclean (ed) *Parenting After Partnering: Containing Conflict After Separation* (Hart, Oxford, 2007); Hunt with Roberts, above (n 9), at 4.

[20] R Mnookin, 'Bargaining in the Shadow of the Law: The Case of Divorce' (1979) *Current Legal Problems* 65.

ten per cent,[21] is separation marked by high levels of conflict requiring legal intervention.[22] These contested cases have attracted a level of political, public and media attention perhaps out of step with their numerical significance. Yet for those involved – mothers, fathers and children,[23] well as grandparents and other kin and friendship networks[24] – these disputes, all too often, are bitter, painful, personally damaging and life-changing. For society, they raise questions about the social costs and economic consequences of relationship breakdown, issues with a particular resonance in the context of neo-liberal imperatives around the privatisation of economic responsibilities.[25]

It is these contested cases therefore, and the political debates to which they have given rise, that have been at the heart of the struggles about the politics of fatherhood and law in recent years. Debates about family law reform have focused to a large degree on the issue of post-separation parenting and related issues of contact, residence and finance. In order to understand *why* this has occurred, it is necessary to consider two further interrelated developments. In the next section, we outline, first, how the idea of the new fatherhood has been constructed in laws around divorce and separation. We consider how fatherhood has been reshaped in this area, and, more specifically, how developments in family policy have repositioned the father figure as a subject of legal intervention. Second, we proceed, in section III, to detail the legal regulation of post-separation fatherhood that has resulted from this shift, and consider how, in particular, law has sought to promote a new kind of responsibility on the part of separated fathers.

[21] See further: Blackwell and Dawe, above (n 11); Hunt with Roberts , above (n 9), who note that between around 50% and 60% of parents agree contact between themselves, with between a fifth and a third having no agreements (with resident and non-resident reports differing as to what constitutes agreement); see further J McIntosh, 'Enduring conflict in parental separation: pathways on child development' (2003) 9 *Journal of Family Studies* 63.

[22] It is important to note, in addition, that there is no 'one' type of conflict; see: B Cantwell, 'Battling Parents in Private Law Proceedings: are they getting the right treatment?' *Family Law* (forthcoming, copy of paper with authors). See also: A Buchanan and V Bream, 'Do some separated parents who cannot agree arrangements for their children need a more therapeutic rather than forensic service?' (2001) 13 *Child and Family Law Quarterly* 535.

[23] See eg: J Dunn *et al*, 'Children's perspectives on their relationships with their non-resident fathers: influences, outcomes and implications' (2003) 45 *Journal of Child Psychology and Psychiatry* 553.

[24] See: F Kaganas, 'Grandparents' Rights and Grandparents' Campaigns' (2007) 19(1) CFLQ 17; F Kaganas and C Piper, 'Grandparents and Contact: "Rights vs Welfare" Revisited' (2001) 15(2) IJLPF 250.

[25] See: S Boyd, 'Legal Regulation of Families in Changing Societies' in A Sarat (ed), *The Blackwell Companion to Law and Society* (Blackwell, London, 2004). See further ch 7.

II A History: Divorce Law, the 'New Consensus' and the Remaking of Post-separation Fatherhood

Fatherhood and the 'Divorce Problem'

It was not until the Matrimonial Causes Act 1857 that a divorce law applicable to the public at large was passed. The numerous Reports, Commissions and Acts of Parliament since this date, alongside a now vast body of case law concerning divorce, has reflected shifts in political, judicial, religious and public attitudes towards parenting, children and 'family life'.[26] The development of the law has reflected changing attitudes, not just towards the legal process[27] and substantive grounds of divorce (for example, and notably, in relation to the issue of fault),[28] but also about child welfare and the institutionalisation of heterosexuality in the form of legal marriage.[29] A rich socio-legal literature has explored the changing status of motherhood in the area of divorce law reform, charting the double standards which have marked this history and the essentialist beliefs embodied in legal pronouncements regarding the 'right' and 'proper' roles of women.[30] In more recent years, however, work has also explored the interconnections between fatherhood and divorce, tracking how assumptions about fathers, as well as mothers, have been bound up with the mutual constitution of (normative) heterosexuality and marriage across a range of discourses concerned with constituting the boundaries of the (heterosexual) 'family'.[31]

Two themes emerge in the studies of fatherhood and divorce law that are of particular significance. First, the figure of the father within law and policy has

---

[26] See further: L Stone, *The Road to Divorce* (Oxford University Press, Oxford, 1991).

[27] Following the introduction of the 'special procedure' in 1977, all undefended divorces could be obtained without a court hearing. Given that about 99% of divorce petitions are undefended this 'special' procedure was itself to become the rule rather than the exception: Law Commission, *Family Law: The Ground for Divorce*, Law Com No 192 (1990) at [2.2].

[28] A Bainham, 'Men and Women Behaving Badly: Is Fault Dead in English Family Law?' (2001) 21 *Oxford Journal of Legal Studies* 210. See further J Eekelaar, *Family Law and Personal Life* (Oxford University Press, Oxford, 2006).

[29] R Collier, 'Men, Heterosexuality and the Changing Family: (Re)constructing Fatherhood in Law and Social Policy' in C Wright and G Jaggar (eds), *Changing Family Values* (Routledge, London, 1999); R Collier, 'Straight Families, Queer Lives? Heterosexual(izing) Family Law' in C Stychin and D Herman (eds), *Sexuality in the Legal Arena* (The Athlone Press, London, 2000).

[30] S Boyd, *Child Custody, Law and Women's Work* (Oxford University Press, Oxford, 2003); C Smart, *The Ties That Bind: Law, Marriage and the Reproduction of Patriarchal Relations* (Routledge Kegan and Paul, London, 1984); See also: M Fineman and I Karpin, *Mothers in Law: Feminist Theory and the Legal Regulation of Motherhood* (Columbia University Press, Columbia, 1995); C Smart (ed), *Regulating Womanhood: Historical Essays on Marriage, Motherhood and Sexuality* (Routledge, London, 1992).

[31] R Collier, *Masculinity, Law and the Family* (Routledge, London, 1995); J Drakich, 'In Search of the Better Parent: The Social Construction of Ideologies of Fatherhood' (1989) 3 *Canadian Journal of Women and the Law* 69; A Dienhart, *Reshaping Fatherhood: The Social Construction of Shared Parenting* (Sage, London, 1998).

been revealed as a male subject encoded, at various historical moments, as both masculine and heterosexual, as responsible and/or irresponsible, as dangerous (to other family members, to society, to himself) or else 'safe'.[32] Second, throughout this history, debates around divorce law have been inseparable from broader political anxieties about the question of what is happening to the status, position, power and authority of fathers in families – and, indeed, to the institution of fatherhood itself. In the nineteenth and early twentieth centuries, for example, we find resonances with contemporary debates in conversations about the 'decline' of the father, and the 'threat' to marriage and the family posed by changes in the lives of women.[33] However, since the enactment of the Divorce Reform Act 1969 (henceforth DRA 1969) and the Matrimonial Causes Act 1973 (MCA 1973),[34] there has occurred a noticeable shift in the way in which the effects of divorce on men have been understood.[35] Each subsequent piece of legislation – for example, the Matrimonial and Family Proceedings Act 1984, the Children Act 1989, the Child Support Act 1991 (as amended), and the Family Law Act 1996 (FLA 1996)[36] – had prompted discussion at the time of enactment regarding the legal rights and responsibilities of men who are fathers. In understanding the period from the late 1960s to the present day as a transition from a discourse of 'women's emancipation' to one, increasingly, of 'sex war', it is possible to chart a number of shifts in how the legal status of the father has been understood.[37]

The reforms introduced by the DRA 1969 and MCA 1973 have been widely interpreted as part of an 'emancipatory moment', marked by a concern to protect women from the consequences of new 'liberalised' divorce laws. In the parliamentary debates which preceded the DRA 1969 and MCA 1973, various assumptions about men and women surfaced, painting them respectively as powerful and powerless familial subjects. It was recognised that 'divorce law must be just to husbands as well as to wives'.[38] However, the combination of men's relative economic power, and assumed 'natural' proclivities towards 'sexual (mis)adventuring',[39] served to constitute the (innocent) wife as the potential primary victim of divorce reform, albeit in ways mediated by assumptions about her social class and sexual propriety. A recurring image in the debates of the late 1960s and early

---

[32] In addition to work cited above at n 29, see: R Collier, 'In Search of the "Good Father": Law, Family Practices and the Normative Reconstruction of Parenthood' (2001) 22 *Studies in Law, Politics and Society* 133; R Collier, 'Anxious Parenthood, the Vulnerable Child and the "Good Father": Reflections on the Legal Regulation of the Relationship Between Men and Children' in J Bridgeman and D Monk (eds), *Feminist Perspectives on Child Law* (Cavendish, London, 2001).

[33] See eg: E Showalter, *Sexual Anarchy* (Virago, London, 1992).

[34] Prior to this legislation divorce law had been strictly fault based, built around the idea that one spouse was 'guilty' of a matrimonial offence whilst the other was 'innocent': Bainham, above (n 28).

[35] J Eekelaar, *Family Law and Personal Life* (Oxford University Press, Oxford, 2006) at 141–3.

[36] See below, p 158.

[37] Collier, above (n 4).

[38] Royal Commission on Marriage and Divorce, *Royal Commission on Marriage and Divorce: Report 1951–1955*, Cmd 9678 (1956) at [46].

[39] See: K O'Donovan, *Family Law Matters* (Pluto, London, 1993) at 77–9.

1970s is of the husband as a (potentially) adulterous man who, given the opportunity, might discard his 'faithful' middle-aged wife for a younger and more sexually attractive woman. This idea translated into widespread concern that the DRA 1969 and MCA 1973 might herald a 'Casanova's Charter' which could result in 'blameless' wives being repudiated by their husbands and left in economic difficulties.[40]

Whilst a desire to regularise and improve the status of the children of new unions remained paramount, a significant theme of these debates, therefore, was the implications of the loss of marital status for the 'innocent' wife, positioned as a potential victim of divorce law. Changes since the early 1970s reflect developments both in the social and economic position of women and men, and in the substance and procedure of divorce law itself. Importantly, however, they also reveal significant shifts in understandings of fatherhood within these debates about how law does (or does not) respond to the 'transformations of intimacy' considered in chapter one,[41] as well as changing beliefs about the place of divorce in society.

We divide our discussion of this issue into two parts. First, we consider the complex amalgam of social, economic, cultural and political shifts that have now repositioned fathers, rather than mothers, as the potential 'victims' of divorce law. Second, running alongside this development, we chart at the level of policy the emergence of a new orthodoxy within family law, which has served to reframe the father figure as an object of legal regulation in the context of post-separation parenting.

Divorce, Law and Social Change: Repositioning the Father as Victim

By the early to mid-1980s in England and Wales, a combination of women's increased employment and other cultural and sexual–political realignments were widely seen as undermining aspects of the economic and social bases of the divorce law reforms of the previous decade.[42] Ideas about equality and justice relating to men and women were advanced, albeit in different ways, in calls for

[40] *Ibid.* O'Donovan notes that in the debates preceding the 1969 DRA, the divorcing husband was constructed as a 'middle-aged Casanova... "a butterfly flitting from flower to flower"' (*Hansard*, 1967–8, HC, vol 758, col 884, cited by O'Donovan, above (n 39) at 78. As she puts it, the assumption was that 'Men desert women. Women are ditched'.

[41] A Giddens, *The Transformations of Intimacy* (Polity, Cambridge, 1992).

[42] Eekelaar, above (n 35). The organisation and registered charity Families Need Fathers, for example, has, since its formation in 1974, sought to provide advice and support on a range of issues to divorced and separated parents 'irrespective of gender or marital status', in such a way as 'to maintain the child's relationship with both parents': Families Need Fathers, Charity Profile (January 2000), <http://www.fnf.org.uk/about-us/charity-profile>, accessed 18 December 2007; see: S Secker, *For the Sake of the Children: The FNF Guide to Shared Parenting* (FNF Publications, London. 2001).

the laws relating to property and financial provision on divorce to be reformed.[43] For men, it was argued, it had become increasingly unfair to have to support a former wife frequently capable of supporting herself (and who, in many cases, would have access to a second partner's finances). For women, such a position served to promote a circle of economic dependence on husbands, damaging women's emancipation by encouraging, in the term imported from North America, 'alimony drones'. Such concerns fuelled debates around the enactment of the Matrimonial and Family Proceedings Act 1984 and the need for a post-divorce 'clean break'. The establishment of the pressure group Campaign for Justice in Divorce, for example, drew on these kinds of concerns about the implications of changing social, economic and sexual roles of women and men for achieving a just, fair, equitable settlement on divorce.[44]

Arguments about the substantive outcomes of divorce continue to resonate, not least in the area of child support (see below). Issues of property and financial settlement figure significantly in accounts of why it has been men, in particular, who emerge from the divorce process feeling aggrieved and embittered. It has been a common scenario within many settlements in England and Wales for the former marital home to be transferred to the wife's sole name, with the children continuing to live with the mother and the husband paying child support until such a point as the children leave full-time education. It is in such a scenario that many fathers can feel that, while retaining a significant financial burden, they have lost meaningful contact with their children, and, indeed, for some at least, that they have 'lost everything' (wife, home and children).

By the mid- to late 1990s, however, a number of influences were beginning to construct the divorced father as a different kind of victim of family (in)justice from that which had existed during the 1970s and 1980s. Increasingly, the issue of fathers' post-separation relationships with their children assumed centre stage in political debates about fatherhood and law. In this process three elements, in particular, were to come together in such a way as to reframe the father as a potential victim of law and the legal process.

First, the enactment of the Child Support Act in 1991 and the establishment of the Child Support Agency (henceforth CSA) brought about a new model of administration for the provision of child maintenance. The significance of this issue cannot be underestimated and is considered in detail below. Second, as seen above,[45] economic, demographic, technological and cultural changes brought about a reappraisal of men's contribution to practices of care and caring and of fathers' responsibilities during, and after, marriage. Third, there was to emerge, by the mid-1990s, a heightened and culturally pervasive (if ill-defined) narrative of

---

[43] Smart (1984), above (n 30).

[44] D Allen, *One Step from the Quagmire* (Campaign for Justice in Divorce, Aylesbury, 1982); P Alcock, 'Remuneration or Remarriage? The Matrimonial and Family Proceedings Act 1984' (1984) 11(3) *Journal of Law & Society* 357. See: Eekelaar, above (n 35).

[45] In chs 1, pp 10–15 and 4 pp 114–118.

'crisis' around fatherhood;[46] and, related to this, a convergence of ideas about crises in the heterosexual family, social risk and the nature of 'safe' and 'dangerous' paternal masculinities.[47] It is during this period, significantly, that a 'new men's movement',[48] marked by diverse strands and perspectives, increasingly sought to engage with the consequences of these changes around marriage and divorce for men and, in particular, for fathers. It is also against the backdrop of each of these debates and concerns that the emergence of a range of fathers' rights groups and what has become known as a distinctive 'fathers' rights movement' has focused on law reform campaigns in the area of divorce and separation.[49]

Taken together, this complex convergence of legal, economic and cultural developments served to reposition men, within both popular consciousness and policy reform debates, as the (potential) victims of family law reform.[50] Interrelated with these developments, however, was a shift in the way in which the non-resident father was understood within family law and policy itself.[51] This development, as we shall see in the following section, has further intensified the politicisation of the relationship between law and fatherhood in this area.

Constructing Consensus? The New Welfare Discourse, Co-parenting Culture and the 'New Fatherhood'

Concern with the (gendered) economic consequences of separation is, we have suggested, part of the history of divorce law reform.[52] More recent debates, however, rely on a general reconstitution of divorce as a particular kind of social problem in need of regulation.[53] Divorce is now widely viewed, not so much as a single moment, a 'one-off' event, but, rather, an ongoing process, one which obliges parents to 'position themselves in relation to a range of often competing

---

[46] Ch 1, p 13.

[47] Above (n 32).

[48] M Messner, *Politics of Masculinities: Men in Movements* (Sage, London, 1997); A Gavanas, *Fatherhood Politics in the United States: Masculinity, Sexuality, Race and Marriage* (Illinois, University of Illinois Press, 2004); R Collier, '"Coming Together?" Post-heterosexuality, Masculine Crisis and the New Men's Movement' (1996) 4(1) *Feminist Legal Studies* 3.

[49] R Collier, '"The Outlaw Fathers Fight Back": Fathers' Rights Groups, Fathers 4 Justice and the Politics of Family Law' in Collier and Sheldon above (n 3); R Collier, 'Fathers 4 Justice, Law and the New Politics of Fatherhood' (2005) 17 *Child and Family Law Quarterly* 511; Reputation Intelligence, *F4J Heralds a New Era in Political Campaigning: Media Report* (Reputation Intelligence, London, 2004).

[50] In the North American context, see eg: T Arendell, *Fathers and Divorce* (Sage, London 1995).

[51] See further C Smart, 'Wishful Thinking and Harmful Tinkering? Sociological Reflections on Family Policy' (1997) 26(3) *Journal of Social Policy* 1; B Neale and C Smart, 'Experiments with Parenthood?' (1997) 31(2) *Sociology* 201; C Smart and B Neale, 'Good enough Morality? Divorce and Postmodernity' (1997) 17(4) *Critical Social Policy* 3.

[52] M Maclean, *Surviving Divorce: Women's Resources After Separation* (Macmillan, London, 1991); M Maclean and J Eekelaar, *The Parental Obligation: A Study of Parenthood Across Households* (Hart, Oxford, 1997).

[53] S Coltrane and M Adams, 'The Social Construction of the "Divorce Problem"' (2003) 52 *Family Relations* 363.

149

discourses (legal, welfare, therapeutic and, more recently, human rights) and to find ways of living alongside them'.[54] Divorce, as a social experience, is 'framed at the intersections of legal practice, social policy, welfare ideology, relationship breakdown and personal pain'.[55] The authorities which have historically defined and delimited divorce as a problem for government by law have been established through, and have worked within, a broader regulatory apparatus concerned with the scrutinising of familial well-being and welfare. Importantly for our present purposes, however, the normative assessments made of the behaviour of women and men transcend any specific or general determination of the vulnerability of children and babies (or, indeed, the importance of marriage and the (hetero) 'sexual family').[56] They address a wide range of social practices and behavioural assessments of parents.

Families Need Fathers? The 'New Paradigm'

An awareness of the contingency and complexity of family policy has a special significance in considering these developments in the regulation of post-separation fatherhood. A new consensus has been identified on the part of politicians and policy makers that it is desirable for the non-resident parent – in the majority of cases the father – to have contact with his children, provided that the arrangements made are considered safe and in the best interests of the child.[57] This assumption has rested on two related ideas: the rethinking of fathers' financial responsibility, noted above, and a new understanding of the place of the separated father within understandings of child welfare and development. Put simply, and for both of these reasons, post-divorce families 'need fathers'. We will briefly address each of these in turn.

Economics: Promoting – and Enforcing – Responsibility: The Case of Child Support

The controversies surrounding child support liability are a significant feature of the politics of fatherhood and law over the past two decades. The troubled

---

[54] F Kaganas and S Day Sclater, 'Contact Disputes: Narrative Constructions of "Good" Parents' (2004) 12(1) *Feminist Legal Studies* 2 at 3; S Day Sclater and F Kaganas, 'Contact Mothers: Welfare and Rights' in A Bainham, B Lindley and M Richards (eds), *Children and their Families: Contact, Rights and Welfare* (Hart, Oxford, 2003).

[55] Kaganas and Day Sclater, above (n 54).

[56] M Fineman, *The Neutered Mother, the Sexual Family and Other Twentieth Century Tragedies* (Routledge, London, 1995); M Fineman, *The Autonomy Myth* (Free Press, New York, 2004).

[57] See: S Day Sclater and C Piper (eds), *Undercurrents of Divorce* (Ashgate, Aldershot, 1999); Neale and Smart, above (n 51); Smart and Neale, above (n 51); C Smart, 'The "New" Parenthood: Fathers and Mothers After Divorce' in E Silva and C Smart (eds), *The New Family?* (Sage, London, 1999); C Smart and B Neale, '"I Hadn't Really Thought About It": New Identities/New Fatherhoods' in J Seymour and P Bagguley (eds), *Relating Intimacies: Power and Resistance* (Palgrave Macmillan, Basingstoke, 1999). See further: C Smart and B Neale, *Family Fragments?* (Polity, Cambridge, 1999).

history of the Child Support Agency (CSA), set up by the Child Support Act 1991, as well as the subsequent amendments to the legislation, is well documented elsewhere.[58] These disputes form one important moment in a long history of contestations around the child maintenance obligation, dating from the time of the Poor Law.[59] The drivers behind the enactment of the 1991 Act are complex and reflect, at least in part, a move in family law towards the privatisation of economic responsibilities, as well as a reappraisal of the relationship between rights, justice and utility, rules and discretion.[60] The Act's introduction of an administrative mechanism to secure economic contributions from non-resident parents via the introduction of a 'child support formula' reflects the greater emphasis on extra-judicial dispute resolution in family law. However, the Act can also be seen as the product of a particular political and moral moment in British society, marked by a coming together of concerns about 'family values', absent fathers, a rising social 'underclass', crime and 'moral breakdown'.[61]

The 1991 Act was enacted at a moment of broad consensus that the existing framework of child maintenance was in need of reform. Following the publication of the 1990 White Paper, *Children Come First*,[62] the Act was initially met with guarded praise from across the political divide, reflecting a 'common sense' agreement about the need for new laws to address existing problems and 'make fathers pay'.[63] There was widespread recognition that less than one in three single mothers received any maintenance payments, notwithstanding fathers' established legal obligations. However, as soon as the new assessments introduced by the 1991 Act began to bite, the workings of the CSA became the object of considerable anger and protest on the part of fathers and their supporters. Significant substantive and procedural flaws were soon apparent in the operation of the CSA,[64] heralding what was to become a procession of reforms and amendments over the following 15 years.[65] What is noticeable about the initial

[58] For detailed discussion of child support see: N Wikeley, *Child Support: Law and Policy* (Hart, Oxford, 2006).

[59] *Ibid*. See also: M Finer and OR McGregor, 'History of the Obligation to Maintain', App 5 in Department of Health and Social Security, *One-parent families: Report of the Committee on One-parent Families*, Cmnd 5629-I (1974).

[60] Boyd, above (n 25); J Herring, *Family Law*, 3rd edn (Pearson Longman, Harlow, 2007) at 20–29; J Dewar, 'Family Law and its Discontents' (2000) 14 *International Journal of Law, Policy and the Family* 59.

[61] R Collier, 'A Father's "Normal Love"? Masculinities, Criminology and the Family' in R Dobash and L Noakes (eds), *Gender and Crime* (University of Wales Press, Cardiff, 1995).

[62] HM Government, *Children Come First: The Government's Proposals on the Maintenance of Children*, Cm 1624 (1990).

[63] Post-divorce orders for children were few in number and rarely paid regularly or in full, and enforcement procedures were widely recognised as ineffective. It is notable that, at the time child support began to be discussed more widely, the numbers of one-parent families on benefit, and their dependence on welfare support, had begun to be documented: J Bradshaw and J Millar, *Lone Parents in the UK*, Department of Social Security Research Report 6 (HMSO, London, 1990).

[64] Social Security Committee, *First Report of Session 1993–4: Operation of the Child Support Act*, HC 69.

[65] These reforms are detailed in Wikeley, above (n 58), especially at ch 5.

protests, however, is both their scale and intensity, and the way in which they drew on the idea of the father as victim of law reform as outlined above. The campaign against the Child Support Act was, in this sense, a sign of things to come in the area of contact.[66]

Three features of the child support debates are of particular significance for discussion of the politics of fatherhood and law. First, along with the enactment of the Children Act 1989,[67] the Child Support Act 1991 constitutes a key moment in shifting understandings of the place of the non-resident father in post-separation family life: both are emblematic of a legal understanding that a father is 'once a parent, always a parent'.[68] The specific focus of the Child Support Act is economic; promoting and enforcing financial responsibility. It is, however, inseparable from the more general attempt to reshape fathers' responsibilities and to bring law 'into line' not only with social change, including the shifting needs, demands and expectations of parents and children, but the requirements of the state itself (notably, a reduction in public expenditure). Since the enactment of the 1991 Act, further law and policy initiatives have developed this idea of refashioning a new kind of responsible post-separation parenting on the part of fathers.

Second, mobilisation around the Child Support Act represents a key moment in the development of political agendas around fathers' rights, a reassertion of fatherhood in the legal arena that has gathered pace in recent years as the debate about contact and residence law has intensified (see below). Criticisms of the CSA were systematically couched in terms of individual fathers being 'wronged' by its operation. The highly visible campaign against the 1991 Act thus marks a significant moment in the construction in the legal and cultural imaginary of the separated father as victim of family law. Third, the arguments deployed against the CSA reflect the conceptual ambiguity of fatherhood itself, in particular a tension between ideas of fathers as breadwinners and carers, a theme we explore in more detail elsewhere in this book.[69]

Notwithstanding the demise of the CSA and, at the time of writing, the proposed introduction of the Child Maintenance and Enforcement Commission,[70] there is no sign that concerns around child support and financial

---

[66] See below, p 159. The similarities with the more recent protests of the group Fathers 4 Justice are striking. At a demonstration in London on 14 February 1994, an eight-year-old child carried a poster declaring Ros Hepplewhite, the much-vilified head of the CSA, to be 'Wanted for crimes against fathers, families and humanity': Collier, above (n 15). Cf Collier (2005), above (n 49).

[67] See below, pp 155–156.

[68] J Roche, 'The Children Act: Once a Parent, Always a Parent' (1991) 5 *Journal of Social Welfare and Family Law* 345.

[69] Ch 4; also Ch 7, p 234.

[70] Following the report by Sir David Henshaw and the subsequent White Paper, the Child Maintenance and Other Payments Bill was published, setting out the reform of policy and delivery of child maintenance: Secretary of State for Work and Pensions, *Recovering Child Support: Routes to Responsibility*, Cm 6894 (2006) (the Henshaw Report); Secretary of State for Work and Pensions, *A New System of Child Maintenance*, Cm 6979 (2006) (White Paper); Child Maintenance and Other

provision will abate. Fathers' rights groups, as well as other stakeholders, continue to express deep concern about the perceived injustice both of the present arrangements and the reforms proposed.[71] Yet these developments around child support provision are, we will suggest in the next section, just one part of the reframing of the father figure that has occurred in the law regulating post separation parenting.

The 'New Father', Child Welfare and the Construction of Conflicted Separation as a Social Problem

The above developments around child support are inseparable from the broader rethinking of the role of non-resident fathers in relation to child welfare and development.[72] Quantitative and qualitative studies have addressed diverse aspects of post-separation parenting, with the result that much more is now known about the behaviour of both residential mothers and non-resident fathers within separated families.[73] Research has explored, for example, the nature and quality of non-resident parent–child and inter-parental relationships, the extent of fathers' participation within post-separation child rearing, and how these dynamics can themselves be mediated by the extent of fathers' maintenance or child support payments.[74] One issue, in particular, has emerged as an object of concern and debate at a policy level: the effects of divorce and conflicted separation on children. More specifically, social science research has been utilised by policy makers, politicians, lawyers and welfare professionals to support the argument that, first, conflict is harmful in and of itself (for children, adults and society) and, second, that ongoing contact between non-resident fathers and their children is not only desirable but should, wherever possible, be legally protected and promoted.[75]

Payments, HC Bill (2006–07) [118] (the 2007 Bill). A new child maintenance delivery organisation, the Child Maintenance and Enforcement Commission, is to replace the CSA, simplifying the way that maintenance is calculated and providing 'tougher' enforcement powers to collect maintenance arrears. For detailed discussion of reform options see: Wikeley, above (n 58), at ch 15, especially pp 491–509.

[71] See eg: Centre for Separated Families, 'CSA Reforms Will Make Little Difference', Press Release (12 December 2006), <www.separatedfamilies.org.uk/news/press_release_121206.htm>, accessed 3 March 2008.

[72] M Lamb (ed), *The Role of the Father in Child Development* (John Wiley, New York, 1997); ME Lamb, 'Father and Child Development: An Introductory Overview and Guide' in M Lamb (ed), *The Role of the Father in Child Development* (John Wiley, New York, 1997).

[73] Wilson, above (n 17); EM Hetherington and MM Stanley-Hagan, 'The Effects of Divorce on Fathers and their Children' in M Lamb (ed), *The Role of the Father in Child Development* (John Wiley, New York, 1997).

[74] Wilson, above (n 17); See eg: V King and HE Heard, 'Non-resident Father Visitation, Parental Conflict, and Mother's Satisfaction: What's best for child well-being?' (1999) 61 *Journal of Marriage and Family* 385.

[75] Wilson, above (n 17). Note also: RA Thompson and PR Amato (eds), *The Post-divorce Family: Children, Parenting, and Society* (Sage, Thousand Oaks, CA, 1999).

Research findings in this area are both complex and contested.[76] Nonetheless, a growing consensus emerged during the late 1980s and the 1990s that the experience of divorce tends to introduce potential risk factors for some children,[77] and that fathers have an important role, notwithstanding separation, in the socialisation and future well-being of children.[78] Thus, lack of contact has been seen to have implications both for the closeness of the mother–child relationship, for the economic contribution of fathers to separated families[79] and for the health of fathers themselves. It is far from clear whether a greater quantity of time spent with non-resident fathers does guarantee 'better' outcomes for children.[80] As Pryor and Rodgers suggest in their much-cited and influential overview of the research literature, the mere presence of fathers is not enough. Monitoring, encouragement, love and warmth and other 'active' positive parenting qualities on the part of fathers, however, are consistently linked with children's well being.[81]

It is not surprising, therefore, to find a growing acceptance at a policy level that the 'stakeholders' in reducing conflict and promoting post-separation contact with non-resident fathers transcend parents and child(ren), and include grandparents and other kin as well as wider friendship networks. In a context of a demographic change in which 'serial parenting' has become an increasingly accepted feature of social life,[82] policy makers and politicians have expressed concern regarding the social consequences of the number of biological fathers who do not live with their children. While the divorce law reforms of the 1970s and 1980s had been intended to facilitate and regulate a 'clean break' for

---

[76] For an excellent summary see Hunt with Roberts, above (n 9). Note, for example, debates in the 1970s and 1980s: J Wallerstein and J Kelly, *Surviving the Breakup: How Children and Parents Cope With Divorce* (Basic Books, New York, 1980); cf: J Goldstein, A Freud and AJ Solnit, *Beyond the Best Interests of the Child* (Burnett Books, London, 1980); J Goldstein, *Before the Best Interests of the Child* (Burnett Books, London, 1980). See generally: J Burgoyne, R Ormrod and M Richards, *Divorce Matters* (Penguin, Harmondsworth, 1987).

[77] See: B Rodgers and J Pryor, *Divorce and Separation: The Outcomes for Children* (Joseph Rowntree Foundation, York, 1998); J Hunt, *Researching Contact* (National Council for One Parent Families, London, 2003); M Cockett and J Tripp, *The Exeter Family Study: Family Breakdown and its Impact on Children* (University of Exeter Press, Exeter, 1994); J Pryor and B Rodgers, *Children in Changing Families: Life After Parental Separation* (Blackwell, Oxford, 2001); Hunt with Roberts, above (n 9).

[78] See also ch 4, p 115.

[79] P Amato and J Galbraith, 'Non Resident Fathers and Children's Well Being: A Meta Analysis' (1999) 61(3) *Journal of Marriage and Family* 557; P Amato, 'Father–Child Relations, Mother–Child Relations and Offspring Psychological Well-being in Early Adulthood' (1994) 56 *Journal of Marriage and Family* 1031.

[80] For discussion: Hunt, above (n 77); Hunt with Roberts, above (n 9); Dunn *et al*, above (n 23); JA Seltzer, 'Relationships between Fathers and Children who Live Apart: The Father's Role After Separation' (1991) 53 *Journal of Marriage and Family* 79.

[81] Rodgers and Pryor, above (n 77). See also: Hunt with Roberts, above (n 9); WJ Doherty, EF Kouneski and MF Erickson, 'Responsible Fathering: An Overview and Conceptual Framework' (1998) 60 *Journal of Marriage and Family* 277; R Parke, 'Father Involvement: A Development Psychological Perspective' (2000) 29 *Marriage and Family Review* 43.

[82] Smart and Neale , 'Family Fragments' (1999), above (n 57).

separating families, we have now moved to a position in which post-separation fathering has itself been reframed as a social problem, with the maintenance of contact an increasingly important goal on the part of policy makers and politicians. And if the desirability of contact per se has not gone unchallenged,[83] the question of what law can do to promote good post-separation fathering has become a central issue within family policy debates.

In the following section, we consider the substantive legal provisions that have been introduced with the aim of reducing conflict and promoting this model of co-operative post-separation parenting. In these debates around contact and residence, we will argue, there has occurred a far-reaching reassessment, and politicisation, of the relationship between fatherhood and law.

III Law, Contact and the 'Responsible' Post-separation Father

Legal Frameworks: Contact, Residence and the Children Act 1989

In 2005 the UK government described as a 'core belief' of family policy that 'both parents should continue to have a meaningful relationship with their children after separation as long as it is safe and in the child's best interests',[84] a vision which can be traced back (at least) to the Children Act 1989. In the intervening years, and interlinked with the promotion and enforcement of fathers' financial responsibilities in the Child Support Act 1991, as discussed above, the central assumption about the desirability of contact with non-resident fathers has been embedded within legislation, case law, policy and legal practice.[85] The positive advantage of contact has been highlighted in a succession of cases, and it has been assumed that to deny contact is to jeopardise the welfare of the child.[86] As the court put it in the case of *Re H*, 'are there any cogent reasons why this father should be denied access to his children; or putting it another way, are there any cogent reasons why these two children should be denied the opportunity of

---

[83] See eg: M King, 'Foreword' in S Day Sclater and C Piper (eds), *Undercurrents of Divorce* (Ashgate, Aldershot, 1999); R Bailey Harris, 'Contact – Challenging Conventional Wisdom' (2001) 13 *Child and Family Law Quarterly* 361.

[84] C Falconer, R Kelly and P Hewitt, 'Ministerial Forward' in HM Government, *Parental Separation: Children's Needs and Parents' Responsibilities: Next Steps*, Cm 6452 (2005).

[85] For an excellent overview of the leading cases and debates in this area see Diduck and Kaganas, above (n 18) at ch 14; Herring, above (n 60) at ch 9; also: G Davis and J Pearce, 'The Welfare Principle in Action' [1999] *Family Law* 237. On shifts in the professional attitudes of lawyers and others: B Neale and C Smart, '"Good" and "Bad'" Lawyers? Struggling in the Shadow of the New Law' (2004) 19 *Journal of Social Work and Family Law* 377.

[86] *Re F (Minors) (Contact: Mother's Anxiety)* [1993] 2 FLR 830.

access to their natural father?'.[87] Likewise, the Court in *Re G* noted 'it is well established by authority that, other things being equal, it is always in a child's welfare to know and, wherever possible, to have contact with both its parents'.[88] The Court of Appeal has further observed how some parents, in particular mothers, can be responsible for alienating children from their fathers without good reason.[89]

Whilst in some cases such opposition by a mother has been taken as a reason for denying contact,[90] the courts have made it clear that residential parents will not be permitted to defy them in relation to the issue of contact.[91] in the presence of what may be considered reasonable grounds for believing that the children are suffering or likely to suffer significant harm, the courts have on occasion viewed the behaviour of mothers who resist contact as so damaging that a care order can be justified. The above issues have had a particular salience in the context of concerns about the consequences of this 'pro-contact culture' for women and children, and debates about the extent and impact of violence. The significance of violence cannot be underestimated and is an issue we consider further in chapter seven.[92]

How has this assumption of the desirability of contact come to have such force in the legal arena? Detailed exploration of the background to and provisions of the Children Act 1989, as well as the subsequent development of case law in this area, is beyond the scope of this chapter.[93] It is also important not to overstate, on one level, what is new about the belief that contact is in the best interests of the child, that fathers should not be 'written out' of their children's lives. We have noted in chapter four how this legislation understood parenthood in terms of *responsibility* rather than *rights*, signifying that both parents are now expected to

---

[87] *Re H (Minors) (Access)* [1992] 1 FLR 148 at 152 (Balcombe LJ). See also: *Re M (Contact: Welfare Test)* [1995] 1 FLR 274.

[88] *Re G (A Minor) (Parental Responsibility Order)* [1994] 1 FLR 505 at 508 (Balcombe LJ).

[89] The literature on this subject is extensive. For a useful overview, see further Hunt, above (n 77); Hunt and Roberts, above (n 9).

[90] *Re P (Contact: Discretion)* [1998] 2 FLR 696; Cf: *Re D (A Minor) (Contact: Mother's Hostility)* [1993] 2 FLR 1, a case in which the court refused to accept a mother's objections notwithstanding concerns about violence and intimidation; see also: *Re P (Contact: Supervision)* [1996] 2 FLR 314.

[91] *Re O (Contact: Imposition of Conditions)* [1995] 2 FLR 124; *Re W (A Minor) (Contact)* [1994] 2 FLR 441. In addition, the passage of time will be a legitimate reason for not facilitating contact with the non-residential parent: *Re S (Uncooperative Mother)* [2004] EWCA Civ 597, [2004] 2 FLR 710.

[92] Ch 7, n 67. Again, the literature on this subject is extensive. For an excellent summary of the relation between contact and domestic violence, including the approach of the courts, see Hunt and Roberts, above (n 22) at 7–9; also Hunt, above (n 77). Note in particular *Re L (Contact: Domestic Violence), Re V (Contact: Domestic Violence), Re M (Contact: Domestic Violence), Re H (Contact Domestic Violence)* [2000] 2 FLR 334; C Sturge and D Glaser 'Contact and Domestic Violence – the Experts' Court Report' (2000) 30 *Family Law* 615; M Hester and L Radford, *Domestic Violence and Child Contact Arrangements in England and Denmark* (The Policy Press, Bristol, 1996). On the court's perceptions of mothers who resist contact see *Re M (Intractable Contact Dispute: Interim Care Order)* [2003] EWHC Fam 1024, [2003] 2 FLR 636; see also: *V v V (Contact: Implacable Hostility)* [2004] EWHC Fam 1215, [2004] 2 FLR 851 at [4] (per Bracewell J). Note: The Right Honourable Justice Wall, 'Enforcement of Court Orders' '[2005] *Family Law* 26.

[93] See: A Bainham, *Children: The Modern Law* 3rd edn (Jordan Publishing, Bristol, 2005).

156

retain equal responsibilities to their children after separation. The terminology adopted in the Act, moving from the language of 'custody' and 'access' towards 'residence' and 'contact', is explicitly premised on the twin assumptions that, first, there should not be 'winners' and 'losers' in divorce, and, second, that parental responsibility is itself ongoing, it does not come to an end on separation. The co-parental role enshrined in the Children Act requires non-resident, separated fathers to engage in family life in such a way as to support their child's best interests. The role of the courts is simply to assist parents in resolving disputes that arise. Thus, in those cases where the parties are unable to agree contact arrangements, the court has jurisdiction to make orders regulating, specifying or prohibiting contact between a child and any person, including a parent or other relative, if the child's welfare so demands. Contact is thus understood as an incident of legal parenthood, although it might also be given to any other person.[94] The courts have available a range of orders which provide for the determination of where, and with whom, a child is to reside,[95] including for contact, requiring the person with whom a child lives to allow the child to visit or stay with the person named in the order.[96]

Importantly, however, there is no *presumption* of contact or shared parenting in the Children Act 1989, a point of particular significance in the debates around fatherhood and fathers' rights that we chart below.[97] The courts are only to intervene if it is considered in the best interests of the child to do so. Contact is thus a qualified right, in that it is subject to the welfare principle and the court's power of intervention. While contact orders can be used to regulate the time a child should have with a non-resident parent, this 'no order' principle of minimum intervention seeks to encourage parents to decide upon and maintain contact arrangements themselves. Decisions as to sole residence and contact orders are taken via reference to a 'welfare checklist' in which the maintenance of the status quo is itself a key feature.[98] Present patterns of residence and contact, in which the majority of children continue to live with their mothers, are thus seen as reflective of a factual situation whereby, during subsisting relationships, it is women who tend to undertake the bulk of the childcare.

---

[94] 'Contact' is used in both the Children Act 1989 and the Children (Scotland) Act 1995 in cases of family breakdown such as separation or divorce, and also where the child is separated from family or carers by the state. It has been suggested that the 'pro-contact culture', in law, psychology and social work, has been most influential in cases of parental separation. It would seem, however, it has also influenced the presumption in favour of contact in cases involving local authority care of children.

[95] Children Act 1989, s 8. Decisions on residence and contact are determined by the welfare principle of Children Act 1989, s 1. See further: J Pearce, G Davis and J Barron, 'Love in a Cold Climate – Section 8 Applications under the Children Act 1989' [1999] *Family Law* 22.

[96] Contact itself can be supervised or unsupervised, direct or indirect. Where the courts do proceed to decide that sole residence is the appropriate course of action, they are also likely, in the majority of cases, to consider whether a child should have regular contact with the non-resident parent (in the majority of cases, the father), and the degree and nature of such contact.

[97] See pp 159–61.

[98] Children Act 1989, s 1(3)(c), which includes reference to the court's need to consider the likely effect on the child of any change in their circumstances.

Before turning to the fathers' rights critique of this framework, it is necessary to consider further how this pro-contact culture is enmeshed with what has become a quite specific understanding of the role of law: as a tool to modify the behaviour of separating parents and to promote 'responsibility'.

Post-separation Fatherhood and the 'New Responsibility': Promoting the 'Good Divorce'

On closer examination, certain features of this new consensus suggest a shift has taken place in understandings of what role law can, and should, play in this area. The evolution of law away from the determination of fault and status in relation to divorce, and towards a concern with process, has been marked by a growing concern with how men and women reach their decisions, rather than what decisions they reach. A model of 'divorcing responsibly', Reece suggests, now captures key features of the legal governance of post-separation parenting.[99] Women and men, in committing to the co-parenting ideal, are to act in ways that are rational, settlement-minded and altruistic. They are to be aware of the social and economic costs of divorce and the risks associated with parental conflict, not least around the refusal of contact with the non-resident father. Given that separation should be as harmonious as possible, the object of legal intervention is to reduce conflict, promote consensus between the parties and, where appropriate, facilitate contact between children and the non-resident parent.

Whilst the origins of this approach can be traced back to the Children Act 1989, tracking to longer-term shifts in the nature of law's governance around the constancy of relationships, this idea of the 'civilised' divorce has had a significant role in shaping debates about law reform, in particular those preceding the enactment of Part II of the FLA 1996. Whilst the specific provisions and fate of the FLA 1996 are considered in detail elsewhere,[100] the development of political agendas around post-separation fatherhood in the period since then can be located in its shadow, particularly the commitment in that legislation to promote the modification of behaviour. As Reece observes in *Divorcing Responsibly*, the model of divorce contained within the FLA 1996 involved some distinctive assumptions about the nature of the divorcing subject. This individual would 'reflect' on and consider their separation, and, given appropriate information,

---

[99] H Reece, *Divorcing Responsibly* (Hart, Oxford, 2003) especially at ch 6. See also: R van Krieken, 'The "Best Interests of the Child" and Parental Separation: on the "Civilising of Parents"' (2005) 68(1) MLR 25; J Dewar, 'The Normal Chaos of Family Law' (1998) 61 MLR 467.

[100] J Walker, *Information Meetings and Associated Provisions within the Family Law Act 1996: Summary of the Final Evaluation Report* (Lord Chancellor's Department, London, 2001); J Walker *et al*, *Picking Up the Pieces: Marriage and Divorce: Two Years After Information Provision* (Department of Constitutional Affairs, London, 2004); R Collier, 'The Dashing of a "Liberal Dream"? The Information Meeting, the "New Family" and the Limits of Law' (1999) 11 *Child and Family Law Quarterly* 257.

learn through engagement with the divorce process.[101] It was not assumed, and has not since been argued, that law alone can solve problems. Far from it:

> changing social expectations, as well as Government action, are both needed. In time, it needs to become socially unacceptable for one parent to impede a child's relationship with its other parent wherever it is safe and in the child's best interests. Equally, it should be unacceptable that non-resident parents absent themselves from their child's development and upbringing following separation. Friends, relatives, the legal profession and the media all have a role to play in emphasising that children require a good and lasting relationship with both their parents wherever it is safe and in the child's best interests to do so.[102]

Notwithstanding the political decision made against implementing the divorce provisions of the FLA 1996,[103] the general philosophy that underpinned the legislation has continued to influence debates about divorce in a number of ways.[104] The measures introduced over the past decade in the field of contact law have, for example, addressed the broader attempt to develop a coherent, 'joined-up' range of policies around children's welfare,[105] policies which reflect the ideas of the 'new democratic family' and parental responsibility discussed in chapter four.[106] Two developments in particular, however, have had a significant bearing on the reshaping of fatherhood in this area of law.

First, it is important to recognise here the significance of an intensified campaign on the part of fathers' rights groups (perhaps most notably, since 2002, Fathers 4 Justice) in shaping the political contours of debates about separated fathers' rights.[107] Against the backdrop of these high-profile campaigns, policy makers, politicians and members of the judiciary have articulated the view that 'something needs to be done' in relation to the laws concerning contact. The present law and related legal practices are generally agreed to have failed adequately to promote a continuing and constructive relationship with both parents. With specific regard to post-divorce parenting, the government has accepted that 'the present legal system is inadequate, failing in the way it deals with contact cases'.[108]

---

[101] Reece, above (n 99).

[102] Falconer, Kelly and Hewitt, above (n 84).

[103] Collier, above (n 100).

[104] In relation, for example, to the provision of information, a focus on the minimising of conflict and early intervention strategies (eg in the form of parenting plans).

[105] The 2003 Green Paper *Every Child Matters* set out a 'new approach' focused on achieving the 'five outcomes' that 'matter for every child': HM Treasury, *Every Child Matters*, Cm 5860 (2003). Combined with the introduction of a Children's Commissioner for England in 2005, the Children's Fund and the provisions of the Children Act 2004, *Every Child Matters* is informed by a broader concern to develop 'integrated planning' and improved multi-disciplinary working in the commissioning and delivery of services for children. For critical discussion: B Daniel *et al*, 'Why Gender Matters for *Every Child Matters*' (2005) 35 *British Journal of Social Work* 1343.

[106] See pp 118–120.

[107] See further: Collier (2005), above (n 49); R Collier, 'The UK Fathers' Rights Movement and Law: Report to the British Academy', British Academy rlf/SRF/2005/88 (2008) (unpublished).

[108] A point acknowledged in the consultation paper, Children Act Sub-committee of the Advisory Board on Family Law, *Making Contact Work. A Report to the Lord Chancellor on the Facilitation of*

Senior figures in the judiciary, meanwhile, have expressed concern about the difficulties they face in dealing with contested cases, notably in relation to the enforcement of court orders.[109] In April 2004, in the midst of Fathers 4 Justice's campaign to raise public awareness of these issues,[110] the government announced its commitment to 'new laws to end the child custody wars'.[111] The 2004 Green Paper *Parental Separation: Children's Needs and Parents' Responsibilities* subsequently outlined a range of proposals aimed at diverting as many divorcing parents as possible from the courts and promoting 'generous parenting' for both.[112]

These developments link to the impact of fathers' rights groups in shaping the political terrain and broader cultural context in which debates around contact have taken place. Second, however, it is also important to note the extent to which the package of measures introduced subsequent to the 2004 Green Paper have themselves continued and developed further the trajectory set by the FLA 1996 in seeking to promote a model of 'divorcing responsibly'. It is important not to overstate in this regard the extent to which these developments have been informed by specific campaigns on the part of fathers' rights groups.

In January 2005, the government published its response to the Green Paper, *Parental Separation: Children's Needs and Parents' Responsibilities, Next Steps*,[113] and Part I of the resulting Children and Adoption Act 2006[114] adopts what is an essentially three-track approach. It is concerned, first, with the facilitation and monitoring of contact,[115] giving some direction regarding the conditions whereby contact will take place. Second, it addresses the issue of enforcement,[116] a key concern for fathers' rights groups, via the introduction of warning notices and provision for compensation for financial loss.[117] Finally, the legislation encapsulates the broader intention, noted above, to educate parents and engage

---

Arrangements for Contact Between Children and their Non-residential Parents and the Enforcement of Court Orders for Contact (Lord Chancellor's Department, London, 2001).

[109] Note, for example, the highly publicised judgement of Munby J in *Re D (A Child) (Intractable Contact Dispute)* [2004] EWHC Fam 727, [2004] 1 FLR 1226. This development prompted the observation on the part of Matt O'Connor of Fathers 4 Justice that 'twelve months ago such judgments would have been unthinkable': F Gibb, 'Judge apologises as justice "fails fathers"', *The Times* (2 April 2004), <http://www.timesonline.co.uk/article/0,,2–1059953,00.html>, accessed 2 January 2008. See M Piercy, 'Intractable Contact Disputes' (2004) Fam Law 815.

[110] See further: Collier (2005), above (n 49).

[111] C Dyer, 'New laws to end child custody wars' *Guardian* (3 April 2004), <http://www.guardian.co.uk/society/2004/apr/03/childrensservices.politics>, accessed 2 January 2008; Transcript of The Today Programme. Radio 4. 3 April 2004. 'Rights for Fathers – Lord Geoff Filkin and Sir Bob Geldof' (GICS Media Monitoring Unit, London, 2004) (copy of transcript with authors).

[112] See C Falconer, R Kelly and P Hewitt, above (n 84).

[113] *Ibid.*

[114] Preceded by the 2005 Children (Contact) and Adoption Bill: J Wallbank, 'Clause 106 of the Adoption and Children Bill: Legislation for the "Good Father"?' (2002) 22 (2) *Legal Studies* 276.

[115] Children and Adoption Act 2006, ss 1–2.

[116] *Ibid*, ss 3–4. It is envisaged that it will be in relatively few cases, in which there has been implacable failure to comply with an order, that the courts will find it necessary to impose such a sanction.

[117] 2006 Act, s 5. See now Children Act 1989, s 11 (J-P).

them in behaviour modification, such as through 'contact activity directions' and the provision of access to information. This has taken the form of encouraging the development of parenting plans,[118] ensuring that advice is widely available at all points in the divorce process[119] and promoting in-court conciliation.[120] Whilst the government has stated that it does not plan to make mediation compulsory, it will 'strongly promote' its use. Co-operation is to be further promoted by counselling and/or the involvement of other external agencies where appropriate.[121]

At the time of writing, notwithstanding the 2006 legislation, significant criticism of the present family justice system continues. For some fathers' rights groups, in the absence of any legal presumption of contact and shared 'equal parenting',[122] law remains grounded in problematic, gendered and discriminatory assumptions. And for a broader coalition of stakeholders, including equal parenting organisations, women's groups and other fathers' organisations, the legal process around separation remains marked by profound 'system failures' – failures which, crucially, have a detrimental impact not only on children but also on separated parents themselves.[123]

Unanswered Questions

Where does this leave us? We have set out above key elements of a new paradigm in law and policy relating to the post-separation family. We have noted, in particular, how the figure of the father has been redrawn within a legal framework seeking to promote non-conflictual separation and a new sense of responsibility on the part of parents. A number of questions pertaining to fatherhood and law are, however, left hanging. First, if it is to be presumed that separated fathers fulfil an essential function in their children's lives post-separation, or at

---

[118] Designed to help parents and other relatives reach agreement about contact arrangements for their children following parental separation and divorce: Department for Education and Skills, 'Parenting Plans: Putting Your Children First: A Guide for Separating Parents', <http://www.dfes.gov. uk/childrensneeds>, accessed 22 December 2007. On shared parenting agreements and family court secrecy: S Clayton, 'The Shared Parenting Agreement', <http://www.parents4protest.co.uk/simon_ clayton.htm>, accessed 13 December 2007. See also: *Re Z (Shared Parenting Plan: Publicity)* [2006] 1 FLR 405.

[119] Such as the new Family Help Service pilot launched via existing Family Advice and Information Service (FAInS) solicitors.

[120] See: L Trinder and J Kellet, *The Longer Term Outcomes of In-Court Conciliation: Ministry of Justice Research Series 15/07* (Ministry of Justice, London, 2007).

[121] Other relevant measures relate to a review of provisions around family assistance orders and risk assessment: Children and Adoption Act 2006, ss 6–7.

[122] The government has, to date, refused to modify the Children Act 1989 emphasis on the welfare of the child as the paramount consideration in any decision affecting that child: 'Some fathers' groups have come to believe that the courts and the law are biased against them. *We do not accept this view*': Falconer, Kelly and Hewitt, above (n 84) at 1 (emphasis added). On the development of fathers' rights agendas in the intervening period see further Collier (2008), above (n 107).

[123] Families Need Fathers *et al*, 'Letter to the Editor: The Government Must Help the Children of Divorcees', *The Times* (12 June 2007) at 16; other signatories included Women's Aid and Fathers Direct.

least that they should do so, it remains far from clear, in law or in policy, precisely what such a role should properly involve.[124] Given the various forms of fatherhood described in this book, the answer is far from obvious. The Children Act 1989, as we have seen, allocates joint responsibilities to both parents for their child's upbringing in the event of separation or divorce. Yet this prescription of co-operation does not appear to differentiate between the resident and non-resident parent. Further uncertainty persists regarding whether contact itself should be understood as a right of the parent or of the child,[125] with the Human Rights Act 1998 and the development of EU laws producing additional questions on this issue.[126]

Second, and with specific reference to the issue of fathers' rights groups, there exists something of a paradox. We have charted a policy shift in family law that, in a number of respects, appears to have empowered fathers through the emergence, embedding and consolidation of the new welfare discourse and co-parenting ideal. At the same time, however, developments over the past decade, in the UK and elsewhere, suggest there is a growing feeling on the part of significant numbers of men – and some women[127] – that law is unjust in how it deals with the social experiences of fathers in the process of divorce and separation. How are we to make sense of this? Are the claims of fathers' rights groups without foundation? Do they exemplify what has been termed a wider anti-feminist 'backlash'?[128] Why it is felt that law is systematically discriminating against men, given the body of research and policy developments discussed above? The law has sought to promote, encourage and enforce contact between separated fathers and their children. Why should this legal framework and the practices to which it has given rise then be the focus of protest on the part of fathers' rights groups? Why, 'given the on-going privileged position of men (politically, economically and

---

[124] Wilson, above (n 17). See: Ch 7 p 234.

[125] A Bainham, 'Contact as a Fundamental Right' (1995) 54 CLJ 255.

[126] See further C McGlynn, *Families and the European Union* (Cambridge University Press, Cambridge, 2006). Claims for contact have been made by adult family members and children under the Human Rights Act 1998, with regard to respecting their private and family life under Art 8 of the European Convention for the Protection of Human Rights and Fundamental Freedoms (European Convention on Human Rights, as amended) (ECHR). Note: Art 8 cannot *establish* a relationship between a family member and a child, it can only protect an existing one: J Herring, 'The Human Rights Act and the Welfare Principle in Family Law – Conflicting or Complementary?' (1999) 11(3) *Child and Family Law Quarterly* 223. See also: H Fenwick, 'Clashing Rights, the Welfare of the Child and the Human Rights Act' (2004) MLR 889.

[127] See eg: The Purplehearts, or Sisters of Mercy, a 'support group for mothers, partners, grandparents, children and other relatives affected by family breakdown and contact disputes': Fathers 4 Justice, 'Purplehearts', <http://www.fathers-4-justice.org/f4j/index.php?option=com_content&task=view&id=27&Itemid=51>, accessed 27 December 2007.

[128] S Boyd, 'Backlash Against Feminism: Canadian Custody and Access Reform Debates of the Late Twentieth Century' (2004) 16(2) *Candian Journal of Women and the Law* 255; S Boyd, 'Backlash and the Construction of Legal Knowledge: The Case of Child Custody Law' (2001) 20 *The Windsor Year Book of Access to Justice* 141; M.Flood, 'Backlash: Angry Men's Movements' in SE Rossie (ed) *The Battle and Backlash Rage On: Why Feminism cannot be Obsolete* (Philadelphia, Xlibris Press, 2004).

culturally) … [is there] felt a need for men to (re)assert their position and status as fathers'?[129] In the next section, we will explore these issues.

IV Reassessing the Politics of Post-separation Fatherhood: Questions of Conflict, Emotion and Gender

A number of interrelated issues, we have seen above, have the potential to come together in such a way as to produce feelings of loss and anger on the part of many fathers.[130] Law, importantly, is implicated in each of them. First, for married men, is the divorce itself, the specific measures of substance and process relating to the ending of a marriage in law, including how law engages with the issue of fault.[131] Second is the legal process pertaining to ancillary matters, whereby marital assets are divided up and financial provision made for affected parties, an issue bound up with the question of child support assessment, discussed above.[132] Third, we have seen, a shift has taken place in understanding of the role and contribution of fathers in the lives of children. There are also other issues, for example relating to tax, the provision of welfare benefits, legal aid and a lack of transparency in the family courts, that all form part of the toxic mixture of factors leading to a sense of injustice and grievance on the part of certain fathers.[133]

From the perspective of fathers' rights groups, therefore, the law is 'out of step' with the social changes discussed in chapter one, failing to reflect the new circumstances of family life in which many men are, and want to be, significant participants, not just in paid employment, but also in childcare and domestic labour.[134] Whilst many fathers wish to establish and maintain meaningful relationships with their children after separation, they see law and the legal process as effectively embodying what is tantamount to a legal presumption of contact with the mother. Moreover, mothers' ability to resist children's contact with fathers has remained, it is argued, effectively unscrutinised by virtue of a largely closed family court system. Thus, notwithstanding the provisions of the Children and Adoption Act 2006, fathers, as non-resident parents, do not have an automatic

---

[129] C Smart, 'Preface' in R Collier and S Sheldon (eds), *Fathers' Rights Activism and Legal Reform in Comparative Perspective* (Hart, Oxford, 2006).

[130] J Arditti and K Allen, 'Understanding Distressed fathers' Perceptions of Legal and Relational Inequities Post-divorce' (1993) 31 *Family and Conciliation Courts Review* 461. Arendell, above (n 50).

[131] For recent discussion of the 'moral' content of family law, including fault on divorce, see: Eekelaar, above (n 35) at 105–11. Contrast the approach of C Smart, *Personal Life* (Polity, Cambridge, 2007).

[132] It is important to note that disagreements around ancillary relief are themselves often the most contested element of proceedings: MCA 1973, s 25.

[133] On tax, see eg: A Mumford, 'Towards a Fiscal Sociology of Tax Credits and the Father's Rights Movement' (2008) 17(2) *Social and Legal Studies* 217. See further Collier, above (n 107).

[134] See ch 4, 114.

legal right to see their children. There is, crucially, no assumption to shared residence or 'equal parenting' arrangements. There is, rather, a lack of political commitment to dealing with, and taking seriously, the specific circumstances of separated fathers. As it was put by one father to one of the authors of this book 'it's a bit like in the Philip Pullman book *Northern Lights*, you know, where the children are being cut from their daemons, they experience this pain. Well being cut away from his child, from something that is part of him, that's what it's like for many fathers.'[135]

A growing literature on the fathers' rights movement, both in the UK and internationally, has sought to address these claims. This work has explored diverse aspects of the emergence and evolution of specific fathers' rights groups, the arguments they advance and the strategies they adopt. Concern has been expressed, in the UK as elsewhere, about the impact some of these groups[136] have had in influencing the direction of case law, the content of legislation and the form of policy debates around contact[137] and shared residence.[138] We have considered these issues elsewhere,[139] and in chapter seven we will return to the questions they raise about the politics of fatherhood and law. For now, we wish at this stage to shift the focus of analysis, and place these developments in the broader context of changes in the legal regulation of fatherhood as detailed in this chapter. Empirical studies of post-separation life suggest that relationships formed during marriage and cohabitation can be reshaped in complex ways following separation. Research indicates, in particular, that different models and understandings of 'good' fathering can emerge from those that prevailed during subsisting relationships. This point is of considerable significance in seeking to understand the political terrain around post-separation fatherhood and law

---

[135] Interview with R Collier, above (n 107). See further, eg: B Geldof, 'The Real Love that Dare Not Speak Its Name' in A Bainham and others (eds), *Children and Their Families* (Hart, Oxford, 2003). Note: Fathers 4 Justice, 'Family Justice On Trial: Opening The Door On Closed Courts', <http://www.fathers-4-justice.org/f4j//index.php?option=com_content&task=view&id=13&Itemid=39>, accessed 27 December 2007.

[136] For Diduck and Kaganas, the 'fathers' rights campaigns [do] appear to have had the effect of galvanising the government and the courts into action against mothers whom they see as obstructive': Diduck and Kaganas, above (n 18) at 561; S Boyd and CF Young, 'Who Influences Family Law Reform? Discourses on Motherhood and Fatherhood in Legislative Reform Debates in Canada' (2002) *Studies in Law, Politics and Society* 43; R Graycar, 'Law Reform by Frozen Chook: Family Law Reform for the New Millennium?' (2000) 24 *Melbourne University Law Review* 737.

[137] H Rhoades, 'The Rise and Rise of Shared Parenting Laws: A Critical Reflection' (2002) 19(1) *Canadian Journal of Family Law* 75; R Bailey-Harris, J Barron, and J Pearce, 'From Utility to Rights? The Presumption of Contact in Practice' (1999) 13 *International Journal of Law, Policy and the Family* 111; C Smart and B Neale, 'Arguments Against Virtue: Must Contact Be Enforced?' [1997] *Family Law* 332.

[138] See: F Kaganas and C Piper, 'Shared Parenting – a 70% Solution?' (2002) 14 *Child and Family Law Quarterly* 365; B Neale, J Flowerdew and C Smart, 'Drifting Towards Shared Residence?' [2003] *Family Law* 904. See also: *Re F (Children) (Shared Residence Order)* [2003] EWCA Civ 592, [2003] 2 FCR 164; *A v A and others* [2004] EWHC 142, [2004] 1 FLR 1195. Cf: *Re H (A Minor) (Shared Residence)* [1994] 1 FLR 717 at 728; *Re D (Children: Shared Residence Orders)* [2001] 1 FLR 495, [2001] 1 FCR 147 at [32].

[139] Collier and Sheldon, above (n 3).

reform. Below, we make two points, considering, first, the gendered dimensions of the experience of separation and (re)location of fathers in relation to what has been termed an 'ethic of care'. Second, we look at how issues of emotion and the psychological dimensions of separation have been dealt with in the legal arena. Each, we suggest, has a particular bearing on understanding the contested nature of the relationship between fatherhood and law in the area of post-separation parenting.

Gendered Lives: Law and the Changing Experience of Fatherhood

We charted above the emergence of a model of 'the responsible divorce', in which law is seen to have a central and distinctive role in encouraging behaviour modification. We also noted the centrality of the father figure to a new paradigm of post-divorce family life. In such a context, it is perhaps unsurprising that the prescriptions for good parenting to be found in law should have, along with related assumptions about what is best for children, 'entered [the] vocabularies' of both parents.[140] Yet, fathers, like mothers, have been seen to 'actively interpret [such prescriptions] according to their own criteria' in ways that reflect their distinctive 'gendered lives' and 'gendered rationalities'.[141] This raises the question of what the gender(ed) experience and expectations of fathers might be at the present moment, as well as those of the wider peer groups and social networks they inhabit. It embraces the issue of how fathering is understood as a situated social practice and how individual life history and biography impact on the experience, not only of post-separation fathering, but also of marriage, the process of divorce and the interpersonal dynamics of any conflicted separation.

Each of these issues is relevant in understanding the contours of current debates around post-separation fathers and law. In studies of post-separation parenting, both fathers and mothers have been seen to negotiate and balance the demands of the new form of personal responsibility and choice contained in law[142] as gendered (as well as, of course, classed, raced) subjects, individuals with particular life histories.[143] Negotiating these processes in a context of life transition such as divorce, however, can result in a tension between the messages about co-operative parenting in law, the family norms we are supposed to live by, as it

---

[140] Kaganas and Day Sclater, above (n 54) at 15.

[141] See further on this idea: S Duncan and R Edwards, *Lone Mothers, Paid Work and Gendered Moral* Rationalities (Palgrave Macmillan, Basingstoke, 1999); S Duncan, A Carling and R Edwards (eds), *Analysing Families: Morality and Rationality in Policy and Practice* (Routledge, London, 2002). See ch 4, p 131.

[142] Reece, above (n 99). See also: R van Krieken, 'Legal Informalism, Power and Liberal Governance' (2001) 19(1) *Social and Legal Studies* 5.

[143] As individuals who experience parenting and socialisation practices, family and interpersonal relationships, the psychological legacy of which can be played out in later adult relations: Cantwell, above (n 22).

were, and those families we actually experience.[144] It is also important to recognise how separation may play out in some distinctive ways for fathers in the context of the legal and cultural reappraisal of 'good' post-separation parenting as outlined in this chapter. Whilst many fathers may have little experience of co-parenting prior to separation,[145] Smart suggests that a perceived inequality of treatment at the time of separation can mean 'the demand for more contact or even residence [then] becomes part of the (inevitable) conflict that surrounds separation and, indeed, even intensifies this conflict'.[146] For many men, the practices associated with being a good father might not equate to 'day-to-day' caring activities and responsibility.[147] This does not mean, however, that they do not love their children,[148] even if a father's love may be perceived as 'rather superficial ... less weighty or emotionally significant'[149] because of how family practices have been gendered in the first place. The dominant pattern of hetero-sexual parenting is one in which 'mothers take overall responsibility for care for children, but ... may delegate out certain activities to fathers'.[150] It is in such a context that the nature and quality of fathering 'in the absence of maternal guidance and supervision' can be experienced by both mothers and fathers as problematic. For men and women, we have suggested, the model of 'divorcing responsibly' outlined above often obliges parents to position themselves in relation to competing discourses.[151] However, negotiating the transition from a situation in which parents may have colluded in maintaining a belief in gender equality in parenting prior to separation would itself appear to be a potential source of anger on the part of many men.[152]

It is perhaps unsurprising, therefore, that at a time when more men identify with the idea of the father as carer, the perceived loss of that role should prove so extremely painful. Nor that the ideal of co-parenting contained in law might itself serve to fuel conflicts between separating parents in cases where it is perceived to be the product, not of co-operation, but of legal coercion. This is precisely the

---

[144] See: A Diduck, *Law's Families* (Lexis Nexis, London, 2003).

[145] See ch 4, p 128.

[146] Smart, above (n 129).

[147] See ch 4, p 130.

[148] It is important to remember that not only do many fathers perceive themselves as 'doing' family precisely through their participation in, and commitment to, paid employment (ch 4), they are viewed as such by others, including their children; see: W Hatten, L Vinter and R Williams, *Dads On Dads: Needs and Expectations at Home and at Work* (Equal Opportunities Commission, Manchester, 2002).

[149] Smart, above (n 129).

[150] *Ibid.* See also: ch 4, p 130.

[151] Kaganas and Day Sclater, above (n 54) at 2–3.

[152] K Backett, 'The Negotiation of Fatherhood' in C Lewis and M O'Brien (eds), *Reassessing Fatherhood: New Observations on Fathers and the Modern Family* (Sage, London, 1987) at 71–90. Backett's work suggests that parents can profess a belief in the equality of contemporary parental roles and yet develop coping mechanisms to avoid confronting what can be the clear mismatch between these ideals and their own practices around childcare, practices which remain heavily gendered: K Backett, *Mothers and Fathers: A Study of the Development and Negotiation of Parental Behaviour* (Macmillan, Basingstoke, 1982).

scenario in many cases involving fathers' rights group activists where there is, for example, more likely to be a history of conflicted separation. For some men, an identification with the model of the father as 'hands-on' carer is experienced as being undercut in a social context in which the father can no longer be valued for 'being there' for his children. Further, it is in this context that the failure of the law to accord fathers equal contact time with their children is perceived as a psychological injury relating to many men's sense of their worth, not just as fathers, but also, importantly, as *men*. The policy rejection of shared parenting might thus appear to some as a symbolic, formal confirmation that fathers are accorded secondary importance in law to their children's mothers. Importantly, these are experiences, feelings of disappointment, frustration and, for some, acute anger (with law, the legal system) that then need to be managed emotionally. This raises the question of the emotive dimensions of post-separation contact, the interconnectedness of the 'everyday' lives of women, men and children and how the question of what fathers emotionally feel and desire can be as important as what they rationally think in shaping behaviour in this area.

Power, Conflict and the Psychology of Separation

We have suggested elsewhere that the relationship between changes in family practices and law reform cannot be reduced to a 'zero-sum' equation where fathers 'lose' rights in direct proportion to the extent that mothers acquire them (and vice versa).[153] Research on post-separation parenting suggests that the reason for the breakdown of contact arrangements can itself be far more complex than that implied by any image of a 'hostile' woman 'refusing' access.[154] Sclater has argued that, far from women deploying a form of uni-directional power (refusing a father access), some mothers may experience a form of 'debilitative power' on the part of fathers; a constraining of their own drive to independence, autonomy and self-development in the period after separation.[155] Equally, it has become increasingly clear that an appreciation of the emotional context of disputes is a critical aspect of developing effective intervention. In particular, and for both mothers and fathers, 'fighting over the child(ren) [can]

---

[153] Collier and Sheldon, above (n 3). Also Collier (2005), above (n 49).

[154] C Smart and V May, 'Why Can't They Agree? The Underlying Complexity of Contact and Residence Disputes' (2004) 26(4) *Journal of Social Welfare and Family Law* 347. See, more generally: A Buchanan *et al*, *Families in Conflict: Perspectives of Children and Parents on the Family Court Welfare Service* (The Policy Press, Bristol, 2001); C Smart and others, *Residence and Contact Disputes in Court: Volume 1*, Research Report No 6/2003 (Department for Constitutional Affairs, London 2003), cited by Margaret Hodge, *Hansard* HC, vol 457, col 67W (5 January 2004); C Smart and others, *Residence and Contact Disputes in Court: Volume 2*, Research Report No 4/2005 (Department for Constitutional Affairs, London, 2005); L Trinder, M Beck and J Connolly, *Making Contact: How Parents and Children Negotiate and Experience Conflict After Divorce* (Joseph Rowntree Foundation, York, 2002); L Trinder *et al*, *A Profile of Applicants and Respondents in Contact Cases in Essex: Research Report No 1/2005* (Department for Constitutional Affairs, London, 2005); Hunt, above (n 77).

[155] S Day Sclater, *Divorce: A Psycho-social Study* (Ashgate, Aldershot, 1999).

167

Post-separation Fatherhood

serve the emotional (often unconscious) purpose of allowing the adults to play out the unresolved feelings associated with the ending of their relationship'.[156]

These psychological and emotional aspects of separation have a particular bearing on political debates around fathers' rights. They render complex, and problematic, the notion of the 'bad', hostile mother simply 'refusing' contact. They also raise questions about the seemingly irrational, litigious father, the question of why, and how, some non-resident fathers may become psychologically 'stuck' in conflict, often seeking to self-represent and control subsequent legal proceedings, draw in extended families and become active in pressure groups.[157] We noted above the central assumption within the new orthodoxy that contact and consensus between the parties on separation is an *a priori* social good. However, Day Sclater suggests, the psychological ambivalences of loss, which often accompany the end of relationships, can jar with this powerful rhetoric of the harmonious divorce and, in particular, function in such a way as to negate the legitimacy of, and deny the space to articulate, feelings of loss, guilt and anger.[158] This cautions against dismissing the protests of fathers as simply misguided or else as the embodiment of an anti-feminist backlash. Writing in 1995, in the context of debates preceding the enactment of the FLA 1996, Day Sclater and Richards put this point well:

> The lawyer translates the expressed wishes and needs of the client into the language of law, because the law does not permit the language of personal emotions. The legal process quickly develops its own momentum, and the parties may experience a further sense of bewilderment, as they lose control over the legal process, which sweeps them along in a direction and at a pace they might not be psychologically equipped for. The two parties may be at different 'stages' of their adjustment, yet the legal process demands that they confront the same issues at the same time, with no regard for their actual capacity to do so.[159]

These psychological processes are, we suggest, deeply enmeshed with the gendered rationalities and lives of men and women, in ways that can mediate how men and women come to experience divorce and engage with law.

There are, Day Sclater and Richards argue, three reasons why an appreciation of this psychology of divorce should inform legal attempts to facilitate positive outcomes for children and parents. First, these are questions about the mental

---

[156] Cantwell, above (n 22).

[157] *Ibid.*

[158] Day Sclater, above (n 155). See also: S Day Sclater, 'Divorce – Coping Strategies, Conflict and Dispute Resolution' [1998] Fam Law 150; S Day Sclater and C Yates, 'The Psycho-politics of Post Divorce Parenting' in A Bainham, S Day Sclater and M Richards (eds), *What is a Parent? A Socio-Legal Analysis* (Hart, Oxford, 1999); J Brown and S Day Sclater, 'Divorce: A Psychodynamic Perspective' in S Day Sclater and C Piper (eds), *Undercurrents of Divorce* (Aldershot, Dartmouth, 1999); Collier, above (n 107).

[159] S Day Sclater and M Richards, 'How Adults Cope with Divorce – Strategies for Survival' [1995] *Family Law* 143 at 145.

168

health of the divorcing population.[160] Second, these psychological processes have an impact on divorce disputes and it is 'in the interests of devising an effective and efficient' means of resolution that these issues are addressed.[161] Third, the 'complexities of adult psychology' have an impact on children, with the quality of children's post-separation relationships with parents a significant influence on outcomes.[162] Arguably, those measures of the Children and Adoption Act 2006 concerning, for example, the provision of information and support seek to achieve precisely these aims. A rather different question, however, concerns how such psychological complexity can be identified and dealt with at various stages in the legal process (for example, in dealings with the Children and Family Court Advisory and Support Service, CAFCASS), what the implications might be of child-responsive and child-focused initiatives for father involvement,[163] what financial resources will be provided for such initiatives 'on the ground' and what the limits of law itself may be in this area.[164]

These issues have a significant bearing on recent debates around post-separation fatherhood and law. The ideal of co-parenting supported by law may itself have served to fuel conflicts between divorcing parents where it is perceived by individuals as the product of not a shared ideology or mutual commitment, but legal or financial coercion, or some other, unresolved, tension. In the cases of some men who participate in fathers' rights organisations, there is reason to believe that these issues, whether relating to finance, property or children, may well, of course, remain unresolved.[165] Legal and cultural pressures for private decisions to run on 'standard biography' lines, meanwhile, can run counter to the (gendered) emotional realities of separation described above. Men, like women, may be focusing on their own emotional needs at a time when law is exhorting them to focus on the collective interests of the family, particularly those of the children. Importantly, all this is taking place within a cultural frame in which many hitherto normative ideas of masculinity and the (hetero)'sexual family' have themselves been fractured and reformed, as we have seen in chapters one and four.[166] It is not difficult to see, in such a context, why the process of separation should appear so fraught and contested for many fathers, nor, perhaps, why the figure of the child should assume such powerful experiential

---

[160] It is known, for example, that divorce can involve, for significant numbers of the adult population, a family transition which 'pose[s] significant threats to their mental health and ability to function': Sclater and Richards, above (n 159) at 146.

[161] *Ibid.* See also: Cantwell, above (n 22).

[162] Sclater and Richards, above (n 159) at 146. See above, p 143.

[163] Sclater and Richards, above (n 159); McIntosh, above (n 21). See also: B Cantwell, 'CAFCASS: In Court Conciliation and Out of Court Mediation' [2006] *Family Law* 389; B Cantwell, 'CAFCASS and Private Law Cases' [2004] *Family Law* 283.

[164] See further: Collier and Sheldon, above (n 3).

[165] Cantwell, above (n 22); Collier, above (n 107).

[166] See: J Lewis, 'The Decline of the Male Breadwinner Model Family' (2001) 8 *Social Politics* 152; K Gerson, *No Man's Land: Men's Changing Commitments to Family and Work* (Basic Books, New York, 1993).

significance in providing meaning to many men's lives at a moment of what can otherwise be disorientating change. At a time when few services seek to reach out and support non-resident fathers, this analysis links to the recognition of importance at a policy level, as above, of engaging with the emotional and relational dynamics of separation and the specific needs of separating parents in developing strategies to defuse conflict and manage post-separation relationships.

Conclusion

It is not so strange that I love you with my whole heart, for being a father is not a tie, which can be ignored. Nature in her wisdom has attached the parent to the child and bound them together with a Herculean knot[167]

We have argued in this chapter that the emergence of a new orthodoxy around post-separation parenthood within family law and policy raises important issues pertaining to fatherhood and law. It involves a model of child welfare that places co-operative parenting and contact with the non-resident parent, in the majority of cases the father, at the centre of children's well-being. Within the 'co-parenting turn', children have been conceptualised as vulnerable, and separation seen as actually or potentially damaging for parents, for children, and for society.[168] Smart and Neale evocatively describe developments in this area as involving nothing less than a clear and determined attempt to effect 'social engineering' in the area of the family,[169] by 'changing the very nature of post-divorce family life'.[170] These changes must also be located in the context of wider shifts in the nature of family law. This is marked by a growing emphasis on extra-judicial dispute resolution, a concern to modify behaviour and 'educate' parents, a move towards the privatisation of economic responsibilities and, more generally, a refiguring of the relationship between rights and utility, welfare and care, rules and discretion.[171] The question, meanwhile, of what constitutes 'good enough' post-divorce parenting on the part of fathers, is not and has never been universally agreed. It concerns struggles over meaning and desired norms, reflecting complex interrelationships between social and legal knowledge(s) and power.[172] Whilst it is

---

[167] B Simpson *et al*, *Post-Divorce Fatherhood: Discussion Document* (Family and Community Dispute Research Centre, Newcastle, University of Newcastle upon Tyne, 1993), citing Sir Thomas More, 1517. See further B Simpson, P McCarthy and J Walker, *Being There: Fathers After Divorce* (Newcastle Centre for Family Studies, University of Newcastle upon Tyne, Newcastle, 1995).

[168] C Henricson and A Bainham, *The Child and Family Policy Divide: Tensions, Convergence and Rights* (Joseph Rowntree Foundation, York, 2005).

[169] Smart and Neale, 'Family Fragments' (1999), above (n 57); see also: Neale and Smart (1997), above (n 57); Smart and Neale (1997), above (n 57).

[170] Smart, above (n 51), 1.

[171] S Parker, 'Rights and Utility in Anglo-Australian Law' (1992) 55 *Modern Law Review* 311: Dewar, above (n 60), (n 99); Boyd, above (n 25), (n 30).

[172] Ch 1, p 32. Boyd, above (n 25).

important not to overstate what is new in these developments,[173] it is possible to identify in conclusion two issues which caution against dismissing recent fathers' rights activism in the legal arena as no more than extreme and minority activity.

Rethinking Divorce

First, the legal changes charted in this chapter have reconstituted divorce as a new and different kind of governable space, one marked by ideas of social responsibility and the promotion of civic responsibility.[174] These shifts, van Krieken observes,[175] are intimately bound up with longer-term historical trends in the governance of family practices, in particular the move towards the 'civilising' of parents.[176] There is, van Krieken suggests, a 'logic of durability' shaping law reform in this area,[177] with law increasingly concerned with attempting to set normative expectations and modify behaviour.[178] Ideas of shared parental authority and the constancy of relationships have come to replace the idea that we might need to choose one parent over another. Rather, the discourse of equal parenting and shared responsibility has become the pursued, desirable outcome for politicians and policy makers alike. It is revealing, nonetheless, that both women and men may perceive divorce as a process now being dominated by an elite; an 'information industry' of therapists, conciliators and mediators who (coercively) prescribe the 'good divorce'.[179] In such a context, Rhoades suggests, recent debates around fathers, contact and residence reflect the emergence of a new *kind* of political conflict in late modernity, one based around the question of how perceived inequalities are distributed and experienced.[180] Far from seeing a 'pendulum swing' against feminism, this would indicate that what is taking place in law is a reconstruction of the rhetoric of equality and liberal legality, a shift which has reshaped the form and content of fathers' narratives within the legal arena.

---

[173] Writing in 1985, for example, Brophy observes how the fathers' rights movement 'continue[s] to make an impact both in terms of conventional wisdom about the treatment of fathers in custody disputes ... and in discussion on law and contemporary legal practice in this field': J Brophy, 'Child Care and the Growth of Power: The Status of Mothers in Custody Disputes' in J Brophy and C Smart (eds), *Women in Law: Explorations in Law, Family, Sexuality* (Routledge and Kegan Paul, London, 1985) at 97, 115.

[174] See: Reece, above (n 99); van Krieken, above (n 99); above (n 142).

[175] van Krieken, above (n 99).

[176] *Ibid.*

[177] *Ibid* at 35. See further: I Thery, '"The Interests of the Child" and the Regulation of the Post-divorce Family' (1986) 14 IJSL 341 at 354.

[178] van Krieken, above (n 99).

[179] Reece, above (n99) 195.

[180] See: H Rhoades, 'The "No Contact Mother": Reconstructions of Motherhood in the Era of the "New Father"' (2002) 16(1) *International Journal of Law, Policy and the Family* 71, citing Z Bauman, *Intimations of Postmodernity* (Routledge, London, 1992) at 198.

Equality, Justice and Care

Second, and given this shift, it is perhaps unsurprising that fathers' claims should be couched increasingly in terms of the caring father, a man who takes an equal share of responsibility for a child (see below). How this relates to the material gendered realities of family practices is, as we saw in chapter four, another matter. Nonetheless, it appears many fathers are now articulating legal claims, not just in a language of rights, justice and entitlement, but also, increasingly, it would seem, via reference to ideas of care, caring and welfare.[181] In this and the preceding chapter, we have located these shifting narratives around fatherhood in the contexts of broader economic and cultural changes around parenting practices, and the reframing of the politico-legal domain around ideas of justice, equality and social cohesion, not least shifts that have occurred in the slipstream of feminism.

The developments concerning post-separation fatherhood discussed in this chapter have evoked ideas of social (in)justice and rights in order to question the perceived unfairness of law, whether in relation to child support legislation, contact or residence. The incorporation of the European Convention on Human Rights through the Human Rights Act 1998 has further entrenched these ideas of equality and rights discourse in the field of family law. It is against this backdrop that fathers' groups are perhaps understandably increasingly seeking to deploy narratives of rights, equality and care within debates on law reform. What is happening, however, reflects the contradictory nature of the cultural shifts around fathers discussed elsewhere in this book in which the 'moral tales' and normative constructions of fatherhood, on the part of both men *and* women, reflect simultaneously the twin ideas of the father as carer, sharer of responsibilities, and as breadwinner, the competing imperatives of 'cash and care'.

It is, ultimately, necessary to recognise therefore the complex and contradictory nature of the reconfiguration of gender relations that has framed these debates about post-separation fatherhood and law. Moreover, and following Smart, it is important to acknowledge the social significance of the 'different registers' of fathers' voices that appear to be emerging around these discourses of welfare, justice and care.[182] We find in the fathers' rights discourse a recognition that men will, and should, deal with feelings of loss and vulnerability by recourse to both legal rights *and* claims couched in terms of an ethic of care.[183] The greater prominence of the fathers' rights movement in the context of post-separation

---

[181] Smart, above (n 2). See also: S Coltrane and N Hickman, 'The Rhetoric of Rights and Needs: Moral Discourse in the Reform of Child Custody and Support Laws' (1992) 39 *Social Problems* 400.

[182] Smart, above (n 2). See also: C Smart, 'Equal Shares – Rights for Fathers or Recognition for Children' (2004) 24 *Critical Social Policy* 484; C Smart, 'Texture of Family Life: Further Thoughts on Change and Commitment' (2005) 34 *Journal of Social Policy* 541; C Smart, 'Changing Landscapes of Family Life: Rethinking Divorce' (2004) 3(4) *Social Policy & Society* 401; Collier, above (n 107).

[183] Smart, above (n 2). See also ch 4, p 120.

fatherhood debates might be understood as one aspect of a complex renegotiation of men's role as parents, one occuring in the light of shifting gender relations, household forms, discourses of parenting and childhood, as well as changes in legal norms and modes of governance. These shifts, as we will see in chapter seven, have significant implications for theorising of the male subject in law. The study of fatherhood, divorce, separation and contact presented in this chapter reveals further aspects of the fragmentation of fatherhood and the contradictory nature of the new fatherhood ideal central to the co-parenting contact culture. In this 'new recognisable narrative',[184] moral claims to rights and justice have been repositioned within debates around fatherhood and law. Discursive shifts around the separated father are, however, symptomatic of wider contradictions and confusions that pervade fatherhood – and, as recent theoretical and empirical research on fathering would suggest, the experiences of many men. Developments around post-separation parenting illustrate the fragmentation of a model of fatherhood held together by a framework of laws and assumptions about paternal responsibility based on economics and the 'cash nexus' between men and families.[185]

What of the future? 'Getting it right' in relation to divorce law reform appears, notwithstanding years of research in the field, to be as elusive as ever. It is unclear, at the time of writing, whether the re-articulation of the narratives of justice, care and welfare advanced by some fathers during separation reflects the emergence of a different consciousness on the part of significant numbers of men. What is equally unclear is whether this is best understood as a (pro-feminist?) 'embrace of responsibility' or no more than a re-articulation of an essentially self-interested form of power.[186] As Day Sclater has argued, however, perhaps real change in this area will require that parents 'of whatever gender' engage with the questions of emotion, pain and loss raised in this chapter and 'find better ways of dealing with the vulnerabilities that separation throws up'.[187] She suggests: 'That's why changing the law won't solve the real problems that fathers face. Solving those is much more difficult, because it means confronting ourselves.'[188]

[184] Smart, above (n 2).
[185] B Hobson (ed), *Making Men into Fathers: Masculinities and the Social Politics of Fatherhood* (Cambridge University Press, Cambridge, 2002) in particular at ch 1.
[186] Smart, above (n 2).
[187] 'We must learn to grieve our losses without acting out or dumping on the children. We can't go on disowning our feelings, imagining that our children, not us, are the vulnerable ones ... These are the displaced emotions that fuel legal battles': S Day Sclater, 'Families Reunited', *FQ Magazine* (Issue 3, Winter, 2003) at 56.
[188] *Ibid.*

173

6

Unmarried Fatherhood

Little is known, said or written about unmarried fathers because society expects them to remove themselves, or even to run away from the situation they have helped to create. Thus it is fair to say that society has clearly delineated expectations of the unmarried father and that it brings considerable pressure to bear upon him to conform to them. They are: to remove himself from the scene and, if possible, to make financial recompense to the unmarried mother and her child. Beyond this he has no function save as an absent object of blame ... The law, which enshrines social attitudes to a large extent, is only concerned with the putative father's financial responsibility.[1]

The consistent theme which characterizes the English reforms and European developments so far is the perceived need to protect unmarried mothers from adverse behaviour by fathers. Throughout the assumption has been that the interests of mother and child are synonymous. This is not unlike the equally dogmatic nineteenth century attitude to parenthood which, albeit in the context of the family within marriage, equated children's interests with their fathers.[2]

Introduction

THESE TWO STATEMENTS, taken respectively from a study of unmarried fathers in the mid-1970s and a legal consideration of their position in the late 1980s, would not be plausible today. While negative stereotypes and allegations of legal bias still exist, as will be seen below, contemporary discussion of unmarried fathers is far more positive. The author of the second quotation has more recently acknowledged this shift, attributing it to a range of factors including a heightened awareness of children's rights, the growing numbers of children born into stable cohabitations, the more assertive claims of fathers themselves and the growing influence of human rights norms.[3] While law makers have remained concerned with financial responsibility and the need to protect mothers from fathers' adverse behaviour, notably violence, greater attention is now paid to the search for ways of recognising, protecting and nurturing unmarried fathers' links with their children. Such concerns are as clear in the

---

[1] D Barber, *Unmarried Fathers* (Hutchinson, London, 1975) at 20.

[2] A Bainham, 'When is a Parent not a Parent? Reflections on the Unmarried Father and His Child in English Law' (1989) 3 *International Journal of Law Policy and the Family* 208 at 234.

[3] A Bainham, *Children: the Modern Law*, 3rd edn (Jordan Publishing, Bristol, 2005) at 184.

decisions of the European Court of Human Rights and domestic courts as they are in the activities of Parliament, which has rolled out a series of statutory reforms to strengthen legal links between non-marital children and their fathers, particularly in the last three decades. Within this body of law, the image of unmarried fathers as unworthy, irresponsible and uninterested in their children has been increasingly supplemented (in many contexts even supplanted) by a very different depiction: of men who are often deeply committed to their children, yet find themselves subject to discrimination, denied access to their children, and unfairly dependent on the whims of selfish, sometimes hostile, mothers.

The coexistence of these two perceptions of unmarried fathers is strongly mediated by assumptions about race and class. As noted in chapter one, the perceived 'crisis' in fatherhood has often focused primarily on children in situations of poverty and deprivation, and Black British men (the group most likely to become unmarried fathers) have sometimes been singled out for a perceived lack of commitment to their children.[4] Where both perceptions cohere, however, is in the idea that unmarried fathers, like separated fathers, present a 'problem' to be 'managed' by law and policy makers, with further reform needed either to force men to accept their responsibilities or to develop the relationships with their children that they want, deserve and are currently unfairly denied. This contrasts with the lack of discussion of the married father in an intact family unit, who, we have seen in chapter four, has, until recent years at least, been relatively invisible. Further, when the parenting of married fathers has been seen as problematic, for example in the case of the work–life balance debate also discussed in chapter four, this is generally constructed as an issue of structural impediments rather than one of individual behaviour.

This ambivalence to unmarried parents was well captured in the then newly elected Labour government's consultation paper of 1998, *Supporting Families,* which used carefully neutral language towards non-marital relationships, while still displaying a clear preference for marriage. Having several times stated that it would not be judgemental about those who choose not to marry, the paper nonetheless notes that:

> [t]he Government believes that marriage provides a strong foundation for stable relationships. This does not mean trying to make people marry, or criticizing or penalizing people who choose not to ... but we do share the belief of the majority of people that marriage provides the most reliable framework for raising children.[5]

Ten years on, while the Conservative party has suggested incentivising marriage through tax breaks, the Labour government's support for the idea of privileging

---

[4] See ch 1.

[5] Home Office, *Supporting Families: A Consultation Document* (HMSO, London, 1998) at [4.3]. For one particularly robust critique of the position taken in this document, see N Dennis and G Erdos, 'Sex and the State: Will *Supporting Families* Help or Harm the Family?' (1999) *Economic Affairs* 20.

marriage reflects an uneasy tension between attempting to promote marriage as the ideal situation in which to raise children while not criticising or penalising those who choose other forms of union.[6] Particular attention in these debates has been focused on those forms of non-marital union that most closely resemble marriage. This has led to the legal recognition of committed relationships between same-sex couples, who can now effectively gain the rights and responsibilities of marriage by entering into civil partnerships.[7] Attention has also focused on long-term cohabitants and the extent to which they should be treated in the same way as married couples.[8]

The unmarried fathers who form the focus of this chapter are an extremely diverse group, including single fathers, long-term committed cohabitants who are actively engaged in parenting and one-off sexual partners who may not even know that they have fathered a child.[9] Given that marriage has historically been a crucial tool for attaching men to children, however, this is a group collectively viewed as posing some quite specific problems for law and policy makers within certain contexts. With the non-marital child historically seen as a 'loose thread in the social fabric',[10] not legally woven into a broader kin network by marriage, how should parental relationships be recognised and regulated here? Non-marital birth historically called into question a child's legal relationship with both the mother and father. Today, however, the key policy problem has been constructed as one of how to recognise, regulate and protect the link between non-marital children and their fathers, where (unlike within marriage) this connection is assumed to require external validation and support. Thus, while much of the discussion of other chapters applies both to married and unmarried fathers, the fact that unmarried fathers have so often been posited as raising specific problems for law and policy and have thus been the targets of reform initiatives grounds the need for a chapter to consider them specifically as such.[11]

In what follows, we discuss policy and legal responses to non-marital birth and the understandings that underpin the legal status, rights and obligations of

---

[6] W Woodward, '£20-a-week Tory tax break plan aims to encourage marriage', *Guardian* (11 July 2007). A policy review issued by the Prime Minister's Strategy Unit notes that: '[t]here is no question that the stability associated with marriage usually provides the best environment in which to bring up children. But to make the promotion of marriage the main focus of family policy would be ineffective and could lead to discrimination against children whose parents have broken up or suffered bereavement...It is the loving atmosphere of a stable environment that makes for good families...So, the aim is to support families in all their variety': Prime Minister's Strategy Unit, *Building on Progress: Families* (Cabinet Office, London, 2007) at 3–4.

[7] Civil Partnership Act 2004.

[8] See: Law Commission, *Cohabitation: The Financial Consequences of Relationship Breakdown*, Consultation Paper, Law Com CP No 179 (2006) for a general consideration of these issues.

[9] We define unmarried fathers here as genetic fathers who have never been legally married to their child(ren)'s biological mothers.

[10] H Krause, *Illegitimacy: Law & Social Policy* (Bobbs-Merrill, Indianapolis, 1971) at 1.

[11] We do not consider child support liability here, as it was discussed in the previous chapter. It should be noted, however, that much of the debate around men's financial liability for their children focused on unmarried fathers and 'irresponsible' procreation outside marriage.

unmarried fathers in different contexts. Across this discussion, we track different constructions of unmarried fathers as, variously, 'feckless', 'deadbeat' or 'irresponsible', to an emergent and, we suggest, increasingly dominant sense of unmarried fathers as a group who are subject to discrimination, potentially vulnerable and a deserving focus of policy initiatives to protect and strengthen their relationships with their children. Developing this latter understanding, we describe the claims made for justice and equality in the name of unmarried fathers, either in comparison to married fathers or to unmarried women, claims now often made with reference to international human rights norms. Finally, picking up on our discussion of this issue in chapter three, we also trace the enhanced significance of the genetic link (rather than marriage or a social relationship with a child) as a way of grounding legal fatherhood.

Below we provide a brief overview of the demographics of unmarried fatherhood, before moving on to discuss the evolution of law regulating non-marital birth, and outlining the gradual erosion of distinctions between married and unmarried fathers. In certain respects, married and unmarried fathers now enjoy the same rights and responsibilities with regard to their offspring. Our focus here is on those legal distinctions between married and unmarried fathers that have survived into recent years. Finally, we analyse the courts' treatment of unmarried fathers in the light of evolving international norms.

I Unmarried Fatherhood and Cohabitation

The proportion of children born outside marriage has quadrupled over the last 25 years, with more than two-fifths of children now born to unmarried parents, a substantial majority of whom are cohabiting. Unmarried fathers form an increasingly significant and highly diverse group, with differences marked along lines of ethnicity, geography, class, sexuality and age. One form of unmarried parenthood, however, has attracted particular attention in recent years: that provided in the context of cohabitation.[12] While cohabiting fathers (as one subset of unmarried fathers) may themselves be a diverse group, a significant amount of research suggests that many such relationships (and the parenting that occurs within them) can be extremely difficult to distinguish from marriage. Whether or not being born to married parents is better for children remains contested, with the social science evidence divided. Some suggest that marriage provides better

---

[12] See generally: A Barlow *et al*, *Cohabitation, Marriage and the Law: Social Change and Legal Reform in the 21st Century* (Hart, Oxford, 2005). 'Cohabitant' is difficult to define precisely. The Law Commission suggests: 'what are commonly referred to "couples", either opposite-sex or same-sex, who live together in intimate relationships', specifically excluding from its definition cohabiting blood relatives, or 'caring' relationships, and 'commercial relationships' such as landlord and tenant. See above (n 8) at [1.19]–[1.21].

outcomes for men, for women, for children and for society more generally.[13] Others find little to distinguish marriage from cohabitation.[14]

In *The Parental Obligation*, Eekelaar and Maclean found that marriage might play an important role in symbolising and confirming an achieved degree of economic security, and therefore be a desirable context within which parenthood can be exercised. However, they also note that the socio-economic status of the parents was much more significant in determining the social capital that parents provide for their children. They conclude that they were 'unable to determine how much *being married* might *in itself* add to the security created by socio-economic circumstances, or whether other types of institutional arrangements (for example, making parental responsibility agreements) might have similar effects'.[15] In a later paper, the same authors advise caution in claiming that marriage is *uniquely* capable of producing certain 'goods', noting that the picture is in fact more complex.[16]

It appears to be true that, statistically, married relationships last longer than unmarried ones. But it is also true that, at times when marriage was more widespread than it is now, the marriages of the young, the poor, and the remarried were at much higher risk of breaking up than those of older, more financially secure, first-time married people. Those risk categories may now be being substantially filled by unmarried cohabitants, so the reasons why married people who were in those circumstances were more likely to separate than others probably apply disproportionately to unmarried cohabitants.[17]

Despite this disagreement regarding the benefits of marriage, what is clear is that, for many, marriage is not seen as a prerequisite for parenthood. In this sense, Lewis has suggested that:

> the real difference between the so-called permissive decade of the 1960s and the position a generation later is the difference between the separation of sex and marriage that took place then and the increasing separation of marriage and parenthood that is taking place now.[18]

This separation of marriage and parenthood, however, poses considerable challenges for a legal system that has historically relied heavily on marriage as a way of cementing relationships between men and their children and has led to an

---

[13] For an overview of the literature in support of this claim, see: R O'Neill, *Experiments in Living: The Fatherless Family* (Civitas, London, 2002).

[14] Eg A Barlow *et al*, above (n 12); C Lewis, A Papacosta and J Warin, *Cohabitation, Separation and Fatherhood* (Joseph Rowntree Foundation, London, 2002).

[15] J Eekelaar and M Maclean, *The Parental Obligation* (Hart, Oxford, 1997) at 69.

[16] J Eekelaar and M Maclean, 'Marriage and the Moral Bases of Personal Relationships' (2004) 31 *Journal of Law and Society* 510, 537.

[17] Ibid.

[18] J Lewis, 'Is Marriage the Answer to the Problems of Family Change?' (2001) *Political Quarterly* 437. See also: J Lewis, *The End of Marriage?* (Edward Elgar, Cheltenham, 2001) and: H Willekens 'Long Term Developments in Family Law in Europe' in J Eekelaar and T Nhlapo, *The Changing Family: Family Forms and Family Law* (Hart, Oxford, 1998) for a historical explanation and contextualisation of this shift in the broader European context.

increasing focus on those obligations that individuals owe as parents, rather than as spouses.[19] Before coming on to an exploration of this current legal position, we provide a brief historical overview of the evolution of the law to the current day.

II The Law of Illegitimacy

For William Blackstone, writing at the end of the eighteenth century, it was clear that the 'illegitimate' child was not related to any broader kinship network.

> The rights which appertain to a bastard are very few, being only such as he can *acquire*; for he can *inherit* nothing, being looked upon as the son of nobody, and sometimes called *filius nullius*, sometimes *filius populi* … The incapacity of a bastard consists principally in this, that he cannot be heir to any one, neither can he have heirs, but of his own body; for being *nullius filius*, he is therefore of kin to nobody, and has no ancestor from whom any inheritable blood can be derived.[20]

The non-marital child was not just cut off from the father but also the mother and any broader kin network. He or she could not inherit in cases of intestacy and, even where named as a beneficiary in a will, would be disadvantaged by the rules of construction. In one case, a bequest to 'our children' was held to refer only to legitimate children, even though none existed.[21] In another, a non-marital child conceived after the making of a disposition could not inherit property because to allow this would encourage immorality.[22] As late as 1841, one court wondered: 'How does the mother of an illegitimate child differ from a stranger?'.[23]

Where the relationship between parent and non-marital child was recognised, however, was in a concern to enforce men's financial responsibility for children, in order to remove that cost from the public purse.[24] Many paternity disputes

[19] G Douglas, 'Marriage, Cohabitation and Parenthood – From Contract to Status?' in S Katz, J Eekelaar and M Maclean (eds), *Cross Currents: Family Law and Policy in the US and England* (Oxford University Press, Oxford, 2000).

[20] W Blackstone, *Commentaries on the Laws of England*, Book 1, 4th edn (Clarendon Press, Oxford, 1770) at 459. This historical section draws heavily on Cretney's impressive history of family law: S Cretney, *Family Law in the Twentieth Century: A History* (Oxford University Press, Oxford, 2003).

[21] Cretney, above (n 20) at 561, citing: *Dorin v Dorin* [1875] LR 7 HL 568 (DC). A further issue concerns the inheritance rights of parents to estates of their non-marital children. Under the Legitimacy Act 1926, the mother was entitled to succeed on her illegitimate child's intestacy as if the child had been born legitimate, but it was not until the Family Law Act 1969 that such rights were also extended to the father.

[22] *Crook v Hill* (1876) 3 Ch D 773; see Cretney, ibid. Further, the definition of 'dependants' in the Inheritance (Family Provision) Act 1938 did not include illegitimate children.

[23] *Re Ann Lloyd* (1841) 3 Man & G 547 at 548; 133 ER 1259 (per Maule J), cited in Church Assembly Board for Social Responsibility, *Fatherless By Law? The Law and the Welfare of Children Designated Illegitimate* (Church Information Office, London, 1966).

[24] An economic nexus between man and child is discussed in ch 5 in the context of child support, pp 150–153.

occurred in the context of affiliation proceedings (applications for maintenance) made by a 'single woman' under the Bastardy Laws Amendment Act 1872.[25] Paternity had to be established only on the balance of probabilities, but in order to 'prevent men being at the mercy of profligate women' who might easily make 'wicked or unfounded charges', corroboration of her evidence was required.[26] Litigation concerning illegitimacy also took place in the divorce courts as evidence of a wife's adultery. Here, the husband would struggle to overcome the presumption of paternity as, for many years, considerations of public decency prevented either spouse from giving evidence that intercourse had not occurred at the relevant time.[27]

Presumptions regarding fatherhood have now been rendered far less significant by scientific advances in paternity testing.[28] They are nonetheless important in indicating that legal certainty regarding paternity was accorded rather more weight than the desire to establish the genetic truth. They also suggest a context where the state had a significant interest in ensuring financial provision for a child, with men far more focused on *dis*proving paternity to avoid such obligations. While this remains a concern, it is seen below that today this coexists with frequent use of paternity tests as part of the 'embrace of fatherhood' discussed in chapters four and five, with men here keen to establish themselves as fathers.

From the beginning of the twentieth century, there was general agreement that the law of illegitimacy was in need of reform,[29] and across the course of the century, the position of non-marital children was improved in three ways. First, the category of those children who counted as 'legitimate' was broadened through allowing children to be legitimated by their parents' subsequent marriage,[30] and recognising as legitimate those children born within a void marriage which one or both parents believed to be lawful at the time.[31] Second, legislation gradually removed many of the legal disadvantages formerly associated with illegitimacy in respect of matters such as maintenance and succession.[32] Third,

---

[25] Cretney, above (n 20) at 530.

[26] *Mash v Darley* [1914] 3 KB 1226 at 1235 (per Phillimore LJ); *Thomas v Jones* [1920] 2 KB 399 at 405 (per Lord Reading CJ). See: Cretney, above (n 20).

[27] Until the Law Reform (Miscellaneous Provisions) Act 1949, neither the husband nor wife was allowed to give evidence of non-access in order to bastardise a child born during marriage: 'it is a rule, founded in decency, morality, and polity, that [the spouses] shall not be permitted to say after marriage, that they have had no connection, and therefore that the offspring is spurious; more especially the mother, who is the offending party': *Goodright ex Dim Stevens v Moss et al* (1777) 2 Cowp 591 at 594; 98 ER 1257 (per Lord Mansfield). Irrefutable evidence that, for example, the husband was serving overseas, was acceptable to rebut the presumption.

[28] See below, p 199.

[29] Pressure groups formed to lobby for this end included the National Council for the Unmarried Mother and Her Child in 1918. See: Cretney, above (n 20) at 546.

[30] Legitimacy Act 1926, s 1. The Legitimacy Act 1926 was a compromise solution. It excluded 'adulterine bastards', but nonetheless operated to legitimate a large number of children. Between 5% and 9% of illegitimate children born between 1921 and 1959 were subsequently legitimated: *ibid.*

[31] Legitimacy Act 1959, s 2.

[32] Eg: Fatal Accidents Act 1976, s 1(5)(b), virtually eliminating the distinction for the purposes of dependency claims brought thereunder; Family Law Reform Act 1969, s 16, changing the law of

the language of illegitimacy was itself removed from the statute books, to be replaced with the less stigmatising, 'non-marital'.[33]

This reform process climaxed in the 1970s and 1980s with a flurry of activity resulting in the Family Law Reform Act 1987. The Law Commission's 1979 working paper on illegitimacy pities the position of those children who have the misfortune to be 'illegitimate'[34] and locates non-marital births as a serious social problem.[35] The document notes that the law discriminated against both the non-marital child and the father, who 'from a strictly legal point of view' was thought 'probably at a greater disadvantage than the child himself'.[36] Intriguingly, having set out a number of problems experienced by the non-marital child and the unmarried father under these headings, the document then lists a number of factors which seem primarily to pose problems for unmarried mothers but fails to describe them as such, preferring the term 'procedural discrimination'.[37] This tends to support Smart's suggestion that the document legitimised a growing disquiet over the supposed power of mothers and marked an important moment in the shift from a 'traditional position' where the unmarried father was perceived as seeking to deny paternity at all costs, towards the current situation where unmarried fathers seek not only the legal status of paternity, but also all the 'rights' of married fathers.[38]

Having canvassed views on whether to remove the adverse consequences of illegitimacy or abolish the distinction altogether, in 1979 the Law Commission came down cautiously in favour of the latter option. In a subsequent report, however, it performed a volte-face, suggesting that it had previously underesti-mated the problems inherent in the complete abolition of illegitimacy.[39] Specifi-cally, granting full parental rights to all unmarried fathers, it was argued, might serve to undermine the mother and disrupt any family unit she had created with a new man. A number of commentators suggested that such rights should thus only be accorded to a category of fathers defined to exclude the 'unmeritorious'.[40] This problem of distinguishing between deserving and undeserving unmarried fathers has continued to dog subsequent policy and reform initiatives,[41] offering an example of the 'good dad/bad dad' binary we have observed in other contexts.

---

inheritance to allow illegitimate children to make claims under a will or (s 14) in the case of their father's intestacy. Many surviving distinctions were swept away by the Family Law Reform Act 1987.

[33] Family Law Reform Act 1987.
[34] Law Commission, 'Family Law: Illegitimacy', Law Com WP No 74 (1979) at [1].
[35] *Ibid* at [1.5].
[36] *Ibid* at [2.11].
[37] *Ibid* at [2.12].
[38] C Smart, '"There is of course the Distinction Dictated by Nature": Law and the Problem of Paternity' in M Stanworth (ed), *Reproductive Technologies: Gender, Motherhood and Medicine*, Feminist Perspectives Series (Polity, Cambridge, 1987) at 110–11.
[39] Law Commission, *Family Law: Illegitimacy*, Law Com No 118 (1982).
[40] See, eg: M Hayes, 'Law Commission Working Paper No 74: Illegitimacy' (1980) 43 MLR 299.
[41] See below, pp 200–201.

After discussing various ways of distinguishing good fathers from bad, the Law Commission decided that some form of judicial scrutiny was essential. Noting that unmarried relationships were 'infinitely variable in their nature and in the intentions of the parties to them', it suggested that scrutiny by a court was a reasonable protection for the interests of all parties.[42] The resulting legislation, the Family Law Reform Act 1987, aimed to remove both the stigmatising label of 'illegitimate' from the statute books, as well as many of the remaining distinctions between the rights and responsibilities of married and unmarried fathers. It did so, however, whilst retaining a distinction between married fathers (who would gain certain rights automatically) and unmarried fathers (who would obtain them only on agreement with the mother, or on application to the courts).[43]

While the Law Commission clearly shows an increased awareness of men's needs here, it nonetheless thought it more acceptable to distinguish between fathers than between children. This distinction attracted some criticism, with one commentator suggesting that it is 'fundamentally flawed with artificiality' and focused on the removal of discriminatory labelling at the expense of fully addressing the more important matters of substance.[44] Yet the Law Commission was not prepared to recognise all fathers as equally worthy. Two different sorts of father populate their working papers and are visible throughout the broader discussions of appropriate reform. First, there is the 'deadbeat', irresponsible or immoral father, seeking to evade his responsibilities to his children. Second, there is the good and caring father who wants to be involved in raising his children but who is offered insufficient support and encouragement to do so, being left dependent on the whims of a potentially hostile mother, who may deny him access to the children he loves. The resonance with the separated father, discussed in chapter five, is in this regard striking. How to recognise and regulate legal fatherhood in a way that responds appropriately to *both* stereotypes is an issue that has continued to exercise policy makers.

In the years to follow, claims to equality for unmarried fathers and their children become increasingly in evidence in this reform process, not least following the introduction of the Children Act 1989.[45] Alongside attempts to disclaim fatherhood, recent years have also seen an increase in reported cases where paternity is asserted against the mother's objection.[46] As noted in chapter five with reference to post-separation parenting, recent debates have involved

---

[42] Law Commission above (n 39) at [4.39].

[43] See, in particular, Family Law Reform Act 1987, s 1, which provides that 'references (however expressed) to any relationship between two persons, shall, unless the contrary intention appears, be construed without regard to whether or not the father and mother of either of them, or the father and mother of any person through whom the relationship is deduced, have or had been married to each other at any time'.

[44] Bainham, above (n 2) at 235.

[45] Ch 4, pp 126–132.

[46] G Douglas, *An Introduction to Family Law*, 2nd edn (Oxford University Press, Oxford, 2004) at 42.

discussions concerning not just child support liability but also fathers' inadequate contact with their children. In the context of unmarried fathers, the perceived disjuncture between liability for child support that is automatic and various rights attached to the status of father, which are not, is an issue that has provoked particular anger.[47]

III   Contemporary Legal Treatment of Unmarried Fathers

We now turn to the contemporary legal treatment of unmarried fathers. Some few statutory distinctions between them and their married counterparts have survived into recent years, and we start by describing those. We begin with the requirements of birth registration. Second, we consider nationality law, where a significant difference in the treatment of married and unmarried fathers has only very recently been removed. Third, we consider the most significant remaining distinction in the legal treatment of married and unmarried fathers, albeit one which has been greatly eroded over the last years: the allocation of parental responsibility (PR).[48] Finally, we consider recent trends in judicial decision-making in this area. Family courts enjoy wide-ranging discretionary powers, and here we track how they have considered the nature of the parents' relationship and the relative importance of the genetic link between father and child in exercising that discretion.

Birth Registration

Married and unmarried fathers have long had radically different legal obligations relating to birth registration, although this distinction is likely to be significantly eroded. Married fathers share a duty with the mother to register a new child within 42 days of birth,[49] while unmarried fathers are currently expressly exempted from this obligation and can only be registered at the request of both parents or following a relevant court order.[50] The mother thus acts as a gatekeeper to recognition of the father, with no duty to disclose his name.[51] We know little about how and why parents decide whether the unmarried father should be named on a birth certificate. What we do know is that the unmarried father's name is recorded in more than four out of five cases, with just over three-quarters of these couples

[47] S Sheldon, 'Unmarried Fathers and Parental Responsibility: a Convincing Case for Reform?' (2001) 2 *Feminist Legal Studies* 93, for discussion in the context of parental responsibility.
[48] We do not consider one further context in which the legal distinction between married and unmarried fathers has been retained: transmission of titles of honour. See: *Re Moynihan* [2001] 1 FLR 113.
[49] Births and Deaths Registration Act 1953. s 2.
[50] *Ibid*, s 10(1); Registration of Births and Deaths (Amendment) Regulations, 1994, SI 1994/1948.
[51] Except in the context of child support: Child Support Act 1991, s 6(7).

184

living at the same address.[52] This leaves a total of around 45,000 birth registrations per year in which no father is named.[53] Unsurprisingly, the registration of fathers' names is higher where the parents are cohabiting and, for non-resident fathers, there is a correlation between registration rates and the closeness of the parents' relationship.[54] Research has also shown that failure to register the father's name is strongly correlated with maternal youth and disadvantage.[55]

This asymmetry in parental obligations would seem to rely on a combination of factors including, first, an understandable reluctance to require women to disclose details of sexual partners (and an obvious difficulty in forcing them to do so). Second, it may reflect the historical notion, further explored with regard to nationality law below, that the non-marital child is not the father's responsibility. Third, Torr has suggested that this is part of a general marginalisation of fathers in the birth process,[56] citing his own experience of registration documentation directed exclusively towards his partner, who was told merely that she 'may, perhaps' wish to discuss registration with him.[57] Whatever the groundings for this asymmetry, however, what is clear is that it is already subject to erosion. The law has been reformed to make it easier for a father to be recognised as such, even where he is opposed by the mother,[58] and further changes in the same broad direction have been canvassed. The government has recently proposed establishing registration of unmarried fathers as a default presumption, with exceptions to be made only where joint registration would be impossible, impracticable or unreasonable. These exceptions pertain where the mother does not know who or where the father is, where pregnancy results from rape or incest, where she fears that the father may be violent, or where there is a dispute about paternity.[59]

The proposed reform would seem to reflect the belief that according unmarried fathers rights will lead them to assume greater responsibility with regard to

---

[52] Office for National Statistics, *Birth Statistics* (ONS, London, 2006). On motivation, see however: Graham *et al*, n 55 below.

[53] This equates to around 7% of all births. About 45% of unregistered fathers are nevertheless believed to be in some kind of contact with child. See Department for Work and Pensions, *Joint Birth Registration: Promoting Parental Responsibility*, Cm 7160 (2007) at [2].

[54] See: K Kiernan and K Smith, 'Unmarried Parenthood: New Insights from the Millennium Cohort Study' (2003) 114 *Population Trends* 26 at 27.

[55] Markers of disadvantage included low educational levels, social tenancy, failure to receive antenatal care, having no one else present at birth (as a sign of isolation), poor health (high smoking rates) and low rates of attempting to breastfeed. See J Graham *et al*, *Sole and Joint Birth Registration: Exploring the Circumstances, Choices and Motivations of Unmarried Parents* (Department for Work and Pensions, Research Report 463, 2007).

[56] See ch 2, n –.

[57] J Torr, *Is There a Father in the House? A Handbook for Health and Social Care Professionals* (Radcliffe, Oxford, 2003) at 56.

[58] Where paternity cannot be presumed through marriage or birth registration, a man's paternity can now also be established by way of a court declaration: Family Law Act 1986, s 55A, introduced by Child Support, Pensions and Social Security Act 2000, s 83.

[59] Department for Work and Pensions, above (n 53) at [57]–[58]; Department for Work and Pensions, *Joint Birth Registration: Recording Responsibility* (Cm 7293, June 2008). Paternity disputes would be left for the courts to resolve in the normal way.

their children, not just in financial provision, but also in terms of contact.[60] This maps to, and is in keeping with, the broader policy agenda of promoting fathers' responsibilities discussed in chapters four and five. In listing potential benefits, the government suggests that such a reform would recognise children's 'right to know that their parents take responsibility for them'[61] and promote 'equal parental status', with children set to benefit if both parents are involved in their upbringing:

> Joint birth registration is one of the very first steps a father can take, regardless of the type of relationship he has with the mother. Parents do not have to live together in order for the father to take an active role in the upbringing of their child and joint birth registration can help to build a culture where a father can feel he has a real purpose and stake in his child's life.[62]

A shift towards increasing the registration of unmarried fathers might be seen within the trend to recognising a child's right to the 'genetic truth'.[63] It should be noted, however, that birth registration has never been treated as exclusively a historical record of genetic 'fact' but also as an important symbolic statement of social roles.[64] The symbolic function of birth registration was seen in our discussion of the Human Fertilisation and Embryology (Deceased Fathers) Act 2003.[65] In this light, the upholding as lawful of a refusal to allow a female-to-male transsexual to be registered as the father of a child born to his partner following donor insemination may seem surprising.[66] In the light of more recent case law, however, it is unlikely that such a refusal would be upheld in the future,[67] and is

---

[60] The Ministerial Foreword to the Green Paper frames the discussion in this way: 'fathers who officially acknowledge the birth of their child from the outset are more likely to stay in contact with that child if their relationship with the child's mother breaks down. And if a father has jointly registered the birth and is later unwilling to pay maintenance, it will be simpler for the mother to claim the child maintenance he owes.' The Green Paper later notes that making joint registration the default position will 'publicly embed an expectation that the usual course of events is for both parents to acknowledge and be involved in the upbringing of their children. Most fathers are fully engaged in bringing up their children. For those who aren't, we want them to realize that they do have a stake in their children's lives and for fewer fathers to have no clear accountability or commitment to their children': DWP, above n 53 at 2 and para 5.

[61] *Ibid* at [17].

[62] *Ibid* at [16].

[63] See ch 3 above. Note Eekelaar's call that 'legal truth' should reflect 'physical truth': J Eekelaar, *Family Law and Personal Life* (Oxford University Press, Oxford, 2006).

[64] As in the case of children born as a result of donated gametes obtained through a licensed clinic; see ch 3. Further, since the introduction of the Gender Recognition Act 2004, transgendered people can ask to have their birth certificates changed to recognise their new gender (a gender which, furthermore, can be acquired without sex reassignment surgery). This possibility had been denied by previous judicial decisions: ch 3, pp 88–89.

[65] See ch 3, pp 79–80.

[66] *X, Y and Z v UK* (App no 21830/93) (1997) 24 EHRR 143, [1997] 2 FLR 892. See further: ch 3, pp 88–89.

[67] See: *Goodwin v UK* (App no 28957/95) (2002) 35 EHRR 447, [2002] 2 FLR 487; *I v UK* (App no 25680/94) (2002) 35 EHRR 447, [2002] 2 FLR 518. This issue has been rendered less pressing as transgender people are now able to acquire legal status in their new gender identity: Gender Recognition Act 2004.

probably best understood as the result of judicial attitudes which would now be seen as outdated. It would not be surprising if the symbolic importance of registration were greater for fathers (whose relationship with a child is not visibly established through pregnancy and birth), and particularly for unmarried fathers (whose relationship is not established by marriage).

Being registered on a birth certificate also has considerable practical legal significance, most notably with regard to the acquisition of PR. The decision to extend PR to those unmarried fathers who were named on the birth certificate relied on the suggestion that signing the birth certificate was 'a formal commitment to family life', an adoption of responsibility analogous to that taken on by married men.[68] As such, the government's suggestion less than ten years on that those men who are 'passive' or 'indifferent' to fatherhood should be specifically targeted and encouraged to be so registered might seem surprising. However, the strengthening and extension of procedures allowing fathers to demand recognition as such can be located within the clear trend noted in chapter five for fathers to make resort to law in order to claim rights, rather than to evade responsibilities towards children, and for law to accommodate such demands. In addition to its importance in the context of PR, birth registration has recently also acquired greater significance in the context of unmarried fathers' ability to transmit UK nationality to their children. It is to these two issues that we turn next.

Nationality and Immigration Law

As part of a raft of provisions designed to 'update' the existing law in order to 'reflect modern thinking about citizenship'[69] and to bring it into line with international law,[70] a long-standing distinction has recently been removed between married fathers (who would transmit UK nationality automatically) and unmarried fathers (who were previously dependent on the Home Office's discretion).[71] Now all British fathers can transmit citizenship to their children automatically. The

---

[68] Advisory Board on Family Law (Lord Chancellor's Department), 'Response to the Consultation Paper on Paternity and Parental Responsibility', Annex C of the Second Annual Report, 1998/1999, <http://www.dca.gov.uk/family/annrep99/annex_c.htm>, accessed 18 July 2007. See below, pp 190–194 for discussion of this reform.

[69] Secretary of State for the Home Department, *Secure Borders, Safe Haven: Integration with Diversity in Modern Britain*, Cm 5387 (2002) at [2.24].

[70] Notably, European Convention on Nationality (1997), Art 5; Convention for the Protection of Human Rights and Fundamental Freedoms (European Convention on Human Rights, as amended), Arts 3, 8 and 14.

[71] Nationality, Immigration and Asylum Act 2002, s 9, amending British Nationality Act 1981, s 50. For a detailed account of this reform, see: S Sheldon, 'Unmarried Fathers and British Citizenship: the Nationality, Immigration and Asylum Act (2002) and British Nationality (Proof of Paternity) Regulations (2006)' (2007) 19(1) *Child and Family Law Quarterly* 1.

only hurdle faced by unmarried fathers will be the need to prove paternity; however, for most that requirement is met by being named on the birth certificate.[72]

The evolution of nationality law to date fits closely with the broader treatment of non-marital children described above. For many years, in line with the principle of coverture, only married fathers (and, exceptionally from 1964, unmarried mothers) could transmit citizenship to their children.[73] From 1981, all mothers were allowed to transmit British nationality, but the law continued to make a firm and significant distinction between unmarried and married fathers, asserting in stark terms that, for the purposes of citizenship law, 'the relationship of father and child shall be taken to exist between a man and any legitimate child born to him' alone.[74] Remaining in place for some 25 years to come, the distinction between marital and non-marital children was thus long to outlive the difficulties of accurate paternity determination and to survive a challenge under the Human Rights Act 1998 brought by an unmarried father.[75]

In the context of citizenship law, unmarried fatherhood is thus revealed as having historically enjoyed a rather contingent status. Until 2006, unmarried fathers were able to pass on UK citizenship only on application to the Home Office. In considering the application, the Home Office would take account of the mother's wishes, reinforcing the idea of mothers as 'gatekeepers' to fathers' rights. That such rights are now to be obtained automatically is further evidence of the gradual erosion of differences between married and unmarried fathers and the rise of the idea of formal equality. Unmarried fathers here gain the right to be treated equally to married fathers and to mothers.

Who counts as a legal parent is also of relevance in immigration law. Historically, the differential treatment of non-marital children of British citizen fathers could be seen in cases such as *C (An Infant) v ECO Hong Kong* (1976).[76] Here, the illegitimate daughter of a Chinese mother and English father had applied to study in the UK and confided to an entry clearance officer that she wanted to remain permanently, wrongly believing that she had a right to abode because of her father's nationality. She was refused entry as a student because she intended to remain indefinitely and was refused settlement in the UK because she was illegitimate. She could not rely on the so-called 'ancestral connection' rule

---

[72] British Nationality (Proof of Paternity) Regulations 2006, SI 2006/1496. Paternity can also be established by other means, eg DNA tests and relevant court orders.

[73] British Nationality (No 2) Act 1964. See generally: Sheldon, above (n 71) for a detailed description of the evolution of the law. Coverture describes the process whereby '[t]he very being or legal existence of the wife is suspended during the marriage or at least incorporated and consolidated into that of the husband under whose wing, protection and cover she performs everything': W Blackstone, *Commentaries on the Laws of England: Volume III* (Dawsons, London, 1967) at 433.

[74] British Nationality Act 1981, s 50(9).

[75] *R (Montana) v Secretary of State for the Home Department* [2001] 1 WLR 552. The plaintiff failed to show that the provision constituted discrimination against him and his child such as to interfere in their enjoyment of family life.

[76] (1976) Imm AR 165.

allowing admittance for settlement to those Commonwealth citizens with a grandparent born in UK, as illegitimate applicants could only rely on their maternal grandparents, not their paternal ones.[77]

The current immigration rules contain a new and more liberal definition that includes both the mother and the father of a non-marital child, where paternity is proven. However, whilst emphasising the importance of family reunification, the rules still attach relevance to marriage in that it is very hard for a non-marital child born overseas to enter the UK to live with one parent while the other is alive and capable of looking after him or her elsewhere. The parent based in the UK must have 'sole responsibility for the child's upbringing' and, further, there must be 'serious and compelling family or other considerations which make exclusion of the child undesirable' and suitable arrangements for the child's care must be demonstrated.[78] Since 1994, there has been provision for parents to come to the UK for contact with UK-resident children.[79]

Parental Responsibility

Finally, we come to the most important remaining statutory distinction between married and unmarried fathers. Since the passing of the Children Act 1989, parental rights have been clustered together in parental responsibility (PR), which includes 'all the rights, duties, powers and responsibilities and authority which by law a parent of a child has in relation to the child and his property'.[80] As we saw in chapter four, this includes the right to administer children's property and to take important decisions regarding their upbringing, including where they will live; how they should be educated; in what religion they should be raised; and what non-essential medical treatment they should receive. PR also accords the right to be heard regarding children's proposed adoption or emigration, and to appoint a guardian for them following one's death.[81] A father without PR may also find himself more vulnerable in certain significant respects. For example, a recent decision of the Court of Appeal has confirmed that where a woman had conceived as the result of a one-night stand, the man concerned had no right to

---

[77] Immigration Rules 1983 (HC 169), para 29.

[78] See: Immigration Rules 1994 (HC 395), para 297(e), (f); *Cenir v Entry Clearance Officer* [2003] EWCA Civ 572; *Sloley v Entry Clearance Officer, Kingston Jamaica* [1973] Imm AR 54.

[79] The rules provide entry for a contact parent where the parent with residence lives permanently in the UK but appear not to do so where the parent with residence wishes to enter or stay in the UK in order to facilitate frequent contact between the British parent and child, a situation described as discriminatory: I Macdonald and F Webber (eds), *Immigration Law and Practice in the UK*, 6th edn (LexisNexis, London, 2005) at [11.76].

[80] Children Act 1989, s 3(1).

[81] An unmarried father without PR will nevertheless typically be joined in the adoption proceedings. See, generally: Bainham, above (n 3), for a detailed account of the rights included within PR.

be informed of the existence of the resulting child nor to be consulted with regard to her being placed for adoption.[82]

Whilst the intention behind the Children Act 1989 may have been to encourage greater parental responsibility, in practice the impact of these provisions has been largely to allocate parental rights (whether exercisable against the state or the other parent) to make decisions with regard to a child's upbringing.[83] No enforceable rights are given against PR holders. The practical significance of PR will be greater when parents are separated and less able to agree over matters to do with schooling or issues such as whether a child should be circumcised, or vaccinated against MMR.[84] In day-to-day parenting, the extent to which a non-resident parent's possession of PR imposes duties on the parent with care to consult is a particularly important issue. The Law Commission believed that to impose such duties would be 'both unworkable and undesirable', and this viewpoint was reflected in the Children Act 1989.[85] However, the courts have held that a parent with PR must be consulted about important decisions, such as a change of school[86] and change of surname.[87]

Until 2002, PR was accorded to an unmarried father only by agreement with the child's mother or on application to the court.[88] Since 2002, however, it has also been granted automatically to unmarried fathers who are named on a child's birth certificate.[89] This change means that whereas formerly most unmarried

---

[82] *Re C (A Child)* [2007] EWCA Civ 1206. Further, a father without PR will normally have no rights under the Hague Convention on the Civil Aspects of International Child Abduction, see: *Re J (A Minor) (Abduction: Custody Rights)* [1990] 3 WLR 492 (HL); Convention on the Civil Aspects of International Child Abduction (adopted 25 October 1980, entered into force 1 December 1983).

[83] Eekelaar has noted that PR can represent two ideas: that parents must behave dutifully towards their children; or that responsibility for childcare belongs to parents, not the state. He argues that the second idea has replaced the first as the dominant conception in the Children Act 1989: J Eekelaar, 'Parental Responsibility: State of Nature or Nature of the State?' (1991) *Journal of Social Welfare and Family Law* 37.

[84] See: K Standing, 'Reasserting Fathers' Rights? Parental Responsibility and Involvement in Education and Lone Mother Families in the UK' (1999) 7 *Feminist Legal Studies* 22; *Re J (Child's Religious Upbringing and Circumcision)* [1999] 2 FCR 307; and *Re C (Welfare of Child: Immunisation)* [2003] 2 FLR 1095 (CA).

[85] Law Commission *Illegitimacy*, Working Paper No. 74 (HMSO, London, 1979) at [2.10]. Under Children Act 1989, s 2(7), where more than one parent has PR, each may act alone, unless some other enactment requires the consent of more than one person, eg under s 13(1), where a residence order is in force, no person can change a child's surname or take him or her outside the UK without leave of the court or agreement of all PR-holders.

[86] *Re G (Parental Responsibility: Education)* [1994] 2 FLR 964. See also *Re C (Disclosure)* [1996] 1 FLR 767, recognising that a parent with PR has the right to information regarding that child. See, generally: Standing, above (n 84), for the argument that the rights and responsibilities of lone mothers are undermined by granting rights to absent fathers in the context of their children's education.

[87] Even where no residence order is in place: *Re T (Change of Surname)* [1998] 2 FLR 620, *Dawson v Wearmouth* [1997] 2 FLR 629, *Re PC (Change of Surname)* [1997] 2 FLR 730.

[88] See: Children Act 1989, s 4(1)(b) and (c), respectively.

[89] Children Act 1989, s 4(1)(a), as amended by the Adoption and Children Act 2002. For more detail, including discussion of the consultation process which preceded reform, see: Sheldon, above (n 47); see above (text at n 52) for birth registration statistics.

fathers did not hold PR, in the future a substantial majority will do so and this figure will be further increased if the proposed reforms concerning birth registration discussed above make their way into the statute books.

The decision to award paternal rights based on birth registration had been rejected in the 1980s on the basis that it might lead to mothers refusing to register fathers. Further, the Law Commission reasoned, registration gives no indication that a father wishes to be involved in a child's upbringing.[90] However, subsequent research revealed a significant disjuncture between unmarried fathers' actual legal situation and popular beliefs regarding what it was and ought to be. It was thought that awarding PR on the basis of birth registration would bring the law more closely into line with public opinion.[91] And, as was noted above, it was suggested that signing the birth certificate represented a 'formal commitment to family life'.[92] The political landscape, as we have seen elsewhere, had itself changed significantly since the 1980s. Whilst the practical inconveniences may have been negligible for most, the symbolism of denying automatic PR to unmarried fathers had provoked increasing hostility, with demands for equality strongly made.[93] The pressure group Families Need Fathers, for example, argued

> Unmarried fathers are a discriminated minority because they do not share the same rights as married parents or unmarried mothers. Their children are a discriminated minority because they do not share the rights to a father enjoyed by children of married parents. They suffer from the last vestiges of bastardy. This is plainly wrong.[94]

One particularly contentious aspect of the discrimination cited was that whereas many unmarried fathers did not have PR, they did have automatic liability to make financial contributions towards the upkeep of their children, a situation likened by one disgruntled individual 'to buying a car on HP but not being allowed to use it'.[95] This argument echoes that made by some separated fathers in relation to the links between child support and contact, noted in chapter five. And given the broader policy context around the promotion of 'active fathering' which we saw in chapter four, unmarried fathers' failure to obtain PR has been of growing concern to a government keen to foster men's commitment to their

---

[90] Law Commission, *Family Law: Illegitimacy*, Law Com No 118 (1982) at [4.40].

[91] Lord Chancellor's Department (LCD), *Court Procedures for the Determination of Paternity and on the Law on Parental Responsibility for Unmarried Fathers* (HMSO, London, 1998) 53; R Pickford, *Fathers, Marriage and the Law* (Family Policy Studies Centre, Cambridge, 1999); see also: Barlow *et al*, above (n 12).

[92] See above (n 68).

[93] See: A Burgess and S Ruxton, *Men and their Children: Proposals for Public Policy* (Institute for Public Policy Research, London, 1996); H Conway, 'Parental Responsibility and the Unmarried Father' (1996) 146 NLJ 782; NV Lowe, 'The Meaning and Allocation of Parental Responsibility – a Common Lawyer's Perspective' (1997) 11 *International Journal of Law, Policy and the Family* 192.

[94] Families Need Fathers, 'Response to the Lord Chancellor's Consultation Paper: Court Procedures for the Determination of Paternity and on the Law on Parental Responsibility for Unmarried Fathers' (April 1998), <http://www.fnf.org.uk/news-events/campaigns/submissions-and-consultation-responses/lcd-consultation-paper-response>, accessed 14 November 2007.

[95] Knight, individual respondent to the LCD consultation.

families in a more general sense. Granting automatic PR is thus seen as a way of entrenching paternal duty to provide for the child's emotional and moral development, as well as their financial needs. Denying this 'stamp of approval' to unmarried fathers,[96] it was suggested, risked alienating them and refusing the vital encouragement necessary for them to take on board family responsibilities,[97] destabilising the family unit and further contributing to the creation of lone-parent families. The claim that according automatic legal status through PR to unmarried fathers will create more stable family units has, however, been challenged by others, who express concerns that this move may destabilise marriage and, ultimately, work to the detriment of children.[98]

PR is not just seen as a practical issue, however; it is also a highly symbolic one, a point well illustrated by a recent dispute concerning a five-year-old child, D.[99] A lesbian couple had advertised for a man who would be interested in fathering a child, intending that such a man should complement their primary care of the child by being a 'real father' but only enjoying relatively infrequent visits. The father had other ideas and obtained a contact order before, some years later, applying for PR. The couple were happy for the man to be recognised as the child's 'father' and for her to see him for regular contact. However, they opposed an order that recognised him as D's 'parent', arguing that *they* were D's parents and that to have a third parent would compromise the child's family unit. The man, however, insisted that he should be recognised not just as a father but also as a parent and saw a PR order as bringing this recognition.[100] In order to gain PR, he made a commitment not to contact the child's school or medical carers without the couple's permission, thus denuding the order of its practical legal significance, and emphasising its symbolic value. The eventual award of PR in this case also illustrates an important trend discussed in chapter three, that is, awarding rights and responsibilities to a man who stands outside the social family unit might be seen as part of a move away from rigid protection of the nuclear family (or, in this case, perhaps the confusion that the recognition of same-sex families may create for this model). In awarding PR, the judge in *Re D* noted:

> I am considerably influenced by the reality that Mr B *is* D's father. Whatever new designs human beings have for the structure of their families, that aspect of nature cannot be overcome. It is to be hoped that as society accepts alternative arrangements more readily, as it seems likely will happen over the next few years, the impulse to hide

---

[96] *Re S (Parental Responsibility)* [1995] 2 FLR 648 (per Ward LJ).

[97] See eg: Interventions by Families Need Fathers, and the Children's Society, cited in Sheldon, above (n 44).

[98] See the commentators discussed in Sheldon, above (n 47), and in the text accompanying n 146, below.

[99] *Re D (Contact and Parental Responsibility: Lesbian Mothers and Known Father) (No 2)* [2006] EWHC 0002 (Fam). See A Diduck, "'If Only We Can Find the Appropriate Terms to Use the Issue will be Solved": Law, Identity and Parenthood' 2007 19(4) *Child and Family Law Quarterly* 458, for an insightful discussion of this case.

[100] [2006] EWHC 0002 (Fam) at [22] (per Black J).

or to marginalise a child's father so as not to call attention to an anomalous family will decline, although accommodating the emotional consequences of untraditional father-hood and motherhood and of the sort of de facto, non-biological parenthood that is experienced by a step-parent or same sex partner will inevitably remain discomfort-ing.[101]

Again, we see here the growing belief that to recognise a father figure standing outwith the boundaries of the social family need not threaten the parenting that occurs within. This case also illustrates the problems that such an approach can pose for mothers who wish to attempt to construct their family unit without involving a man.[102]

The result of the reform of PR law is to assimilate to a marital norm those unmarried fathers who, through birth certification, have made a formal acknowl-edgment of paternity. Others, of course, retain the possibility of obtaining PR via agreement or court order, although such procedures are still relatively rarely used.[103] The distinction between meritorious fathers (who are worthy of recog-nition and should thus acquire rights automatically) and others (who should not acquire them without undergoing some form of scrutiny) thus remains, although we would suggest the line has been redrawn in such a way as to extend rights to significantly greater numbers of men. Those who do not have automatic PR and fall on the wrong side of this line are in the weaker position of being able to gain it only at the discretion of a court and in revocable form. The test which the courts apply uses criteria of commitment, attachment and motivation. In the words of Butler-Sloss LJ:

> A father who has shown real commitment to the child concerned and to whom there is a positive attachment ... ought ... to assume the weight of those duties and cement that commitment and attachment by sharing the responsibilities for the child with the mother.[104]

---

[101] *Ibid* at [89]. McCandless points out the implicit hierarchy in the court's choice of letters to designate the various adults in this case. The birth mother is Ms A, the genetic father, Mr B and the co-mother, Ms C: J McCandless, 'Status and Anomaly: Considerations of the "Sexual Family" and Fatherhood in *Re D (contact and parental responsibility: lesbian mothers and known father)* [2006]', 'Gender Unbound' conference at the University of Keele, 9–11 July 2007.

[102] See also: *X v Y* (2002) SLT (Sh Ct) 161, where a gay man agreed to provide sperm for a lesbian couple. The nature of his future involvement in the life of the resulting child was unclear, but he visited often, introduced the child to his broader family, and sought to provide some financial support. Later, following the deterioration of his relationship with the lesbian couple, he sought parental rights and responsibilities. The court held that the biological mother and her partner did not constitute a family and preferred to take the biological parents as the starting point for the family unit. The finding that a lesbian couple cannot constitute a 'family' is, at best, surprising in the light of other legal developments.

[103] 8,835 PR orders were made in 2005. See: Department for Constitutional Affairs, *Judicial Statistics (Revised): England and Wales for the year 2005*, Cm 6903 (2006) at table 5.3.

[104] *Re S (Parental Responsibility)* [1995] 2 FLR 648.

While the majority of applications for PR are accepted, the courts have refused them where the father was serving a prison sentence for robbery,[105] had previously injured a child and acted in a cruel and sadistic way,[106] and where it was believed that he would use PR inappropriately to interfere with the mother's parenting.[107] As seen in chapter five, fear of violence thus imposes important limitations on men's parenting.

Where a father does not succeed in obtaining PR, he finds himself at a legal disadvantage. For example, he is less able to oppose a child's adoption. He does have the right to be party to proceedings if he is paying maintenance,[108] or if the court thinks it appropriate, but there is no presumption in favour of including him. Again, the courts here grapple with the problem of distinguishing meritorious and unmeritorious fathers.

> There will be cases in which the natural father will have little merit and, accordingly, very little entitlement to consideration. At the other end of the scale, there will be cases in which the natural father should be given what will be something akin to the statutory right that s. 16 of the Adoption Act 1976 confers.[109]

This is well illustrated by another case, where two mothers had placed children for adoption with a local authority asking that confidentiality be observed. In the first case, where the parents had cohabited and had another child who had contact with the father, the court held that the father must nonetheless be consulted. In the second, where the parties had never cohabited and had lost touch, there was no need to inform the father.[110]

Trends in Judicial Treatment of Unmarried Fathers

As the law has evolved in a context that is now heavily influenced by international norms, we begin our consideration of the judicial treatment of unmarried fathers by briefly reviewing some cases brought before the European Court of Human Rights. We then discuss the evolution of the judicial treatment of unmarried fathers across a number of areas of domestic law, focusing particularly on litigation surrounding residence, contact, paternity testing and disputes regarding a child's name. As some of these areas of law are considered in earlier chapters, our discussion here is limited to assessing how unmarried fathers fare in these contexts. In a useful overview, Jane Fortin describes a considerable degree of judicial confusion as to how unmarried fathers should be treated, while nonetheless noting a gradual entrenchment of their legal position, with the courts

---

[105] *Re P (Parental Responsibility)* [1997] 2 FLR 722.
[106] *Re H (Parental Responsibility)* [1998] 1 FLR 855.
[107] *Re M (Contact: Parental Responsibility)* [2001] 2 FLR 342.
[108] Adoption Rules 1984, SI 1984/265.
[109] *Re G (Adoption Order)* [1999] 1 FLR 400 (per Thorpe LJ).
[110] *Re H, Re G (Adoption: Consultation of Unmarried Fathers)* [2001] 1 FLR 646.

coming to attribute greater significance to the genetic tie.[111] Claims of equality also play an increasingly important role here, with the general pattern to emerge being one of equalisation of the rights of unmarried fathers to those enjoyed by married fathers.

As noted in earlier chapters, since the introduction of the Human Rights Act 1998, the European Convention on Human Rights has been directly enforceable in the UK courts and the jurisprudence of the European Court of Human Rights has gained more influence. A series of the decisions of that Court have helped to sketch the contours of the rights and obligations of fatherhood, drawing particularly on the right to respect for family and private life under Article 8, often coupled with Article 14, which prohibits discrimination in the exercise of Convention rights. The United Nations Convention on the Rights of the Child is also relevant in this context. In particular, it upholds the right of the child as far as possible to know both parents from birth and to receive care from them thereafter.[112] The European Convention rights are phrased in more general terms and the European Court has adopted a more nuanced position in its interpretation of them, recognising the diversity of unmarried fathers.[113] It has been held that Article 8 implies an obligation on the state to act in a manner calculated to allow ties between near-relatives to develop normally;[114] that the law must protect natural family ties between unmarried parents and their children;[115] and that the bond amounting to family life can exist between a child and parents at birth, even where the parents are not cohabiting.[116] A mere genetic link is insufficient, however: some form of social life between a man and his child is necessary.[117] Legal presumptions, based on the fact that the mother was currently married to another man, should not be allowed to block recognition of the biological and social reality of a paternal relationship.[118] However, this does not mean that a man will always be able to insist on a paternity test, particularly where the child concerned is being happily raised in a secure marital unit by another social father.[119]

---

[111] J Fortin, 'Parenthood in Child Law – What is its Real Significance?' in D Pearl and R Pickford (eds), *Frontiers of Family Law: Part 1* (John Wiley and Sons, Chichester, 1995).

[112] Convention on the Rights of the Child (adopted 20 November 1989, entered into force 2 September 1990) 1577 UNTS 3 (CRC); Arts 7(1) and 18(1). Bainham suggests that this requires states to take positive action to try to establish both maternity and paternity whenever a child is born: Bainham, above (n 3) at 216.

[113] Eg: *B v UK* [2000] 1 FLR 1, noting that relationships between unmarried fathers and their children vary 'from ignorance and indifference to a close stable relationship indistinguishable from the conventional family-based unit': *ibid* at 5.

[114] *Marckx v Belgium* (App no 6833/74) (1979) 2 EHRR 330.

[115] *Johnston v Republic of Ireland* (App no 9697/82) (1987) 8 EHRR 203.

[116] *Kroon v Netherlands* (App no 18535/91) (1994) 19 EHRR 263; *Lebbink v Netherlands* (App no 45582/99) ECHR, 1 June 2004, [2004] 2 FLR 463; *Berrehab v Netherlands* (App no 10730/84) (1988) 11 EHRR 322.

[117] *G v Netherlands* (App no 16944/90) (1990) 16 EHRR 38.

[118] (1994) 19 EHRR 263.

[119] *MB v UK* (App no 22920/93) (1994) 77 A DR 108.

A series of recent cases brought against Germany have provided the most emphatic endorsement of the rights of unmarried fathers. In *Sahin*, the Court held that German law, which allowed mothers to restrict unmarried fathers' contact with their children, was discriminatory since no similar restriction applied to married but separated fathers.[120] For a child born of a relationship where the parents had cohabited, there was no sufficiently weighty reason to discriminate on the grounds of the father's marital status. Law should not be applied in such a way as to prevent the genetic tie between a parent and child being used as the basis for legal recognition, at least where this is bolstered by evidence of social parenthood. However, the Court also held that, in determining whether automatic rights should accrue to the genetic father, it was permissible to distinguish between married and unmarried fathers, denying the latter the same rights which were automatically bestowed on the former in order to limit the benefits of legal fatherhood to 'meritorious' unmarried fathers, who may be required to prove 'fitness' before gaining equal rights. In a further recent case, tax breaks that were only offered to married fathers after divorce, but not to separated unmarried fathers, were similarly deemed discriminatory. Scant credence was given to the UK government's argument that providing tax deductions for child support payments only to married fathers post-divorce, and not to unmarried fathers post-separation, might somehow promote the institution of marriage.[121]

This evolving human rights context has inevitably made its mark on the decisions of the domestic courts. It has been suggested that *Sahin*, taken together with another German case *Elsholz*, means that there is now a prima facie right of contact as an aspect of family life, and that the courts must be careful not to discriminate between married and unmarried parents in this respect.[122] It remains true, however, that while unmarried fathers have come to enjoy a more favourable reception in such disputes, they have found the courts more receptive where they are not opposed by the mother.

We turn now to the domestic courts, beginning with consideration of residence disputes. For many years, the leading authority in this area was *J v C* (1970), which held that the claims of birth parents, while important, carried no overriding weight.[123] The significance of the blood tie was just one factor to be placed in the balance when determining the best interests of the child.[124] More recently, however, in line with shifts in understandings of child welfare and development, greater weight has been attached to the genetic link. In the words of Lord Templeman:

---

[120] *Sahin v Germany* (App no 30943/96) (2003) 36 EHRR 33. See also: *Elsholz v Germany* (App no 25735/94) ECHR, 13 July 2000, [2000] 2 FLR 486.

[121] *PM v UK* (App no 6638/03) ECHR, 19 July 2005.

[122] Bainham, above (n 3) at 214.

[123] [1970] AC 688. See further ch 5, pp 155–58.

[124] See also: *Re M (A Minor: Custody Appeal)* [1990] 1 FLR 291.

The best person to bring up a child is the natural parent. It matters not whether the parent is wise or foolish, rich or poor, educated or illiterate, provided the child's moral and physical health are not endangered. Public authorities cannot improve on nature.[125]

Subsequent decisions have held that in deciding where a child should live, the correct approach is not to consider where he or she would get the better home. Rather, a birth parent must be 'entirely unsuitable' before another parent can be considered,[126] or we risk slipping into social engineering.[127] This approach, not easily reconciled with the principle that the child's welfare should be paramount,[128] provides a clear illustration of the significance now attached to the genetic link between father and child.

As was noted above, fathers' claims have proved stronger in the context where they are opposing a third party rather than the mother. In the case of *Re K* (1990), following the mother's suicide, her step-sister and husband cared for the child for around one year. A lower court refused to remove the child from them in order to return him to his father, who had cohabited with the mother for some time. The Court of Appeal criticised the failure to apply what they saw as a rebuttable presumption that there was a 'right of every child, as part of its general welfare, to have the ties of nature maintained wherever possible with the parents who gave it life', seeing no ground for ordering:

> that the father should be displaced from his normal role in the care and upbringing of his child ... no circumstances had been demonstrated which made it necessary that, in the interests of the welfare of the child, the father's "right" to bring him up should be displaced.[129]

This again demonstrates the weight attached to the genetic link (in this case leading to the removal of a child from a home where he was settled and happy) and evidences the growing currency of talk of fathers' 'rights'. Fortin suggests it is 'remarkable' that the Court found such language appropriate and argues that *Re K* is unsound, not least because no attempt was made to evaluate the quality of the father's relationship with his son. The Court contented itself, rather, with applauding his good qualities as an adult and assuming that a good relationship would exist just because of their blood tie.[130] In another, more recent, case both the maternal grandmother and the father wished to provide a home for a three-year-old boy.[131] Neither had yet done so and there were grounds for doubt

---

[125] *Re KD (A Minor) (Ward: Termination of Access)* [1988] AC 806 at 812.

[126] *Re K (A Minor) (Ward: Care and Control)* [1990] 1 WLR 431, [1990] 3 All ER 795.

[127] *Re K (Wardship: Adoption)* [1991] 1 FLR 57 at 62.

[128] Children Act 1989, s 1(1).

[129] [1990] 3 All ER 795 at 799 (per Fox LJ). See also: *Re O (A Minor) (Custody: Adoption)* [1992] 1 FLR 77 at 79, where Butler-Sloss LJ suggested it would be 'social engineering' to suggest that the father's known defects should be balanced against some idealised adoptive parents.

[130] Fortin, above (n 111) at 173.

[131] *Re D* [1999] 1 FLR 134. See: J Fortin, '*Re D (Care: Natural Parent Presumption)*: Is Blood Really Thicker than Water?' (1999) 11(4) *Child and Family Law Quarterly* 435.

regarding the parenting ability of each. The lower court favoured the grand-mother, as this would foster the child's relationship with his half-siblings, who were already in her care. The Court of Appeal, however, again found that there should be a presumption in favour of the child's natural parent, which could only be overridden by compelling evidence to the contrary. Here the genetic link with the father is prioritised over those with grandparents and half-siblings. Fortin suggests, therefore, that the blood tie's significance is confined to the parent–child relationship.[132] Given the context in which these cases are brought, however, it might be more accurately suggested that the blood tie's particular significance is narrower still, being emphasised in cases involving the *father*–child relationship: what we are witnessing here is, in fact, a powerful strengthening of the genetic reading of fatherhood.[133]

A similar trajectory can be discerned in cases concerning contact. As was seen in chapter five, the courts, in certain respects at least, have been sympathetic to the contact claims of separated married fathers. For a significant time they were much less so to similar actions on behalf of unmarried fathers.[134] In *Re W* (1989), a lower court was called to account for placing too much weight on the blood tie and being insufficiently concerned to prevent disruption to the social family, having failed to consider:

> that this mother had been fortunate enough to find and fall in love with a man against whom not a word of criticism had been made, who had offered marriage and who accepted with love and kindness her child by another man … For a mother in these circumstances to seek to make a fresh start in marriage, with the blessing of her own family and that of her fiancé's, must be, one would have thought, not only very desirable for her, but also in [her child]'s interests.[135]

More recently, however, the judiciary has tended increasingly to emphasise the benefits to a child of retaining contact with both natural parents.[136] Wall J has summarised the present law on contact in three propositions. First, wherever possible, a child should get to know his or her estranged parent, with cogent reasons being needed in order to deny contact. Second, no court should deprive the child of contact with a natural parent unless wholly satisfied that it should cease, a conclusion that it should be very slow to reach. Third, the normal assumption is that a child would benefit from continued contact with a natural parent.[137] Further, as was seen in the previous chapter, this approach is linked to a new readiness to 'get tough' with those unmarried mothers who display an

---

[132] Fortin, above (n 131) at 443.
[133] Fortin notes a few exceptions to this approach, in particular in cases that involve children with strong attachments to long-term foster carers: *ibid* at 440–41.
[134] Fortin, above (n 111) at 167–8.
[135] *Re W (A Minor: Access)* [1989] 1 FLR 163 at 168.
[136] See Fortin's overview of the relevant case law: above (n 111) at 170.
[137] *Re M (Contact: Conditions)* [1994] 1 FLR 272 at 279; *Re D (Contact: Interim Order)* [1995] 1 FLR 495 at 504.

'implacable hostility' to fathers' desire for contact.[138] Again, the focus here is on the 'natural' parent, with no weight attached to whether the parents' relationship had been a marital one.

The strengthening of the position of the 'natural' father is also clear in the case law regarding paternity testing. The legal presumptions regulating paternity establishment were born of an era when no certain means existed of deciding genetic fatherhood and the rules governing rebuttal of a marital presumption made it difficult for a married man to exclude paternity. Today, however, it is relatively easy to establish paternity with a very high degree of certainty through DNA testing. Recent years have witnessed a far greater openness to requests for paternity tests, even when this will introduce a father figure outside the social family unit within which a child is being raised, and even when the mother and her current partner strongly oppose the test or where the test is strongly opposed by the child him or herself.[139] Again, the courts might be seen as less concerned than previously to protect the nuclear family from outside challenge and more convinced of a child's need to know the truth about her/his origins. Indeed, here as in some of the other areas discussed in this book, the courts recognise that these two considerations are not necessarily in conflict and, perhaps for this reason, have been increasingly keen to assert the importance of the genetic tie.[140] Fortin has described this as a movement away from the 'gooseberry bush' approach, which held that, provided a child had a stable home, it did not much matter 'who she called daddy'.[141] This greater judicial willingness to order paternity tests has coincided with an important shift in the way in which the tests are used, which echoes one of the points made above. Historically, paternity tests tended to be sought primarily in order to enforce financial responsibility on a reluctant putative father. Now, while this is still one reason for requesting tests, increasingly they are also sought by men who wish to assert their paternity as a basis for claiming paternal rights and responsibilities with regard to a child.[142] This is broadly in keeping with the social shifts around fatherhood detailed in chapters one and four.

Finally, disputes have also arisen regarding the naming of a child. The unmarried mother with sole PR has the right to name a child, although the father may challenge her in court and a specific issue order can be used to determine the

---

[138] *Re J (A Minor: Contact)* [1994] 1 FLR 729 at 736 (per Balcombe LJ).

[139] The courts' power to order such tests is contained in the Family Law Reform Act 1969, s 21(3) (as amended by the Child Support, Pensions and Social Security Act 2000, s 82). See *Re D* [2006] EWHC 3545 for a case involving a ten-year-old child who strongly opposed a test. While concern for the child's emotional well-being meant that the test could be deferred, the child's guardian was charged with explaining to the child that the issue of paternity could not be put off indefinitely.

[140] In the context of paternity testing, see for example: *Re H (Paternity: Blood Test)* [1996] 2 FLR 65 at 80 (per Ward LJ): 'if [the child] grows up knowing the truth, that will not undermine his attachment to his father-figure, and he will cope with knowing that he has two fathers'; and *Re H and A (Paternity: Blood Tests)* [2002] EWCA Civ 383.

[141] J Fortin, '*Re F*: The Gooseberry Bush Approach' (1994) MLR 296.

[142] See Douglas, above (n 46).

child's name. Once the family name is registered, however, it cannot be changed without the consent of the other parent.[143] The courts have suggested that a child's name is a 'profound issue', a 'biological label which tells the world at large that the blood of the name flows in its veins'.[144] Further, it is possible that the child's name may be a more significant matter for fathers, as greater uncertainty regarding one's parenthood may underpin the need for public affirmation of one's connection with a child, a need which may be all the stronger where the mother, father and child are not (any longer) seen as constituting an 'intact' family group.

Conclusion

In chapter four, we traced the regulation of law's traditional 'ideal' family and the father figure assumed within it: the marital breadwinner. This chapter and the previous both consider family situations that, in different ways, fall outside this ideal. In chapter five we discussed the regulation of fatherhood in families that are fragmented across households, with fathers separated from children with whom they had previously shared a home. Here, our focus has been on unmarried parents.

It was suggested above that, in a context where marriage has been a crucial tool for attaching men to children, unmarried fathers have posed particular problems for policy makers. This problem has often been described in a clearly value-laden way, which reproduces familiar gendered binaries of good and bad fathers: how should law distinguish between the 'meritorious' who have demonstrated commitment to their children (or partners) and exclude the 'unmeritorious' who have not? Or should the law rather recognise all unmarried fathers in order to grant the 'meritorious' the rights they need and deserve, perhaps through such recognition providing encouragement for all fathers to become more closely involved with their children? The general challenge for law makers might thus be perceived as that of developing legal rules which best accommodate the diversity of unmarried fathers.

---

[143] This is certainly the case where the father has PR, and possibly the case even where he does not; see Bainham, above (n 3) at 135. Where a residence order is in force, the name of a child cannot be changed without either the consent of all of those with PR or leave of the court. Where there is no residence order in force, it had been thought that one person with PR could change a child's name with no need for consent. This was rejected in *Dawson v Wearmouth* [1997] 2 FLR 629 (CA), aff'd [1999] 1 FLR 1167 (HL); *Re W, Re A, Re B (Change of Name)* [1999] 2 FLR 930. Cf: *Re PC (Change of Surname)* [1997] 2 FLR 730, where it was held that one person with PR could unilaterally change a child's name.

[144] See the similar tone of the Canadian Supreme Court in *Trociuk v British Columbia (AG)* [2003] 1 SCR 835, 2003 SCC 34. On choice of name as a significant issue for couples, see: J Lewis, 'Marriage and Cohabitation and the Nature of Commitment' (1999) 11(4) *Child and Family Law Quarterly* 355 at 358.

Conclusion

How is this to be done? The evolution of the law described above reflects a substantial consensus that the genetic link is important to fatherhood. However, precisely how unmarried fathers should be recognised has varied in different contexts and at different times. This response might be seen as ranging between three approaches. First, the *pure genetics approach* recognises (virtually) all unmarried fathers on the basis of the genetic link alone (for example, in child support liability).[145] Second, the *genetics plus individual action approach* awards rights automatically, but on a basis that requires the father to do more than merely provide evidence of the genetic link (for example, in PR acquired through birth registration). Third, and finally, the *genetics plus scrutiny approach* accords rights only following assessment of the suitability of the unmarried father and the strength of his connection with the child (for example, in contact, residence or PR orders). These latter two possibilities reflect an ongoing desire to distinguish between unmarried fathers and to recognise the meritorious alone. As such, it is not surprising that the clearest example of a *pure genetics approach* is in an area of law where, as we saw in chapter five, debate has been focused on fathers perceived as seeking to evade their responsibilities and how to hold them to account.

The analysis in this chapter leaves open a number of questions which, no doubt, will continue to provoke debate for many years to come. First, is the inevitable end point of the trends described above that marriage should lose any role at all in grounding fathers' legal status? In a context where research reveals long-term, committed cohabitation to be virtually indistinguishable from marriage in terms of partners' commitment to each other and to their children, is it right that all married fathers should gain full legal rights as parents automatically, while a significant number of unmarried fathers have to resort to law to acquire such a status? Or should the position be one of complete formal equality between married and unmarried fathers? Some of the traditional factors cited as mandating such a distinction (the problems inherent in determining paternity and questions of public decency and morality in recognising non-marital birth) are no longer compelling. Others have more contemporary resonance. Concern persists, for example, that recognising the rights of unmarried fathers may serve to undermine the position of mothers, who will generally be children's primary carers. And while long-term cohabitants may closely resemble married fathers in terms of their commitment and involvement with their children, non-cohabiting unmarried fathers are an inevitably more disparate group. Further, it has been suggested that according rights to unmarried fathers rewards the unmeritorious and wrongly accords the benefits of parenthood unencumbered by the responsibilities that come with the commitment to the child or the mother said to be

---

[145] Exceptions might allow for this legal status to be severed, eg in cases of adoption or conception by sperm donor in a licensed clinic.

201

evidenced by marriage. As such, some claim that recognising unmarried fathers removes the incentive to marry and will thus lead to greater familial instability.

> Applying a contractual approach, if the father wants all the rights appertaining to a married father, he should marry the mother. If he does not want to make that permanent connection, then he is asking for rights without the *quid pro quo* of responsibilities. If she does not want to marry him, she should not be forced into a quasi-marital situation by being subjected to fathers' rights, such as they are, save where imposed by a court in the interests of the child.[146]

This statement, made some years ago by Ruth Deech, also raises a second concern: that it is wrong for the state to impose the rights and responsibilities which go with marriage onto those who have made a conscious and autonomous decision not to marry.[147] While there is logic to this argument, it is not clear to what extent it withstands the body of empirical research conducted since it was made. Notably, it is clear that many unmarried partners believe that they *are* making a powerful commitment, but one that requires neither religious nor state endorsement through marriage vows.[148] That they should do so is fully in keeping with the cultural and social shifts relating to the fathering practices discussed in this book. In such a context, the clear public ignorance of the true legal position of unmarried fathers does not square easily with the contractual approach advocated by Deech, which assumes a conscious opting in or out of particular legal relationships: many believe that the unmarried father already has the same parental rights as his married counterpart.[149] Further, and perhaps more fundamentally, the argument fails to take account of the separation of marriage and parenthood discussed above. Men (like women) may wish to make a commitment to their children without making a marital commitment to a partner. These commitments are clearly seen by many, perhaps most, as separable: one can become or remain a committed father in the absence of an ongoing relationship with a child's mother. Further, as we noted above in discussion of PR and birth registration reform, recognising unmarried fathers is seen by many as an important positive stamp of approval, which will encourage men to assume responsibilities with regard to their children. Such a view would hold it mistaken to require men to prove themselves 'meritorious' before granting them rights as fathers, rather suggesting that granting such rights is a crucial aspect of encouraging paternal involvement and thus setting fathers on the path to becoming 'meritorious'.

Finally, if marriage is not a prerequisite to obtaining paternal rights, what should take its place? Should the genetic connection be all that is needed to gain

---

[146] R Deech, 'The Unmarried Father and Human Rights' (1992) 4 *Journal of Child Law* 3 at 4.

[147] See eg: M Freeman and C Lyon, *Cohabitation Without Marriage* (Gower, Aldershot, 1983) at 34.

[148] Pickford's study, for example, found no difference between married and unmarried fathers in terms of the level of commitment shown to their children: above (n 91). See also: Barlow *et al*, above (n 12).

[149] *Ibid.*

the full rights and responsibilities of fatherhood? If not, should the test be one of social fatherhood or intention to fulfil the duties of fatherhood? The answer which English law has given to this question thus far is complex. In some instances, however, it seems that birth registration is taking the place of marriage as grounding men's rights. This is now central to determining unmarried fathers' rights in the context of parental responsibility and plays an important evidential role, for example in the context of nationality. These changes can be seen as part of a rolling out of the rights and responsibilities of marriage to those relationships which most closely resemble it: here, fathers are to be recognised on the basis of a formal and legally recognised declaration of paternity. Yet, with the exception of the study noted above, we know little about why couples make the decision to register the father's name on a birth certificate and equally little about why they decide not to do so.[150]

In conclusion, we have seen dramatic changes in the legal rights and responsibilities of unmarried fathers over the last century, changes which have been particularly marked in the last three decades. The evolving law can be seen both as a response to developments in how people choose to organise their family lives and as part of the context in which those choices are made. A close analysis has revealed a decentring of marriage, a greater weight attributed to the genetic link between fathers and children and the increased prevalence of demands for equality. We have also highlighted the extent to which mothers operate as 'gatekeepers' to unmarried fathers' relationships with their children. In the final chapter, we develop some of these ideas, bring them together with themes emerging from other chapters of the book and locate them in a broader context.

---

[150] Graham et al, above (n 55). In addition to noting a correlation between sole registration and maternal youth and disadvantage, this study cited relationship failure and communication breakdown; the unplanned nature of a pregnancy; and a positive decision which negated the possibility of joint registration (eg where a child had been born to a lesbian couple) as factors which contributed to sole registration. It also found that parents were poorly informed both about the legal significance of registering a father's name and the practicalities of joint registration.

7

Fragmenting Fatherhood

Introduction

FRAGMENTING FATHERHOOD has explored how fatherhood has been understood and regulated at different moments across diverse areas of English law and social policy. In the preceding pages, we suggested that legal understandings of fatherhood have evolved unevenly over time, interacting in complex ways with the economic, cultural and political contexts in which particular ideas about parenthood are produced. Legal approaches to fatherhood have themselves proved highly context-specific, with various ways of awarding paternal rights and responsibilities foregrounded at different times and in different areas of law. We have tracked shifting ideas of what constitutes a 'good' father, a man deemed worthy of recognition in law, as well as a 'bad' father, who is not. Finally, and importantly, we have traced the diverse and conflicting ways in which fatherhood has itself been 'problematised' within this evolving legal and policy context.

In this analysis, we have resisted a simple linear interpretation of changes in the legal regulation of fatherhood, rejecting the idea (explored in chapter four) that the movement from paternal rights to parental responsibilities involves an inevitable diminution or displacement of the figure of the father in law. Likewise, we resisted a 'zero-sum' approach to the power of law, arguing against accounts that suggest that something akin to a 'pendulum swing' has occurred within family law, from a historical bias towards the interests of fathers, as at the end of the nineteenth century, to a systematic prioritisation of the interests of mothers.[1] We have equally questioned, however, the assertion that the development of contemporary fathers' rights activism can itself be reduced to a 'backlash' against any such perceived maternal bias.[2] The emergence of a multi-layered and frequently contradictory father-victim discourse results from social shifts more intricate than any simple manifestation of 'anti-women' sentiment on the part of

---

[1] A particular theme in the fathers' rights discourse discussed in ch 5. See eg: B Geldof, 'The Real Love that Dare not Speak its Name' in A Bainham *et al* (eds), *Children and Their Families: Contact, Rights and Welfare* (Hart, Oxford, 2003).

[2] See ch 5, pp 163–170 and below.

205

some men. The legal and social changes relating to gender and families detailed in the preceding chapters are, we have suggested, far more complex.

The importance attached to legally establishing a father figure in families has emerged as a dominant theme across each of the areas of law studied in this book. The basis on which the father should be recognised in law, however, has changed considerably from the time when fathers would be left with 'the responsibility of exercising the power which nature has given him by birth of the child'.[3] The result is a shifting, complex and contradictory web of legal rights and responsibilities. The renegotiation of men's role in the family has been shaped by a reconfiguration of gender relations that has occurred in the light of shifting household forms, evolving discourses of parenting, childhood and intimacy, as well as changes in legal norms and modes of governance. Situating our analysis within these social, historical and cultural shifts, and recognising the interconnected nature of the simultaneous reconstruction of both motherhood and childhood, we have suggested that fatherhood has been constituted as a specific, distinctive kind of social problem within particular legal contexts, and is a subject requiring study in its own right.

One particularly noteworthy challenge for law and policy over the past three decades, and an important part of the background to our own research, has been the issue of how fathers should be recognised in a social context marked by the decline of marriage – where understood as lifelong commitment – and the correlative, so-called 'fragmentation' of families.[4] In response to these changes, as well as to related shifts in understandings of the place of the father in child welfare and development, we have noted how law's focus has moved from a concentration on horizontal relationships (that is, between adult partners) towards vertical relationships (between adult and child). This shift implies new ideas about social responsibility on the part of both parents, and, importantly, envisages a new role for law itself in setting out normative expectations, 'radiating messages' about desirable conduct and seeking to modify behaviour.[5] These developments are not, we have suggested, a recent phenomenon, and track to longer-term shifts in law's governance of family practices, forming part of a wider

---

[3] 'It is for the general interest of families, and for the general interest of children, and really for the interests of the particular infant, that the court should not, except in very extreme cases, interfere with the discretion of the father but leave him the responsibility of exercising the power which nature has given him by birth of the child'; *Re Agar-Ellis* (1883) 24 Ch D 317 at 334 (per Cotton LJ).

[4] For discussion, ch 1, p 3.

[5] See eg: J Eekelaar, 'Family Law: Keeping Us "On Message"' (1999) 11 *Child and Family Law Quarterly* 387.

'civilising process'[6] in which significant changes have occurred in understandings of responsibility,[7] rights and discretion in law.[8]

Why did we choose to focus on the idea of 'fragmentation' as a way of approaching this study of fatherhood in law? We began, in chapter one, by noting the emergence of this term over the past decade within a broader literature on families and parenting.[9] Whilst not arguing that it captures all significant aspects, we suggested that the idea of fragmentation has considerable analytical purchase in explaining a number of important developments with regard to fatherhood and law. Notably, the term suggests the disintegration of an ideal type of marital fatherhood in law, as discussed in particular in chapter four. It denotes a consequent 'sub-division' of fatherhood, where the work of fathering is legally recognised as shared between two or more men, perhaps following the separation and re-partnering of a child's genetic parents, or where a genetic father seeks to develop a relationship with a child who is being raised within another family unit.[10] Fragmentation here captures something of the law's response to these situations, reflecting the legal treatment of fatherhood as a bundle of rights and responsibilities that may be split up and shared between different men, allocated on different bases in different contexts. Further, drawing on both relevant empirical research and recent theoretical studies of masculinities, identity and subjectivity, we noted that the idea of fragmentation might itself reflect aspects of the lived experience of many contemporary fathers. This opens up the possibility of contradiction and tension between different aspects of fathering identity (around, for example, what it means to be a 'good' father or a 'family man').[11]

---

[6] R van Krieken, 'The "Best Interests of the Child" and Parental Separation: on the "Civilising of Parents"' (2005) 68(1) MLR 25. Note also the argument of J Dewar, 'The Normal Chaos of Family Law' (1998) 61 MLR 467; J Dewar, 'Family Law and its Discontents' (2000) 14 *International Journal of Law, Policy and the Family* 59.

[7] H Reece, *Divorcing Responsibly* (Hart, Oxford 2003); H Reece, 'From Parental Responsibilty to Parenting Responsibly' in M Freeman (ed), *Law and Sociology* (Current Legal Issues Series, Oxford University Press, Oxford, 2005). See further, for discussion of these shifting ideas of responsibility across diverse areas of law, the 2008 Special Issue of the *Journal of Law and Society*, in particular: V Gillies, 'Perspectives on Parenting Responsibility: Contextualizing Values and Practices' (2008) 35(1) *Journal of Law and Society* 95; C Henricson, 'Governing Parenting: Is There a Case for a Policy Review and Statement of Parenting Rights and Responsibilities?' (2008) 35(1) *Journal of Law and Society* 150. See also: J Bridgeman, C Lind and H Keating (eds), *Responsibility, Law and the Family* (Ashgate, Aldershot, 2008, in press).

[8] S Parker, 'Rights and Utility in Anglo-Australian Law' (1992) 55 MLR 311; Dewar (1998), above (n 6).

[9] Ch 1, pp 4–7. The idea has, intriguingly, now entered media accounts of fathering. See eg: Editorial, 'Not Broken, Fractured: Communities Without Fathers Are Likely to Become Enclaves of Their Own', *The Times* (25 August 2007), <http://www.timesonline.co.uk/tol/comment/leading_article/article2324204.ece>, accessed 18 March 2008. The theme, moreover, cuts across political perspectives. See: ME David (ed), *The Fragmenting Family: Does it Matter?* (Institute of Economic Affairs, Health and Welfare Unit, London, 1998).

[10] See chs 5 and 6, respectively.

[11] On the idea of the 'family man', see S Coltrane, *Family Man: Fatherhood, Housework and Gender Equality* (Oxford University Press, Oxford, 1996); R Collier, *Masculinity, Law and the Family* (Routledge, London, 1995).

In developing the idea of fragmentation, we have also sought to avoid the dangers that can inhere in deconstructive attempts within law to 'reveal' or 'unpack' the gendered subject(s) of legal discourse.[12] Such engagements run the risk of ignoring the significant affective dimensions of social relations, effacing the complexity and interconnectedness of the 'everyday' lives of women, men and children, and erasing the 'real lives' of individuals.[13] One challenge in studying the relationship between fatherhood and law is thus to avoid a form of analysis whereby 'real people and their lives ... become a kind of grist to a pre-existing theoretical mill ... reduced to ciphers for a culturally and historically specific knowledge-building industry'.[14] Understood as distinctive family practices, experiences of fathering (and of being father*ed*) are inevitably mediated by a variety of factors, such as age, class, geographical location, religion, ethnicity, sexuality, health and disability. Further, beyond the significant differences that exist between different social groups, what it means to be a father will itself vary enormously between individual men, depending on the specificities of life history and biography as well as the social contexts that situate fathering practices (for example, the different relationships with the child's mother and living arrangements discussed in chapters four, five and six).[15] Such experience may itself vary for any one man across his own life course. We hope that the idea of fragmentation helps to preserve something of this diversity and fluidity of contemporary fathering practices and experiences whilst, at the same time, indicating real substantive changes that have occurred at the level of legal regulation.

In this concluding chapter, we draw out and explore a number of the more significant themes to have arisen over the course of the preceding pages, and we develop further some of the issues that emerge from them. We begin, in section I, by considering how law has sought to promote certain messages about 'good' fatherhood, building on the discussion in chapter four of the increasingly dominant model of the 'new father' within social policy. We explore here how some contradictory assumptions about fatherhood, not least in terms of discourses of 'cash and care', have come to inform the emergence of normative ideals about paternal rights and responsibilities across diverse areas of law and policy.[16] We proceed, in section II, to focus on the evolution of fatherhood in a more general sense as a distinctive 'social problem' for law, arguing that recent policy agendas around fatherhood reflect deeper social tensions in how ideas about

---

[12] For discussion of these issues in relation to the construction of masculinities in law see: R Collier, (2003) 'Reflections on the Relationship Between Law and Masculinities: Rethinking The "Man Question"' 56 *Current Legal Problems* 345.

[13] In foregrounding this concern, we here follow Smart, drawing on the discussion, for example, in B Skeggs, *Formations of Class and Gender* (Sage, London 1997); and P Johnson, *Love, Heterosexuality and Society* (Routledge, London, 2005); C Smart, *Personal Life* (Polity, Cambridge 2007).

[14] Smart, *ibid* at 190.

[15] See further on 'situating' fathering practices: W Marsiglio, K Roy and G Litton Fox (eds), *Situated Fathering: a Focus on Physical and Social Spaces* (Rowman & Littlefield, Lanham, MD, 2005).

[16] See further, and generally: B Hobson (ed), *Making Men into Fathers: Masculinities and the Social Politics of Fatherhood* (Cambridge University Press, Cambridge, 2002).

men, masculinities and men's parenting are now understood. In section III, we turn to the closely related ideas of equality, gender convergence and geneticisation, each of which have emerged as central themes in our consideration of fatherhood and law in this book. Finally, in section IV, we outline some theoretical implications and further questions arising from our study, before concluding by drawing out a number of significant tensions, inconsistencies and points of fragmentation within contemporary legal understandings of fatherhood.

I. Beyond the 'New Fatherhood'

In chapter four, focusing primarily on the rights and responsibilities of the father within the context of intact marital relationships, we traced how a nexus of economic, cultural and political shifts reframed legal ideas about 'good' and 'responsible' fatherhood from the late nineteenth century to the present. We tracked, in particular, the emergence of the ideal of the 'new fatherhood', involving a man who is not (or, at least, not just) seen as primary breadwinner, but is also, increasingly, a 'hands-on' carer, an individual who is (or who should be) emotionally engaged and involved in the day-to-day care of his children.[17] We described the emergence of a distinctive social policy agenda which, responding to this idea, has served to promote, in particular in the years since 1997, the development of father-inclusive practice across a range of areas of law and policy. The impact of these discourses around the new father was evident, in chapter two, in the context of debates around men's involvement in reproduction. Equally, in our discussion of post-separation fatherhood in chapter five, we saw that many men now frame legal claims, not just via a language of rights, justice and entitlement, but also, increasingly, by evoking appeals to the welfare of the child and ideas about men's capacity and willingness to care. Such claims deploy a model of fatherhood that transcends the traditional breadwinning role, encompassing a new set of norms around men's parenting and masculinities.[18]

However, while the idea of this shift from 'cash to care' in law and policy undoubtedly captures aspects of real changes that have occurred in fathering practices and identities, to identify these developments in terms of a linear narrative of progression, or as a process of modernisation of fatherhood, offers too superficial an analysis. What is more revealing, we have suggested, is to

---

[17] These terms are themselves, of course, contested. Note E Dermott, *Intimate Fatherhood: A Sociological Analysis* (Routledge, London, 2007); E Dermott, 'The "Intimate Father": Defining Paternal Involvement' (2003) 8(4) *Sociological Research Online* <http://www.socresonline.org.uk/8/4/dermott.html>, accessed 18 March 2008.

[18] See: C Gattrell, 'Whose Child is It Anyway?: The Negotiation of Paternal Responsibilities Within Marriage' (2007) 55(2) *Sociological Review* 352; A Hill, 'Fathers fight for lead role in childcare', *Observer* (20 January 2008).

consider the shifting ways in which fatherhood has been constituted and conceptualised as a distinctive object of intervention within debates around law reform. The theoretical framework set out in chapter one thus sought to allow us scope for:

> [b]oth the examination of how social phenomena come to be seen as social problems and also for an acceptance that material reality (in this case, what men are *really* like) will affect the construction of social problems ... The processes whereby issues become social problems involves mediation of concerns by media, academia, government and street-level bureaucracy.[19]

To this list, we would add law and legal regulation. This approach served to reveal how the emergence of the active, nurturing father, as envisaged in the new fatherhood ideal, has reconstituted fathers as a different *kind* of desirable presence within families and in the lives of their children. The belief that fathers have a central role to play in meeting the day-to-day needs of children has informed the development of policy across each of the areas of law discussed in this book.[20] As such, the lack of a suitably 'engaged' father has frequently been cited as a significant social problem, and ensuring and protecting such a paternal presence is now widely accepted as a worthy end of government intervention. Yet the analysis of earlier chapters also revealed the tenacious hold of some more traditional ideas of fatherhood that cut-across this model of the new father in certain respects. Whether in relation to the responsibilities of the marital father described in chapter four, the separated father discussed in chapter five or the unmarried father in chapter six, fathers continue also to appear in law as family providers, as exemplars of a distinctly gendered role model and as the symbolic means of 'completing' the nuclear (sexual) family.

Every one of these understandings of 'the father' was seen to be relevant in the complex determinations of fatherhood in the assisted conception context discussed in chapter three. As we saw there, these diverse normative ideals for fatherhood have, inevitably, sometimes pulled the law in different directions. This central tension, between ideas of fathers as involved carers and as breadwinners, is also evident in the analysis of chapter four, where the juxtaposition of conflicting paternal responsibilities is a key feature of recent debates around the issue of work–life balance. The need to juggle financial and caring responsibilities further informs ideas of the father as 'victim' of law, discussed in particular in relation to post-separation parenting in chapter five. In this context, the spectre

---

[19] J Scourfield and M Drakeford, 'New Labour and the "Problem of Men"' (2002) 22 *Critical Social Policy* 619 at 622.

[20] See further, and generally: K Stanley, *Daddy Dearest? Active Fatherhood and Public Policy* (Institute for Public Policy Research, London, 2005); S Dex and K Ward, *Parental Care and Employment in Early Childhood: Working Paper 57* (Equal Opportunities Commission, Manchester, 2007). This is not to deny that the 'new father' ideal may stand in an uncertain relation to what is known about the material (gendered) realities of 'everyday' caring practices within the majority of contemporary households. See below pp 230–231.

of the 'ruined' man, living in fear of Child Support Agency (CSA) assessments, has become a particularly powerful and culturally resonant image within broader debates around family law reform.[21] What is becoming clear, however, is that the tensions between these two imperatives play out not just at the policy level, but also in terms of the lived experiences and perceptions of 'good' fathering on the part of individual men, women and children. Thus, across a range of personal accounts, men describe a stark conflict between these caring and financial imperatives,[22] experiencing difficulties in balancing cash and care responsibilities, and negotiating the seemingly mixed messages emerging from law and policy. Some may feel themselves to be and, indeed be perceived as, falling short of the moral imperatives of the new fatherhood ideal.[23]

Against this backdrop of potentially conflicting ideas about what being a good father entails, it is perhaps little wonder that there has been a heightened politicisation of the relationship between fatherhood and law in recent years.[24] For some fathers' rights groups,[25] the criticism that law sees men as little more than 'cheque-signing machines' dovetails with a demand for greater contact and residence rights for separated fathers. In these accounts, the practice of the CSA is viewed as reducing complex emotional relationships between fathers and children to a simple (or, more accurately, not so simple) financial equation, an approach to fatherhood castigated as radically at odds with the model of the nurturing, caring father dominant in other policy contexts. Here, fathers' rights groups explicitly connect a rejection of the breadwinner image of fatherhood with an embrace of a model of paternal responsibility more in keeping with the new fatherhood ideal. However, such arguments have been seen by some feminist

---

[21] See eg: R Collier, 'The Campaign against the Child Support Act, "Errant Fathers" and "Family Men"' [1994] *Family Law* 384; J Wallbank, 'The Campaign for Change of the Child Support Act: Reconstituting the "Absent" Father' (1997) 6 *Social and Legal Studies* 191.

[22] See Dex and Ward, above (n 20). This is itself a recurring theme within fathers' rights discourse. For discussion of the connections between payments and contact: GB Wilson, 'The Non-Resident Parental Role for Separated Fathers: A Review' (2006) *International Journal of Law, Policy and the Family* 1. See also: J Hunt with C Roberts, *Child Contact with Non-Resident Parents*, Family Policy Briefing Paper 3 (Department of Social Policy and Social Work, University of Oxford, Oxford, 2004).

[23] On fathers' perceptions of their roles and responsibilities, see further: Equal Opportunities Commission, *Fathers and the Modern Family* (Equal Opportunities Commission, Manchester, 2007); W Hatten, L Vinter and R Williams, *Dads on Dads: Needs and Expectations at Home and Work* (Equal Opportunities Commission, Manchester, 2002); Equal Opportunities Commission, *Fathers: Balancing Work and Family* (Equal Opportunities Commission, Manchester, 2003); J Warin *et al*, *Fathers, Work and Family Life* (Family Policy Studies Centre, London, 1999). Some accounts have been sceptical of this dilemma, suggesting that not all men are reluctant to concentrate on their work lives at the expense of spending time with their families. See further, and generally: D Perrons *et al*, *Gender Divisions and Working Time in the New Economy: Changing Patters of Work, Care and Public Policy in Europe and North America* (Edward Elgar, Cheltenham, 2007).

[24] R Collier and S Sheldon (eds), *Fathers' Rights Activism and Legal Reform in Comparative Perspective* (Hart, Oxford, 2006).

[25] There is, of course, no 'one' fathers' rights perspective: Collier and Sheldon, above (n 24). See also: R Collier, *The UK Fathers' Rights Movement and Law: Report to the British Academy* (2008) (unpublished).

critics as themselves nothing more than a re-articulation of familiar appeals to authority and prerogative on the part of men. Thus, the claims made for contact and residence rights for fathers in the legal arena and, in particular, for the institution of a presumption of shared equal parenting in law are criticised as a way of maintaining control over women and children. Moreover, the historical failure of many fathers to meet their responsibilities in relation to child support is likewise attacked as representing, not so much an embrace, but something more akin to a 'flight from' commitment.[26]

The causes and very concepts of 'father absence' and 'father distance' have been, therefore, and remain deeply contested,[27] explained variously as due to the irresponsibility of individual men or as the product of institutional barriers to men spending more time with children.[28] In chapter five, we saw how these contrasting understandings play out in a particularly high-profile and politically resonant way in the area of contact law and in relation to separated fathers' legal rights. On closer examination, disputes in this area are pervaded by conflicting ideas about fathers as, variously, holders of legal rights, representatives of a new form of paternal responsibility, victims of the legal system, embodiments of traditional forms of men's power, and self-interested figures who, individually and collectively, seek to resist social change, and pose, in some contexts, significant risks to children. These disputes reflect a stark contrast between images of men as victims of social structures and forces beyond their control, and, simultaneously, ideas of men as empowered perpetrators who have direct responsibility for a range of actual or potential social harms to children, their partners and society more generally. We return to this point below.

It is against the backdrop of these shifting and conflicting ideas about fatherhood that much energy has been devoted to the question of whether the 'new father' really exists. As we noted in chapter four, there is limited empirical evidence to suggest that men's participation in domestic labour and childcare is matching up to the projected notion of active fatherhood contained within the

---

[26] Cf: B Ehrenreich, *The Hearts of Men and the Flight from Commitment* (Pluto, London, 1983). This argument is contested, however, by evidence suggesting that many mothers, as well as fathers, have failed to meet child support liabilities. See: D Hencke, 'Seven out of 10 absent parents pay maintenance for children', *Guardian* (10 April 2006), <http://www.guardian.co.uk/money/2006/apr/10/childrensservices.freedomofinformation>, accessed 18 March 2008.

[27] Note, for example, different interpretations of father absence in the exchange between Lord Geoff Filkin and Sir Bob Geldof on the *Today* programme in April 2004: Lord Geoff Filkin and Sir Bob Geldof, 'Rights for Fathers', Transcript, *Today* programme, Radio 4, 3 April 2004 (GICS Media Monitoring Unit, London, 2004) (copy of transcript with authors). Contrast the readings of father absence by A McMahon, *Taking Care of Men* (Cambridge University Press, Cambridge, 1999). See also: B Campbell, *Goliath: Britain's Dangerous Places* (Methuen, London, 1993).

[28] See: A Burgess and S Ruxton, *Men and Their Children: Proposals for Public Policy* (Institute for Public Policy Research, London, 1996); A Burgess and G Russell, 'Fatherhood and Public Policy' in G Barker *et al*, *Supporting Fathers: Contributions From the International Fatherhood Summit 2003* (Early Childhood Development: Practice and Reflections Series, Bernard van Leer Foundation, The Hague 2004); Stanley, above (n 20); A Burgess and S Ruxton, 'Men and Their Children' in J Franklin (ed), *Social Policy and Social Justice* (Polity, Cambridge, 1998).

new father ideal.[29] Changes at the level of culture, that is, might appear out of step with social practice. However, it would be a mistake to assume that because things have not changed entirely they have not changed at all. Further, if change has not been as marked as some would suggest, the explanation for this is complex and inevitably owes something to the tension between fathers' cash and care responsibilities outlined above and to questions of individual agency on the part of both fathers and mothers.

More generally, the very question of the existence of the 'new fatherhood' is one, as Haywood and Mac an Ghaill observe,[30] that reveals much about the poverty of contemporary thinking about fathers, reflecting a reductionist model of fatherhood based on ideas about bad (traditional) and good (new) categories of behaviour. Historical research, as we have seen in this book, highlights the diverse nature of paternal attitudes and behaviour, the plurality of fathering experiences,[31] and the dangers inherent in reading the past through the gaze of the present.[32] This should lead us to guard against any assumption that the development of paternal responsibilities in law necessarily reflects or can be mapped to real changes in fathering practices, or that it can usefully be understood in terms of stark dichotomies between progress and regress (or stasis) – or, indeed, in terms of 'new' and 'old', or 'good' and 'bad' fathers.[33] Social practice is rarely so clear-cut.

II. Fatherhood, Masculinities and the 'Problem of Men'

If the idea of new fatherhood has been an important driver of recent law and policy initiatives, however, it has been by no means the only one. A set of competing imperatives focus on men who fall outside the frame of familial

---

[29] A view supported by cross-European research suggesting that gendered patterns have not significantly changed: J Hearn and K Pringle, *European Perspectives on Men and Masculinities* (Palgrave Macmillan, Basingstoke 2006); K Pringle *et al*, *Men and Masculinities in Europe* (London, Whiting and Birch, 2006). For discussion of the commitments of one group of professional men, note G Ranson, 'Men at Work: Change – or No Change? – in the Era of the "New Father"' (2001) 4(1) *Men & Masculinities* 3. See also: McMahon, above (n 27). See further: C Grbich, 'Male Primary Caregivers and Domestic Labour: Involvement or Avoidance?' (1995) 1(2) *Journal of Family Studies* 14.

[30] C Haywood and M Mac an Ghaill, *Men and Masculinities: Theory, Research and Social Practice* (Open University Press, Buckingham, 2003).

[31] An example of this diversity throughout the life course can be found in: D Henry and JA McPherson (eds), *Fathering Daughters: Reflections by Men* (Beacon Press, Boston, MA, 1998). See further D Lupton and L Barclay, *Constructing Fatherhood: Discourses and Experiences* (Sage, London, 1997)

[32] See: J Tosh, *A "Man's Place": Masculinity and the Middle-class Home in Victorian England* (Yale University Press, London, 1999) at 195; JR Gillis, *A World of Their Own Making: Myth, Ritual and the Quest for Family Values* (Harvard University Press, Cambridge, MA, 1996); R Larossa, *The Modernization of Fatherhood: A Social and Political History* (University of Chicago Press, Chicago, IL, 1997).

[33] Haywood and Mac an Ghaill, above (n 30); F Furstenberg, 'Good Dads–Bad Dads: Two Faces of Fatherhood' in AJ Cherlin (ed), *The Changing American Family and Public Policy* (Changing Domestic Priorities Series, Urban Institute Press, Washington, DC, 1988).

relationships, men who continue, particularly in certain contexts, to be ascribed the status of the deviant, dysfunctional and (potentially) dangerous male.[34] Such concerns have come to the fore in recent years in the emergence of policy agendas around families, crime and citizenship that have served to reconstitute fatherhood, men and masculinity as a social problem in a number of very different – and by no means consistent – ways. We now go on to explore some of the tensions that have emerged between these ideas of fatherhood, in what has become a broader discussion and debate about 'the problem of fathers'.

Engaging Fathers

If the issue of how to promote ongoing, 'healthy' relationships between men and children has a long history, it is one that has become increasingly central to social policy debates around fathers over the past decade. Fitting closely with the new fatherhood ideal discussed above, and underscored by the evidence base suggesting that men have a major impact on children's lives and well-being, the distinctive role and contribution of fathers has been explicitly recognised within a range of policy frameworks seeking to promote and integrate 'father-inclusive' practice within the delivery of social services.[35] The issue of 'engaging fathers' has, more generally, become an increasingly visible theme within much political and policy discussion. For example, it is now a strategic requirement that all Children's Services in England and Wales[36] consider the inclusion of fathers as

[34] For further discussion of these divisions see R Collier, *Masculinities, Crime and Criminology: Men, Heterosexuality and the Criminal(ised) Other* (Sage, London, 1998). See also: R Collier, 'Dangerousness, Popular Knowledge and the Criminal Law: A Case Study of the Paedophile as Socio-cultural Phenomenon' in P Alldridge and C Brants (eds), *Personal Autonomy, the Private Sphere and the Criminal Law: A Comparative Study* (Hart, Oxford, 2001); R Collier, 'Anxious Parenthood, the Vulnerable Child and the "Good Father": Reflections on the Legal Regulation of the Relationship Between Men and Children' in J Bridgeman and D Monk (eds), *Feminist Perspectives on Child Law* (Cavendish, London, 2001). See also below p 218.

[35] See D Bartlett, A Burgess and K Jones, *A Toolkit for Developing Father-Inclusive Practice* (Fathers Direct, London, 2007); The Fatherhood Institute, *The Difference a Dad Makes* (Fatherhood Institute, London, 2007); D Bartlett and A Burgess, *Working with Fathers: Six Steps Guide* (Fathers Direct, London, 2005); T Lloyd, *What Works With Fathers?* (Working with Men, London, 2001).

[36] A policy agenda laid out, for example, in the Department for Education and Skills paper *Every Parent Matters*, as well as in Children's Centre Guidance, The National Service Framework for Children, Young People and Maternity Services, the Teenage Pregnancy Strategy, the Gender Equality Duty (Sex Discrimination Act 1975, s 76A, inserted by the Equality Act 2006), the Childcare Act 2006, and *Aiming High for Children: Supporting Families*. See: Department for Education and Skills, *Every Parent Matters* (Department for Education and Skills, London, 2007); Department of Education and Skills, 'Children's Centre Practice Guidance', Surestart website, revised November 2006, <http://www.surestart.gov.uk/publications/?Document=1500>, accessed 4 January 2008; Department of Health, Department for Education and Skills, *The National Service Framework for Children, Young People and Maternity Services* (Department of Health/Department for Education and Skills, London 2004); Department for Children, Schools and Families, 'Teenage Pregnancy Strategy', Every Child Matters website, 2007, <http://www.everychildmatters.gov.uk/health/teenagepregnancy/about/>, accessed 18 March 2008; HM Treasury/Department for Education and Skills, *Aiming High for Children: Supporting Families* (HMSO, London, 2007). See further: Bartlett, Burgess and Jones, above (n 35); Burgess

users of services provided for parents. Such an imperative is to be found explicitly in central government policy and in the delivery of local services, informing debates about, for example, household economics, the reduction of child poverty, the interlinking of parenting, child socialisation and criminality, and in relation to broader attempts to 'support families'. A growing research literature, meanwhile, highlights the challenges that can exist in this regard,[37] revealing the extent to which much service provision continues to fail adequately to engage with fathers, in particular vulnerable fathers and those belonging to ethnic and other minority groupings,[38] and also how difficult it can be to get fathers 'involved' in service provision.[39]

Scourfield and Drakeford offer a particularly insightful analysis of how a distinctive 'problem of men' has been articulated within New Labour's social policy in this regard.[40] In relation to attempts to 'engage fathers', they suggest that there has been a marked degree of 'policy optimism' about men around issues located primarily inside the home.[41] For example, the attempts that have been made to support men as fathers in the family, which we discussed in chapter four, have often begun from the premise not only that are men changing, but also – and crucially – that men want to change. From this perspective, institutional and organisational barriers are cited as the obstacles impeding 'active fathering'. Accordingly, a key role is envisaged for law and government in seeking to remove these barriers, in order to help men accomplish what they are already trying to achieve – to become 'better' fathers. As a result, we have seen fathers acquire new rights to take parental leave, to restrict their maximum working hours, to request

and Russell, above (n 28), See also: B Daniel *et al*, 'Why Gender Matters for "Every Child Matters"' (2005) 35 *British Journal of Social Work* 1343, on the lack of gender analysis in much of recent debate. See further: B Featherstone and L Trinder, 'New Labour, Families and Fathers' (2001) 21(4) *Critical Social Policy* 534; B Featherstone, M Rivett and J Scourfield, *Working With Men in Health and Social Care* (Sage, London, 2007).

[37] In addition to work cited in ch 4 and n 36 above, see eg: C Ashley *et al*, *Fathers Matter: Research Findings on Fathers and Their Involvement with Social Care Services* (Family Rights Group, London, 2006); B Daniel and J Taylor, *Engaging With Fathers: Practice Issues for Health and Social Care* (Jessica Kingsley, London, 2001); M Ryan, *Working with Fathers* (Radcliffe Medical Press, Abingdon 2000); J.Scourfield, 'The Challenge of Engaging Fathers in the Child Protection Process' (2006) 26 (2) *Critical Social Policy* 440.

[38] Note in particular the resources offered by the Fatherhood Institute (formerly Fathers Direct) in this regard: Fathers Direct and the An-Nisa Society, *Working with Muslim Fathers: A Guide for Practioners* (Fathers Direct, London, 2007); G Waugh, *Working with Asian Fathers: A Guide* (YMCA, Bradford, 2007); and further specific internet resources, aimed at, for example, young, Muslim, African-Caribbean, imprisoned and disabled fathers: The Fatherhood Institute, 'The UK's fatherhood thinktank', <http://www.fatherhoodinstitute.org/>, accessed 18 March 2008; A.Phoenix and F.Husain, *Parenting and Ethnicity* (Joseph Rowntree Foundation, York, 2007).

[39] Bartlett, Burgess and Jones, above (n 35); see further: Ashley and others, above (n 37); Daniel and Taylor, above (n 37).

[40] Scourfield and Drakeford, above (n 19).

[41] These authors contend that precisely the opposite is true for women. For discussion, see: Scourfield and Drakeford, above (n 19) at 625–7, 632–3.

flexible working and so forth.[42] Funding has been provided to develop father-inclusive and 'father-friendly' initiatives at both national and local level, and to source wider information provision and policy development on diverse aspects of fathering.[43] Within this perspective, fatherhood is seen as providing a unique and much desired opportunity for men to express their nurturing feelings, and take on a more equal role in parenting in a way that their own fathers, it is often supposed, did not.[44] Law, crucially, is seen as having a central role in achieving this objective.

Fatherhood and the 'Problem of Men'

In stark contrast, however, to the optimism regarding men's ability to change within the home, Scourfield and Drakeford describe a very different set of assumptions about men outside it. They suggest that thinking in that context has tended, rather, to be dominated by a set of assumptions more associated with a deficit model of fathering.[45] This identifies a lack of appropriate paternal involvement (particularly amongst certain social groups) as underpinning a range of social problems, with blame laid firmly at the doors of individual men and women.[46] Importantly, very different ideas about responsibility, masculinities and fatherhood are deployed in these discussions of law and policy, relating to issues such as youth criminality, anti-social behaviour,[47] the educational undera-chievement of boys,[48] safety issues pertaining to men working with children, men's health and illness,[49] child support and paternal 'irresponsibility'.[50] Paternal disengagement is here seen to reflect the absence of more traditional models of fatherhood, evoking ideas of the father as authority figure, disciplinarian and provider of a distinctive (gendered) socialisation. As was noted above, little optimism regarding men's ability and willingness to change tends to be expressed

[42] Ch 4, pp 120–126.

[43] For discussion, see Ch 4, p 125.

[44] Just as it is important not to judge fathering practices of the past by the standards of the present, the complexity and diversity of fathering at earlier moments is also to be noted: above, n 32. See also: R Griswold, *Fatherhood in America: A History* (Basic Books, New York, 1992); A Burgess, *Fatherhood Reclaimed: The Making of the Modern Father* (Vermilion, London, 1997).

[45] AJ Hawkins and DC Dollahite, *Generative Fathering: Beyond Deficit Perspectives* (Sage, Thousand Oaks, CA, 1997).

[46] As evident, for example, in variations of underclass theory: C Murray, *The Emerging British Underclass* (Institute for Economic Affairs, Health and Welfare Unit, London, 1990). See further: Collier (1998), above (n 34) at ch 5.

[47] Scourfield and Drakeford, above (n 19) at 629; M Drakeford and I Butler, 'Curfews for Children: Testing a Policy Proposal in Practice' (1998) 62 *Youth & Policy* 1.

[48] D Epstein *et al* (eds), *Failing Boys? Issues in Gender and Achievement* (Open University Press, Buckingham, 1998).

[49] Scourfield and Drakeford, above (n 19) at 628; S Robertson, *Understanding Men's Health: Masculinity, Identity and Well-Being* (Open University Press, Buckingham, 2007).

[50] F Williams, 'Troubled Masculinities in Social Policy Discourses: Fatherhood' in J Popay, J Hearn and J Edwards (eds), *Men, Gender Divisions and Welfare* (Routledge, London, 1998).

in these contexts, with their failings seen more as a reflection of self-interest and a desire to maintain social power relative to women and children.

How might we account for these differences? As with the 'new fatherhood' ideal, considered above, such discussion of the 'problem of men' reveals not a unitary discourse stemming from a homogenous set of concerns, but comes 'from several different directions and focuses on a variety of behaviours'.[51] While sharing a central concern with fatherhood as a social problem for law, two highly contrasting characterisations of men appear within these discussions: first, that of men as perpetrators, and, second, that of men as victims.[52] Crucially, each of these ideas engages law in different ways. The idea of men as perpetrators tends to envisage men as 'a source of danger and disorder, an anti-social influence'[53] drawing on powerful (gendered) discourses circulating in the field of crime and criminal justice. The focus is then on how dominant ideas of masculinity and the 'gender order' serve to privilege men in general, with the issue of men's violence, in particular, identified as a key element within a broader cultural configuration of (hegemonic) masculinity.[54] In such accounts, individual men are often seen as at fault, their vested self-interest emerging as an impediment to change. This approach is evident both within a significant strand of feminist thought and in writings within the critical study of men and masculinities, as well as within much political discourse.

By contrast, the idea of men as victims highlights the broader disadvantages seen to befall men in general, and certain groups of men in particular. It focuses on the costs and 'crises' of contemporary masculinity, including the displacement of men from the workplace, and, in particular, from the family.[55] This recalls themes central to the fathers' rights discourses discussed in chapter five. It also resonates, however, with ideas that can be found within a rather different body of feminist thought – as well as within some scholarship on men and masculinities – that seeks to emphasise the need for men to take on a more caring role within families. 'Changing men' is seen as essential not only in addressing ongoing female disadvantage, but also in meeting men's own needs.[56] Both of these ideas of, first, men as perpetrators and, second, as victims can be seen to have informed government policies around men's parenting, as well as pervading much media discussion about the 'future of fatherhood'.[57] Each, however, pulls law in different

---

[51] Scourfield and Drakeford, above (n 19) at 621.

[52] *Ibid* at 621.

[53] *Ibid.*

[54] See further below, pp 230–33.

[55] See eg: S Faludi, *Stiffed: The Betrayal of the Modern Man* (Chatto and Windus, London, 1999); A Clare, *On Men: Masculinity in Crisis* (Chatto and Windus, London, 2000).

[56] Note, eg, the argument of Lynne Segal: L Segal, *Is the Future Female? Troubled Thoughts on Contemporary Feminism* (Virago, London, 1987); L Segal, *Slow Motion: Changing Masculinities, Changing Men* (Virago, London, 1990). Cf: R Coward, *Sacred Cows: Is Feminism Relevant for the New Millennium?* (Harper Collins, London, 1999) especially at 152–5.

[57] As evident in the debates on diverse aspects of fatherhood, prompted on a regular basis in the media either by the publication of a relevant research study or the comments of newspaper

directions, and draws on different ideas about the nature of fatherhood and possibilities of legal intervention, as was clear in our discussion above of debates around father 'absence' and father 'distance'.[58]

This diversity of approaches reflects, in part, the conceptual ambiguity of fatherhood itself, a theme addressed at various stages of this book. Seen in this light, what is at issue in debates around, for example, contact and residence rights, is not just the content of specific legal decisions, reforms or policy initiatives, but these broader questions about the changing nature of fatherhood, struggles over its meaning and value and how law might respond to contemporary 'transformations' of intimacy and 'personal life'.[59] It should not surprise that recent debates within both the legal and cultural realms are marked by what appears to be a simultaneous devaluing[60] and celebration[61] of fathers, nor that conflict in the legal arena should have proved so resistant to a resolution satisfactory to all parties.[62] What is also becoming clear, however, is that such private law conflicts around fatherhood relate in complex ways to the emergence of wider policy agendas concerned with tackling the 'problem of men' as a perceived solution to a range of social issues. Such policy initiatives, as we shall see in the next section, have been particularly central to debates about men's crime, criminality and social disorder.

Men, Violence and Crime: The 'Bigger Picture'?

In much of this book, we have focussed on issues relating to fatherhood that might be seen as primarily, if by no means exclusively, lying within the field of family law. It is also important, however, to locate our analysis in the context of the study of men and masculinities in a more general sense, and in relation to

---

columnists. See eg: L Brooks, 'Dumbed-Down Masculinity Erases Men from Parenting', *Guardian* (5 December 2007), Comment & Debate 32; 'Putting Fathers in the Picture' *Guardian* (8 December 2007), Leaders & Reply 43.

[58] See p 142.

[59] A Giddens, *The Transformations of Intimacy* (Polity, Cambridge, 1992); U Beck and E Beck Gernsheim, *The Normal Chaos of Love* (Polity, Cambridge, 1995). For discussion see Smart, above (n 13), for whom the term 'personal' 'incorporates all sorts of families, all sorts of relationships ... allows for the role of agency and personal meanings, but also retains notions of connectedness and embeddedness in and with the social and cultural': *ibid* at 188. Note also J Lewis, *The End of Marriage? Individualism and Intimate Relations* (Edward Elgar, Cheltenham, 2001); L Jamieson *et al*, 'Friends, Neighbours and Distant Partners: Extending or Decentring Family Relationships? (2006) 11(3) <http://www.socresonline.org.uk/11/3/jamieson.html> accessed 18 March 2008.

[60] See eg: Burgess, above (n 44) on negative contemporary images of fathers and a 'devaluing of fatherhood in late twentieth century Europe': *ibid* at 19–20.

[61] Itself, it has been suggested, a distinctive theme within New Labour social policy. See: Featherstone and Trinder, above (n 36).

[62] Itself, Dewar observes, unsurprising given the nature of the conflicts and 'normal chaos' (following Beck and Beck Gernsheim) central to family law's governance of intimate relations: Dewar (1998), above (n 6).

work on fatherhood, crime and men's violence(s) in particular.[63] Men dominate crime in almost all of its forms and remain much more likely than women to be the perpetrators of violence.[64] One strand of writing in contemporary criminology has sought to advance a theoretical and political engagement with the concept of masculinity by exploring precisely this relationship between men and crime, and, in this work, questions around the prevalence, causes and consequences of men's violence(s) have been central.[65]

This scholarship has a threefold bearing on our discussion of fatherhood. First, in any account of how fatherhood has been constituted as a social and legal problem, it is essential to recognise the historical scale and prevalence of men's violence, both in general terms and, in particular for our present discussion, within families. Over the past three decades, and in no small part down to feminist interventions, the development of understanding around issues such as domestic violence and child sexual abuse has not only revealed a 'hidden history' of family life; it has also raised important questions about the legal safeguarding of men's power within families historically, and the capacity of law adequately to protect the women and children therein. This reappraisal of the gendered nature of violence has been part of a broader cultural reshaping of the contours of 'acceptable' masculinity,[66] one that has, without doubt, profoundly disturbed ideas about what constitutes the 'safe' and the 'dangerous' father. In our discussion of post-separation parenting and fathers' rights in chapter five, for example, we have seen that concerns about violence have been central to debates around contact and residence. It is difficult to overstate, indeed, how significant and divisive the issue of violence has been in this area.[67] It has become a cipher for

---

[63] See eg: JW Messerschmidt, *Masculinities and Crime: Critique and Reconceptualization of Theory* (Rowman and Littlefield, Lanham, MD, 1993); Collier, above (n 34); T Jefferson, 'Introduction' (1996) 35 *British Journal of Criminology* 1337; T Jefferson, 'Masculinities and Crime' in M Maguire, R Morgan, and R Reiner (eds), *The Oxford Handbook of Criminology*, 2nd edn (Oxford University Press, Oxford, 1997); T Newburn and EA Stanko (eds), *Just Boys Doing Business? Men, Masculinities and Crime* (Routledge, London, 1994).

[64] Crime statistics, whether in the form of victimisation or self-report studies, have long revealed what is now generally accepted to be the male dominance of crime. We recognise, however, that the issue of the gendering of crime is itself a contested issue, particularly in relation to certain areas.

[65] See the work cited in n 63, above.

[66] Note B Gough, '"Biting your Tongue": Negotiating Masculinities in Contemporary Britain' (2001) 10(2) *Journal of Gender Studies* 169.

[67] The literature on this subject is extensive. For a useful overview of the relation between contact and domestic violence, including the approach of the courts, see Hunt and Roberts, above (n 22) at 7–9. *Re L (Contact: Domestic Violence), Re V (Contact: Domestic Violence), Re M (Contact: Domestic Violence), Re H (Contact Domestic Violence)* [2000] 2 FLR 334 (the latter is a key case in which the Court of Appeal sought to acknowledge the dangers to mothers and children posed by violence by non-resident fathers). This case has itself been subject to critique for the way in which the risk and dynamics of violence are conceptualised. See further: H Reece, 'UK Women's Groups' Child Contact Campaign: "So long as it is safe"' (2006) 18(4) *Child and Family Law Quarterly* 538: B Featherstone and S Peckover, 'Letting Them Get Away With it: Fathers, Domestic Violence and Child Welfare' (2007) 27(2) *Critical Social Policy* 181; C Sturge and D Glaser 'Contact and Domestic Violence – the Experts' Court Report' (2000) 30 *Family Law* 615; H Saunders, *Twenty-Nine Child Homicides: Lessons to be Learnt on Domestic Violence and Child Protection* (Women's Aid, London, 2004); H Saunders,

wider debates and anxieties about, for example, the extent to which law does (or does not) reflect the power of men, and whether a new ideology of masculinity indicates real changes in men's practices. Violence, in short, has been seen as inextricably linked to the 'doing' of family life for men in ways that raise important questions about its relationship to understandings of 'normal' fatherhood.[68]

Second, recent theoretical elaborations of masculinities and the growing literature around the analytic strengths and weaknesses of the concept of 'hegemonic masculinity' in particular have directly addressed questions of violence which bear on this discussion of fatherhood.[69] Whether understood in terms of the social practice and the structuring of gender relations, via a language of hegemonic and subordinated masculinities,[70] or else as psycho-social engagements with men's criminal behaviour,[71] this work speaks to concerns that are central to developing an understanding of the relationship between fatherhood and law. What we find in this literature are accounts of the interconnections between the structures which inform men's practices,[72] the social significance of normative conceptions of masculine behaviour, and an attempt to understand the place of social practice as a 'resource' for specific groups of men in their 'accomplishment' of masculinity within particular contexts.[73] From this perspective, 'doing' fatherhood, like 'doing' crime, can be viewed as a resource that will vary between different men, depending on their location in relation to structures of class, gender and race. Questions of fathering and violence interconnect in an

---

Failure to Protect? Domestic Violence and the Experiences of Abused Women and Family Courts (Women's Aid, Bristol, 2003). There exist profoundly strong disagreements in this area, around, for example, the scale and prevalence of domestic violence, the appropriateness of mandatory risk assessment and around the need for resources (including facilities for safe contact and treatment programmes for perpetrators). See generally discussion in: RE Dobash and RP Dobash *Violence Against Wives: A Case Against the Patriarchy* (Free Press, New York, 1979); RE Dobash and RP Dobash, *Women, Violence and Social Change* (Routledge, London, 1992).

[68] An issue that has received particular attention in the context of a growing debate about what have been termed 'family annihilators', men who kill their children, and often themselves, in an act of revenge directed against their partners: L Martin, 'Fathers Who Kill Their Children', *Observer* (5 November 2006), Focus 20; Saunders (2004), above (n 67). Violence has itself been a central theme within the critical study of men and masculinities: see J Hearn, *The Violences of Men* (Sage, London, 1998).

[69] We consider these issues in more depth below in the context of our discussion of the male subject, see pp 230–233.

[70] Messerschmidt, above (n 63); RW Connell, *Gender and Power* (Polity, Cambridge, 1987).

[71] See eg: Jefferson, 1997, above (n 63); also: D Gadd, 'Masculinities, Violence and Defended Psycho-Social Subjects' (2000) 4 *Theoretical Criminology* 429; D Gadd, 'Masculinities and Violence Against Female Partners' (2002) 11 SLS 61.

[72] See further: Connell, above (n 70); RW Connell, *Masculinities* (Polity, Cambridge, 1995); RW Connell, *The Men and the Boys* (University of California Press, Berkeley, 2000). Note: S Ervo and T Johansson, *Among Men: Moulding Masculinities* (Ashgate, Aldershot, 2003).

[73] See eg: Messerschmidt, above (n 63). Elsewhere, relational accounts of masculinities have sought to acknowledge the significance of the 'sexed' body in ways that avoid a collapse into biological essentialism. On how ideas of sex/gender have been conceptualised in these debates see: Collier, above (n 34); R Collier, 'Men, Masculinities and Crime' in C Sumner (ed), *The Blackwell International Companion to Criminology* (Blackwell, Oxford, 2003).

explanatory framework that sees fatherhood itself in terms of the performance of masculinity: the 'doing' of gender within a particular structural frame.

Third, to return to the tensions that inhere in policy agendas around the 'problem of men' discussed above, it is important to note the extent to which men's involvement in the lives of their children has been cast as the key to the success of various policy initiatives seeking to address questions of crime and criminality, social disorder and violence. In relation to such diverse areas as, for example, the development of Respect agendas, issues of social exclusion, anti-social behaviour and issues of community cohesion, the 'father figure' has variously appeared as both a cause of, and solution to, a range of social problems. It is important to remember in this context that, for all the funding that has been provided to the fathering initiatives and projects aimed at 'engaging fathers' in families, the major policy priority in terms of government spending on men has been, and remains, in the areas of crime, employment and social cohesion.[74] Engaging fathers is here seen as integral to promoting social order and stability, with efforts to do so targeted towards particular communities in ways that have relied on some class-specific ideas about the nature of the social problems posed by unemployed, anti-social and 'irresponsible' men (ideas that have themselves, of course, been racialised in complex ways).[75] As Scourfield and Drakeford note:

> the concern within government about men in relation to work, crime, health and education is a gender-specific twist on conservative underclass theories, combined with feminist critiques of social problems that have originated on the political left.[76]

The different ways in which these ideas about fatherhood, 'father-presence'[77] and paternal responsibility have been deployed are, however, problematic in a number of respects. As we noted above, promoting father involvement in an effort to address issues such as youth crime and boys' educational (under)a-chievement has tended to rely on a mobilisation of ideas of masculinity quite different from those informing the policy agendas around 'engaging fathers' discussed in chapter four. In the former, fathers are seen as necessary for their contribution to authority and discipline, as figures with a distinctive (gendered) presence in the socialisation of children. 'Active' fathering is thus necessary to

---

[74] Scourfield and Drakeford, above (n 19) at 632.

[75] This raises the question of how the 'father-inclusive' policy agenda may represent a reframing of, rather than a challenge to, dominant ideas of hegemonic masculinity in the way certain negative qualities have been projected on subordinated groups of men (with the 'new father' embodying the 'virtues' of balancing his nurturing and breadwinning roles in ways others may be less able to). See further K Henwood and J Proctor, 'The "good father": reading men's accounts of paternal involvement during the transition to first-time fatherhood' (2003) 42(3) *British Journal of Social Psychology* 337. Generally, see Collier, above (n 34). Note: S Hall, 'Daubing the Drudges of Fury: Men, Violence and the Piety of the "Hegemonic Masculinity" Thesis' (2002) 6(1) *Theoretical Criminology* 35; P Bagguley and K Mann, '"Idle Thieving Bastards"?: Scholarly Representations of the Underclass' (1992) 6(1) *Work, Employment & Society* 113.

[76] Scourfield and Drakeford, above (n 19) at 632.

[77] Like father absence (above n 27), 'father presence' is, of course, itself a contested concept: Collier, above (n 11).

221

ensure the presence of qualities deemed less likely to be present in the mother, however capable she may be of providing love and care. Further, father absence is frequently evoked to explain the poverty of single-parent families, the vast majority of which are headed by women, thus further reinforcing perceptions of the need for a father as breadwinner. In this context, focusing on the absence of fathers and of an appropriate paternal masculinity can be seen to efface any engagement with wider questions of social structure, power and inequality, as well as the material basis of these social relations.

At the very moment a body of feminist legal scholarship has sought to reclaim a place for autonomy in the family,[78] therefore, a form of 'gendered authoritarianism'[79] has been seen to underpin initiatives that have served to reconstitute the family, and the behaviour of mothers, fathers and children,[80] as a site for a reassessment of 'acceptable' normative behaviour. Such a 'remoralising' of the family, in particular in relation to questions of crime, criminality and social order, can itself be seen as a hallmark of neo-liberal governance, forming part of a marked 'ratcheting up' of social control of specific populations.[81] In accounting for fatherhood as a social problem, not all fathers are seen as problems for law in quite the same way.

III Equality, Gender Convergence and 'Geneticisation'

We turn now to equality, a central theme in our discussion of the evolving legal rights and responsibilities of fatherhood. The pre-eminence of ideas of equality can be seen as partly due to a changing legal context framed by concerns with gender neutrality and the rise of the 'new democratic family'.[82] It is also, however, closely interrelated with the increasing significance of genetic factors to how we

---

[78] See eg: M Fineman, *The Autonomy Myth* (The New Press, New York, 2004).

[79] Scourfield and Drakeford, above (n 19) at 630. See also: V Gillies, *Marginalised Mothers: Exploring Working Class Experiences of Parenting* (Routledge, London, 2006).

[80] On a recent 'blending' of paradigms in relation to children, for example, see: F Kaganas and A Diduck, 'Incomplete Citizens: Changing Images of Post-separation Children' (2004) 67(6) MLR 959.

[81] C Piper and S Day Sclater, 'Remoralising the Family? Family Policy, Family Law and Youth Justice' (2000) 12(2) *Child and Family Law Quarterly* 135. See further: L Koffman, 'Holding Parents to Account: Tough on Children, Tough on the Causes of Children' (2008) 35 *Journal of Law and Society* 113; AL James and A James, 'Tightening the Net: Children, Community and Control' (2001) 52 *British Journal of Sociology* 211; C Walsh, 'Imposing Order: Child Safety Orders and Local Child Curfew Schemes' 21(2) *Journal of Social Welfare and family Law* 135. See also: Gillies, above (n 79).

[82] A Giddens, *The Third Way: The Renewal of Social Democracy* (Polity, Cambridge, 1998). See generally, on changing conceptions of rights and responsibilities in this area of law over the past decade: J Eekelaar, *Family Law and Personal Life* (Oxford University Press, Oxford, 2006). Contrast this reading of 'personal life' with that of Smart, above (n 13). For further discussion, ch 4, p 118. Note also the influence in relation to New Labour thinking of A Etzioni, *New Communitarian Thinking: Persons, Virtues, Institutions and Communities* (University Press of Virginia, Charlottesville, VA, 1995); A Etzioni (ed), *The Essential Communitarian Reader* (Rowman and Littlefield, Lanham, MD, 1998).

think about fatherhood, and a 'gender convergence' in understandings of men's and women's roles and responsibilities in reproduction, employment and care.[83]

Equality, Rights and the Evolving Legal Context

Fathers' claims to equal treatment have been bolstered by a reliance on rights discourses which have become politically resonant in the UK following the incorporation of the European Convention on Human Rights through the Human Rights Act 1998. Additionally, ideas of equality have been further entrenched as, across diverse contexts, EU policy agendas have sought to promote the 'mainstreaming' of gender equality within member states,[84] and have informed the emergence of a now distinctive jurisprudence around 'law's families' in EU law.[85] Fathers, as we have seen in this book, have sought to deploy rights discourse in a variety of ways in staking out equality claims in the legal arena.[86] Such equality arguments often appear to resist the traditional vision of parenting as based on a clear-cut and gendered division of labour, whereby reproduction and child-rearing are seen largely as 'women's business', with fathers somehow an optional supplement to mothers. They also challenge the perceived naturalness of gendered differences in parenting in a more general sense, disrupting the idea, for example, that men are more able to provide discipline and guidance, and women more likely to provide nurture.

Equality claims by fathers, and the contestations around rights with which they have been associated, have nonetheless played out in very different ways across the legal contexts discussed in this book and have enjoyed varying degrees of success. As we saw in chapter five, the use of equal rights claims in contact and residence disputes has undoubtedly shaped the political and cultural framework in which debates about family law reform now play out.[87] Such equality claims, however, have had limited impact in other respects, notably failing to achieve key legal changes which some fathers' rights groups have sought.[88] A further issue raised by fathers' demands for equal rights is the extent to which the deployment of such ostensibly progressive rhetoric may mask the continuation of gendered

---

[83] See ch 1, p 13.

[84] S Mazey, *Gender Mainstreaming in the EU: Principles and Practice* (Kogan Page, London, 2001); V Schmidt, *Gender Mainstreaming: An Innovation in Europe? The Institutionalisation of Gender Mainstreaming in the European Commission* (Verlag Barbara Burich, Leverkusen Opladen, 2005).

[85] See C McGlynn, *Families and the European Union* (Cambridge University Press, Cambridge 2006); H Salford, 'Concepts of Family Under EU Law – Lessons from the ECHR' (2002) 16 *International Journal of Law, Policy and the Family* 410.

[86] For further discussion of the changing status of equality and rights in family law see: Eekelaar, above (n 82).

[87] See, for example, the contributions to the collection edited by Collier and Sheldon, above (n 24), particularly the chapter by Susan Boyd.

[88] Notably, the institution of a legal presumption of shared residence and 'equal' parenting. It is open to question how close the British government may have been, in the period from 2004 to 2006, to seriously considering the introduction of such a presumption: Collier, above (n 25).

divisions of parenting labour, underpinned by issues of differential social power and vested interests in maintaining existing structures of family practices. For one writer, therefore, at the present moment 'men who love their children':

> are assumed to be sharing equally in the work of the family ... [yet] the social conversation about men and the sexual political issue of domestic work omits the most significant fact about male resistance to change – that it suits men. This seems to be too unpalatable to be made explicit – to say it about gender relations undermines the romantic ideology ... Meanwhile men's interests continue to be served by the same discourses which deny them, and which continue to invite us to wait until men are ready to change.[89]

Yet there is, we would suggest, nothing intrinsically 'pro-' or 'anti'-women (or pro- or anti-feminist) about the fact that calls for equality are marshalled by fathers within the diverse contexts in which some men do appear increasingly keen to assert their rights and, it would seem, embrace responsibilities with regard to children.[90] Rather, the deployment of ideas of equality can be seen as one part of a complex renegotiation of what it means to be a father in a context where the legal and political terrain has shifted considerably under the weight of cultural and economic changes and evolving understandings of parental responsibilities, child welfare, development and protection. Rethinking the relationship between fatherhood, rights and equality raises significant questions about what it means to engage with the idea of men as gendered, 'responsible' subjects, as well as what such changes mean for understandings of men and women's relationships to wider shifts around parenting, economy and society.[91]

Gender Convergence

The rise of the discourse of equality is closely interrelated with another theme to emerge from the preceding chapters: the deeply contested idea of gender convergence in parenting. Significantly, if it is the case that men and women can, do or should parent in much the same way, there can be little basis for seeking to treat mothers and fathers differently, in law, policy or otherwise.[92] In our discussion of men's involvement in 'natural' reproduction in chapter two, we described a movement away from a view that fathers have a more distant, even vicarious, relationship to reproduction. We suggested, rather, that legal provisions relevant to this area (taking the examples of liability for congenital disability and foetal

---

[89] McMahon, above (n 27) at 7–8.

[90] See Jocelyn Crowley's empirical investigation of the use of equality arguments in the context of the US fathers' rights movement: JE Crowley, 'Adopting "Equality Tools" from the Toolboxes of their Predecessors: the Fathers' Rights Movement in the United States' in R Collier and S Sheldon, *Fathers' Rights Activism and Legal Reform* (Hart, Oxford, 2006). See further: Collier, above (n 25).

[91] See the work cited above at nn 6, 7 and 59.

[92] See eg: A Doucet, *Do Men Mother? Fatherhood, Care and Domestic Responsibility* (University of Toronto Press, Toronto, 2006).

protection legislation) had fossilised understandings of male and female bodies characteristic of an earlier time, treating men's and women's reproductive functioning as somehow radically distinct. We argued that significant social changes are implicated in shifting beliefs about men's fertility and reproductive health that, it would appear, increasingly mirror understandings of female fertility and reproductive health.

These developments around the place of the father in reproduction – as well as related ideas about masculinities, men's health and male sexuality[93] – parallel the changes which we then went on to outline in later chapters, where we discussed fathers' evolving role within the family. Perhaps most notably, the 'new fatherhood' discussed in chapter four is seen as reflecting a belief that men are capable of parenting in ways historically associated with women: that men too can nurture, provide 'hands-on' care, and carry out the day-to-day tasks of raising a child. Further, and crucially, fathers are now often stated to be just as necessary as mothers to that child's psychological, educational and emotional development. However, this is not to deny the continued presence in law and policy of powerful and still resonant assumptions that women are somehow 'naturally' more connected to their children, and more directly involved as parents than are men.[94] In some contexts, as we have seen, fathering remains associated with a largely vicarious experience of parenting, one that is significantly mediated through the agency of the mother. Often, the father's responsibilities as a parent are constituted in terms of a primary financial responsibility and an ability to provide economically for his family.[95] As we noted above, the ongoing struggle between these different understandings of fatherhood represents a significant and ongoing point of tension in law.

The Geneticisation of Fatherhood

Closely related to these themes of equality and gender convergence, *Fragmenting Fatherhood* has charted an enhanced focus on genetic links in grounding the rights and responsibilities associated with fatherhood across diverse areas of law. The geneticisation of understandings of what it means to be a father is one aspect of the enhanced focus on vertical, as opposed to horizontal, relationships noted above, with men's relationships with their children increasingly seen as direct, rather than mediated through or dependent on their relationship with a child's mother. 'Geneticisation' can thus be seen, at least in part, as a response to the

---

[93] See further: Robertson, above (n 49).

[94] A central theme, for example, in much feminist criminological work, which has sought to analyse how these gendered assumptions can play out in contradictory ways within the criminal justice system. See eg: N Naffine, *Feminism and Criminology* (Polity, Cambridge, 1997); N Naffine (ed), *Gender, Crime and Feminism* (Aldershot, Dartmouth, 1995); L Gelsthorpe and A Morris (eds), *Feminist Perspectives in Criminology* (Open University Press, Buckingham, 1990); C Smart, *Law, Crime and Sexuality: Essays in Feminism* (Sage, London, 1995).

[95] Ch 4, p 109.

decline in marriage as a lifelong commitment to one partner, a development which has provoked the need to find other ways of grounding men's relationships with their children. While on its own a genetic link might not be either necessary or sufficient to claim the rights associated with fatherhood, it is now legally accepted as forming an important basis on which a father may claim the right to develop a relationship with his child.[96] In chapter six, we saw the courts' growing willingness to recognise the rights of the genetic father, even where such recognition might be seen as posing a risk to the stability of a social family unit and to challenge the role played by another man within it. In chapter three we saw the growing relevance of the genetic link in the regulation of reproductive technologies (albeit that this relevance is one which does not always play out in straightforward ways).[97]

This 'geneticisation' of fatherhood is, we suggest, integrally linked to the rise of the discourse of equality discussed above. A reliance on genetics serves to emphasise men's and women's contributions (and thus responsibilities) to a child as equal, giving further weight to a presumption that law adopts a policy of formal equality in dealing with men's and women's claims.[98] One particularly vivid example of this was provided by our discussion of the embryo dispute in *Evans*, where a reliance on the significance of genetic links resulted in an erasure of the additional gestational contribution that women make to reproduction. This added weight to the trial judge's description of the legal treatment of the parties as entirely even-handed, and the dismissal of Ms Evans' claims that she had been subject to discrimination.[99]

IV Fatherhood and Law: Theoretical Issues

The analysis of this book raises a number of further issues for future theoretical engagements with fatherhood, and, before concluding, we outline some of the more important here.

---

[96] Ch 6, p 195.

[97] As in the case of *The Leeds Teaching Hospitals NHS Trust v Mr A, Mrs A and others* [2003] EWHC 259 (QB), [2003] 1 FLR 1091.; see ch 3, pp 85–8.

[98] It should be noted that where the mother both contributes the egg and gestates the pregnancy, then the presence of mitochondrial DNA will mean that her genetic contribution is very slightly greater than that of the father.

[99] Ch 3, p 96. *Evans v Amicus Health Care* [2003] EWHC Fam 2161, [2004] EWCA Civ 727. See further: S Sheldon, 'Gender Equality and Reproductive Decision Making' (2004) 12(3) FLS 303. Our criticism here is not necessarily of the outcome in *Evans*, but merely of this aspect of the judge's framing of what was at stake in the dispute.

Fatherhood and Families

We suggested, in chapter one, that feminist scholarship was first to place the study of fatherhood on the agenda as an object in its own right within legal studies. Developments within the critical study of men and masculinities in law have been the natural corollary of earlier feminist explorations of the 'woman of legal discourse'.[100] Feminism may also take some credit for having contributed to the framing of subsequent reform initiatives pertaining to fatherhood. The provisions for maternity, paternity and parenting leave discussed in chapter four,[101] for example, may be seen as built upon a groundwork laid by feminist ideas, which created the conditions for progressive dialogue to occur among policy and law makers.[102] Such success, however, has been subject to certain limitations. For example, feminist critiques of the way in which personal life is structured, and the 'private family' conceptualised, have largely failed to permeate into political discourse. Notably, far from generating increased support for families through public funds, the privatisation of responsibilities within neo-liberal political and economic agendas would appear to have had a particularly hard impact on already vulnerable social groups, including some groups of fathers.[103] In this very significant sense, law has remained largely impervious to feminist engagements with the political and conceptual limits of the 'private' family,[104] as well as recent sociological, political, philosophical and economic analyses of personal life, intimacy, care, relationality and social dependency.[105]

The transformation of fatherhood, we have suggested, is central to these debates about the changing relation between families and law. Writing in the US context, Fineman has observed how the 'private family is assumed ideally to

---

[100] See further: Collier, above (n 12).

[101] See further: D Smeaton and A Marsh, *Maternity and Paternity Rights and Benefits: Survey of Parents 2005*, Employment Relations Research Series No 50 (Department for Work and Pensions, London, 2006), suggesting an increase in take-up of paid paternity leave by fathers. Note also M Thompson, L Vinter and V Young, *Dads and their Babies: Leave Arrangements in the First Year* (Equal Opportunities Commission, Manchester, 2005).

[102] A Diduck and K O'Donovan, 'Feminism and Families: Plus Ça Change?' in A Diduck and K O'Donovan, *Feminist Perspectives on Family Law* (Routledge-Cavendish, Abingdon, 2006) at 16.

[103] S Boyd, 'Legal Regulation of Families in Changing Societies' in A Sarat (ed), *The Blackwell Companion to Law and Society* (Blackwell, London, 2004); Gillies, above (n 79); S Boyd, *Child Custody, Law and Women's Work* (Oxford University Press, Oxford, 2003); M Fineman, 'Cracking the Foundational Myths: Independence, Autonomy, and Self-sufficiency' (2000) 13 *Journal of Gender, Social Policy and Law* 13.

[104] See: Fineman, above (n 78); M Fineman, *The Neutered Mother, The Sexual Family, and Other Twen-tieth Century Tragedies* (Routledge, New York, 1995).

[105] See eg: Smart, above (n 13); Fineman, above (nn 78 and 104). See also: W Hollway, *The Capacity to Care: Gender and Ethical Subjectivity* (Routledge, London, 2006); S Roseneil and S Budgeon, 'Cultures of Intimacy and Care Beyond "the Family": Personal Life and Social Change in the Early 21st Century' (2004) *Current Sociology* 135; M Urban Walker, *Moral Understandings: A Feminist Study in Ethics* (Routledge, New York, 1998); JC Tronto, *Moral Boundaries* (Routledge, London 1993); S Sevenhuijsen, *Citizenship and the Ethics of Care: Feminist Considerations about Justice, Morality and Politics* (Routledge, London, 1998); S Benhabib *Situating the Self: Gender, Community and Postmodernism in Contemporary Ethics* (Routledge, London, 1992).

operate independently of the state and the market in fulfilling its caretaking responsibilities.'[106] This claim must be qualified in the UK context, which is characterised both by an infrastructure of social care unlike that of the US, at least in certain significant respects, and rather different assumptions about what is appropriate in terms of state involvement. Nonetheless, Fineman's work requires us to address the issue of how a form of familial independence 'is not accomplished unless the family is able to produce both economic support and caretaking labor, tasks historically allocated along gendered lines'.[107] She explains:

> Men's role as economic providers serves an essential function in an ideological system in which dependency is privatized and will not be readily displaced until there is some greater public responsibility for the provision of essential goods ... change will necessitate recasting our societal expectations for fatherhood so that it is more than just an economic relationship with the family. However, expectations that fathers (or breadwinners generally) also engage in caretaking will cause as many complications as has the expectation that caretakers engage in market work.[108]

This analysis offers a broader perspective within which to locate our discussion of changes in fathers' family practices and paternal responsibilities. It provokes questions about the way society presently values care, dependency and vulnerability, recognising the gendered nature of caring practices and of a cultural and political economy which make it so difficult to balance the demands of parenting, for both women and men, alongside those of paid work.[109] Ignoring structural factors results in a debate about fatherhood that itself conceptualises social change in a superficial way, leaving questions of aspiration, expectation and the shifting nature of 'personal life' undisturbed.[110] Yet the percolation of these kinds of questions into the law and policy-making arena in the UK remains, we suggest, limited.

Gender and Power

Our analysis also raises important questions for contemporary accounts of male power. We have argued throughout against the idea that power can be usefully conceptualised in 'zero-sum' terms, whereby as men (or fathers) 'lose' power, women (or mothers) somehow 'gain' it, and vice versa. While a 'zero-sum' understanding might resonate with certain strands of both feminist and fathers' rights thinking, each curiously mirroring the other in terms of seeing legal reform as having 'winners' and 'losers', law's relation to social change is far more complex. Indeed, a more accurate picture is provided by those authors who have

---

[106] Fineman, above (n 78) at 199.
[107] *Ibid.*
[108] *Ibid.*
[109] Above, n 100.
[110] A central theme, for example, in the work of Martha Fineman, above (n 78). See also: Boyd, above (n 103).

described a general 'normative pluralism' and 'conceptual chaos' within the family law field.[111] However, a vast literature in the field of masculinity studies has charted the extent to which men continue, notwithstanding the social changes we have discussed, to hold political and economic power. In the UK, as elsewhere, men dominate the main institutions of government, the judiciary and the legal system, the military and the world of business.[112] The question that then arises is whether it is possible to hold on simultaneously to this sense of 'conceptual chaos', complexity and confusion, whilst still engaging in a broader, structural critique of men's power and theorising of gender (dis)advantage and the agency of individuals in ways that can then inform political action and legal reform.[113]

Further, we would note here a significant question, not least for feminism, regarding how appropriate account can be taken of *women's* agency and power within the context of the debates about fatherhood discussed in this book. If it is right to criticise a system which, in the compelling language of Czapanskiy,[114] often sees mothers as 'draftees' and men as 'volunteers', is this necessarily and exclusively to women's disadvantage? Specifically: while appearing in law as 'volunteers' may make it easier for fathers to evade responsibilities, to what extent does it also make it harder for them to claim rights? In the preceding pages, we noted a number of instances in which mothers act in some way as gatekeepers to fathers' involvement with a child, from the moment – for example – that an unmarried mother can choose whether to reveal the existence of a child to a man, or consent to his being named on a birth certificate.[115] Does the rise of the new fatherhood ideal of engaged fathers, and the authority claims with which it is now being associated, pose significant challenges to this power, threatening an ideal of motherhood that may itself, of course, be experienced at a personal level by some women as contradictory and conflicted? What political and policy questions then emerge from refocusing attention towards social processes that might facilitate the greater 'involvement' of fathers?[116]

In chapter five we saw how these issues play out in the context of a reframing of the non-resident father as a figure potentially in need of support and service provision. As Fineman asks:

> What has been missing from policy and reform discussions thus far is a debate about the nature of fatherhood and the transformation of the role of the father in response to

---

[111] Parker, above (n 8); Dewar, above (n 6).

[112] See eg: Connell, above (n 72); S Whitehead, *Men and Masculinities* (Polity, Cambridge, 2002)

[113] See, on recent attempts within sociology to engage with these issues, Smart, above (n 13).

[114] K Czapanskiy, 'Volunteers and Draftees: The Struggle for Parental Equality' (1991) 38 *UCLA Law Review* 415.

[115] See *Re C (A Child)* [2007] EWCA Civ 1206, discussed at pp 189–190 above; and the requirements of birth registration, discussed in ch 6, pp 184–187.

[116] Lewis, above (n 59).

changing expectations, norms and practices. How does the desire for gender neutrality and the ideal of egalitarianism play a role in the creation of a new set of norms for fatherhood?[117]

Yet what, we might add, would such a 'new set of norms for fatherhood' look like?[118] What re-visioning of legal concepts and categories might such change entail?[119] And what would this all mean for women? What might the implications be for women's own relationship to and investments in motherhood? Greater paternal involvement may be a twin-edged sword for mothers, challenging their own authority with regard to their children and forcing them into a continued relationship where one is no longer desired, for example in the post-separation context or following a brief sexual relationship. As such, in rethinking father-hood, we need also to question the implications for women's aspirations, desires and investments, in relation to both employment and to parenting, and to recognise the potentially contradictory, conflicted nature of both women's and men's subjectivity. We live, as Smart has observed, in 'interesting times'.[120]

Rethinking the Male Subject

This sense of complexity is particularly important in how we conceptualise the male subject in these discussions of fatherhood. Feminists have been alive to the dangers of essentialism in thinking about women.[121] Yet this pitfall has perhaps been less successfully avoided in thinking about men and fatherhood, not least in the context of the often highly politically polarised debates discussed in this book. How might diversity in the lives of men be accommodated in accounts of, for example, recent social movements around fatherhood?[122] Do common inter-ests really exist between fathers across other axes of power and discrimination, such as race, class and sexuality? To what extent has the entire debate about 'the future of fatherhood' itself been part of a process that has served to exacerbate social divisions, absolving some men from responsibility 'to change' whilst casting others as the 'bad' fathers, and, in so doing, pathologising men's parenting in a more general sense?[123] We would suggest that the 'good father' ideal in law has been premised historically on certain assumptions that have had far-reaching implications for how the parenting practices of men from certain social groups, but not others, are then assessed and subject to surveillance.[124] To what extent,

---

[117] Fineman, above (n 78) at 195.
[118] *Ibid.*
[119] See Fineman, above (n 78) for further discussion.
[120] C Smart, 'Preface' in R Collier and S Sheldon (eds), *Fathers' Rights Activism and Legal Reform in Comparative Perspective* (Hart, Oxford, 2006).
[121] See eg: E Spelman, *Inessential Woman* (Beacon Press, Boston, 1990).
[122] See further: Collier, above (n 25).
[123] See eg: Hall, above (n 75), and, by way of response: RW Connell, 'On Hegemonic Masculinity and Violence: A Response to Jefferson and Hall' (2002) 6 *Theoretical Criminology* 89.
[124] See: Hall, above (n 75). See also: Gillies, above (n 79).

230

therefore, have contemporary debates about fatherhood and, with it, men and masculinities, been pervaded with normative ideas about social class, race, ethnicity and (hetero)sexuality?[125]

A further question can be asked about how these issues have themselves been engaged with in the context of legal studies. How, we asked above, do ideas about fatherhood contained in legal discourse relate to the 'real lives' of individuals? What cannot be ascertained from an 'unpacking' or 'deconstruction' of representations of fatherhood in law is any knowledge of the cultural, economic and psychological investments specific individuals may make in adapting to (or, indeed, resisting) social practices, attitudes and values. In order to address such issues it would be necessary to ask some rather different questions. Why is it that some men 'turn to' or invest in a particular subject position (such as 'fathers' rights activist'), and others do not? And why do some parents, and not others, become 'stuck' in conflict around separation?[126] These questions relate to the specificities of individual biographies, life histories and experience. How do broader social shifts around identity and aspiration, along with ideas of community, belonging and intimacy, ideas that are themselves socially situated and historically contingent, link to the psycho-social and emotional aspects of legal disputes? Why are some men violent, and how might a more adequate conceptualisation of the male subject facilitate and inform policy engagements around such violence?[127]

Recent work in the field of masculinities, drawing on developments in sociology, psychology and cultural studies, has sought to address these issues and, foregrounding emotional and psychological factors, explore the active production of identity formations in an attempt to (re)conceptualise the male subject.[128] The essentially contested nature of the concept of 'masculinity' has received far greater attention in recent years and is a subject beyond the scope of this book.[129] Crucially, however, this work has recognised that fathers can occupy potentially contradictory subject positions.[130] Moving away from exclusively rationalist

---

[125] See: B Featherstone, 'Taking Fathers Seriously' (2003) 33(2) *British Journal of Social Work* 239.

[126] See ch 5, p 168.

[127] Gadd (2000, 2002), above (n 71).

[128] For general discussion, and in addition to the work cited above see: M Wetherell and N Edley, 'Negotiating Hegemonic Masculinity: Imaginary Positions and Psycho-Discursive Practices' (1999) 9 *Feminism & Psychology* 335; J Hearn, 'From Hegemonic Masculinity to the Hegemony of Men' (2004) 5(1) *Feminist Theory* 49; Collier, above (nn 12 and 34); RW Connell and J Messerschmidt, 'Hegemonic Masculinity: Rethinking the Concept' (2005) 19 *Gender & Society* 829; DZ Demetriou, 'Connell's Concept of Hegemonic Masculinity: A Critique' (2001) 30 *Theory & Society* 327; C Brickell, 'Masculinities, Performativity and Subversion: A Sociological Appraisal' (2005) 8 *Men & Masculinities* 24. See further: S Whitehead, 'Hegemonic Masculinity Revisited' (1999) 6 *Gender, Work & Organization* 58; Hall, above (n 75); Connell, above (n 72).

[129] See above n 128. See also: R Collier, *The Man of Law: Essays on Law, Men and Gender* (Routledge, London, forthcoming); J MacInnes, *The End of Masculinity* (Open University Press, Buckingham, 1998).

[130] See further: Wetherell and Edley, above (n 128); S Frosh, *Sexual Difference: Masculinity and Psychoanalysis* (Routledge, London, 1994). See also: S Frosh, A Phoenix and R Pattman, *Young*

accounts of the male subject, it has sought to acknowledge how 'what fathers *emotionally* feel and desire is as important as what they *rationally* think in shaping paternal behaviour'.[131] For example, in the field of private law disputes around contact, discussed in chapter five, we find a growing recognition of the importance of engaging with the emotional and relational dynamics of separation.[132] This shift in focus potentially opens out the study of fatherhood and law to a more complex analysis of power, rendering visible the interconnections between social, psychological and interpersonal aspects of personal life, alongside recognition of the significance of men's emotional histories.[133] It does so, importantly, in ways that, far from effacing women and women's agency (and, importantly, the agency of children[134]), might seek to integrate the social agency, interdependency and psychological complexity of all parties.

A growing research base suggests that an appreciation of the psychological complexity of parenting is central to understanding the form and content of legal disputes of the kind addressed in this book. By imposing 'an a priori theoretical/ conceptual frame on the psychological complexity of men's behaviour,'[135] however, there has been a frequent tendency in law to negate these questions of the embodied,[136] contradictory and affective dimensions of personal life: the very issues that have themselves become increasingly salient within more recent sociological scholarship.[137] Whilst the contours of this literature and the debates to which it has given rise transcend the scope of this book, this work has

---

Masculinities: Understanding Boys in Contemporary Society (Palgrave Macmillan, Basingstoke, 2001); S Frosh, *After Words: The Personal in Gender, Culture and Psychotherapy* (Palgrave Macmillan, Basingstoke, 2002); A Samuels, 'The Good-Enough Father of Whatever Sex' (1995) 5(4) *Feminism & Psychology* 511.

[131] Haywood and Mac an Ghaill, above (n 30) (italics in original).

[132] See eg: Letter, 'The Government Must Help the Children of Divorcees', *The Times* (12 June 2007), Comment 16. Note also the conclusions of L Trinder and J Kellet, *The Longer Term Outcomes of In-Court Conciliation* (Ministry of Justice, London, 2007). For further discussion see ch 5, p 161. On developments in relation to support and advice for parents, see: R Roberts, 'Adult Approach: Interview with Dorit Braun, Parentline Plus', *Guardian* (25 April 2007), Society 5.

[133] For discussion, Smart (n 13).

[134] Note, for example, in relation to the inclusion of children in family law dispute resolution (and the possible consequences for fathers: J McIntosh, 'Child Inclusion as a Principle and as Evidence-Based Practice: Applications to Family Law Services and Related Sectors' (Australian Institute of Family Studies, Melbourne, 2007).

[135] Collier, above (n 34) at 22.

[136] By this, we mean that the 'lived' male body is itself a ubiquitous presence within family law. Family practices are bodily practices, concerned with bodies that not only move across time and space but may be healthy or ill, fertile or infertile, which experience ageing, psychological and physical harm and which have been positioned by law in particular spatial relationships to children. As Morgan observes, 'family themes and family concerns revolve around issues of birth, death and sexuality and the connections and relationships that are made and unmade through these': D Morgan, *Family Connections* (Polity, Cambridge, 1996). He cites Shilling: 'Our daily experiences of living . . . are intrinsically bound up with experiencing and managing our own and other people's bodies' *ibid* at 113–14, citing C Shilling, *The Body and Social Theory* (Sage, London, 1993) 22. See further: R Collier, 'Male Bodies, Family Practices' in A Bainham *et al* (eds), *Body Lore and Laws* (Hart, Oxford, 2002).

[137] For discussion, see generally: Smart, above (n 13). See also: Morgan, above (n 136); L Jamieson, *Intimacy: Personal Relationships in Modern Society* (Polity, Cambridge, 1998); Lewis, above (n 59).

significant implications for understanding the social practices of fathers across each of the legal contexts discussed in the preceding chapters. In ways aligned to recent feminist engagements with materiality[138] and an ethics of care,[139] these developments seek to recognise the complex psychosocial dynamics of legal disputes, issues all too often effaced by a strict adherence to legality and abstract principles of justice and welfare within legal analysis.[140]

Representations of fatherhood in law, therefore, far from being pre-constituted, unmediated artefacts, constitute a nexus of the physical and cognitive realms, of knowledge and experience, of self and society, and of ideas about how individual subjectivity is articulated and constituted. In endeavouring to value different styles of parenting, the recognition of the gendered dimensions of social experience raises further questions for the development of intervention around inclusive and gender-sensitive practices within specific policy contexts. For example, in the context of debates around non-resident fathers discussed in chapter five, what are the implications of re-conceptualising separated fathers as a distinctive social group with specific, if diverse, needs?[141] Far from negating the experience and voices of children,[142] or positioning them as somehow 'outside' legal disputes around fatherhood (conflicts that are then understood primarily in terms of adult relations),[143] such an approach can be further aligned to recent attempts to locate the child her or himself as an active subject within a complex – and shifting – set of social relations.[144]

---

[138] R Hennessy, *Materialist Feminism and the Politics of Discourse* (Routledge, London 1992); R Hennessy and C Inghram (eds), *Materialist Feminism: A Reader in Class, Difference and Women's Lives* (Routledge, London 1997).

[139] Above n 105.

[140] Cf: Smart, above (n 13); contrast Eekelaar, above (n 82).

[141] For discussion of this issue in the context of fathers' rights agendas in law see: Collier, above (n 25).

[142] See further: J McIntosh, above (n 134); C Smart and B Neale, "'It's My Life Too" – Children's Perspectives on Post-Divorce Parenting' [2000] *Family Law* 163; V May and C Smart, 'Silence in Court? Hearing Children in Residence and Contact Disputes' (2004) *Child and Family Law Quarterly* 305; F Kaganas and A Diduck, 'Incomplete Citizens: Changing Images of Post-Separation Children' (2004) 67(6) MLR 959. See generally: C Smart, B Neale and A Wade, *The Changing Experience of Childhood – Families and Divorce* (Polity, Cambridge, 2001).

[143] F Kaganas and S Day Sclater, 'Contact Disputes: Narrative Constructions of "Good" Parents' (2004) 12(1) *Feminist Legal Studies* 1.

[144] See eg McIntosh, above (n 134). Debates about childhood have encompassed in a more general sense (and cannot be confined to) questions about the changing nature of adult interdependencies and, increasingly, issues of risk, anxiety and security associated with the physical safety and psychological well-being of children; see eg: F Furedi, *Paranoid Parenting* (Allen Lane, London, 2002); C Jenks, *Childhood* (Routledge, London, 1996). See also: C Henricson and A Bainham, *The Child and Family Policy Divide: Tensions, Convergence and Rights* (Joseph Rowntree Foundation, York, 2005). For broader discussion in the European context, see: J Hearn and K Pringle, 'Men, Masculinities and Children: Some European Perspectives' (2006) 26(2) *Critical Social Policy* 365.

V Conclusion: Fragmentation, Tension and Contradiction

Whilst typically 'still used as a single unitary concept',[145] we have suggested that the idea of fatherhood is better understood as open-ended, fluid and fragmented. As a final illustration of this central theme, we end by highlighting some of the more significant tensions, contradictions and inconsistencies in law and policy initiatives regarding fatherhood that have been visible in the course of the preceding chapters.

First, we have charted clear tensions and contradictions in the way in which changes around fatherhood have served to fragment and disturb the legal parameters of 'the sexual family'. This term was coined by American feminist legal theorist Martha Fineman to describe the 'ideal' family type, which has informed so much family law in the UK, as in the US.[146] The 'sexual family' describes the nuclear family unit with a heterosexual, formally celebrated union at its core. Within the sexual family, then, all possible aspects of fatherhood are united in the person of one man, who will be the mother's husband and the children's genetic and social father. Yet the social reality that the sexual family ideal purports to reflect is now widely reported to be in significant transition, if not decline.[147] A noteworthy increase in the rate of non-marital births and the decline in marriage as a lifelong permanent commitment to one person has increasingly resulted in 'genetic families' split across households, with children living apart from at least one of their genetic parents, typically the father.[148] Further, same-sex couples are now able to enter into legally binding civil partnerships, and jointly to adopt children, and, should the reforms described in chapter three pass into law, lesbian couples will gain the right jointly to be recognised as the legal parents of a child born to them as a result of licensed infertility treatment services.[149] Such changes, we have suggested, pose clear challenges for legal orders that have traditionally relied on (heterosexual) marriage as the formal means of connecting men to their children.[150] The first point of tension and contradiction we would note, therefore, lies between the tenacious hold of this ideal family type on the legal imagination, and the simultaneous pull of the recognition that law needs to

---

[145] S Sevenhuijsen, 'Fatherhood and the Political Theory of Rights: Theoretical Perspectives of Feminism' (1986) 14 *International Journal of the Sociology of Law* 329 at 338.

[146] Fineman, above (n 104) at 143.

[147] Ch 1, p 4.

[148] See ch 1, pp 10–15.

[149] See respectively the Civil Partnership Act 2004, the Adoption and Children Act 2002, and the Human Fertilisation and Embryology Bill 2007, discussed in ch 3. The fast-track adoption procedure following surrogacy, foreseen in s 30 of the Human Fertilisation and Embryology Act 1990, is likewise set to be extended to both female and male same-sex couples.

[150] See: S Sheldon, 'Reproductive Technologies and the Tenacious Hold of the Sexual Family' *Current Legal Problems* Lecture, UCL (7 February 2008). See also: A Diduck, 'Shifting Familiarity' (2005) 58 *Current Legal Problems* 235.

234

support those familial, caring relationships which are significant to children, whether they occur within a (hetero)sexual family or not.[151]

Closely interrelated to the above, we have shown that the term 'father' is now being used to denote a range of roles and relationships between men and children. Within the diverse and changing social contexts sketched above, the different kinds of relationship which were previously contained within the sexual family (marriage to and cohabitation with a child's mother, intention to create or to father a child with her, demonstrated commitment to and social parenting of a born child, a genetic link) may now be spread amongst several men. In many instances, then, law has had to navigate between competing claims predicated on these different kinds of fatherhood. As noted, in recent years greater weight has been accorded in law and policy to the asserted 'truth' of the genetic link.[152] In keeping with our theme of fragmentation, however, we have suggested that the weight given to genetic factors has not been won *at the expense of* other visions of fatherhood. Rather, the figure of the genetic father who exists outside the nuclear family unit, has been reinterpreted as no longer constituting a significant threat to the child's relationship with the social father parenting within it. The idea that contact with both a genetic and social father may be a psychologically enriching, rather than confusing and damaging, experience for children, emerged as a clear theme in our discussion of the developments considered in chapters three, five and six.

A second tension, linked to the discrepancy between the unitary and plural senses of 'fatherhood' noted above, lies in the relationship between fatherhood and motherhood. We have seen that fatherhood continues to be defined in opposition to activities identified with mothering in a number of respects. 'Successful' fatherhood is still routinely portrayed as connected to a particular set of culturally masculine attributes (authority, rationality, discipline and so on) as opposed to the 'feminine' qualities associated with the mother (warmth, emotionality, nurture and hands-on care). Fatherhood, furthermore, tends to be perceived as 'the product of acquired knowledge and mastery of action', while motherhood 'still tends to be represented as having an instinctive core'.[153] However, co-existing alongside this more traditional vision, we have suggested, lie other ideas of fatherhood, ideas which strongly resemble our understandings of motherhood (seeing men, for example, as equally capable of nurturing and hands-on childcare). As such, there is a tension between cultural ideas of fatherhood as the same as motherhood, and more traditional visions of fatherhood as different from motherhood but complementary to it.

These tensions pervade debates in the legal arena, raising complex questions of how men and women parent, and whether 'fathering' is itself no more than what happens when the activity of parenting is carried out by a man, or whether it

---

[151] For our discussion of this tension in New Labour family policy, see p 135.
[152] See pp 225–226. For discussion: Eekelaar, above (n 82).
[153] Lupton and Barclay, above (n 31).

involves some specific attributes and activities.[154] Further, as we argued above, these issues of gender sameness and difference in parenting mean that it can be extremely difficult to make sense of the demand for legal 'equality' in this context. Relatedly, we noted the tension between still resonant constructions of fathers as breadwinners and as hands-on carers. This tension marks current policy initiatives, legal reforms and the experiences of individual men in negotiating the competing imperatives involved in being a 'good dad'.[155]

Third, we traced further contradictions between ideas of fathers as victims of institutional and structural impediments (battling to parent 'against the odds'),[156] and ideas of fathers as perpetrators (whose own selfishness and failure to square up to their responsibilities lies at the root of a range of social problems).[157] Men's parenting continues, in certain policy areas in particular, to be 'depicted as a social problem rather than a social strength', fathers becoming 'only visible in terms of their absence: working long hours, not living with their children or lacking legal rights as parents'.[158] We suggested that the legacy of a deficit model of fatherhood, one which relies on very different assumptions from those underpinning policy initiatives aimed at engaging fathers with their children, remains particularly powerful in areas relating to crime and social order.[159]

The picture that we have sought to paint in *Fragmenting Fatherhood*, then, is one of complexity, change, inconsistency and contradiction. There is a richness, texture and subtlety to the 'gendered lives' of men that cannot be comprehended through the deployment of binaries of 'good' and 'bad' dads, 'new' and 'traditional' fathers, or, indeed, in terms of whether fathering is to be understood as the 'same as' or 'different from but complementary to' mothering. We have argued that understanding law's engagement with fatherhood is a vital – and often neglected – dimension to understanding this complex and shifting picture. Yet the nature of law's involvement here has itself emerged as equally complex. Law has served as an important focal point for political frustrations produced by social changes around fatherhood, as well as operating as a significant symbolic discourse that offers a state-sanctioned account of who is, and who is not, worthy of recognition as a father, in what form and to what extent. Law has also played a central part in the redrawing of the contours of fatherhood as a social problem.

---

[154] For discussion: Doucet, above (n 92); Fineman, above (n 104). The most recent manifestation of these debates, still current as this book goes to press, are discussions regarding the 'need for a father' provision in s 13(5) of the Human Fertilisation and Embryology Bill 2007. See ch 6, and below pp 237–238.

[155] S Dex and K Ward, *Parental Care and Employment in Early Childhood: Working Paper 57* (Equal Opportunities Commission, Manchester, 2007); M O'Brien, *Shared Caring: Bringing Fathers into the Frame* (Equal Opportunities Commission, Manchester, 2005).

[156] See eg: W Farrell, *Father and Child Reunion: How to Bring the Dads We Need to the Children We Love* (Penguin Putnam, New York, 2001).

[157] A strong theme, of course, within strands of both feminist and masculinities scholarship.

[158] C Lewis, *A Man's Place In the Home: Fathers and Families in the UK* (Josepth Rowntree Foundation, York, 2000) at 7.

[159] See pp 218–222.

236

Further, many parties – not least, as we have noted elsewhere, fathers' rights activists themselves – continue to place considerable faith in the ability of legal reform to solve the social problems now associated with fatherhood, a faith that socio-legal research suggests may itself be misplaced.[160]

At the time that this book goes to press, the Human Fertilisation and Embryology Bill 2007 has finished its passage through the House of Lords and is currently before the House of Commons.[161] If, as seems certain, the Bill makes its way onto the statute books, it will introduce complex and wide-ranging reforms. Yet among its many controversial provisions, those relating to fatherhood have excited perhaps most attention in the media, in the House of Lords and in the public consultation processes prior to the Bill's arrival there.[162] The debates provide, in a microcosm, a vivid illustration of the continuing resonance of each of the various tensions described above. Discussion of extending legal parenthood to the lesbian partner of a woman who conceives using regulated technologies shows law attempting to recognise new family forms, while the manner of this extension clearly reveals the 'tenacious hold of the sexual family'.[163] The question of whether fatherhood ought to be grounded in a genetic link, the relationship with a child's mother, or commitment to a (future) child, remains a thorny and central issue, with new provisions for the determination of fatherhood striking an uneasy balance between these various criteria. The significance of genetics in grounding fatherhood received renewed attention, in further debates regarding the rights of children born of donor insemination to know their genetic fathers. The focus on concerns regarding fatherhood clearly demonstrate that the question of men's roles in families remains a matter of considerable contemporary anxiety, with specific concerns about fathers easily generalised to evoke broader fears regarding social stability.[164]

Further, and finally, these debates echo the considerable confusion about the role of men in families, and what law should be doing to entrench and support them, which we have witnessed in other contexts in this book. One peer complains:

---

[160] Collier and Sheldon, above (n 24) at 19.

[161] See ch 3 for further discussion of this Bill.

[162] In particular, many hours of discussion in the House of Lords were devoted to the deletion of the 'need for a father' from s 13(5) of the Human Fertilisation and Embryology Act 1990, with particular concern for what symbolic message this would send out. The various consultation processes and reports which preceded the Bill are usefully listed by the Joint Committee on the Human Tissue and Embryos (Draft) Bill; 'Human Tissue and Embryos (Draft) Bill: Volume I: Report' HC (2006–07) 630-I [243] 11.

[163] Sheldon, above (n 150).

[164] For example, Baroness Williams notes: 'Unless we give men a full sense of what it is to be a father, a member of a family, and a proud and in many ways a very rich potential, we will simply find ourselves with more and more dysfunctional families': *Hansard*, HL, vol 696, col 687 (19 November 2007). Lord Northbourne concurs, suggesting that without the presence of a father, children may end up finding a male role model in a 'gang leader on the streets': *Hansard*, HL, vol 696, col 850 (19 November 2007). See also Lord Patten: *Hansard*, HL, vol 697, col 30 (10 December 2007).

The Government are able to define the meaning of 'mother' … Yet flip over [the] page and off we go into a magical mystery tour about what on earth the word 'father' might mean in different times and places, as a sign. This leads me to the conclusion that the Government, either by design or, as I suspect, by a muddled series of accidents, have ended up attempting to deconstruct the meaning of fatherhood in the Bill, divorcing male parenthood from biological reality as well as from practical and moral responsibilities.[165]

Yet the analysis of this book gives the lie to any suggestion that earlier law had contained a clear, unitary conception of fatherhood. The shifting legal recognition of the rights and responsibilities of fathers is part of a significant ongoing renegotiation of men's roles in families in the light of the broad social shifts we have described elsewhere in this book. The fragmentation of fatherhood took place long before, and will continue to take place far beyond, the confines of this particular legal reform. We have here attempted to track some of the changing contours of that fragmentation.

---

[165] *Hansard*, HL, vol 697 col 30 (10 December 2007) (per Lord Patten).

Bibliography

ABBOTT, P and WALLACE, C, *The Family and the New Right* (Pluto, London, 1992).

ADVISORY BOARD ON FAMILY LAW, LORD CHANCELLOR'S DEPARTMENT, 'Response to the Consultation Paper on Paternity and Parental Responsibility', Annex C of the Second Annual Report, 1998/1999, <http://www.dca.gov.uk/family/annrep99/annex_c.htm>, accessed 18 July 2007.

ALCOCK, P, 'Remuneration or Remarriage?: The Matrimonial and Family Proceedings Act 1984' (1984) 11(3) *Journal of Law & Society* 357.

ALLEN, D, *One Step from the Quagmire* (Campaign for Justice on Divorce, Aylesbury, 1982).

ALMOND, B, *The Fragmenting Family* (Clarendon Press, Oxford, 2006).

AMATO, P, 'Father–Child Relations, Mother–Child Relations and Offspring Psychological Well-being in Early Adulthood' (1994) 56 *Journal of Marriage and Family* 1031.

AMATO, P and GALBRAITH, J, 'Non Resident Fathers and Children's Well Being: A Meta Analysis' (1999) 61(3) *Journal of Marriage and Family* 557.

ANDERSON, RA, 'Hormonal Contraception in the Male' (2000) 56(3) *British Medical Bulletin* 717.

ANNESLEY, C, 'New Labour and Welfare' in S Ludlam and MJ Smith (eds), *New Labour in Government* (Macmillan, London, 2001).

ARDITTI, J and ALLEN, K, 'Distressed Fathers' Perceptions of Legal and Relational Inequities Post-Divorce' (1993) 31 *Family and Conciliation Courts Review* 461.

AREIAS, ME *et al*, 'Correlates of Postnatal Depression in Mothers and Fathers' (1996) 169 *British Journal of Psychiatry* 36.

ARENDELL, T, *Fathers and Divorce* (Sage, London, 1995).

ASHLEY, C *et al*, *Fathers Matter: Research Findings on Fathers and Their Involvement with Social Care Services* (Family Rights Group, London, 2006).

ATKINS, S and HOGGETT, B, *Women and the Law* (Blackwell, Oxford, 1984).

AUCHMUTY, R, 'Unfair Shares for Women: The Rhetoric of Equality and the Reality of Inequality' in A Bottomley and H Lim (eds), *Feminist Perspectives on Land Law* (Routledge-Cavendish, London, 2007).

BABY CENTRE, 'Diet For A Healthy Dad-To-Be' (article reviewed 2007), <http://www.babycentre.co.uk/preconception/dadstobe/dietforadadtobe/>, accessed 25 October 2007.

BACKETT, K, *Mothers and Fathers: A Study of the Development and Negotiation of Parental Behaviour* (Macmillan, Basingstoke, 1982).

—— , 'The Negotiation of Fatherhood' in C Lewis and M O'Brien (eds), *Reassessing Fatherhood: New Observations on Fathers and the Modern Family* (Sage, London, 1987).

Bibliography

BAGGULEY, P and MANN, K, '"Idle Thieving Bastards"?: Scholarly Representations of the Underclass' (1992) 6(1) *Work, Employment & Society* 113.

BAILEY, MJ, 'England's First Custody of Infants Act' (1994) 20 *Queen's Law Journal* 391.

BAILEY-HARRIS, R, 'Contact – Challenging Conventional Wisdom' (2001) 13 *Child and Family Law Quarterly* 361.

BAILEY-HARRIS, R, BARRON, J and PEARCE, J, 'From Utility to Rights? The Presumption of Contact in Practice' (1999) 13 *International Journal of Law, Policy and the Family* 111.

BAINHAM, A, 'When is a Parent not a Parent? Reflections on the Unmarried Father and His Child in English Law' (1989) 3 *International Journal of Law, Policy and the Family* 208.

——, 'Contact as a Fundamental Right' (1995) 54 *Cambridge Law Journal* 255.

——, 'Sex, Gender and Fatherhood: Does Biology Really Matter?' (1997) *Cambridge Law Journal* 512.

——, 'Men and Women Behaving Badly: Is Fault Dead in English Family Law?' (2001) 21 *Oxford Journal of Legal Studies* 210.

——, *Children: The Modern Law*, 3rd edn (Jordan Publishing, Bristol 2005).

BARBER, D, *Unmarried Fathers* (Hutchinson, London, 1975).

BARKER, G *et al*, *Supporting Fathers: Contributions from the International Fatherhood Summit 2003*, Early Childhood Development: Practice and Reflections Series (Bernard van Leer Foundation, The Hague, 2004).

BARKER, RW, *Lone Fathers and Masculinities* (Ashgate, London, 2004).

BARKER, S and EINSTEIN, A, *How to Be a Great Divorced Dad* (Foulsham, Slough, 2007).

BARLOW, A *et al*, *Cohabitation, Marriage and the Law: Social Change and Legal Reform in the 21st Century* (Hart, Oxford, 2005).

BARLOW, A and DUNCAN, S, 'New Labour's Communitarianism, Supporting Families and the "Rationality Mistake": Part I' (2000) 22(2) *Journal of Social Welfare and Family Law* 23.

——, 'New Labour's Communitarianism, Supporting Families and the "Rationality Mistake": Part II' (2000) 22(2) *Journal of Social Welfare and Family Law* 129.

BARLOW, A, DUNCAN, S and JAMES, G, 'New Labour, the Rationality Mistake and Family Policy in Britain' in A Carling, S Duncan and R Edwards (eds), *Analysing Families: Morality and Rationality in Policy and Practice* (Routledge, London, 2002).

BARRETT, M, and MCINTOSH, M, *The Anti-Social Family* (Verso, London, 1982).

BARRY, A, OSBORNE, T and ROSE, N (eds), *Foucault and Political Reason: Liberalism, Neo-liberalism and Rationality of Government* (UCL Press, London, 1996).

BARTLETT, D, and BURGESS, A, *Working with Fathers: Six Steps Guide* (Fathers Direct, London, 2005).

BARTLETT, D, BURGESS, A and JONES, K, *A Toolkit for Developing Father-inclusive Practice* (Fathers Direct, London, 2007).

BBC NEWS (WORLD SERVICE), 'Gay Dads' Twins Stay in Britain' (25 January 2000), <http://news.bbc.co.uk/1/hi/world/europe/618862.stm>, accessed 22 November 2007.

BBC NEWS, 'Shame Bad Fathers Says Cameron' (22 February 2007), <http://news.bbc.co.uk/1/hi/uk_politics/6385781.stm>, accessed 30 March 2008.

BECK, U, *Risk Society: Towards a New Modernity* (Sage, London, 1992).

——, 'Democratization of the Family' (1997) 4(2) *Childhood* 151.

240

Bibliography

BECK, U and BECK-GERNSHEIM, E, *The Normal Chaos of Love* (Polity, Cambridge, 1995).

——, *Individualization* (Sage, London, 2002).

BEDFORD, VA and JOHNSON, N, 'The Role of the Father' (1998) 4 *Midwifery* 190.

BELFIELD, T, 'It Takes Two: Men and Contraception' (2005) 31(1) *Journal of Family Planning & Reproductive Health Care* 3.

BENHABIB, S, *Situating the Self: Gender, Community and Postmodernism in Contemporary Ethics* (Routledge, London, 1992).

BEVAN, S *et al*, *Family Friendly Employment: The Business Case* (Department for Education and Employment, London, 1999).

BEVERIDGE, F, NOTT S and STEPHEN, K (eds), *Making Women Count: Integrating Gender into Law and Policy-making* (Ashgate, Aldershot, 2000).

BIGGS, H, 'Madonna Minus Child Or: Wanted: Dead or Alive! The Right to Have a Dead Partner's Child' (1997) 5(2) *Feminist Legal Studies* 22.

BLACKSTONE, W, *Commentaries on the Laws of England*, Book 1, 4th edn (Clarendon Press, Oxford 1770).

——, *Commentaries on the Laws of England: Volume I* (Clarendon Press, Oxford, 1765).

——, *Commentaries on the Laws of England: Volume III* (Dawsons, London, 1967).

BLACKWELL, A and DAWE, F, *Non-Resident Parental Contact: Based on Data from the National Statistics Omnibus Survey for The Department for Constitutional Affairs: Final Report* (Office for National Statistics, London, 2003).

BLAKENHORN, D, *Fatherless America: Confronting Our Most Urgent Social Problem* (Basic Books, New York, 1995).

BLANK, RH, *Fetal Protection in the Workplace* (Columbia University Press, New York, 1993).

BLUNKETT, D and HARMAN, H, 'Foreword' in *Meeting the Childcare Challenge: A Summary* (Department for Education and Employment, London, 1998).

BOND, S *et al*, *Family Friendly Working? Putting Policy Into Practice* (The Policy Press, Bristol, 2002).

BOYD, S, 'From Gender Specificity to Gender Neutrality? Ideologies in Canadian Child Custody Law' in J Brophy and C Smart (eds), *Child Custody and the Politics of Gender* (Routledge, London, 1989).

——, 'Is there an Ideology of Motherhood in (Post)modern Child Custody Law?' (1996) 5 *Social and Legal Studies* 495.

—— (ed), *Challenging the Public Private Divide: Feminism, Law, and Public Policy* (University of Toronto Press, Toronto, 1997).

——, 'Backlash and the Construction of Legal Knowledge: The Case of Child Custody Law' (2001) 20 *The Windsor Year Book of Access to Justice* 141.

——, *Child Custody, Law, and Women's Work* (Oxford University Press, Oxford, 2003).

——, 'Backlash Against Feminism: Canadian Custody and Access Reform Debates of the Late Twentieth Century' (2004) 16(2) *Canadian Journal of Women and the Law* 255.

——, 'Legal Regulation of Families in Changing Societies' in A Sarat (ed), *The Blackwell Companion to Law and Society* (Blackwell, London, 2004).

BOYD, S and YOUNG, CF, 'Who Influences Family Law Reform? Discourses on Motherhood and Fatherhood in Legislative Reform Debates in Canada' (2002) *Studies in Law, Politics and Society* 43.

BOZETT, F and HANSON, S (eds), *Fatherhood and Families in Cultural Context* (Springer, New York, 1991).

241

BRADLEY, DC, 'A Woman's Right to Choose' (1978) 41(4) MLR 368.

BRADSHAW, J *et al, Absent Fathers?* (Routledge, London, 1999).

BRADSHAW, J and MILLAR, J, *Lone Parents in the UK*, Department of Social Security Research Report 6 (HMSO, London, 1990).

BRAZIER, M, 'Reproductive Rights: Feminism or Patriarchy?' in J Harris and S Holm (eds), *The Future of Human Reproduction* (Oxford University Press, Oxford, 2000).

BRICKELL, C, 'Masculinities, Performativity and Subversion: A Sociological Appraisal' (2005) 8 *Men & Masculinities* 24.

BRIDGEMAN, J, LIND, C and KEATING, H (eds), *Responsibility, Law and the Family* (Ashgate, Aldershot, 2008 in press).

BRISTOW, J, 'Seeds of Suspicion' *Spiked*, 21 January 2004, <http://www.spiked-online. com>.

BRITISH PREGNANCY ADVISORY SERVICE, 'Background Information on Men and Abortion', Press release (14 May 2001).

——, *Men Too!* (abortion information leaflet) (British Pregnancy Advisory Service, London, 2006), <http://www.bpas.org/images/pdfs/Men_Too_Mar06_FINAL.pdf>, accessed 25 October 2007.

BRITTAN, A, *Masculinity and Power* (Blackwell, Oxford, 1989).

BROOKS, L, 'Dumbed-Down Masculinity Erases Men from Parenting', *Guardian* (5 December 2007), Comment & Debate 32.

BROPHY, J, 'Child Care and the Growth of Power: The Status of Mothers in Custody Disputes' in J Brophy and C Smart (eds), *Women in Law: Explorations in Law, Family, Sexuality* (Routledge & Kegan Paul, London, 1985).

BROPHY, J and SMART, C (eds), *Women in Law: Explorations in Law, Family, Sexuality* (Routledge & Kegan Paul, London, 1985).

BROUGHTON, TL and ROGERS, H (eds), *Gender and Fatherhood in the Nineteenth Century* (Palgrave Macmillan, London, 2007).

BROWN, J and BARKER, G, 'Global Diversity and Trends in Patterns of Fatherhood' in G Barker *et al, Supporting Fathers: Contributions from the International Fatherhood Summit 2003* (Early Childhood Development: Practice and Reflections Series, Bernard van Leer Foundation, The Hague, 2004).

BROWN, J and DAY SCLATER, S, 'Divorce: A Psychodynamic Perspective' in S Day Sclater and C Piper (eds), *Undercurrents of Divorce* (Aldershot, Dartmouth, 1999).

BRUZZI, S, *Bringing Up Daddy: Fatherhood and Masculinity in Post-war Hollywood* (British Film Institute, London, 2005).

BUCHANAN, A and BREAM, V, 'Do Some Separated Parents who Cannot Agree Arrangements for their Children Need a More Therapeutic Rather than Forensic Service?' (2001) 13 *Child and Family Law Quarterly* 535.

BUCHANAN, A *et al, Families in Conflict: Perspectives of Children and Parents on the Family Court Welfare Service* (The Policy Press, Bristol, 2001).

BURCHELL, G, GORDON, C and MILLER, P (eds), *The Foucault Effect: Studies in Governmentality* (Harvester Wheatsheaf, London, 1991).

BURGESS, A, *Fatherhood Reclaimed: The Making of the Modern Father* (Vermilion, London, 1997).

——, 'Fathers and Public Service', in K Stanley (ed), *Daddy Dearest? Active Fatherhood and Public Policy* (Institute for Public Policy Research, London, 2005).

BURGESS, A and BARTLETT, D, *Working With Fathers* (Fathers Direct, London, 2004).

Bibliography

BURGESS, A and RUSSELL, G, 'Fatherhood and Public Policy' in G Barker *et al*, *Supporting Fathers: Contributions from the International Fatherhood Summit 2003* (Early Childhood Development: Practice and Reflections Series, Bernard van Leer Foundation, The Hague, 2004).

BURGESS, A and RUXTON, S, *Men and Their Children: Proposals for Public Policy* (Institute for Public Policy Research, London, 1996).

——, 'Men and Their Children' in J Franklin (ed), *Social Policy and Social Justice* (Polity, Cambridge, 1998).

BURGHES, L, CLARKE, L and CRONIN, N, *Fathers and Fatherhood in Britain* (Family Policy Studies Centre, London, 1997).

BURGOYNE, J, ORMROD, R and RICHARDS, M, *Divorce Matters* (Penguin, Harmondsworth, 1987).

BURTON, S, REGAN, L and KELLY, L, *Supporting Women and Challenging Men: Lessons from the Domestic Violence Intervention Project* (The Policy Press, Bristol, 1998).

CAMPBELL, B, *Goliath: Britain's Dangerous Places* (Methuen, London, 1993).

CANTWELL, B, 'CAFCASS and Private Law Cases' [2004] *Family Law* 283.

——, 'CAFCASS: In Court Conciliation and Out of Court Mediation' [2006] *Family Law* 389.

CANTWELL, B, 'Battling Parents in Private Law Proceedings: are they Getting the Right Treatment?' *Family Law* (forthcoming).

CARABINE, J, 'Heterosexuality and Social Policy' in D Richardson (ed), *Theorising Heterosexuality: Telling it Straight* (Open University Press, Buckingham, 1996).

CARBONE, J, *From Partners to Parents: The Second Revolution in Family Law* (Columbia University Press, New York, 2000).

CARRIGAN, T, CONNELL, B and LEE, J, 'Toward a New Sociology of Masculinity' (1985) 14(5) *Theory & Society* 551.

CEALEY HARRISON, W and HOOD WILLIAMS, J, *Beyond Sex and Gender* (Sage, London, 2002).

CENTRE FOR SEPARATED FAMILIES, 'CSA Reforms Will Make Little Difference', Press Release (12 December 2006), <www.separatedfamilies.org.uk/news/press_release_121206.htm>, accessed 3 March 2008.

CHALMERS, B and MEYER, D, 'What Men Say About Pregnancy, Birth and Parenthood' (1996) 17 *Journal of Psychosomatic Obstetrics and Gynecology* 47.

CHAMBERS, D, *Representing the Family* (Sage, London, 2001).

CHANCELLOR OF THE EXCHEQUER, *Investing For Our Future: Fairness and Opportunity for Britain's Hard-Working Families: 2005 Budget Report* (HM Treasury, London, 2005).

CHEAL, D, *Family and State Theory* (Harvester Wheatsheaf, Hemel Hempstead, 1991).

CHILDREN ACT SUB-COMMITTEE OF THE ADVISORY BOARD ON FAMILY LAW, *Making Contact Work: A Report to the Lord Chancellor on the Facilitation of Arrangements for Contact Between Children and their Non-Residential Parents and the Enforcement of Court Orders for Contact* (Lord Chancellor's Department, London, 2001).

CHOUDHRY, S and FENWICK, H, 'Taking the Rights of Parents and Children Seriously – Confronting the Welfare Principle under the Human Rights Act' (2005) 25 *Oxford Journal of Legal Studies* 453.

CHRISAFIS, A, 'Parenthood Postponed', *Guardian* (20 February 2001), <http://www.guardian.co.uk/law/story/0,,440294,00.html>, accessed 21 November 2007.

Bibliography

CHURCH ASSEMBLY BOARD FOR SOCIAL RESPONSIBILITY, *Fatherless By Law? The Law and the Welfare of Children Designated Illegitimate* (Church Information Office, London, 1966).

CLARE, A, *On Men: Masculinity in Crisis* (Chatto & Windus, London, 2000).

CLAYTON, S, 'The Shared Parenting Agreement', <http://www.parents4protest.co.uk/simon_clayton.htm>, accessed 13 December 2007.

COCKETT, M and TRIPP, J, *The Exeter Family Study: Family Breakdown and its Impact on Children* (University of Exeter Press, Exeter, 1994).

CODD, H, 'Slippery Slope to Sperm Smuggling' (2007) 15 *Medical Law Review* 220.

COLBORN, T, DUMANOSKI, D and MYERS, JP, *Our Stolen Future: How We are Threatening Our Fertility, Our Intelligence and Our Survival* (Plume Books, New York, 1997).

COLLIER, R, '"The Art of Living the Married Life": Representations of Male Heterosexuality in Law' (1992) 1 *Social and Legal Studies* 543.

——, 'The Campaign Against the Child Support Act, "Errant Fathers" and "Family Men"' [1994] *Family Law* 384.

——, 'A Father's "Normal Love"? Masculinities, Criminology and the Family' in R Dobash and L Noakes (eds), *Gender and Crime* (University of Wales Press, Cardiff, 1995).

——, *Masculinity, Law and the Family* (Routledge, London, 1995).

——, '"Coming Together?" Post-heterosexuality, Masculine Crisis and the New Men's Movement' (1996) 4(1) *Feminist Legal Studies* 3.

——, *Masculinities, Crime and Criminology: Men, Heterosexuality and the Criminal(ised) Other* (Sage, London, 1998).

——, '"Feminising the Workplace"? (Re)constructing the "Good Parent" in Employment Law and Family Policy' in A Morris and T O'Donnell (eds), *Feminist Perspectives on Employment Law* (Cavendish, London, 1999).

——, 'From "Women's Emancipation" to "Sex War"?: Beyond the Masculinized Discourse of Divorce', in S Day Sclater and C Piper (eds), *Undercurrents of Divorce* (Aldershot, Dartmouth, 1999).

——, 'Men, Heterosexuality and the Changing Family: (Re)constructing Fatherhood in Law and Social Policy' in C Wright and G Jaggar (eds), *Changing Family Values* (Routledge, London, 1999).

——, 'The Dashing of a "Liberal Dream"?: The Information Meeting, the "New Family" and the Limits of Law' (1999) 11 *Child and Family Law Quarterly* 257.

——, 'Straight Families, Queer Lives? Heterosexual(izing) Family Law' in C Stychin and D Herman (eds), *Sexuality in the Legal Arena* (The Athlone Press, London, 2000).

——, 'A Hard Time to be a Father? Law, Policy and Family Practices' (2001) 28 *Journal of Law & Society* 520.

——, 'Anxious Parenthood, the Vulnerable Child and the "Good Father": Reflections on the Legal Regulation of the Relationship Between Men and Children' in J Bridgeman and D Monk (eds), *Feminist Perspectives on Child Law* (Cavendish, London, 2001).

——, 'Dangerousness, Popular Knowledge and the Criminal Law: A Case Study of the Paedophile as Socio-cultural Phenomenon' in P Alldridge and C Brants (eds), *Personal Autonomy, the Private Sphere and the Criminal Law: A Comparative Study* (Hart, Oxford, 2001).

——, 'In Search of the "Good Father": Law, Family Practices and the Normative Reconstruction of Parenthood' (2001) 22 *Studies in Law, Politics and Society* 133.

Bibliography

——, 'Male Bodies, Family Practices', in A Bainham, S Day Sclater and M Richards (eds), *Body Lore and Laws* (Hart, Oxford, 2002).

——, 'Men, Masculinities and Crime' in C Sumner (ed), *The Blackwell International Companion to Criminology* (Blackwell, Oxford, 2003).

——, 'Reflections on the Relationship Between Law and Masculinities: Rethinking The "Man Question"' (2003) 56 *Current Legal Problems* 345.

——, 'Fathers 4 Justice, Law and the New Politics of Fatherhood' (2005) 17 *Child and Family Law Quarterly* 511.

——, 'Feminist Legal Studies and the Subject(s) of Men: Questions of Text, Terrain and Context in the Politics of Family Law and Gender' in A Diduck and K O'Donovan (eds), *Feminist Perspectives on Family Law* (Routledge-Cavendish, Abingdon, 2006).

——, '"The Outlaw Fathers Fight Back": Fathers' Rights Groups, Fathers 4 Justice and the Politics of Family Law' in Collier and Sheldon (eds) *Fathers' Rights Activism and Legal Reform in Comparative Perspective* (Hart, Oxford, 2006).

——, 'The UK Fathers' Rights Movement and Law: Report to the British Academy' (2008) (unpublished).

——, *The Man of Law: Essays on Law, Men and Masculinities* (Routledge, London, forthcoming).

COLLIER, R and SHELDON, S (eds), *Fathers' Rights Activism and Legal Reform in Comparative Perspective* (Hart, Oxford, 2006).

——, 'Fathers' Rights, Fatherhood and Law Reform – International Perspectives' in R Collier and S Sheldon (eds), *Fathers' Rights Activism and Law Reform in Comparative Perspective* (Hart, Oxford, 2006).

COLTRANE, S, 'The Future of Fatherhood: Social, Demographic, and Economic Influences on Men's Family Involvements' in W Marsiglio (ed), *Fatherhood: Contemporary Theory, Research, and Policy* (Sage, Thousand Oaks, CA, 1995).

——, *Family Man: Fatherhood, Housework and Gender Equality* (Oxford University Press, Oxford, 1996).

COLTRANE, S and ADAMS, M, 'The Social Construction of the "Divorce Problem"' (2003) 52 *Family Relations* 363.

COLTRANE, S and ALLAN, K, '"New" Fathers and Old Stereotypes: Representations of Masculinity in 1980s Television Advertising' (1994) 2(4) *Masculinities* 43.

COLTRANE, S and HICKMAN, N, 'The Rhetoric of Rights and Needs: Moral Discourse in the Reform of Child Custody and Support Laws' (1992) 39 *Social Problems* 400.

COMINOS, P, 'Late Victorian Sexual Respectabilty and the Social System' (1963) 8 *International Review of Social History* 18.

COMMITTEE ON HUMAN FERTILISATION AND EMBRYOLOGY, *Report of the Committee of Inquiry into Human Fertilisation and Embryology* ('the Warnock Report'), Cmnd 9314 (1984).

CONAGHAN, J, 'Reassessing the Feminist Theoretical Project in Law' (2000) 27 *Journal of Law & Society* 351.

CONNELL, RW, *Gender and Power* (Polity, Cambridge, 1987).

——, *The Men and the Boys* (University of California Press, Berkeley, CA, 2000).

——, 'On Hegemonic Masculinity and Violence: A Response to Jefferson and Hall' (2002) 6 *Theoretical Criminology* 89.

CONNELL, RW and MESSERSCHMIDT, J 'Hegemonic Masculinity: Rethinking the Concept' (2005) 19 *Gender & Society* 829.

CONWAY, H, 'Parental Responsibility and the Unmarried Father' (1996) 146 NLJ 782.

245

Bibliography

COOPER, D and HERMAN, D, 'Getting "The Family Right": Legislating Heterosexuality in Britain, 1986–1991' (1991) 10 *Canadian Journal of Family Law* 41.

COREA, G, *The Mother Machine: Reproductive Technologies from Artificial Insemination to Artificial Wombs* (The Women's Press, London, 1988).

COSSMAN, B, 'Family Feuds: Neo-conservative and Neo-liberal Visions of the Reprivatization Project' in J Fudge and B Cossman (eds), *Privatization, Law and the Challenge to Feminism* (University of Toronto Press, Toronto, 2002).

COTTERRELL, R, 'Subverting Orthodoxy, Making Law Central: A View of Socio-legal Studies' (2002) 29(4) *Journal of Law & Society* 632.

COWARD, R, *Sacred Cows: Is Feminism Relevant for the New Millennium?* (Harper Collins, London, 1999).

COYLE, CT, 'Men and Abortion: A Review of Empirical Reports Concerning the Impact of Abortion on Men' (2007) 3(2) *The Internet Journal of Mental Health*, <http://www.ispub.com/ostia/index.php?xmlFilePath=journals/ijmh/vol3n2/abortion.xml>, accessed 25 October 2007.

CREASEY, R *et al*, 'Family networks and parenting support in England and Wales' in C Attwood *et al*, *2001 Home Office Citizenship Survey: People, Families and Communities* (Home Office Research, Development and Statistics Directorate, London, 2003).

CRETNEY, S, '"What will women want next?" The Struggle for Power Within the Family 1925–1975' (1996) 12 *Law Quarterly Review* 110.

——, *Family Law in the Twentieth Century: A History* (Oxford University Press, Oxford, 2003).

CROMPTON, R, *Restructuring Gender Relations and Employment: The Decline of the Male Breadwinner* (Oxford University Press, Oxford, 1999).

CROMPTON, R and LYONETTE, C, *Who Does the Housework? The Division of Labour Within the Home: British Social Attitudes 24th Report* (National Centre for Social Research/Sage, London, 2008).

——, 'Gender, Attitudes to Work and Work Life Balance' in R Crompton and C Lyonette, 'Project Seven: Class, Gender, Employment and Family', <http://www.genet.ac.uk/projects/project7.htm>, accessed 31 January 2008.

CROWLEY, JE, 'Adopting "Equality Tools" from the Toolboxes of their Predecessors: the Fathers' Rights Movement in the United States' in R Collier and S Sheldon, *Fathers' Rights Activism and Legal Reform* (Hart, Oxford, 2006).

CURRAN, L, and ABRAMS, S, 'Making Men into Dads: Fatherhood, the State, and Welfare Reform' (2000) 14(5) *Gender & Society* 662.

CZAPANSKIY, K, 'Volunteers and Draftees: The Struggle for Parental Equality' (1991) 38 *UCLA Law Review* 415.

DANIEL, B and J TAYLOR, *Engaging with Fathers: Practice Issues for Health and Social Care* (Jessica Kingsley, London, 2001).

DANIEL, B *et al*, 'Why Gender Matters for "Every Child Matters"' (2005) 35 *British Journal of Social Work* 1343.

DANIELS, CR, *At Women's Expense: State Power and the Politics of Fetal Rights* (Harvard University Press, Cambridge, MA, 1993).

——, 'Between Fathers and Fetuses: The Social Construction of Male Reproduction and the Politics of Fetal Harm' (1997) 22(3) *Signs* 579.

—— (ed), *Lost Fathers: The Politics of Fatherlessness in America* (St Martin's Press, New York, 1998).

Bibliography

——, *Exposing Men: The Science and Politics of Male Reproduction* (Oxford University Press, Oxford 2006).

DAVID, ME (ed), *The Fragmenting Family: Does it Matter?* (Health and Welfare Unit, Institute of Economic Affairs, London, 1998).

DAVIDOFF, L and HALL, C, *Family Fortunes* (Hutchinson, London, 1987).

DAVIDOFF, L et al, *The Family Story: Blood, Contract and Intimacy, 1830–1960* (Addison Wesley Longman, Harlow, 1999).

DAVIS, G and PEARCE, J, 'The Welfare Principle in Action' [1999] *Family Law* 237.

DAVIS, G et al, *Child Support in Action* (Hart Publications, Oxford, 1998).

DAY SCLATER, S, 'Divorce – Coping Strategies, Conflict and Dispute Resolution' [1998] *Family Law* 150.

——, *Divorce: A Psycho-social Study* (Ashgate, Aldershot, 1999).

——, 'Families Reunited', *FQ Magazine* (Issue 3, Winter, 2003).

DAY SCLATER, S and KAGANAS, F, 'Contact Mothers: Welfare and Rights' in A Bainham, B Lindley and M Richards (eds), *Children and their Families: Contact, Rights and Welfare* (Hart, Oxford, 2003).

DAY SCLATER, S and PIPER, C (eds), *Undercurrents of Divorce* (Ashgate, Aldershot, 1999).

DAY SCLATER, S and RICHARDS, M, 'How Adults Cope with Divorce – Strategies for Survival' [1995] *Family Law* 143.

DAY SCLATER, S and YATES, C, 'The Psycho-Politics of Post Divorce Parenting' in A Bainham, Day Sclater, S and M Richards, *What is a Parent? A Socio-Legal Analysis* (Hart, Oxford, 1999).

DAY SCLATER, S, BAINHAM, A and RICHARDS, M, 'Introduction', in A Bainham, S Day Sclater and M Richards (eds), *What is a Parent? A Socio-legal Analysis* (Hart, Oxford, 1999).

DAYCARE TRUST, *Informal Childcare: Bridging the Childcare Gap for Families* (Daycare Trust, London, 2003).

DEAN, M, *Governmentality: Power and Rule in Modern Society* (Sage, London, 1999).

DEECH, R, 'The Unmarried Father and Human Rights' (1992) 4 *Journal of Child Law* 3

——, 'Family Law and Genetics' (1998) 61 *Modern Law Review* 697.

——, 'Assisted Reproductive Techniques and the Law' (2001) 69 *Medico-Legal Journal* 13.

DE GAMA, K, 'Posthumous Pregnancies: Some Thoughts on "Life" and Death' in S Sheldon and M Thomson (eds), *Feminist Perspectives on Health Care Law* (Cavendish, London, 1998).

DEMETRIOU, DZ, 'Connell's Concept of Hegemonic Masculinity: A Critique' (2001) 30 *Theory & Society* 327.

DENCH, G, *The Place of Men in Changing Family Cultures* (Institute of Community Studies, London, 1996).

DENNIS, N and ERDOS, G, *Families Without Fatherhood* (Institute of Economic Affairs, London, 1993).

——, 'Sex and the State: Will *Supporting Families* Help or Harm the Family?' (1999) *Economic Affairs* 20.

DEPARTMENT FOR BUSINESS ENTERPRISE AND REGULATORY REFORM, 'Working Time Opt-out' (Information resource), http://www.berr.gov.uk/employment/employment-legislation/working-time-regs/opt-out/page24607.html, accessed 28 January 2008.

247

DEPARTMENT FOR CHILDREN, SCHOOLS AND FAMILIES, 'Teenage Parents Next Steps: Guidance for Local Authorities and Primary Care Trusts' (Department for Children, Schools and Families, London, 2007).

——, 'Teenage Pregnancy Strategy', Every Child Matters website, 2007, <http://www.everychildmatters.gov.uk/health/teenagepregnancy/about/>, accessed 18 March 2008.

——, 'About Sure Start: Sure Start and the Government' (Sure Start website) <http://www.surestart.gov.uk/aboutsurestart/about/thesurestartunit2/>, accessed 25 January 2008.

——, 'Childcare Act 2006: First ever Early Years and Childcare Act' Information Resource Surestart website, <http://www.surestart.gov.uk/resources/general/childcareact>, accessed 4 January 2008.

DEPARTMENT FOR CONSTITUTIONAL AFFAIRS, *Judicial Statistics (Revised): England and Wales for the year 2005*, Cm 6903 (2006).

DEPARTMENT FOR EDUCATION AND EMPLOYMENT, DEPARTMENT OF STATE FOR SOCIAL SECURITY and MINISTER FOR WOMEN, *Meeting the Childcare Challenge: A Framework and Consultation Document*, Cm 3959 (1998).

DEPARTMENT FOR EDUCATION AND SKILLS, 'Planning and Performance Management Guidance', Surestart website, revised November 2006, <http://www.surestart.gov.uk/publications/?Document=1852>, accessed 4 January 2008.

——, 'Children's Centre Practice Guidance', Surestart website, 2006 <http://www.surestart.gov.uk/publications/?Document=1500>, accessed 4 January 2008.

——, *Every Parent Matters* (Department of Education and Skills, London, 2007).

——, 'Parenting Plans: Putting Your Children First: A Guide for Separating Parents', <http://www.dfes.gov.uk/childrensneeds>, accessed 22 December 2007.

DEPARTMENT FOR TRADE AND INDUSTRY, *Fairness at Work*, Cm 3968, (1998).

——, *Work and Families: Choice and Flexibility: A Consultation Document* (Department for Trade and Industry, London, 2005).

DEPARTMENT FOR WORK AND PENSIONS, *A New System of Child Maintenance*, Cm 6979 (2006).

——, *Recovering Child Support: Routes to Responsibility*, Cm 6894 (2006).

——, *Joint Birth Registration: Promoting Parental Responsibility*, Cm 7160 (2007).

——, *Joint Birth Registration: Recording Responsibility* Cm 7293 (June 2008).

DEPARTMENT OF HEALTH, 'Donor Information: Providing Information about Sperm, Egg and Embryo Donors' (Consultation paper) (20 December 2001) <http://www.dh.gov.uk/en/Publicationsandstatistics/Publications/PublicationsPolicyAndGuidance/DH_4005810> accessed 22 November 2007.

DEPARTMENT OF HEALTH/DEPARTMENT FOR EDUCATION AND SKILLS, *The National Service Framework for Children, Young People and Maternity Services* (Department of Health/Department for Education and Skills, London, 2004).

DERMOTT, E, 'The "Intimate Father": Defining Paternal Involvement' (2003) 8(4) *Sociological Research Online* <http://www.socresonline.org.uk/8/4/dermott.html>, accessed 18 March 2008.

——, 'Time and Labour: Fathers' Perceptions of Employment and Childcare' in L Pettinger *et al* (eds), *A New Sociology of Work?* (Sociological Review Monographs (Blackwell, Oxford, 2006).

——, *Intimate Fatherhood: A Sociological Analysis* (Routledge, London, 2007).

DEWAR, J, *Law and the Family*, 2nd edn (Butterworths, London, 1992).

——, 'The Normal Chaos of Family Law' (1998) 61 MLR 467.

Bibliography

——, 'Family Law and its Discontents' (2000) 14 *International Journal of Law, Policy and the Family* 59.

DEX, S, *Families and Work in the Twenty-First Century* (Joseph Rowntree Foundation, York, 2003).

DEX, S and SMITH, C, *The Nature and Pattern of Family-Friendly Employment Policies in Britain* (The Policy Press, Bristol, 2002).

DEX, S and WARD, K, *Parental Care and Employment in Early Childhood: Working Paper 57* (Equal Opportunities Commission, Manchester, 2007).

DEY, I and WASOFF, F, 'Mixed Messages: Parental Responsibilities, Public Opinion and the Reforms of Family Law' (2006) 20 *International Journal of Law, Policy and the Family* 225.

DIDUCK, A, 'Legislating Ideologies of Motherhood' (1993) 2 *Social and Legal Studies* 461.

——, 'In Search of the Feminist Good Mother' (1998) 7(1) *Social and Legal Studies* 129.

——, 'Fairness and Justice for All? The House of Lords in *White v White*' (2001) 9 *Feminist Legal Studies* 173.

——, *Law's Families* (Lexis Nexis, London, 2003).

——, 'Shifting Familiarity' 58 *Current Legal Problems* 235.

——, '"If Only we can Find the Appropriate Terms to Use the Issue will be Solved": Law, Identity and Parenthood' (2007) 19(4) *Child and Family Law Quarterly* 458

DIDUCK, A and KAGANAS, F, *Family Law, Gender and the State: Text, Cases and Materials*, 2nd edn (Hart, Oxford, 2006).

DIDUCK, A and O'DONOVAN, K (eds), *Feminist Perspectives on Family Law* (Routledge-Cavendish, Abingdon, 2006).

——, 'Feminism and Families: Plus Ça Change?' in A Diduck and K O'Donovan (eds), *Feminist Perspectives on Family Law* (Routledge-Cavendish, Abingdon, 2006).

DIENHART, A, *Reshaping Fatherhood: The Social Construction of Shared Parenting* (Sage, London, 1998).

DJERASSI, C, *This Man's Pill: Reflections on the 50th Birthday of the Pill* (Oxford University Press, Oxford, 2001).

DOBASH, RE and DOBASH, RP, *Violence Against Wives: A Case Against the Patriarchy* (Free Press, New York 1979).

——, *Women, Violence and Social Change* (Routledge, London, 1992).

DOHERTY, WJ, KOUNESKI, EF and ERICKSON, MF, 'Responsible Fathering: An Overview and Conceptual Framework' (1998) 60 *Journal of Marriage and Family* 277.

DOUCET, A, 'Fathers and Responsibility for Children: A Puzzle and a Tension' (2004) 28(2) *Atlantis* 103.

——, *Do Men Mother? Fatherhood, Care and Domestic Responsibility* (University of Toronto Press, Toronto, 2006).

DONZELOT, J, *The Policing of Families* (Hutchinson, London, 1980).

DOUGLAS, G, *Law, Fertility and Reproduction* (Sweet & Maxwell, London, 1991).

——, 'Assisted Reproduction and the Welfare of the Child' (1993) 5 *Current Legal Problems* 53.

——, 'Marriage, Cohabitation and Parenthood – From Contract to Status?' in S Katz, J Eekelaar and M Maclean (eds), *Cross Currents: Family Law and Policy in the US and England* (Oxford University Press, Oxford, 2000).

——, *An Introduction to Family Law*, 2nd edn (Oxford University Press, Oxford, 2004).

DOUGLAS, M, *Implicit Meanings: Selected Essays in Anthropology*, 2nd edn (Routledge, London, 1999).

Bibliography

DOWD, N, *Redefining Fatherhood* (New York University Press, New York, 2000).

DRAKEFORD, M, and BUTLER, I, 'Curfews for Children: Testing a Policy Proposal in Practice' (1998) 62 *Youth & Policy* 1.

DRAKICH, J, 'In Search of the Better Parent: The Social Construction of Ideologies of Fatherhood' (1989) 3 *Canadian Journal of Women and the Law* 69.

DRAPER, J, 'Whose Welfare in the Labour Room? A Discussion of the Increasing Trend of Fathers' Birth Attendance' (1997) 13 *Midwifery* 132.

——, '"It was a real good show": The Ultrasound Scan, Fathers and the Power of Visual Knowledge' (2002a) 24(6) *Sociology of Health & Illness* 771.

——, '"It's the first scientific evidence": Men's Experience of Pregnancy Confirmation' (2002) 39(6) *Journal of Advanced Nursing* 563.

——, 'Blurring, Moving and Broken Boundaries: Men's Encounters with the Pregnant Body' (2003) 25(7) *Sociology of Health & Illness* 743.

DRUCKER, J, *Families of Value: Gay and Lesbian Parents and their Children Speak Out* (De Capo Press, New York, 1998).

DUDGEON, MR and INHORN, MC 'Men's Influences on Women's Reproductive Health: Medical Anthropological Perspectives' (2004) 59 *Social Science & Medicine* 1379.

DUNCAN, S and EDWARDS, R *Lone Mothers, Paid Work and Gendered Moral Rationalities* (Palgrave Macmillan, Basingstoke, 1999).

DUNCAN, S, CARLING, A and EDWARDS, R (eds), *Analysing Families: Morality and Rationality in Policy and Practice* (Routledge, London, 2002).

DUNCAN, S *et al*, 'Motherhood, Paid Work and Partnering: Values and Theories' (2002) 17 *Work, Employment & Society* 309.

DUNCAN SMITH, I, 'Now They Want to Abolish Fatherhood', *Mail on Sunday* (18 November 2007) News 29.

DUNN, J *et al*, 'Children's Perspectives on their Relationships with their Non-Resident Fathers: Influences, Outcomes and Implications' (2003) 45 *Journal of Child Psychology and Psychiatry* 553.

DYER, C, 'New Laws To End Child Custody Wars', *Guardian* (3 April 2004), <http://www.guardian.co.uk/society/2004/apr/03/childrensservices.politics>, accessed 2 January 2008.

EARLY, R, 'Men as Consumers of Maternity Services: A Contradiction in Terms' (2001) 25 *International Journal of Consumer Studies* 160.

EDWARDES, C and ALDERSON, A, 'Women Bypass Sex in Favour of "Instant Pregnancies"' *Daily Telegraph* (25 September 2005), http://www.telegraph.co.uk/global/main.jhtml?xml=/global/2005/09/25/nivf25.xml, accessed 21 November 2007.

EDWARDS, R and GILLIES, V, 'Support in Parenting: Values and Consensus Concerning Who to Turn to' 33(4) *Journal of Social Policy* 623.

EEKELAAR, J, *Family Law and Social Policy*, 2nd edn (Weidenfeld & Nicholson, London, 1984).

——, 'Family Law: Keeping Us "On Message"' (1999) 11 *Child and Family Law Quarterly* 387.

——, 'Parental Responsibility: State of Nature or Nature of the State?' (1991) *Journal of Social Work and Family Law* 37.

——, *Family Law and Personal Life* (Oxford University Press, Oxford, 2006).

EEKELAAR, J and MACLEAN, M, *Maintenance After Divorce* (Clarendon Press, Oxford, 1986).

——, *The Parental Obligation* (Hart, Oxford, 1997).

Bibliography

——, 'Marriage and the Moral Bases of Personal Relationships' (2004) 31 *Journal of Law and Society* 510.

EHRENREICH, B, *The Hearts of Men and the Flight from Commitment* (Pluto, London, 1983).

ELSHTAIN, JB, *The Family in Political Thought* (Harvester Press, Sussex, 1982).

EPSTEIN, D *et al* (eds), *Failing Boys? Issues in Gender and Achievement* (Open University Press, Buckingham, 1998).

EQUAL OPPORTUNITIES COMMISSION, *Fathers: Balancing Work and Family* (Equal Opportunities Commission, Manchester, 2003).

——, *Facts About Men and Women in Great Britain 2006* (Equal Opportunities Commission, Manchester, 2007).

——, *Fathers and the Modern Family* (Equal Opportunities Commission, Manchester, 2007).

ERVO, S and JOHANSSON, T, *Among Men: Moulding Masculinities* (Ashgate, Aldershot, 2003).

ETZIONI, A, *The Parenting Deficit* (Demos, London, 1993).

——, *New Communitarian Thinking: Persons, Virtues, Institutions and Communities* (University Press of Virginia, Charlottesville, VA, 1995).

—— (ed), *The Essential Communitarian Reader* (Rowman & Littlefield, Lanham, MD, 1998).

FALCONER, C, KELLY, R and HEWITT, P, 'Ministerial Forward' in HM Government, *Parental Separation: Children's Needs and Parents' Responsibilities: Next Steps*, Cm 6452 (2005).

FALUDI, S, *Backlash: The Undeclared War Against Women* (Chatto & Windus, London, 1991).

——, *Stiffed: The Betrayal of the Modern Man* (Chatto & Windus, London, 1999).

FAMILIES NEED FATHERS, 'Response to the Lord Chancellor's Consultation Paper: Court Procedures for the Determination of Paternity and on the Law on Parental Responsibility for Unmarried Fathers' (April 1998), <http://www.fnf.org.uk/news-events/campaigns/submissions-and-consultation-responses/lcd-consultation-paper-response>, accessed 14 November.

——, Charity Profile (January 2000), <http://www.fnf.org.uk/about-us/charity-profile>, accessed 18 December 2007.

FAMILIES NEED FATHERS *et al*, 'Letter to the Editor: The Government Must Help the Children of Divorcees', *The Times* (12 June 2007).

FAMILY AND PARENTING INSTITUTE, 'About Us', <http://www.familyandparenting.org/aboutUs>, accessed 29 January 2008.

FAMILY PLANNING ASSOCIATION, 'Male and Female Sterilisation' <http://www.fpa.org.uk/information/leaflets/documents_and_pdfs/detail.cfm?contentID=157>, 11 December 2007

FAMILY WELFARE ASSOCIATION, 'About Us', <http://www.fwa.org.uk/about.html>, accessed 29 January 29 2008.

FARRELL, W, *Father and Child Reunion: How to Bring the Dads We Need to the Children We Love* (Penguin Putnam, New York, 2001).

FATHERHOOD INSTITUTE, THE, *The Difference a Dad Makes* (The Fatherhood Institute, London, 2007).

—— 'The UK's Fatherhood Thinktank', <http://www.fatherhoodinstitute.org/>, accessed 18 March 2008.

251

Bibliography

FATHERS 4 JUSTICE, 'Family Justice On Trial: Opening The Door On Closed Courts', <http://www.fathers-4-justice.org/f4j//index.php?option=com_ content&task=view&id=13&Itemid=39>, accessed 27 December 2007.

——, 'Purplehearts', <http://www.fathers-4-justice.org/f4j/index.php?option=com_ content&task=view&id=27&Itemid=51>, accessed 27 December 2007.

FATHERS DIRECT, 'Family Sector Leaders Meet Government and Issue Call for Transformation of Separated Family Policy', Press release (2 May 2006), <http://www. fatherhoodinstitute.org/index.php?id=4&cID=467>, accessed 29 January 2008.

FATHERS DIRECT and THE AN-NISA SOCIETY, *Working with Muslim Fathers: A Guide for Practioners* (Fathers Direct, London, 2007).

FEATHERSTONE, B, 'Taking Fathers Seriously' (2003) 33(2) *British Journal of Social Work* 239.

——, 'Fathers Matter: A Research Review' (2004) 18 *Children & Society* 312.

FEATHERSTONE, B and PECKOVER, S, 'Letting Them Get Away With it: Fathers, Domestic Violence and Child Welfare' (2007) 27(2) *Critical Social Policy* 181.

FEATHERSTONE, B, RIVETT, M and SCOURFIELD, J, *Working with Men in Health and Social Care* (Sage, London, 2007).

FEATHERSTONE, B and TRINDER, L, 'New Labour, Families and Fathers' (2001) 21(4) *Critical Social Policy* 534.

FEGAN, E, 'Fathers, Fetuses and Abortion Decision Making' (1996) 5 *Social and Legal Studies* 75.

FERRI, E and SMITH, K, *Step-parenting in the 1990s* (Family Policy Studies Centre, London, 1998).

FENWICK, H, 'Clashing Rights, the Welfare of the Child and the Human Rights Act' (2004) MLR 889.

FILKIN, G and GELDOF, B, 'Rights for Fathers', Transcript, *Today* programme, Radio 4, 3 April 2004 (GICS Media Monitoring Unit, London, 2004) (copy of transcript with authors).

FINE-DAVIS, M *et al*, *Fathers and Mothers: Dilemmas of the Work-Life Balance*, Social Indicators Research Series (Kluwer Academic Publishers, Dordrecht, 2004).

FINEMAN, M, *The Illusion of Equality: The Rhetoric and Reality of Divorce Reform* (University of Chicago Press, London, 1991).

——, 'Feminist Legal Scholarship and Women's Gendered Lives' in M Cain and C Harrington (eds), *Lawyers in a Postmodern World* (Open University Press, Buckingham, 1994).

——, *The Neutered Mother, The Sexual Family, and Other Twentieth Century Tragedies* (Routledge, New York, 1995).

——, 'Cracking the Foundational Myths: Independence, Autonomy, and Self-Sufficiency' (2000) 13 *Journal of Gender, Social Policy and Law* 13.

——, *The Autonomy Myth* (The New Press, New York, 2004).

FINEMAN, M and KARPIN, I (eds), *Mothers in Law: Feminist Theory and the Legal Regulation of Motherhood* (Columbia University Press, New York, 1995).

FINER, M and MCGREGOR, OR, 'History of the Obligation to Maintain', Appendix 5 in Department of Health and Social Security, *One-parent Families: Report of the Committee on One-parent Families*, Cmnd 5629-I (1974).

FISCH, H, *The Male Biological Clock: The Startling News About Aging, Sexuality, and Fertility in Men* (Free Press, New York, 2005).

Bibliography

FLOOD, M 'Backlash: Angry Men's Movements' in SE Rossie (ed) *The Battle and Backlash Rage On: Why Feminism Cannot be Obsolete* (Philadelphia, Xlibris Press, 2004).

FLOURI, E, *Fathering and Child Outcomes* (John Wiley & Sons, Chichester, 2005).

FORTIN, J, 'Legal Protection for the Unborn Child' (1988) 51 MLR 54.

——, '*Re F*: The Gooseberry Bush Approach' (1994) MLR 296.

——, 'Parenthood in Child Law – What is its Real Significance?' in D Pearl and R Pickford (eds), *Frontiers of Family Law: Part 1* (John Wiley & Sons, Chichester, 1995).

——, '*Re D (Care: Natural Parent Presumption)*: Is Blood Really Thicker than Water?' (1999) 11(4) *Child and Family Law Quarterly* 435.

FOUCAULT, M, *Madness and Civilisation* (Tavistock, London, 1967).

FOUCAULT, M, *The History of Sexuality: Volume 1: An Introduction* (Penguin, Harmondsworth, 1981).

——, 'Governmentality' in G Burchell, C Gordon and P Miller (eds), *The Foucault Effect: Studies in Governmentality* (Harvester Wheatsheaf, London, 1991).

FOX, L, *Conceptualising Home: Theories, Power, Policies* (Hart, Oxford, 2006).

FREEMAN, MDA, 'Towards a Critical Theory of Family Law' (1985) 38 *Current Legal Problems* 153.

—— (ed), *State, Law, and the Family: Critical Perspectives* (Tavistock, London, 1984).

FREEMAN, MDA and LYON, C, *Cohabitation Without Marriage* (Gower, Aldershot, 1983).

FREEMAN, T and RICHARDS, M, 'DNA Testing and Kinship' in F Ebtehaj, B Lindley and M Richards (eds), *Kinship Matters* (Hart, Oxford, 2006).

FRENCH, S (ed), *Fatherhood* (Virago, London, 1993).

——, *Sexual Difference: Masculinity and Psychoanalysis* (Routledge, London, 1994).

——, *After Words: The Personal in Gender, Culture and Psychotherapy* (Palgrave Macmillan, Basingstoke, 2002).

FROSH, S, PHOENIX, A and PATTMAN, R, *Young Masculinities: Understanding Boys in Contemporary Society* (Palgrave Macmillan, Basingstoke, 2001).

FUREDI, F, *Paranoid Parenting* (Allen Lane, London, 2002).

FURSTENBERG, F, 'Good Dads–Bad Dads: Two Faces of Fatherhood' in AJ Cherlin (ed), *The Changing American Family and Public Policy* (Urban Institute Press, Washington, DC, 1988).

GADD, D, 'Masculinities, Violence and Defended Psycho-social Subjects' (2000) 4 *Theoretical Criminology* 429.

——, 'Masculinities and Violence Against Female Partners' (2002) 11 *Social and Legal Studies* 61.

GATTRELL, C, 'Whose Child is It Anyway?: The Negotiation of Paternal Responsibilities Within Marriage' (2007) 55(2) *Sociological Review* 352.

GAUTHIER, AH, SMEEDING, T and FURSTENBERG, F 'Are Parents Investing Less Time in Children? Trends in Selected Industrialized Countries' (2004) 30(4) *Population and Development Review* 647.

GAVANAS, A, *Fatherhood Politics in the United States: Masculinity, Sexuality, Race and Marriage* (Illinois, University of Illinois Press, 2004).

GAVIGAN, S, 'Legal Forms and Family Norms: What is a Spouse?' (1999) 14 *Canadian Journal of Law & Society* 127.

GELDOF, B, 'The Real Love that Dare Not Speak Its Name' in A Bainham *et al* (eds), *Children and Their Families* (Hart, Oxford, 2003).

253

Bibliography

GELSTHORPE, L and MORRIS, A (eds), *Feminist Perspectives in Criminology* (Open University Press, Buckingham, 1990).

GERSON, K, *No Man's Land: Men's Changing Commitments to Family and Work* (Basic Books, New York, 1993).

GHATE, D, SHAW, C and HAZEL, N, *Fathers and Family Centres: Engaging Fathers in Preventative Services* (Joseph Rowntree Foundation, York, 2000).

GIBB, F, 'Judge Apologises As Justice "Fails Fathers"', *The Times* (2 April 2004), <http://www.timesonline.co.uk/article/0,,2–1059953,00.html>, accessed 2 January 2008.

GIDDENS, A, *The Transformations of Intimacy* (Polity, Cambridge, 1992).

——, *The Third Way: The Renewal of Social Democracy* (Polity, Cambridge, 1998).

GILLIES, V, 'Meeting Parents' Needs? Discourses of "Support" and "Inclusion" in Family Policy' (2005) 25(1) *Critical Social Policy* 70.

——, *Marginalised Mothers: Exploring Working Class Experiences of Parenting* (Routledge, London, 2006).

——, 'Perspectives on Parenting Responsibility: Contextualizing Values and Practices' (2008) 35(1) *Journal of Law and Society* 95.

GILLIS, JR, *A World of Their Own Making: Myth, Ritual and the Quest for Family Values* (Harvard University Press, Cambridge, MA, 1996).

GLASIER, AF *et al*, 'Contraception: Would Women Trust their Partners to Use A Male Pill?' (2000) 15(3) *Human Reproduction* 646.

GLENDON, MA, *The Transformation of Family Law: State, Law and Family in the United States and Western Europe* (University of Chicago Press, Chicago, IL, 1989).

GOLDBERG-HILLER, J, 'The Status of Status: Domestic Partnership and the Politics of Same-Sex Marriage' (1999) 19 *Studies in Law, Politics & Society* 3.

GOLDSTEIN, J, *Before the Best Interests of the Child* (Burnett Books, London, 1980).

GOLDSTEIN, J, FREUD, A and SOLNIT, AJ, *Beyond the Best Interests of the Child* (Burnett Books, London, 1980).

GOLOMBOK, S *et al*, 'The European Study of Assisted Reproduction Families: the Transition to Adolescence' (2002) 17(3) *Human Reproduction* 830.

GOUGH, B, '"Biting your Tongue": Negotiating Masculinities in Contemporary Britain' (2001) 10(2) *Journal of Gender Studies* 169.

GRAHAM, J *et al*, *Sole and Joint Birth Registration: Exploring the Circumstances, Choices and Motivations of Unmarried Parents* (Department for Work and Pensions, Research Report 463, 2007).

GRAUDT, J, 'The Reckoning', *Observer* (24 April 2005).

GRAYCAR, R, 'Law Reform by Frozen Chook: Family Law Reform for the New Millennium?' (2000) 24 *Melbourne University Law Review* 737.

——, 'Sex, Golf and Stereotypes: Measuring, Valuing and Imagining the Body in Court' (2002) 10 *Torts Law Journal* 205.

GRBICH, C, 'Male Primary Caregivers and Domestic Labour: Involvement or Avoidance?' (1995) 1(2) *Journal of Family Studies* 14.

GREER, G, *Daddy, We Hardly Knew You* (Penguin, Harmondsworth, 1990).

GRIMSHAW, D and RUBERY, J, *The Gender Pay Gap: A Research Review* (Equal Opportunities Commission, Manchester, 2001).

GRISWOLD, R, *Fatherhood in America: A History* (Basic Books, New York, 1992).

GROSZ, E, 'A Note on Essentialism and Difference' in S Gunew (ed), *Feminist Knowledge: Critique and Construct* (Routledge, London, 1990).

Bibliography

——, *Volatile Bodies: Towards a Corporeal Feminism* (Allen & Unwin, St Leonards, New South Wales, 1994).

GROSZ, E and PROBYN, E (eds), *Sexy Bodies: Strange Carnalities of Feminism* (Routledge, London, 1995).

GUARDIAN EDITOR, 'The Conservatives and Family Policy: Fatherhood and Apple Pie', *Guardian* (21 June 2006) Comment 32.

GUARDIAN LETTERS, 'Putting Fathers in the Picture', *Guardian* (8 December 2007), Leaders & Reply 43.

HAAS, L, HWANG, P and RUSSELL, G (eds), *Organisational Change and Gender Equity: International Perspectives on Fathers and Mothers in the Workplace* (Sage, London, 2000).

HAIMES, E, 'Recreating the Family? Policy Considerations Relating to the "New" Reproductive Technologies' in M McNeil, I Varcoe and S Yearley (eds), *The New Reproductive Technologies* (Macmillan, Basingstoke, 1990).

HALL, J, 'Attendance Not Compulsory' (1993) 89(46) *Nursing Times* 69.

HALL, S, 'Daubing the Drudges of Fury: Men, Violence and the Piety of the "Hegemonic Masculinity" Thesis' (2002) 6(1) *Theoretical Criminology* 35.

HANDY, C, *The Empty Raincoat: Making Sense of the Future* (Arrow, London, 1994).

HARKE, L and LEWIS, S, 'Work Life Policies: Where Should the Government Go Next?' in N Birkitt (ed), *A Life's Work: Achieving Full and Fulfilling Employment* (Institute for Public Policy Research, London, 2001).

HARRISON, J, HENDERSON, M and LEONARD, R, *Different Dads: Fathers' Stories of Parenting Disabled Children* (Jessica Kingsley, London, 2007).

HATTEN, W, VINTER, L and WILLIAMS, R, *Dads on Dads: Needs and Expectations at Home and Work* (Equal Opportunities Commission, Manchester, 2002).

HAWKINS, AJ and DOLLAHITE, DC, *Generative Fathering: Beyond Deficit Perspectives* (Sage, Thousand Oaks, CA, 1997).

HAYES, M, 'Law Commission Working Paper No 74: Illegitimacy' (1980) 43 MLR 299.

——, 'Relocation cases: is the Court of Appeal applying the correct principles?' (2006) 18(3) *Child and Family Law Quarterly* 351.

HAYWARD, B, FONG, B and THORNTON, A, *The Third Work–Life Balance Employer Survey: Main Findings*, Employment Relations Research Series 86 (Department for Business, Enterprise and Regulatory Reform, London, 2007).

HAYWOOD, C and MAC AN GHAILL, M, *Men and Masculinities: Theory, Research and Social Practice* (Open University Press, Buckingham, 2003).

HEARN, J, *Birth and Afterbirth: A Materialist Account* (Achilles Heel, London, 1983).

——, 'Child Abuse and Men's Violence' in Violence Against Women Study Group (ed), *Taking Child Abuse Seriously* (Unwin Hyman, London, 1990).

——, *Men in the Public Eye* (Routledge, London, 1992).

——, *The Violences of Men* (Sage, London, 1998).

——, 'From Hegemonic Masculinity to the Hegemony of Men' (2004) 5(1) *Feminist Theory* 49.

HEARN, J and PRINGLE, K, 'Men, Masculinities and Children: Some European Perspectives' (2006) 26(2) *Critical Social Policy* 365.

——, *European Perspectives on Men and Masculinities* (Palgrave Macmillan, Basingstoke, 2006)

HEINEMANN, K *et al*, 'Attitudes toward Male Fertility Control: Results of a Multinational Survey on Four Continents' (2005) 20(2) *Human Reproduction* 549.

Bibliography

HENCKE, D, 'Seven out of 10 absent parents pay maintenance for children', *Guardian* (10 April 2006), <http://www.guardian.co.uk/money/2006/apr/10/childrensservices. freedomofinformation>, accessed 18 March 2008.

HENNESSY, R, *Materialist Feminism and the Politics of Discourse* (Routledge, London, 1992).

HENNESSY, R and INGHRAM, C (eds), *Materialist Feminism: A Reader in Class, Difference and Women's Lives* (Routledge, London, 1997).

HENRICSON, C, *Government and Parenting: Is there a Case for a Policy Review?* (Joseph Rowntree Foundation, York, 2003).

——, 'Governing Parenting: Is There a Case for a Policy Review and Statement of Parenting Rights and Responsibilities?' (2008) 35(1) *Journal of Law and Society* 150.

HENRICSON, C and BAINHAM, A, *The Child and Family Policy Divide: Tensions, Convergence and Rights* (Joseph Rowntree Foundation, York, 2005).

HENRY, D and MCPHERSON, JA, *Fathering Daughters: Reflections by Men* (Beacon, Boston, MA, 1999).

HENWOOD K and PROCTOR, J, 'The "Good Father": Reading Men's Accounts of Paternal Involvement During the Transition to First-time Fatherhood' (2003) 42(3) *British Journal of Social Psychology* 337.

HERRING, J, 'The Human Rights Act and the Welfare Principle in Family Law – Conflicting or Complementary?' (1999) 11(3) *Child and Family Law Quarterly* 223.

——, *Family Law*, 3rd edn (Pearson Longman, Harlow, 2007).

HESTER, M and RADFORD, L, *Domestic Violence and Child Contact Arrangements in England and Denmark* (The Policy Press, Bristol, 1996).

HETHERINGTON, EM and STANLEY-HAGAN, MM, 'The Effects of Divorce on Fathers and their Children' in M Lamb (ed), *The Role of the Father in Child Development* (John Wiley, New York, 1997).

HILL, A, 'Fathers Fight for Lead Role in Childcare' *Observer*, (20 January 2008) News 27.

HINSLIFF, G, 'Blunkett Blasted for "Intrusion" in Kimberly Quinn Paternity Battle', *Observer* (6 March 2005), <http://observer.guardian.co.uk/politics/story/0,,1431623, 00.html>, accessed 21 November 2007.

HM GOVERNMENT, *Children Come First: The Government's Proposals on the Maintenance of Children*, Cm 1624 (1990).

——, Response to the Report from the Joint Committee on the Human Tissue and Embryos (Draft) Bill, Cm 7209 (HMSO, London, 2007).

HM TREASURY, *Every Child Matters*, Cm 5860 (2003).

——, *Child Poverty Review* (HM Treasury, London, 2004).

HM TREASURY/DEPARTMENT FOR EDUCATION AND SKILLS, *Aiming High for Children: Supporting Families* (HMSO, London, 2007).

HM TREASURY *et al*, *Choices for Parents, The Best Start for Children: A Ten Year Strategy for Childcare* (HM Treasury, London, 2004).

HOBSON, B (ed), *Making Men into Fathers: Men, Masculinities and the Social Politics of Fatherhood* (Cambridge University Press, Cambridge, 2002).

HOBSON, B, DUVANDER, AZ and HALLDÉN, K, 'Men's Capabilities and Agency to Create a Work Family Balance: The Gap Between European Norms and Men's Practices', Paper given at 'Fatherhood in Late Modernity: Cultural Images, Social Practices, Structural Frames', Conference (April 2007) (copy of paper with authors).

HOCHSCHILD, AR, *The Second Shift: Working Parents and the Revolution at Home* (Piatkus, London, 1989).

Bibliography

——, 'Understanding the Future of Fatherhood' in M van Dongen, G Frinking and M Jacobs (eds), *Changing Fatherhood* (Thesis Publishers, Amsterdam, 1995).

——, *The Time Bind: When Work Becomes Home and Home Becomes Work* (Metropolitan Books, New York, 1997).

HOGARTH, T *et al, Work Life Balance 2000: Baseline Study of Work Life Balance Practices in Great Britain* (Department for Education and Employment, London, 2000).

HOLCOMBE, L, *Wives and Property: Reform of the Married Women's Property Acts* (University of Toronto Press, Toronto, 1983).

HOLLWAY, W, 'Recognition and Heterosexual Desire' in D Richardson (ed), *Theorising Heterosexuality: Telling it Straight* (Open University Press, Buckingham, 1996).

——, *The Capacity to Care: Gender and Ethical Subjectivity* (Routledge, London, 2006).

HOME OFFICE, *Supporting Families: A Consultation Document* (HMSO, London, 1998).

——, *Secure Borders, Safe Haven: Integration with Diversity in Modern Britain*, Cm 5387 (2002).

HORSEY, K, 'Older Fathers May Increase Chance of Dying Before Adulthood', http://www.bionews.org.uk/new.lasso?storyid=3862 (accessed 13 June 2008).

HOUSE OF COMMONS SCIENCE AND TECHNOLOGY SELECT COMMITTEE, 'Human Reproductive Technologies and the Law', HC (2004–05) 7-I.

——, *Scientific Developments Relating to the Abortion Act 1967, Twelfth Report of Session 2006–07 (Volume I)*, HC 1045-I.

HOUSE OF COMMONS SOCIAL SECURITY COMMITTEE, *First Report of Session 1993–4: Operation of the Child Support Act* , HC 69.

HOUSTON, D and WAUMSLEY, JA, *Attitudes to Flexible Working and Family Life*, Family and Work Series (The Policy Press, Bristol, 2003).

HOWEY, N and SAMUELS, E, *Out of the Ordinary: Essays on Growing Up With Gay, Lesbian and Transgender Parents* (St Martins Press, New York, 2000).

HUMAN FERTILISATION AND EMBRYOLOGY AUTHORITY, 'Who are the UK's Sperm Donors? Fertility Regulator Presents National Picture of the People Who Donate', Press release, October 2005, <http://www.hfea.gov.uk/en/1109.html>, accessed 22 November 2007.

——, 'Code of Practice: Edition 7.0' (2007), <http://cop.hfea.gov.uk/cop>. accessed 21 November 2007.

——, 'Revised Guidance: Welfare of the Child and the Assessment of those Seeking Treatment', < http://www.hfea.gov.uk/en/505.html>, accessed 21 November 2007.

——, 'Factsheet on Sperm, Egg and Embryo Donation' (Human Fertilisation and Embryology Authority, London, 2004).

HUNT, J *Researching Contact* (National Council for One Parent Families, London, 2003)

HUNT, J with ROBERTS, C, *Child Contact with Non Resident Parents*, Family Policy Briefing 3 (Department of Social Policy and Social Work, University of Oxford, Oxford, 2004).

HYDE, A, *Bodies of Law* (Princeton University Press, Princeton, NJ, 1997).

IVES, J, 'Becoming a Father/Refusing Fatherhood: How Paternal Responsibilities and Rights are Generated' (DPhil thesis, University of Birmingham, 2007).

JAMES, AL and JAMES, A, 'Tightening the Net: Children, Community and Control' (2001) 52 *British Journal of Sociology* 211.

JAMES, A and PROUT, A (eds), *Constructing and Reconstructing Childhood* (Falmer Press, London, 1990).

JAMES, A, JENKS, C and PROUT, A, *Theorizing Childhood* (Polity, London, 1998).

257

Bibliography

JAMIESON, L, *Intimacy: Personal Relationships in Modern Society* (Polity, Cambridge, 1998).

JAMIESON, L *et al*, 'Friends, Neighbours and Distant Partners: Extending or Decentring Family Relationships? (2006) 11(3) *Sociological Research Online* <http://www.socresonline.org.uk/11/3/jamieson.html>, accessed 18 March 2008.

JEFFERSON, T, 'Introduction' (1996) 35 *British Journal of Criminology* 1337.

——, 'Masculinities and Crime' in M Maguire, R Morgan, and R Reiner (eds), *The Oxford Handbook of Criminology*, 2nd edn (Oxford University Press, Oxford, 1997).

JENKS, C, *Childhood* (Routledge, London, 1996).

JOHNSON, M, 'A Biomedical Perspective on Fatherhood', in A Bainham *et al* (eds), *What is a Parent? A Socio-legal Analysis* (Hart, Oxford, 1999).

——, 'Genes, Genealogies and Paternity: Making Babies in the Twenty-first Century' in A Pedain and J Spencer (eds), *Freedom and Responsibility in Reproductive Choice* (Hart, Oxford, 2006).

JOHNSON, M and BAKER, S, 'Co-occurrence of Positive and Negative Affect Following Miscarriage', ESCRC Report; RES-000–22–0192.

JOHNSON, P, *Love, Heterosexuality and Society* (Routledge, London, 2005).

JOINT COMMITTEE ON THE HUMAN TISSUE AND EMBRYOS (DRAFT) BILL, Volume 1: Report, HC (2006–07) 630-I.

JORDAN, PL, 'Laboring for Relevance: Expectant and New Fatherhood' (1990) 39(1) *Nursing Research* 11.

KAGANAS, F, 'Grandparents' Rights and Grandparents' Campaigns' (2007) 19(1) *Child and Family Law Quarterly* 17.

KAGANAS, F and DAY SCLATER, S, 'Contact Disputes: Narrative Constructions of "Good" Parents' (2004) 12(1) *Feminist Legal Studies* 1.

——, 'Contact Disputes: Narrative Constructions of "Good" Parents' (2004) 12(1) *Feminist Legal Studies* 1.

KAGANAS, F and DIDUCK, A, 'Incomplete Citizens: Changing Images of Post-separation Children' (2004) 67(6) *Modern Law Review* 959.

KAGANAS, F and PIPER, C, 'Grandparents and Contact: "Rights vs Welfare"' Revisited' (2001) 15(2) IJLPF 250.

——, 'Shared Parenting – a 70% Solution?' (2002) 14 *Child and Family Law Quarterly* 365.

KENNEDY, H, *Eve was Framed* (Vintage, London, 1993).

KERO, A, LALOS, A and HOGBERG, U, 'Ethics and Society: The Male Partner Involved in Legal Abortion' (1999) 14(10) *Human Reproduction* 2669.

KERRIDGE, T, PÖRKSEN, J and ROBOTHAM, S, *Into View: Views on Vasectomy: The Male Experience* (Marie Stopes International, London, 2003).

KIERNAN, K and SMITH, K, 'Unmarried Parenthood: New Insights from the Millennium Cohort Study' (2003) 114 *Population Trends* 26.

KILKEY, M, 'New Labour and Reconciling Work and Family Life: Making it Fathers' Business?' 5 *Social Policy & Society* 167.

KIMMELL, M, *The Gender of Desire: Essays on Male Sexuality* (SUNY Press, New York, 2005).

KING, M, 'Foreword' in S Day Sclater and C Piper (eds), *Undercurrents of Divorce* (Ashgate, Aldershot, 1999).

KING, M and PIPER, C, *How the Law Thinks About Children*, 2nd edn (Arena, Aldershot 1995).

Bibliography

KING, M and TROWELL, J, *Children's Welfare and the Law: The Limits of Legal Intervention* (Sage, London, 1992).

KING, V and HEARD, HE, 'Non-resident Father Visitation, Parental Conflict, and Mother's Satisfaction: What's Best for Child Well-being?' (1999) 61 *Journal of Marriage and Family* 385.

KITSUSE, JI and SPECTOR, M, 'The Definition of Social Problems' (1973) 20(4) *Social Problems* 407.

KOFFMAN, L, 'Holding Parents to Account: Tough on Children, Tough on the Causes of Children' (2008) 35 *Journal of Law and Society* 113.

KRAUSE, H, *Illegitimacy: Law & Social Policy* (Bobbs-Merrill, Indianapolis, 1971).

LACEY, N, *Unspeakable Subjects: Feminist Essays in Legal and Social Theory* (Hart, Oxford, 1998).

LAMB, ME (ed), *The Role of the Father in Child Development* (John Wiley, New York, 1997).

——, 'Father and Child Development: An Introductory Overview and Guide' in ME LAMB (ed), *The Role of the Father in Child Development* (John Wiley, New York, 1997).

LAND, H, 'The Family Wage' (1980) 6 *Feminist Review* 55.

LANGLEY, C, 'Anti-Abortion Man Raises Baby Alone', *Sunday Times* (17 January 1988).

LAQUEUR, TW, 'The Facts of Fatherhood' in M Hirsch and E Fox (eds), *Conflicts in Feminism* (Routledge, New York, 1990).

LAROSSA, R, 'Fatherhood and Social Change' (1988) 37 *Family Relations* 451.

——, *The Modernization of Fatherhood: A Social and Political History* (University of Chicago Press, Chicago, 1997).

LASCH, C, *Haven in a Heartless World: The Family Besieged* (Basic Books, New York, 1977).

LATTIMER, M, 'Abortion Discourses: An Exploration of the Social, Cultural and Organisational Context of Abortion Decision-Making in Contemporary Britain' (DPhil thesis, University of Sussex, 2000).

LAW COMMISSION, *Report on Injuries to Unborn Children*, Cmnd 60 (1974).

——, *Illegitimacy* Working Paper No 74 (1979).

——, *Family Law: Illegitimacy*, Law Com No 118, (1982).

——, *Family Law: The Ground for Divorce*, Law Com No 192 (1990).

——, *Cohabitation: the Financial Consequences of Relationship Breakdown*, Consultation Paper, Law Com CP No 179 (2006).

——, 'Cohabitation: The Financial Consequences of Relationship Breakdown', Law Com No 307, Cm 7182 (2007).

LAVILLE, S et al 'Kennedy Rushes to Pregnant Wife' *Guardian* (12 April 2005)

LEE, E, *et al*, A Matter of Choice? Explaining National Variations in Teenage Abortion and Motherhood (Joseph Rowntree Foundation, York, 2004).

LEE, RG and MORGAN, D, *Human Fertilisation and Embryology: Regulating the Reproductive Revolution* (2nd edn Blackstones, London 2001).

LEWIS, C, *Becoming a Father* (Open University Press, Milton Keynes, 1986).

——, *A Man's Place in the Home: Fathers and Families in the UK* (Joseph Rowntree Foundation, York, 2000).

259

Bibliography

LEWIS, C and LAMB, ME, 'Fathers: The Research Perspective' in G Barker *et al*, *Supporting Fathers: Contributions from the International Fatherhood Summit 2003* (Early Childhood Development: Practice and Reflections Series, Bernard van Leer Foundation, The Hague, 2004).

——, *Understanding Fatherhood: A Review of Recent Research* (Joseph Rowntree Foundation, Lancaster University, 2007).

LEWIS, C and O'BRIEN, M, *Reassessing Fatherhood: New Observations on Fathers and the Modern Family* (Sage, London, 1987).

LEWIS, C, PAPACOSTA, A and WARIN, J, *Cohabitation, Separation and Fatherhood* (Joseph Rowntree Foundation, London, 2002).

LEWIS, J, 'Marriage and Cohabitation and the Nature of Commitment' (1999) 11(4) *Child and Family Law Quarterly* 355.

——, *The End of Marriage? Individualism and Intimate Relations* (Edward Elgar, Cheltenham, 2001).

——, 'Is Marriage the Answer to the Problems of Family Change?' (2001) *Political Quarterly* 437.

——, 'The Decline of the Male Breadwinner Model Family' (2001) 8 *Social Politics* 152.

——, 'Individualisation, Assumptions about the Existence of an Adult Worker Model and the Shift towards Contractualism' in A Carling, S Duncan and R Edwards (eds), *Analysing Families: Morality and Rationality in Policy and Practice* (Routledge, London, 2002).

——, 'The Problem of Fathers: Policy and Behaviour in Britain' in B Hobson (ed), *Making Men into Fathers: Men, Masculinities and the Social Politics of Fatherhood* (Cambridge University Press, Cambridge, 2002).

——, 'Balancing Work and Family: The Nature of the Policy Challenge and Gender Equality' (Working Paper for GeNet Project 9, *Tackling Inequalities in Work and Care Policy Initiatives and Actors at the EU and UK Levels*) (ESRC Gender Equality Network, Cambridge, 2007).

LEWIS, J and GUILLARI, S, 'The Adult Worker Model Family, Gender Equality and Care: The Search for New Policy Principles and the Possibilities and Problems of a Capabilities Approach' (2005) 34(1) *Economy & Society* 76.

LEWIS, J and KIERNAN, K, 'The Boundaries between Marriage, Non Marriage, and Parenthood: Changes in Behavior and Policy in Postwar Britain' (1996) 21 *Journal of Family History* 372.

LEWIS, S, 'Family Friendly Employment Policies' (1997) 4(1) *Gender, Work and Organization* 13.

LEWIS, S and LEWIS, J (eds), *The Work–Family Challenge: Rethinking Employment* (Sage, London, 1996).

——, 'Work, Family and Well-Being: Can the Law Help?' (1997) 2 *Legal and Criminal Psychology* 155–67.

LLOYD, A, *Doubly Deviant, Doubly Damned* (Penguin, Harmondsworth, 1995).

LLOYD, N, O'BRIEN, M and LEWIS, C, *Fathers in Sure Start: The National Evaluation of Sure Start (NESS)* (Institute for the Study of Children, Families and Social Issues, Birkbeck, University of London, London, 2003).

LLOYD, T, *Fathers Group Evaluation* (Working With Men, London, 1996).

——, *What Works With Fathers?* (Working with Men, London, 2001).

Bibliography

LORD CHANCELLOR'S DEPARTMENT, *Court Procedures for the Determination of Paternity and on the Law on Parental Responsibility for Unmarried Fathers* (HMSO, London, 1998).

LOW PAY COMMISSION, *The National Minimum Wage: Protecting Young Workers: Fifth Report* (HMSO, London, 2004).

LOWE, N, 'The Legal Status of Fathers: Past and Present' in L McKee and M O'Brien (eds), *The Father Figure* (Tavistock, London, 1982).

——, 'The Meaning and Allocation of Parental Responsibility – A Common Lawyer's Perspective' (1997) 11 *International Journal of Law, Policy and the Family* 192.

LUPTON, D and BARCLAY, L, *Constructing Fatherhood: Discourses and Experiences* (Sage, London, 1997).

LYCETT, E *et al*, 'Offspring Created as a Result of Donor Insemination: A Study of Family Relationships, Child Adjustment, and Disclosure' (2004) 82(1) *Fertility & Sterility* 172.

MCCANDLESS, J, 'Status and Anomaly: Considerations of the "Sexual Family" and Fatherhood in *Re D (Contact and Parental Responsibility: Lesbian Mothers and Known Father)* [2006]', 'Gender Unbound' conference at the University of Keele, 9–11 July 2007.

MCCARTHY, S, 'A Couple's Deal to Use Birth Control is a Deal', *Dallas Morning News* (20 November 1998).

MCDONNELL, K, *Not an Easy Choice: A Feminist Re-examines Abortion* (Women's Press, Ontario, 1984).

MCGLYNN, C, *Families and the European Union* (Cambridge University Press, Cambridge, 2006).

MCINTOSH, J, 'Enduring Conflict in Parental Separation: Pathways on Child Development' (2003) 9 *Journal of Family Studies* 63.

——, 'Child Inclusion as a Principle and as Evidence-Based Practice: Applications to Family Law Services and Related Sectors' (Australian Institute of Family Studies, Melbourne, 2007).

MCKEE, L and O'BRIEN, M (eds), *The Father Figure* (Tavistock, London, 1982).

MCLAREN, A, *A History of Contraception: From Antiquity to the Present Day* (Basil Blackwell, Cambridge, MA, 1990).

MCLEAN, S, *Old Law, New Medicine: Medical Ethics and Human Rights* (Pandora, London, 1999).

——, *Review of the Common Law Provisions Relating to the Removal of Gametes and of the Consent Provisions in the Human Fertilisation and Embryology Act 1990* (Department of Health, London, 1998).

MCMAHON, A, *Taking Care of Men* (Cambridge University Press, Cambridge, 1999).

MCNEIL, M, 'Putting the Alton Bill in Context' in S Franklin, C Lury, and J Stacey (eds), *Off-centre: Feminism and Cultural Studies* (HarperCollins Academic, London, 1991).

MACKAY, Lord, 'Perceptions of the Children Bill and Beyond' (1989) 139 NLJ 505.

MACDONALD, I and WEBBER, F (eds), *Immigration Law and Practice in the UK* 6th edn (LexisNexis, London, 2005).

MACINNES, J, *The End of Masculinity* (Open University Press, Buckingham, 1998).

MACKINNON, C, 'Feminism, Marxism, Method and the State: An Agenda for Theory' (1983) 8 *Signs* 635.

——, *Feminism Unmodified: Discourses on Life and Law* (Harvard University Press, Cambridge, MA, 1987).

MACLEAN, M, *Surviving Divorce: Women's Resources After Separation* (Macmillan, London, 1991).

——, (ed), *Parenting After Partnering: Containing Conflict After Separation* (Hart, Oxford, 2007).

MACLEAN, M and EEKELAAR, J, *The Parental Obligation: A Study of Parenthood Across Households* (Hart, Oxford, 1997).

MACLEAN, M and RICHARDS, M, 'Parents and Divorce: Changing Patterns of Public Intervention' in A Bainham, B Lindley and M Richards (eds), *Children and their Families: Contact, Rights and Welfare* (Hart, Oxford, 2003).

MACONOCHIE, N, DOYLE, P and CARSON, C, 'Infertility among Male UK Veterans of the 1990–1 Gulf War: Reproductive Cohort Study' (2004) 329 BMJ 196.

MAIDMENT, S, *Child Custody and Divorce: The Law in Social Context* (Croom Helm, London, 1984).

MALLENDER, P and RAYSON, J, *The Civil Partnership Act 2004: A Practical Guide* (Cambridge University Press, Cambridge, 2005).

MANDER, R, *Men and Maternity* (Routledge, London and New York, 2004).

MANGAN, J and WALVIN, J (eds), *Manliness and Morality: Middle Class Masculinity in Britain and America 1800–1940* (Manchester University Press, Manchester, 1987).

MANNING, A and PETRONGOLO, B, *The Part-time Pay Penalty* (Women and Equality Unit, London, 2004).

MARKS, G and HOUSTON, DM 'Attitudes Towards Work and Motherhood Held by Working and Non-Working Mothers' (2002) 16(3) *Work, Employment and Society* 523.

MARSIGLIO, W, *Fatherhood: Contemporary Theory, Research and Social Policy* (Sage, New York, 1995).

——, *Procreative Man* (New York University Press, New York, 1998).

——, *Stepdads: Stories of Love, Hope and Repair* (Rowman & Littlefield, Lanham, MD, 2004).

MARSIGLIO, W and HINOJOSA, R, 'Managing the Multifather Family: Stepfathers as Father Allies' (2007) 69 *Journal of Marriage & Family* 862.

MARSIGLIO, W and PLECK, JH, 'Fatherhood and Masculinities' in M Kimmell, J Hearn and RW Connell (eds), *The Handbook of Studies on Men and Masculinities* (Sage, Thousand Oaks, CA, 2004).

MARSIGLIO, W, DAY, RD and LAMB, M, 'Exploring Fatherhood Diversity: Implications for Conceptualizing Father Involvement' (2000) 29(4) *Marriage & Family Review* 269.

MARSIGLIO, W, ROY, K and LITTON FOX, G (eds), *Situated Fathering: A Focus on Physical and Social Spaces* (Rowman & Littlefield, Lanham, MD, 2005).

MARTIN, L, 'Fathers Who Kill Their Children', *Observer* (5 November 2006), Focus 20.

MASON, JK, MCCALL SMITH, RA and LAURIE, GT, *Law and Medical Ethics* (Butterworths, London, 2002).

MASON, MA, *From Father's Property to Children's Rights: The History of Child Custody in the United States* (Columbia University Press, New York, 1994).

MAY, V and SMART, C, 'Silence in Court? Hearing Children in Residence and Contact Disputes' (2004) *Child and Family Law Quarterly* 305.

MAZEY, S, *Gender Mainstreaming in the EU: Principles and Practice* (Kogan Page, London, 2001).

MEN'S HEALTH FORUM, 'Private Parts, Public Policy: Improving Men's Sexual Health', Report by the Men's Health Forum (2003) <http://www.menshealthforum.org.uk/uploaded_files/mhfprivateparts.pdf>, accessed 25 October 2007.

MESSERSCHMIDT, J, *Masculinities and Crime: Critique and Reconceptualization of Theory* (Rowman & Littlefield, Lanham, MD, 1993).

MESSING, K, *One-eyed Science: Occupational Health and Women Workers* (Temple University Press, Philadelphia, 1998).

MESSNER, M, *Politics of Masculinities: Men in Movements* (Sage, London, 1997).

METCALF, H and KOROU, A, *Towards a Closing of the Gender Pay Gap* (Department of Trade and Industry, London, 2003).

MILLNS, S, 'Making Social Judgments which Go Beyond the Medical' in J Bridgeman and S Millns (eds), *Law and Body Politics: Regulating the Female Body* (Aldershot, Dartmouth, 1995).

MISCARRIAGE ASSOCIATION, THE, *Men & Miscarriage* (The Miscarriage Association, Wakefield, 2006).

MITCHELL, J and GOODY, J, 'Feminism, Fatherhood and the Family in Britain' in A Oakley and J Mitchell (eds), *Who's Afraid of Feminism? Seeing Through the Backlash* (Hamish Hamilton, London, 1997).

MNOOKIN, R, 'Bargaining in the Shadow of the Law: The Case of Divorce' (1979) *Current Legal Problems* 65.

MORAN, L, 'A Study of the History of Male Sexuality in Law: Non-Consummation' (1990) 1 *Law and Critique* 155.

MORGAN, D, 'Risk and Family Practices: Accounting for Change and Fluidity in Family Life' in E Silva and C Smart (eds), *The 'New' Family?* (Sage, London, 1999).

——, *Family Connections: An Introduction to Family Studies* (Polity, Cambridge, 1999).

MORGAN, D and LEE, R, *Blackstone's Guide to the Human Fertilisation and Embryology Act 1990*, 1st edn (Blackstone, London, 1991).

——, 'In the Name of the Father? *Ex parte Blood*: Dealing with Novelty and Anomaly' (1997) 60 MLR 840.

MORGAN, P, *Farewell to the Family? Public Policy and Family Breakdown in Britain and the USA* (Health and Welfare Unit, Institute of Economic Affairs, London, 1995).

MORT, F, *Cultures of Consumption: Masculinities and Social Space in Late Twentieth Century Britain* (Routledge, London, 1996).

MORRISON, B, *And When Did You Last See Your Father?*, 2nd edn (Granta, London, 2006).

MOSS, P (ed), *Father Figures: Fathers in the Families of the 1990s* (HMSO, Edinburgh, 1995).

MUMFORD, A 'Working Towards Credit for Parenting: A Consideration of Tax Credits as a Feminist Enterprise' in A Diduck and K O'Donovan, *Feminist Perspectives on Family Law*, Feminist Perspectives Series (Routledge-Cavendish, London, 2006).

——, 'Towards a Fiscal Sociology of Tax Credits and the Father's Rights Movement' (2008) 17(2) *Social and Legal Studies* 217.

MURRAY, C, *Losing Ground* (Basic Books, New York, 1984).

——, *The Emerging British Underclass* (Institute of Economic Affairs, Health and Welfare Unit, London, 1990).

MURRAY, TH and KNAEBNICK, GE, 'Genetic Ties and Genetic Mixups' (2003) 29 *Journal of Medical Ethics* 68.

NAFFINE, N, *Law and the Sexes: Explorations in Feminist Jurisprudence* (Allen & Unwin, Sydney, 1990).

——, (ed), *Gender, Crime and Feminism* (Aldershot, Dartmouth, 1995).

——*Feminism and Criminology* (Polity, Cambridge, 1997).

NEALE, B and SMART, C, 'Experiments with Parenthood?' (1997) 31(2) *Sociology* 201.

——, 'Caring, Earning and Changing: Parenthood and Employment after Divorce' in A Carling, S Duncan and R Edwards (eds), *Analysing Families: Morality and Rationality in Policy and Practice* (Routledge, London, 2002).

——, '"Good" and "Bad"' Lawyers? Struggling in the Shadow of the New Law' (2004) 19 *Journal of Social Work and Family Law* 377.

NEALE, B, FLOWERDEW, J and SMART, C, 'Drifting Towards Shared Residence?' [2003] *Family Law* 904.

NEWBURN, T and STANKO, EA (eds), *Just Boys Doing Business? Men, Masculinities and Crime* (Routledge, London, 1994).

NEW WAYS TO WORK, *Balanced Lives: Changing Work Patterns for Men* (New Ways to Work, London, 1995).

NEWSPLANET STAFF, 'UK Dads First With US Birth Cert.', <http://www.planetout.com/news/article-print.html?1999/10/28/5>, accessed 22 November 2007.

NICHOLSON, L, 'The Myth of the Traditional Family' in HL Nelson (ed), *Feminism and Families* (Routledge, London, 1997).

NOLAN, M, 'Caring for Fathers in Antenatal Classes' (1994) 4(2) *Modern Midwife* 25.

NORDQVIST, C, 'Infertility affects 2.5 million males in the UK' *Medical News Today* (13 September 2005), <http://www.medicalnewstoday.com/articles/30585.php>, accessed 25 October 2007.

NOVAS, C and ROSE, N, 'Genetic Risk and the Birth of the Somatic Individual' (2000) 29(4) *Economy & Society* 485.

O'BRIEN, M, *Fathers and Family Support* (National Family and Parenting Institute, London, 2004).

——, Social Science and Public Policy Perspectives on Fatherhood' in ME Lamb (ed) *The Role of the Father in Child Development* (John Wiley, New Jersey, 2004).

——, *Shared Caring: Bringing Fathers into the Frame* (Equal Opportunities Commission, Manchester, 2005).

O'BRIEN, M and SHEMILT, I, *Working Fathers: Earning and Caring* (Equal Opportunities Commission, Manchester, 2003).

O'DONOVAN, K, *Sexual Divisions in Law* (Weidenfeld & Nicholson, London, 1985).

——, *Family Law Matters* (Pluto, London, 1993).

O'MALLEY, P, *Risk, Uncertainty and Government* (The Glasshouse Press, London, 2004).

O'NEILL, R, *Experiments in Living: The Fatherless Family* (Civitas, London, 2002).

OAKLEY, A, *The Sociology of Housework* (Martin Robertson, London, 1974).

OFFICE FOR NATIONAL STATISTICS, *UK 2000 Time Use Survey: Dataset,* 2nd edn (Office for National Statistics, London, 2002).

——, *Key Statistics for Local Authorities in England and Wales: Census 2001* (Office for National Statistics, London, 2003).

——, Living in Britain: General Household Survey 2002, Chapter 3: Households, families and people' (2004) <http://www.statistics.gov.uk/cci/nugget.asp?id=819>, accessed 3 January 2008.

Bibliography

——, Living in Britain: General Household Survey 2002, Chapter 10: Contraception' (2004) <http://www.statistics.gov.uk/lib2002/downloads/contraception.pdf>, accessed 25 October 2007.

——, *NHS Contraceptive Services, England: 2004–05* (Office for National Statistics, London, 2005).

——, *Birth Statistics* (Office for National Statistics, London, 2006).

——, 'Divorce' (2007) <http://www.statistics.gov.uk/cci/nugget.asp?id=170>, accessed 3 January 2008.

——, *Population Trends* (Palgrave Macmillan, London, 2008), http://www.statistics.gov.uk/downloads/theme_population/Population_Trends_131_web.pdf, accessed 30 March 2008.

OKIN, SM, *Justice, Gender and the Family* (Harper Collins, London, 1989).

OLSEN, F, 'The Family and the Market: A Study of Ideology and Legal Reform' (1983) 96 *Harvard Law Review* 1497.

——'The Myth of State Intervention in the Family' (1985) 18(4) *University of Michigan Journal of Law Reform* 835.

OUDSHOORN, N, '"Astronauts in the Sperm World": The Renegotiation of Masculine Identities in Discourses on Male Contraception' (2004) 6(4) *Men & Masculinities* 349.

OVORTROP, J et al (eds), *Childhood Matters: Social Theory, Practices and Politics* (Avebury Press, Aldershot, 1994)

PARENTLINE PLUS, *Stepfamilies: New Relationships, New Challenges*, Report (Parentline Plus, London, 2005).

——, 'Who We Are', <http://www.parentlineplus.org.uk/index.php?id=15>, accessed 29 January 2008.

PARKE, R, *Fatherhood* (Harvard University Press, Cambridge, MA, 1996).

——, 'Father Involvement: A Development Psychological Perspective' (2000) 29 *Marriage and Family Review* 43.

PARKER, S, 'Rights and Utility in Anglo-Australian Law' (1992) 55 MLR 311.

PARSONS, T, 'The American Father: Its Relation to Personality and to Social Structure' in T Parsons and RF Bales (eds), *Family, Socialization and Interaction Process* (The Free Press, New York, 1955).

PARSONS, T and BALES, F, *Family, Socialization and Interaction Process* (The Free Press, Glencoe, 1955).

PATEMAN, C, *The Sexual Contract* (Cambridge University Press, Cambridge, 1988).

PAULSON, JF, with DAUBER, S, and LIEFERMAN, JA, 'Individual and Combined Effects of Postpartum Depression in Mothers and Fathers on Parenting Behavior' (2006) 118(2) *Paediatrics* 659.

PEARCE, J, DAVIS, G and BARRON, J, 'Love in a Cold Climate – Section 8 Applications under the Children Act 1989' [1999] *Family Law* 22.

PERRONS, D et al, *Gender Divisions and Working Time in the New Economy: Changing Patters of Work, Care and Public Policy in Europe and North America* (Edward Elgar, Cheltenham, 2007).

PETERS, EH et al, *Fatherhood: Research, Interventions and Policies* (Haworth, New York, 2000).

PHOENIX, A, WOOLLETT, A, and LLOYD, E, *Motherhood: Meanings, Practices, Ideologies* (Sage, London, 1991).

PHOENIX, A and HUSAIN, F, *Parenting and Ethnicity* (Joseph Rowntree Foundation, York, 2007).

Bibliography

PICKFORD, R, *Fathers, Marriage and the Law* (Family Policy Studies Centre, Cambridge, 1999).

PIERCY, M 'Intractable Contact Disputes' (2004) *Family Law* 815.

PINCHBECK, I and HEWITT, M, *Children in English Society: Volume 1: From Tudor Times to the Eighteenth Century* (Routledge & Kegan Paul, London, 1969).

——, *Children in English Society, Volume II: From the Eighteenth Century to the Children Act 1948* (Routledge & Kegan Paul, London, 1973).

PIPER, C and DAY SCLATER, S, 'Remoralising the Family? Family Policy, Family Law and Youth Justice' (2000) 12(2) *Child and Family Law Quarterly* 135.

PLANT, R, 'Citizenship and Social Security' (2003) 24(2) *Fiscal Studies* 153.

PLECK, J, 'American Fathering in Historical Perspective' in M Kimmell (ed), *Changing Men: New Directions in Research on Men and Masculinity* (Sage Focus Editions, Sage, Beverly Hills, CA 1987).

PLOMER, A, SMITH, I and MARTIN-CLEMENT, N, 'Rationing Policies on Access to In Vitro Fertilisation in the NHS, UK' (1999) 7 *Reproductive Health Matters* 60.

POWELL, M (ed), *New Labour, New Welfare State* (The Policy Press, Bristol, 1999).

PRASAD, R, 'The Sperm that Turned', *Guardian* (11 February 1999).

PRIME MINISTER'S STRATEGY UNIT, *Building on Progress: Families* (Cabinet Office, London, 2007).

PRINGLE, K *et al*, *Men and Masculinities in Europe* (London, Whiting and Birch, 2006).

PROBERT, R, *Cretney's Family Law* (London, Sweet and Maxwell, 2006).

PRYOR, J and RODGERS, B, *Children in Changing Families: Life After Parental Separation* (Blackwell, Oxford, 2001).

QUINTON, D, POLLOCK, S and GOLDING, J, *The Transition to Fatherhood for Young Men: Influences on Commitment* (ESRC Trust for the Study of Adolescence, University of Bristol, Bristol, 2002).

QVORTRUP, J *et al* (eds), *Childhood Matters: Social Theory, Practices and Politics* (Avebury Press, Aldershot 1994).

RAKE, K, 'Gender and New Labour's Social Policies' (2001) 30(2) *Journal of Social Policy* 209.

RANSON, G, 'Men at Work: Change – or No Change? – in the Era of the "New Father"' (2001) 4(1) *Men & Masculinities* 3.

REECE, H, 'The Paramountcy Principle: Consensus or Construct?' (1996) 49 *Current Legal Problems* 267.

——, *Divorcing Responsibly* (Hart, Oxford, 2003).

——, 'From Parental Responsibilty to Parenting Responsibly' in M Freeman (ed), *Law and Sociology* (Current Legal Issues Series, Oxford University Press, Oxford, 2005).

——, 'UK Women's Groups' Child Contact Campaign: "So long as it is safe"' (2006) 18(4) *Child and Family Law Quarterly* 538.

REICHENBERG, A, *et al*, 'Advancing Paternal Age and Autism' (2006) 63(9) *Archives of General Psychiatry* 1026.

REPUTATION INTELLIGENCE, *F4J Heralds a New Era in Political Campaigning: Media Report* (Reputation Intelligence, London, 2004).

REYNAUD, E, *Holy Virility: The Social Construction of Masculinity* (Pluto, London, 1983).

RHOADES, H, 'The "No Contact Mother": Reconstructions of Motherhood in the Era of the "New Father"' (2002) 16(1) *International Journal of Law, Policy and the Family* 71.

——, 'The Rise and Rise of Shared Parenting Laws: A Critical Reflection' (2002) 19(1) *Canadian Journal of Family Law* 75.

Bibliography

RIBBENS, J, *Mothers and their Children: A Feminist Sociology of Childrearing* (Sage, London, 1994).

RICHARDS, M, 'Fatherhood, Marriage and Sexuality: Some Speculations on the English Middle-class Family' in C Lewis and M O'Brien (eds), *Reassessing Fatherhood: New Observations on Fathers and the Modern Family* (Sage, London, 1987).

RICHARDSON, A, *Fathers Plus: An Audit of Work With Fathers Throughout the North East of England 1998* (Children North East, Newcastle, 1998).

ROBERTS, D, 'The Genetic Tie' (1995) 62 *University of Chicago Law Review* 209.

——, *Killing the Black Body: Race, Reproduction and the Meaning of Liberty* (Vintage Books, New York, 1997).

ROBERTS, R, 'Adult Approach: Interview with Dorit Braun, Parentline Plus', *Guardian* (25 April 2007), Society 5.

ROBERTSON, S, *Understanding Men's Health: Masculinity, Identity and Well-Being* (Open University Press, Buckingham, 2007).

ROCHE, J, 'The Children Act: Once a Parent, Always a Parent' (1991) 5 *Journal of Social Welfare and Family Law* 345.

RODGERS, B and PRYOR, J, *Divorce and Separation: The Outcomes for Children* (Joseph Rowntree Foundation, York, 1998).

ROSE, N, 'Beyond the Public/Private Division: Law, Power and the Family' (1987) 14 *Journal of Law & Society* 61.

——, 'Expertise and the Government of Conduct' (1994) 14 *Studies in Law, Politics and Society* 359.

——, *Governing the Soul* (Routledge, London, 1995).

ROSE, N and MILLER, P, 'Political Power Beyond the State: Problems of Government' (1994) 43(2) *British Journal of Sociology* 173.

ROSE, N and VALVERDE, M, 'Governed by Law?' (1998) 7(4) *Social and Legal Studies* 541.

ROSENEIL, S and BUDGEON, S, 'Cultures of Intimacy and Care Beyond "the Family": Personal Life and Social Change in the Early 21st Century' (2004) *Current Sociology* 135.

ROSH WHITE, N, 'About Fathers: Masculinity and the Social Construction of Fatherhood' (1994) 30(2) *Journal of Sociology* 119.

ROTH, R, *Making Women Pay: The Hidden Costs of Fetal Rights* (Cornell University Press, Ithaca, NY, 2000).

ROTUNDO, EA, 'Patriarchs and Participants: A Historical Perspective on Fatherhood' in M Kaufman (ed), *Beyond Patriarchy: Essays by Men on Pleasure, Power and Change* (Oxford University Press, Toronto, 1987).

ROYAL COMMISSION ON MARRIAGE AND DIVORCE, *Royal Commission on Marriage and Divorce: Report 1951–1955*, Cmd 9678 (1956).

RUDDICK, S, 'Thinking About Fatherhood' in M Hirsch and E Fox Keller (eds), *Conflicts in Feminism* (Routledge, New York, 1990).

RUSSELL, G, *The Changing Role of the Father* (University of Queensland Press, London, 1983).

RYAN, M, *Working with Fathers* (Radcliffe Medical Press, Abingdon, 2000).

SACHS, A and WILSON, JH, *Sexism and the Law: A Study of Male Beliefs and Judicial Bias* (Martin Robertson, Oxford 1978).

SALFORD, H, 'Concepts of Family Under EU Law – Lessons from the ECHR' (2002) 16 *International Journal of Law, Policy and the Family* 410.

Bibliography

SAMUELS, A, 'The Good-Enough Father of Whatever Sex' (1995) 5(4) *Feminism & Psychology* 511.

SANDELOWSKI, M, 'Channels of Desire: Fetal Ultrasonography in Two Use Contexts' (1994) 4(3) *Qualitative Health Research* 262.

——, 'Separate but Less Unequal: Fetal Ultrasonography and the Transformation of Expectant Mother/Fatherhood' (1994) 8(2) *Gender & Society* 230.

SAUNDERS, H, *Failure to Protect? Domestic Violence and the Experiences of Abused Women and Family Courts* (Women's Aid, Bristol, 2003).

——, *Twenty-Nine Child Homicides: Lessons to be Learnt on Domestic Violence and Child Protection* (Women's Aid, London, 2004).

SAYER, L, GAUTHIER, AH and FURSTENBERG, F 'Educational Differences in Parental Time with Children: Cross-national Variations' (2004) *Journal of Marriage and Family* 1152.

SCHMIDT, V, *Gender Mainstreaming: An Innovation in Europe? The Institutionalisation of Gender Mainstreaming in the European Commission* (Verlag Barbara Burich, Leverkusen Opladen, 2005).

SCOURFIELD, J 'The Challenge of Engaging Fathers in the Child Protection Process' (2006) 26(2) *Critical Social Policy* 440.

SCOURFIELD, J and DRAKEFORD, M, 'New Labour and the "Problem of Men"' (2002) 22 *Critical Social Policy* 619.

SECKER, S, *For the Sake of the Children: The FNF Guide to Shared Parenting* (FNF Publications, London, 2001).

SEGAL, L, *Is the Future Female? Troubled Thoughts on Contemporary Feminism* (Virago, London, 1987).

——, *Slow Motion: Changing Masculinities, Changing Men* (Virago, London, 1990).

——, *Straight Sex: The Politics of Pleasure* (Virago, London, 1994).

SEIDLER, V, *Rediscovering Masculinity* (Routledge, London, 1989).

SELTZER, JA, 'Relationships Between Fathers and Children Who Live Apart: The Father's Role After Separation' (1991) 53 *Journal of Marriage and Family* 79.

SEN, A, 'Capability and Well-being' in M Nussbaum and A Sen (eds), *The Quality of Life* (Oxford University Press, Oxford, 2003).

SENNETT, R, *The Corrosion of Character: Personal Consequences of Work in the New Capitalism* (WW Norton, New York, 1999).

SEVENHUIJSEN, S, 'Fatherhood and the Political Theory of Rights: Theoretical Perspectives of Feminism' (1986) 14 *International Journal of the Sociology of Law* 329.

——, 'The Gendered Juridification of Parenthood' (1992) 1 *Social and Legal Studies* 71.

——, *Citizenship and the Ethics of Care: Feminist Considerations about Justice, Morality and Politics* (Routledge, London, 1998).

SHAKESPEARE, T, GILLESPIE-SELLS, K and DAVIES, D, *The Sexual Politics of Disability: Untold Desires* (Cassell, London, 1996).

SHAPIRO, JL, 'When Men are Pregnant' in JL Shapiro, MJ Diamond and M Greenberg (eds), *Becoming a Father: Contemporary, Social, Developmental and Clinical Perspectives* (Springer, New York, 1995).

SHELDON, S, *Beyond Control: Medical Power and Abortion Law* (Pluto, London, 1997).

——, 'The Abortion Act 1967: a Critical Perspective' in E Lee (ed), *Abortion Law and Politics Today* (Macmillan, Basingstoke, 1998).

——, '*Re*Conceiving Masculinity: Imagining Men's Reproductive Bodies in Law' (1999) 26(2) *Journal of Law & Society* 129.

Bibliography

——, 'Sperm Bandits, Birth Control Fraud and the Battle of the Sexes' (2001) 21(3) *Legal Studies* 460.

——, 'Unmarried Fathers and Parental Responsibility: a Convincing Case for Reform?' (2001) 2 *Feminist Legal Studies* 93.

——, 'Gender Equality and Reproductive Decision Making' (2004) 12(3) *Feminist Legal Studies* 303.

——, '*Evans v Amicus Health Care:* Revealing Cracks in the "Twin Pillars"?' [2004] *Child and Family Law Quarterly* 437.

——, 'Fragmenting Fatherhood: The Regulation of Reproductive Technologies' (2005) 68(4) *Modern Law Review* 523.

——, 'Reproductive Choice: Men's Freedom and Women's Responsibility?' in A Pedain and J Spencer (eds), *Freedom and Responsibility in Reproductive Choice* (Hart, Oxford, 2006).

——, 'Unmarried Fathers and British Citizenship: the Nationality, Immigration and Asylum Act (2002) and British Nationality (Proof of Paternity) Regulations (2006)' (2007) 19(1) *Child and Family Law Quarterly* 1.

——, 'Reproductive Technologies and the Tenacious Hold of the Sexual Family' (2008) *Current Legal Problems*, lecture, UCL (7 February 2008).

SHERR, L and N BARRY, 'Fatherhood and HIV-positive Men' (2004) 5 *HIV Medicine* 258.

SHILLING, C, *The Body and Social Theory* (Sage, London, 1993).

SHOSTAK, AB, MCLOUTH, G and SENG, L, *Men and Abortion: Lessons, Losses and Love* (Praeger, New York, 1984).

SHOWALTER, E, *Sexual Anarchy* (Virago, London, 1992).

SILVA, E (ed), *Good Enough Mothering? Feminist Perspectives on Lone Motherhood* (Routledge, London, 1996).

SILVA, E and SMART, C (eds), *The New Family* (Sage, London, 1999).

SIMPSON, B, *Changing Families: An Ethnographic Approach to Divorce and Separation* (Berg, Oxford, 1998).

SIMPSON, B, JESSOP, JA, and MCCARTHY, P, 'Fathers After Divorce' in A Bainham, B Lindley and M Richards (eds), *Children and their Families: Contact, Rights and Welfare* (Hart, Oxford, 2003).

SIMPSON, B, MCCARTHY, P and WALKER, J, *Being There: Fathers After Divorce* (Newcastle Centre for Family Studies, University of Newcastle upon Tyne, Newcastle, 1995).

——, *Post-Divorce Fatherhood: Discussion Document* (Family and Community Dispute Research Centre, Newcastle, University of Newcastle upon Tyne, 1993).

SINGH, D and NEWBURN, M, *Becoming a Father* (National Childbirth Trust, London, 2000).

SKEGGS, B, *Formations of Class and Gender* (Sage, London, 1997).

SMART, C, *The Ties That Bind: Law, Marriage and the Reproduction of Patriarchal Relations* (Routledge & Kegan Paul, London, 1984).

——, 'Feminism and Law: Some Problems of Analysis and Strategy' (1986) 14 *International Journal of the Sociology of Law* 109.

——, '"There is of course the Distinction Dictated by Nature": Law and the Problem of Paternity' in M Stanworth (ed), *Reproductive Technologies: Gender, Motherhood and Medicine*, Feminist Perspectives Series (Polity, Cambridge, 1987).

——, *Feminism and the Power of Law* (Routledge, London, 1989).

——, (ed), *Regulating Womanhood: Historical Essays on Marriage, Motherhood and Sexuality* (Routledge, London, 1992).

——, 'The Woman of Legal Discourse' (1992) 1 *Social and Legal Studies* 29.

——, *Law, Crime and Sexuality: Essays in Feminism* (Sage, London, 1995).

——, 'Collusion, Collaboration and Confession: on Moving Beyond the Heterosexuality Debate' in D Richardson (ed), *Theorising Heterosexuality: Telling it Straight* (Open University Press, Buckingham, 1996).

——, 'Desperately Seeking Post-Heterosexual Woman' in J Holland and L Adkins (eds), *Sex, Sensibility and the Gendered Body* (Macmillan, Basingstoke, 1996).

——, 'Wishful Thinking and Harmful Tinkering? Sociological Reflections on Family Policy' (1997) 26(3) *Journal of Social Policy* 1.

——, 'The "New" Parenthood: Fathers and Mothers After Divorce' in E Silva and C Smart (eds), *The New Family?* (Sage, London, 1999).

——, 'Changing Landscapes of Family Life: Rethinking Divorce' (2004) 3(4) *Social Policy & Society* 401.

——, 'Equal Shares – Rights for Fathers or Recognition for Children' (2004) 24 *Critical Social Policy* 484.

——, 'Texture of Family Life: Further Thoughts on Change and Commitment' (2005) 34 *Journal of Social Policy* 541.

——, 'Preface' in R Collier and S Sheldon (eds), *Fathers' Rights Activism and Legal Reform in Comparative Perspective* (Hart, Oxford, 2006).

——, 'The Ethic of Justice Strikes Back', in A Diduck and K O'Donovan (eds), *Feminist Perspectives On Family Law* (Routledge-Cavendish, London, 2006).

——, *Personal Life* (Polity, Cambridge, 2007).

SMART, C and V MAY, 'Why Can't They Agree? The Underlying Complexity of Contact and Residence Disputes' (2004) 26(4) *Journal of Social Work and Family Law* 347

SMART, C and NEALE, B, 'Arguments Against Virtue: Must Contact Be Enforced?' [1997] *Family Law* 332.

——, 'Good enough Morality? Divorce and Postmodernity' (1997) 17(4) *Critical Social Policy* 3.

——, *Family Fragments?* (Polity, Cambridge, 1999).

——, '"I hadn't really thought about it": New Identities/New Fatherhoods' in J Seymour and P Bagguley (eds), *Relating Intimacies: Power and Resistance* (Palgrave Macmillan, Basingstoke, 1999).

——, '"It's my life too" – Children's Perspectives on Post-Divorce Parenting' [2000] Family Law 163.

SMART, C and SEVENHUJSEN, S (eds), *Child Custody and the Politics of Gender* (Routledge, London, 1989).

SMART, C, NEALE, B and WADE, A, *The Changing Experience of Childhood – Families and Divorce* (Polity, Cambridge, 2001).

SMART, C *et al*, *Residence and Contact Disputes in Court: Volume 1*, Research Report No 6/2003 (Department for Constitutional Affairs, London, 2003).

——, *Residence and Contact Disputes in Court: Volume 2*, Research Report No 4/2005 (Department for Constitutional Affairs, London, 2005).

SMEATON, D and MARSH, A, *Maternity and Paternity Rights and Benefits: Survey of Parents 2005*, Employment Relations Research Series No 50 (Department for Work and Pensions, London, 2006).

Bibliography

SMITH, J 'The First Intruder: Fatherhood, a Historical perspective' in P Moss (ed), *Father Figures: Fathers in the Families of the 1990s* (HMSO, Edinburgh, 1995).

SMITH, M *et al*, *A Study of Step Parents and Step Parenting* (Thomas Coram Research Unit, Institute of Education, London, 2003).

SOCIAL POLICY JUSTICE GROUP, 'Fractured Families: The State of The Nation Report', (Policy Statement (December 2006), <http://www.centreforsocialjustice.org.uk/default.asp?pageRef=174>, accessed 17 December 2007.

SPEAK, S, CAMERON, S and GILROY, R, *Young Single Fathers: Participation in Fatherhood – Bridges and Barriers* (Family Policy Studies Centre, London, 1997).

SPELMAN, EV, *Inessential Woman: Problems of Exclusion in Feminist Thought* (Beacon Press, Boston, 1990).

STANDING, K, 'Reasserting Fathers' Rights? Parental Responsibility and Involvement in Education and Lone Mother Families in the UK' (1999) 7 FLS 22.

STANLEY, K, (ed), *Daddy Dearest? Active Fatherhood and Public Policy* (Institute for Public Policy Research, London, 2005).

STEINBERG, D, *Bodies in Glass: Genetics, Eugenics Embryo Ethics* (Manchester University Press, Manchester, 1997).

STEWART, M, 'Judicial Redefinition of Marriage' (2004) 21 *Canadian Journal of Family Law* 11.

STONE, L, *The Road to Divorce* (Oxford University Press, Oxford, 1991).

STURGE, C and GLASER, D, 'Contact and Domestic Violence – the Experts' Court Report' (2000) 30 *Family Law* 615.

STYCHIN, C, 'Family Friendly? Rights, Responsibilities and Relationship Recognition' in A Diduck and K O'Donovan (eds), *Feminist Perspectives on Family Law* (Routledge-Cavendish, Abingdon, 2006).

SUNDERLAND, J, 'Baby Entertainer, Bumbling Assistant and Line Manager: Discourses of Fatherhood in Parentcraft Texts' (2000) 11(2) *Discourse & Society* 249.

TAYLOR, R, *The Future of Work Life Balance* (Economic and Social Research Council, Swindon, 2002).

TEMPLE-BONE, G (2000) 'Fathers, Parental Responsibility and Care Proceedings' *Family Law* 55.

THERY, I, '"The Interests of the Child" and the Regulation of the Post-Divorce Family' (1986) 14 *International Journal of the Sociology of Law* 341.

THOMAS, P (ed), *Socio-legal Studies* (Dartmouth, Aldershot, 1997).

THOMPSON, C, *Making Parents: The Ontological Choreography of Reproductive Technologies* (MIT Press, Cambridge, MA, 2005).

THOMPSON, M, VINTER, L and YOUNG, V, *Dads and their Babies: Leave Arrangements in the First Year*, Working Paper Series No 37 (Equal Opportunities Commission, Manchester, 2005).

THOMPSON, RA and AMATO, PR (eds), *The Post-divorce Family: Children, Parenting, and Society* (Sage, Thousand Oaks, CA, 1999).

THOMSON, M, 'Employing the Body: the Reproductive Body and Employment Exclusion' (1996) 5 *Social and Legal Studies* 243.

——, *Reproducing Narrative: Gender, Reproduction and the Law* (Ashgate, London, 1998).

——, *Endowed: Regulating the Male Sexed Body* (Routledge, New York, 2007).

THORNTON, M, 'The Public Private Dichotomy: Gendered and Discriminatory' (1991) 18(4) *Journal of Law & Society* 448.

271

——, 'Neoliberal Melancholia: The Case of Feminist Legal Scholarship' (2004) 20 *Australian Feminist Law Journal* 7.

TIMES EDITORIAL, 'Not Broken, Fractured: Communities Without Fathers Are Likely to Become Enclaves of Their Own', *The Times* (25 August 2007), <http://www.timesonline.co.uk/tol/comment/leading_article/article2324204.ece>, accessed 18 March 2008.

TIMES LETTER, 'The Government Must Help the Children of Divorcees', *The Times* (12 June 2007), Comment 16.

TINCKNELL, E, *Mediating the Family: Gender, Culture and Representation* (Hodder Arnold, London, 2005).

TIZZARD, J, 'Who's the Daddy?', *Bionews* (3 March 2003), <http://www.ivf.net/ivf/index.php?page=out&id=132>, accessed 22 November 2007.

TORR, J, *Is There a Father in the House? A Handbook for Health and Social Care Professionals* (Radcliffe, Oxford, 2003).

TOSH, J, *A Man's Place: Masculinity and the Middle-class Home in Victorian England* (Yale University Press, New Haven, CT, 1999).

TREMLETT, G, '"Hate mail drove us out of Britain. Now we've found a place in the sun"', *Observer* (8 February 2004), <http://observer.guardian.co.uk/uk_news/story/0,,1143435,00.html>, accessed 22 November 2007.

TRINDER, L, BECK, M and CONNOLLY, J, *Making Contact: How Parents and Children Negotiate and Experience Conflict After Divorce* (Joseph Rowntree Foundation, York, 2002).

TRINDER, L and J KELLET, *The Longer Term Outcomes of In-Court Conciliation* (Ministry of Justice, London, 2007).

TRINDER, L *et al*, *A Profile of Applicants and Respondents in Contact Cases in Essex*, Research Report No 1/2005 (Department for Constitutional Affairs, London, 2005).

TRONTO, JC, *Moral Boundaries* (Routledge, London, 1993).

URBAN WALKER, M, *Moral Understandings: A Feminist Study in Ethics* (Routledge, New York, 1998).

VALVERDE, M, *Law's Dream of a Common Knowledge* (Princeton University Press, Princeton, NJ, 2003).

VAN KAMMEN, J and OUDSHOORN, N, 'Gender and Risk Assessment in Contraceptive Technologies' (2002) 24(4) *Sociology of Health & Illness* 436.

VAN KRIEKEN, R, 'Legal Informalism, Power and Liberal Governance' (2001) 19(1) *Social and Legal Studies* 5.

——, 'The "Best Interests of the Child" and Parental Separation: On the "Civilising of Parents"' (2005) 68(1) MLR 25.

VOBEJDA, B, 'Sexual Commodities', *Minneapolis Star Tribune* (24 November 1998).

WALBY, S, *Gender Transformations* (Routledge, London, 1997).

WALKER, J, *Information Meetings and Associated Provisions within the Family Law Act 1996: Summary of the Final Evaluation Report* (Lord Chancellor's Department, London, 2001).

WALKER, J *et al*, *Picking Up the Pieces: Marriage and Divorce: Two Years After Information Provision* (Department of Constitutional Affairs, London, 2004).

WALL, The Rt Hon Justice, 'Enforcement of Court Orders' '[2005] *Family Law* 26

WALLBANK, J, 'The Campaign for Change of the Child Support Act: Reconstituting the "Absent" Father' (1997) 6 *Social and Legal Studies* 191.

Bibliography

——, 'Clause 106 of the Adoption and Children Bill: Legislation for the "Good Father"?' (2002) 22 (2) *Legal Studies* 276.

WALLERSTEIN, J and KELLY, J, *Surviving the Breakup: How Children and Parents Cope With Divorce* (Basic Books, New York, 1980).

WALSH, C, 'Imposing Order: Child Safety Orders and Local Child Curfew Schemes' 21(2) *Journal of Social Work and Family Law* 135.

WARIN, J *et al*, *Fathers, Work and Family Life* (Family Policy Studies Centre, London, 1999).

WARNOCK, M, *Making Babies: Is there a Right to Have Children?* (Oxford University Press, Oxford, 2002).

WASOFF, F and DEY, I, *Family Policy* (Gildridge, Eastbourne, 2000).

WAUGH, G, *Working with Asian Fathers: A Guide* (YMCA, Bradford, 2007).

WEBB, RE, and DANILUK, JC, 'The End of the Line: Infertile Men's Experience of Being Unable to Produce a Child' (1999) 2(1) *Men & Masculinities* 6.

WEBSTER, P, 'Flexible Working Hours for Millions' *The Times* (7 November 2007), <http://ste-edition.timesonline.co.uk/tol/news/politics/article2821194.ece>, accessed 24 January 2008.

WEEKS, J, *Sex, Politics and Society: The Regulation of Sexuality Since 1800* (Longman, Harlow, 1989).

WEEKS, J, HEAPHY, B and DONOVAN, C, *Same-Sex Intimacies: Families of Choice and Other Life Experiments* (Routledge, London, 2001).

WESTWOOD, S, '"Feckless Fathers": Masculinity and the British State' in M Mac an Ghaill (ed), *Understanding Masculinities: Social Relations and Cultural Arenas* (Open University Press, Buckingham, 1996).

WETHERELL, M and EDLEY, N, 'Negotiating Hegemonic Masculinity: Imaginary Positions and Psycho-Discursive Practices' (1999) 9 *Feminism & Psychology* 335.

WHITEHEAD, S, 'Hegemonic Masculinity Revisited' (1999) 6 *Gender, Work & Organization* 58.

——, *Men and Masculinities* (Polity, Cambridge, 2002).

WIKELEY, N, *Child Support: Law and Policy* (Hart, Oxford, 2006).

WILKINSON, H and BRISCOE, I, *Parental Leave: The Price of Family Values?* (Demos, London, 1996).

WILLEKENS, H, 'Long Term Developments in Family Law in Europe' in J Eekelaar and T Nhlapo (eds), *The Changing Family: Family Forms and Family Law* (Hart, Oxford, 1998).

WILLIAMS, F, 'Troubled Masculinities in Social Policy Discourses: Fatherhood' in J Popay, J Hearn and J Edwards (eds), *Men, Gender Divisions and Welfare* (Routledge, London, 1998).

WILLIAMS, F and CHURCHILL, H, *Empowering Parents in Sure Start Local Programmes* (HMSO, London, 2003).

WILLIAMS, J, *Unbending Gender: Why Family and Work Conflict and What To Do About It* (Oxford University Press, New York, 2000).

WILSON, GB, 'The Non-resident Parental Role for Separated Fathers: A Review' (2006) *International Journal of Law, Policy and the Family* 1.

WINTOUR, P, 'Fathers Told: Do More For Your Children' *Guardian* (27 February 2007) News 1.

WOMEN AND EQUALITY UNIT, *Improving Life at Work: Advancing Women in the Workplace* (Department of Trade and Industry, London, 2003).

273

Bibliography

——, *Individual Incomes of Men and Women 1996/97 to 2002/03: A Summary* (Department of Trade and Industry, London, 2004).

WOODWARD, W, 'Gay Couple Celebrate Birth of Twins Aspen and Saffron', *Guardian* (London, 13 December 1999), <http://www.guardian.co.uk/uk_news/story/0,, 245638,00.html>, accessed 22 November 2007.

——, '£20-a-week Tory Tax Break Plan Aims To Encourage Marriage'. *Guardian* (11 July 2007).

YOUNG, M and WILMOTT, P, *Family and Kinship in East London* (Pelican, Harmondsworth, 1957).

——, *The Symmetrical Family* (Penguin, Harmondsworth, 1973).

ZARETSKY, E, *Capitalism, The Family, and Personal Life* (Harper & Row, New York, 1976).